People in the Presence of God

BARRY LIESCH

People in the Presence of God

MODELS AND DIRECTIONS FOR WORSHIP

Foreword by Donald P. Hustad

ZondervanPublishingHouse
Grand Rapids, Michigan

A Division of HarperCollinsPublishers

PEOPLE IN THE PRESENCE OF GOD
Copyright © 1988 by Barry W. Liesch
Requests for information should be addressed to:
Zondervan Publishing House
Academic and Professional Books
Grand Rapids, Michigan 49530

Library of Congress Cataloging in Publication Data

Liesch, Barry Wayne, 1943–
　　People in the presence of God.

　　Includes index.
　　1. Public worship. I. Comanda, Joseph. II. Smith, Michael G. (Michael
Gary), 1947–　　. III. Title.
BV15.L54　　1988　　　　264　　　　88-9279
ISBN 0-310-31601-4

All Scripture quotations, unless otherwise noted, are taken from the HOLY
BIBLE: NEW INTERNATIONAL VERSION (North American Edition).
Copyright © 1973, 1978, 1984, by the International Bible Society. Used by
permission of Zondervan Bible Publishers. Italics used in Scripture quotations are
usually added for emphasis.

Edited by Joseph Comanda and Michael G. Smith
Designed by Louise Bauer and James E. Ruark

Printed in the United States of America

95 96 97 98 99 00 01 02 03 / DH / 14 13 12 11 10 9 8 7 6

Jacob Liesch (1909–1974)

Jesse, my son, I pass on to you two things my father Jacob Liesch told my brother Don and me. He said, "Boys, when you play for the Lord, let it be from the heart."

When Dad was dying, Don and I and other friends and relatives gathered around his bedside and sang Christmas carols to him. We asked him, "Are you getting tired, Dad, should we stop?" He replied, "You can never sing too much."

Contents

Foreword

It should be apparent to every alert observer of the evangelical scene that our worship customs are changing these days. This must signal a *renewal* of some sort, certainly a freshening of modes of expression, and, one hopes, the beginning of a full renewing of the church by the Holy Spirit.

Curiously enough, not all the changes move in the same direction. Some churches are recapturing liturgical traditions (such as observance of the Church Year and use of artistic symbolism) that we have lost in our continuing stance as persistent iconoclasts who reject much of our pre-Reformation heritage. Others are attracted to the more emotional fervor of modern-day charismatic worship (as illustrated by the repetitious use of praise choruses or the appearance of dance), even though they may not accept the theology or even the ultimate worship practices of Pentecostalism. Still others are combining these apparently antithetical styles, because, as someone said, "In our day the liturgical is often wedded to the charismatic." The truth is, the oldest Christian worship traditions (those of the first five centuries after Christ) probably witnessed that same coupling.

The reaction of evangelical scholars to these phenomena has been expressed in a "modest spate" of books on worship—the first such outpouring in my lifetime! They have dealt rather thoroughly and most helpfully with the development of a biblical and theological rationale for worship, but have largely ignored the question "How should we practice worship in a corporate setting?"

One of the few liturgical rubrics Jesus gave is the instruction to worship the Father "in spirit and in truth" (John 4:24). Other New Testament books tell us something of how early Christians worshiped, but there are no clear commands that are commonly understood to apply to the historic and continuing church (other than those concerning the Lord's Supper in 1 Corinthians 11).

From many modern evangelical writers we might get the impression that an exegesis of Jesus' command answers all the significant questions, and that worship (like the exegesis) is mostly a rational, left-brain activity that is connected mainly with words. Other authorities remind us that "worshiping in spirit" says something about the response of the *emotional* selfhood—the intuitive—in which the right side of the human brain is involved. Communication to "the spirit" depends largely on such nonverbal symbols as space, architecture, music, silence, and movement—elements that have traditionally been viewed as "nonspiritual" by Evangelicals.

Corporate worship in most cultures must take place in a building, and Jesus did not say what kind of structure it should be, in shape or in decoration. Again, worship must be expressed somehow, and Jesus did not give any instructions about what words or musical sounds or gestures or artwork should speak to us or for us. Evidently He (and the apostle Paul also) understood that modes of expression vary according to culture and that they could be left to be determined by the wisdom given to all beings because of "common grace."

This book is important because it begins where others have left off, emphasizing the "how" of corporate evangelical worship. At the same time, it too draws heavily on Scripture, both Old and New Testaments. One of its most distinctive contributions is the reminder that several forms of worship appeared in pre-Christian Jewish history, and that New Testament Christians in Corinth or in Rome had different practices from those in Jerusalem. In each of these traditions, and in those of the continuing church during the past nineteen hundred years, Barry Liesch finds justification for contemporary concepts and actions that may signal that the wind of the Spirit is creating a new breeze in our day!

Probably no single reader will agree with everything this book contains. For one thing, the author deals with most of the phenomena that characterize modern worship; thus it would appear that he belongs with the group who tend to unite liturgical and charismatic styles. Further, it is in the nature of human beings that those subjects which strongly involve our emotions tend to be approached more emotionally than rationally. Reading the manuscript, at times I was not sure that I could agree sufficiently to write this foreword. But I continued to read—and discovered that there is much here that will be helpful to any reasonable person. As Liesch himself says in chapter 19: "The goal is to present issues strongly and encourage thoughtful consideration so that 'iron may sharpen iron.' Readers who do not accept the whole argument may find parts of it valid." So I urge every reader to *read on!* My final judgment is that, though I may disagree in many details, and though his Southern California culture may accept some metaphors that Midwesterners find to be extreme, Liesch is on the right track biblically, theologically, liturgically, and aesthetically.

In delineating the various types of worship—in the home, the small group, and the large gathering—and in the helpful suggestions for initiating healthy change in the local church, Liesch has reminded us that, for the Christian believer, *all of life should be worship.* It is our constant affirming and transforming response to God, as He has revealed Himself in the world of things and of people, in the Scriptures, and supremely in Jesus Christ. To experience full and authentic worship, "in spirit and in truth," is the greatest need of the church today.

—*Donald P. Hustad*
Senior Professor of Church Music
Southern Baptist Theological Seminary
Louisville, Kentucky

Preface

"I've got the right way! Worship my way!" This is the message impressed upon me time and time again in my reading some fifty books and several hundred articles while doing research for this book over the last ten years. We all know that styles and philosophies of worship vary widely. Is there a correct way?

I discovered a startling fact while doing research for this book. *The Oxford Dictionary of Religion* (1981) reports there are 20,280 Christian denominations in the world. That is also fascinating, because it suggests there could be 20,280 approaches to worship! Then I discovered that worship was culturally differentiated in the Bible, according to the time period and the ethnic group involved. I gradually came to think in terms of five basic models of worship in the Bible: pre-Sinai (family worship modeled by the patriarchs), tabernacle-temple, synagogue, Pauline, and worship in the Book of Revelation.

I believe that our different styles of worship arise because every Christian group from Fundamentalists to Roman Catholics emphasizes different elements of biblical worship. Ancient, traditional, and contemporary forms can all be related to Scripture. For example, Roman Catholics draw heavily on the tabernacle-temple model, Charismatics on Pauline worship, and the typical Protestant church on the synagogue pattern.

I try to keep Scripture up front in this book. What the Bible has to say about worship has always struck me with the greatest force. As Martin Luther said, "The Bible is alive, it speaks to me; it has hands, it lays hold on me."

In employing the five models as a launching point for worship possibilities in contemporary church culture, I make no claim that they strike the perfect balance or are all-comprehensive. Rather, I think they provide a useful framework and serve to prevent a lot of distortion.

A pastor told me, "I've worked hard. I've studied the theology of worship, but I don't know how to implement it in my church. Would you serve as a worship consultant at our church for a few months?" I hope this book helps people who have this pastor's problem. The book has already been field tested by worship committees, Sunday school classes, and college classes on church music. This has helped to sort out the significant issues from the inconsequential. Many of the discussion questions at the end of each chapter were generated in these settings.

Other people may have a different problem. They *think* they know what worship is all about. They speak extemporaneously in their worship and music committee meetings; they see no need to study about worship. They surmise, "Isn't worship after all a natural thing—purely and simply a matter of the heart? Why get so fussy about it?" The result? Some churches flounder through lack of knowledge. They do not have a well-thought-out rationale for what they are doing. I hope this book meets that problem also.

I do not expect every part of this book to appeal to every congregation, although I hope everyone's perspective will be broadened. If this book is used by a Sunday school class or a worship committee, I suggest the following course of action. Choose a person who has the confidence of the pastor to lead the group. If possible, have the pastor initiate the first meeting with his blessing. This opens the way for him to be invited to subsequent sessions when it is appropriate. Keep the pastor informed on the group's reactions to the ideas presented. Be sure to include him when discussion turns toward implementing specific ideas.

If the book is used as teaching text, identify the ideas and insights that you think will stimulate the class and relate best to your situation; then arrange the material as you like. A single chapter may well have enough material for one session. Use the discussion questions. In a classroom, written responses to the questions might be advisable.

Much of my time outside the classroom has been devoted to helping small, struggling churches. I have had these churches very much on my mind during my writing, although I have sought to make the book helpful to churches of all sizes. The examples and suggestions come from practical experience in small churches as well as assemblies involving two or three thousand people in a Christian university setting.

It is my hope that this book will be a catalyst for change with the recognition that extensive change is not likely to come quickly. We can all, however, learn to grow, adapt, and become better equipped to glorify God and assist worshipers to enjoy Him forever.

BARRY W. LIESCH

Acknowledgments

I wish to thank my editors, Michael Smith, James Ruark, and Joseph Comanda, for their openness, wise counsel, and the many improvements they have made to this book. I always had the feeling you were working *with* me. I sensed, too, that you were striving for a work of the highest quality possible.

I wish to thank music colleagues Dr. William Lock, for encouraging me to stick with my initial intuition regarding the spiral structure of this book, and Dr. Ed Childs, for preparing the computer printout of the music examples.

I wish to thank my friends Prof. Barry Krammes, Wayne Peterson, J. Paul Sattem, and Barney Kinnard for their careful critiquing of parts of the text, and my dear friend Prof. Marlin Owen for his emotional support during a time of stress.

I express special thanks to my journalist friend and colleague, Lowell ("Doc") Saunders, who was a constant source of encouragement and voluntarily pre-edited the entire book before I sent the manuscript to Zondervan. Your kindness really moved me, Doc.

My thanks to my music-worship classes of 1987 and 1988 who read the manuscript and made insightful suggestions.

My thanks to those in the Biola University academic community who so generously critiqued parts of the manuscript or made invaluable suggestions in private conversations: Ann Bowman, Beth Brown, John Carter, Daniel Cornell, Paul Enns, Tom Finley, Bob Harrison, Del Hanson, Bingham Hunter, Lloyd Kmast, Sherwood Lingenfelter, Larry Marshburn, Marvin Mayers, Curtis Mitchell, Richard Rigsby, Jim Rosscup, Jack Schwarz, Robert Saucy, Randy West, Leland Wilshire, and Tony Wong. I owe you one!

My thanks also to Dr. Clyde Cook, president of Biola University, for letting me try out many of the ideas I perceived in Revelation worship in Christmas and Easter All-University worship services.

My thanks finally to Biola University for a sabbatical leave, a summer grant to study the worship models, and a reduction in my teaching load for one semester that made possible the writing of this book.

I am grateful to the following publishers for permission to use extensive quotations or other materials from their publications:

Martin Blogg, *Dance and Christian Faith* (London: Hodder and Stoughton, 1985).

Brent Chambers, "The Celebration Song." Copyright © 1977 by Scripture in Song. Administered by Maranatha! Music.

J. G. Davies, *Liturgical Dance: An Historical, Theological and Practical Handbook* (London: SCM Press, 1984).

J. G. Davies, *New Perspectives on Worship Today* (London: SCM Press, 1978).

"Drabble" comic strip. Copyright © 1986 by United Feature Syndicate.

George Eldon Ladd, *A Theology of the New Testament* (Grand Rapids: Wm. B. Eerdmans Publishing Co., 1974).

Ralph P. Martin, *The Worship of God: Some Theological, Pastoral, and Practical Reflections* (Grand Rapids: Wm. B. Eerdmans Publishing Co., 1982).

Wayne A. Meeks, *The First Urban Christians: The Social World of the Apostle Paul* (New Haven: Yale University Press, 1983).

Nolene Price, "Holy, Holy, Holy Is the Lord." Copyright © 1976 by Scripture in Song. Administered by Maranatha! Music.

Introduction: Getting the Idea

People in the Presence of God is a book for pastors; full-time and part-time directors of music and worship; worship leaders and worship committees; artists and performers of all kinds; teachers of college, seminary, and Sunday school classes; and readers who want to be aroused to think about worship.

The text of the book weaves together worship principles and practical suggestions throughout. Four appendixes offer further examples for implementing worship ideas in practical ways, including a statement of philosophy, a sample worship participation form, a worship service involving congregational reading of Scripture, and a reader's theater presentation for Easter. Suggested readings with each chapter and extensive notes at the back of the book provide additional resources for research and discussion. Each chapter offers questions for discussion.

The book unfolds in ever-widening circles, beginning with worship in the family, then small groups and large groups, and culminating in worship in the Book of Revelation (see diagram next page). These five worship models are grouped according to size.

> Family worship
>   Pre-Sinai model: Parent-led worship in the family
>
> Small-group worship
>   Pauline model: Body life-charismatic worship
>   Synagogue model: Lay-led disciplined worship
>
> Large-group worship
>   Tabernacle-temple model
>   Revelation model: worship in heaven

The spiral form also provides a foreshadowing quality: topics introduced early on are developed later. As each scriptural element of worship is introduced and explored, it is hoped the rich tapestry of possibilities available even to a small church will stimulate the imagination.

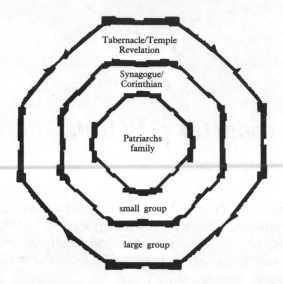

The five models form part of the biblical and historical record and serve as prototypes for worship practices today. They are not mutually exclusive; each adds a dimension to the whole. They show the way worship can be organized and presented to God. They demonstrate how people can come into the presence of the Lord to worship Him.

When these models are put in order according to their size—not their chronological appearance in the Scriptures—they suggest a natural growth pattern. They contain valuable insights for pastors and worship leaders who anticipate changes in organization as a body grows from informal meetings (in a home or school, for example) into perhaps a sprawling, multiple-staff church.

Churches and individuals are very likely to feel tension with each worship model when it is viewed in isolation. But the models are not to be left all alone. I believe they will enlarge our vision and provide guidance for decision making as we allow all of them to affect our thinking. This broad base of information will contribute to our making good decisions and can help us avoid the pitfall of copying without adaptation what we see another group do, either inside or outside our own congregation.

OVERVIEW OF THE MODELS

In the pre-Sinai model of worship, the patriarchs are priests to their own families. They build altars, offer sacrifices, and gather families together in worship. Their worship in the course of everyday living highlights its intergenerational aspects.

In the Pauline model we sense the dynamics of improvisation, Spirit-guided unity, the maximum participation obtainable in small groups, and the special intimacy that transpires in a home setting: "When you come together, everyone has a hymn, or a word of instruction, a revelation, a tongue or an interpretation" (1 Cor. 14:26). Synagogue worship, basic to many Protestant churches, emphasizes structured liturgy and accords a prominent place to prayer, Scripture reading, and biblical exposition.

Large-group worship includes the tabernacle-temple and Revelation models. The former helps us to broaden our perspective to include such elements of worship as drama, symbolism, the fine arts, and Davidic praise. Temple festivals (special-events worship) offer guidance on such matters as using movement in worship, organizing Davidic praise, and evaluating musical styles. Revelation worship includes elements from all the other models but relates most to the tabernacle-temple model. Its overarching conception is inclusive, consummate, and timeless.

BLENDING THE MODELS IN YOUR CHURCH

Experience with denominational differences indicates it is certainly possible to blend or alternate elements between and within these models. Small churches can blend aspects of Pauline and synagogal worship. Large groups can combine body-life participation and Spirit-guided improvisation (Corinthian worship) with choirs and orchestras (temple worship) in the Sunday morning assembly. Other churches may wish to attempt a blend of charismatic worship and expository teaching. Or a large church may use both the temple and Pauline-Corinthian styles by developing meticulously planned Sunday morning services while maintaining intimacy through small groups on Sunday evenings or weeknights.

It may be possible—and even desirable—for aspects of all the five models to be operational in the life experience of even a small church. If a worship committee works toward the goal of encouraging its people to obtain a multilevel experience of worship in the family, small groups, and the general assembly, it will have gone a long way toward meeting the concern of Jesus that no separation, dichotomy, or inconsistency occur between private and public worship (Matt. 6:1–6). This concern with building bridges between private and public worship outside the confines of the church building needs attention in many congregations today.

AWESOME: PEOPLE IN THE PRESENCE OF GOD

I hope that reading this book will be an adventure like setting out to scale a mountain peak. Each chapter prepares you step by step to appreciate the ultimate summit of worship expression: Revelation worship. *God* designed it! It is mind-boggling! An unparalleled creative explosion! I believe the final chapters offer the book's most distinctive contribution to worship literature.

God is unmistakably at the center of Revelation worship. The people assemble around His throne. This is why the image suggested by the title—*People in the Presence of God*—continues to grip and motivate me. More and more I believe this is what worship is all about. I hope that reading this book enriches your life *half* as much as writing it has enriched mine.

PART I

Principles of Worship

CHAPTER ONE

Old Testament Principles

If I took a microphone into the foyer of your church and asked people why they had come, what do you think I would hear? I suspect I'd hear reasons like these:

To obtain some new thought from the Word

To hear Pastor speak—he's an outstanding preacher

To be built up

To fellowship with other believers

To really feel and be moved by the music and worship

I think you'll agree that these are fairly typical responses. Maybe you too would say you worship for one or another of these reasons. As good as these reasons are, though, some critical reasons are missing from the list.

Why *do* we worship? Why do you and your church worship? And more important, what is the *real* purpose of worship? What does the Bible have to say about it?

We will start out by looking at three Old Testament principles of worship in this chapter.

PRINCIPLE 1: COME *INTO HIS PRESENCE* AND SING *TO* HIM

In worship we draw near to God, the One who has called us to worship. That's what is missing from the response of these worshipers: the expectation that they assemble to meet with God. When we lose sight of that central purpose of worship, we begin to misdirect our efforts. We start to think in terms of getting something out of worship—good feelings or good teaching—or we make worship into a means to some other end.

Feelings are valid and play an important role in worship. Children, who cannot comprehend what is going on intellectually, learn about worship from the feelings present in the worship environment. Warm feelings benefit all, but the major emphasis should not be on generating good feelings; we shouldn't think that we have not worshiped if on a particular Sunday we "feel nothing." Instead, the experience of healthy emotions will come from focusing on a God who, by His very character, loves to bless His people. We come to Him; He graciously comes to us.

Many church leaders believe that worship is for teaching. Scripture choruses, they point out, can help people memorize the Bible; hymns and Bible readings can reinforce church doctrines. Alternatively, pastors may view worship as a preparation for the sermon—when the real teaching takes place. True worship will stimulate in us a desire to be changed, and as we draw close to the Lord in worship and see His person more clearly we will be changed. But even edification—certainly a worthy purpose—is only a minor part of what worship is all about.

Other leaders want "good" worship because they think it promotes church growth. In southern California many of the growing churches are actively involved in worship as an experience that attracts nonmembers. Others see a connection between worship and evangelism; they believe that corporate worship can be used to prepare the unsaved for the gospel "like nothing else." These and many other benefits derive from worship, including a cleansed conscience, inner peace, and tranquillity.

Yet all these reasons for worship fall short of the real purpose. We should worship God because He is deserving and worthy of our praise. We should worship because we want God.

> And we, who with unveiled faces all reflect the Lord's glory, are being transformed into his likeness with ever-increasing glory, which comes from the Lord, who is the Spirit (2 Cor. 3:18).

Graham Kendrick calls this "transformation through adoration."[1] Change comes inevitably. When Moses came down from Mount Sinai, he glowed because he had met with God. In that meeting, God's character and presence visibly transformed him.

Change for us, as for Moses, will come by being in God's presence and by directing our worship to Him. Ministering, serving, and performing "to the Lord" is a core idea of Christian worship. The preposition *to* here is everything. There is an enormous difference between singing *to* the Lord and merely singing *about* him. There is an enormous difference between praying to each other *about* God and actually entering into His presence. In more than one hundred references in the Psalms, worshipers sing *to* the Lord. More than twenty passages speak of worshipers "ministering" *to* the Lord. Offerings ascend to make a soothing aroma "to the LORD" (Lev. 1:9).

Similarly, when you consult a concordance, you discover an overwhelming consistency in the Bible's language from Genesis to Revelation. The people come *before* God—they come before His presence to praise Him. Over one hundred passages describe the worshiper as "approaching" or appearing *before* the Lord. As Bruce Leafblad has observed, we have forgotten in our churches that we perform our worship—our singing, our praying, and our offering—before the Lord.[2]

God's real and visible presence in the tabernacle lay at the heart of the covenant. The tabernacle stood in the center of the camp. It was erected so that God's presence could become a permanent, living reality. God told Moses:

> "There I will meet you and speak to you; there also I will meet with the Israelites. . . . I will dwell among the Israelites and be their God" (Exod. 29:42–45).

The tabernacle, or "tent of meeting," literally means "tent of appointment" or "rendezvous tent."[3]

Yet, not only was God to be present in corporate worship, but the whole of life was to be lived out in the presence of God. The thundering refrain often repeated in the Old Testament—"I am the LORD your God" (Lev. 18:2)—encompassed all of life. The Gospel of John, moreover, alludes to the life of Christ in terms of the tabernacle image: "The Word became flesh and made his dwelling ['tabernacled'] among us" (1:14).

PRINCIPLE 2: OFFER WORSHIP THAT COSTS YOU SOMETHING

If I could, I would teach every congregation to offer up costly worship. Cheap worship is a contradiction in terms.[4] In the tabernacle, worshipers always brought an offering. The most frequent offering, the burnt offering, was also the most costly. Only unblemished animals were to be presented, and they had to be burned whole; no meat remained for the priest or offerer. Moreover, Pentateuchal ceremonies invariably elevated the importance of the shedding of blood. Only the priests were allowed to officiate during that part of the ceremony. Blood was daubed on the altars, the veil, the mercy seat, and even the priests and their vestments. During the ceremony in the desert when the Israelites publicly assented to the Sinai covenant, Moses took the blood, threw it over the people, and said, "This is the blood of the covenant that the LORD has made with you" (Exod. 24:8).

With even greater poignancy, Jesus at the Last Supper told His disciples to drink (symbolically) His blood: "Drink from it, all of you. This is my blood of the covenant which is poured out for many for the forgiveness of sins" (Matt. 26:27–28). *True worship costs everyone concerned, both God and man.* When Jesus and the disciples sat and watched the crowds put their money into the temple treasury, it was the widow putting in two small copper coins who attracted His attention: "They all gave out of their wealth; but she, out of her poverty, put in everything—all she had to live on" (Mark 12:44). Similarly, David, with great perception in acquiring the site for the temple, refused to accept the land as an outright gift. "I will not sacrifice to the LORD my God," he insisted, things "that cost me nothing" (2 Sam. 24:24).

Throughout the Scriptures true worship costs. The primary word for worship in the Old Testament is *abodah*, which is translated "service." The Greek equivalent in the New Testament, *latreia*, has the same meaning.[5] Both words are used in the sense of rendering a "service" of costly worship. *Abodah* is used in reference to Old Testament priests who dedicated their lives to serve the Lord in the temple.

Latreia is also closely related to our word *liturgy*. Accordingly, when students of worship talk about the *liturgy* of worship, they are speaking about the "work" or "service" of worship directed to God by both leaders and congregation. This "work" may involve any of the following in liturgically oriented churches: liturgical movement, action, drama, symbolism, dance, texts, lectionaries, creeds, furniture, and vestments. When the word *liturgical* is used in this book, it will often be in reference to one of the above.

Liturgical churches often have a fixed order to their worship with fixed prayers, multiple Scripture readings, and extensive symbolism (altar, cross, candles, incense). They also tend to offer Communion each Sunday and adhere to the liturgical year. Nonliturgical churches may have a less formal pattern to their worship, characterized by more spontaneity or greater simplicity.

Whatever your church is like, the important question is this: what can you do to make your worship more costly? The Book of Romans urges worshipers to offer their bodies in an entire lifestyle of worship.

> Therefore, I urge you, brothers, in view of God's mercy, to offer your bodies as living sacrifices, holy and pleasing to God—this is your spiritual act of worship (Rom. 12:1).

The Book of Hebrews also suggests that praise and good works should be natural expressions of worship.

> Through Jesus, therefore, let us continually offer to God a *sacrifice of praise*—the fruit of lips that confess his name. And do not forget to

do good and to *share with others*, for with such sacrifices God is pleased (Heb. 13:15–16).

As for costly praise, we can learn to bring more of our total person before God in worship. We can kneel, prostrate ourselves, or lift our hands in private or public prayer as a way of making a more complete response. At home we can invest costly time and energy in preparing a solo, a prayer to be offered, a reading to be rendered, an inventive keyboard harmonization that will spur the people toward inspired singing. We can take the time to prepare our Sunday school lesson well. We can learn to turn the radio off on the way to church and focus on the Lord in preparation for worship. In the service itself we can take risks by singing out less tentatively than we normally do and by attempting to sing that "high" note. Afterward we can offer a listening ear at the end of the service to someone who is hurting. All these can be costly offerings that we bring to Sunday morning worship.

Resentments between Christians can sap the very strength of worship. Jesus commanded us to take the initiative in resolving differences we have with others *before* we come to worship (see Matt. 5:23–24), and that too is one of the costs of worship. I once attended a Communion service where an old gentleman took this command to heart before our eyes. His obedient response strengthened the congregation's integrity in worship.

Costly acts of compassion like the one in the parable of the Good Samaritan (Luke 10) also fall into a broader definition of worship to our Lord Jesus. Jesus has told us, "Whatever you did for one of the least of these brothers of mine, you did for me" (Matt. 25:40).

One Sunday I came to church with a seemingly unsolvable problem. When the congregation sang "Amazing Grace"—"Through many dangers, toils, and snares I have already come"—I began to sob and could not stop. I tried to leave quietly so as not to disturb others, but an older man I had never met followed me out, put his arms around me, and cried with me for about ten minutes. In reaching out to me, that man made a costly, priceless offering that morning. Nor did it stop there! Later in the summer, he and his wife interrupted their vacation and drove two hundred miles out of their way to spend time with me. Sometimes when I lead people in worship, this incident flickers across my mind and revitalizes me! I am stirred to worship by the graciousness of a God who loved and cared for me. The foundation of worship is a love for God and man that results in costly worship.

PRINCIPLE 3: FOCUS ON THE CHARACTER OF GOD, ESPECIALLY HIS TRANSCENDENCE

Our worship stands or falls on our understanding of the character of God. A list of God's attributes would at least include God's wisdom, goodness, righteousness, justice, love, eternal existence, changelessness, omnipresence, omniscience, and omnipotence. It would be a valuable exercise to evaluate which attributes of God receive weight and repetition in our weekly selection of hymns and choruses and in our public prayers. Remember that through the act of singing we project both verbal and nonverbal images of what God is like. In our singing we are involved in concept formation; a concept of God is being formed in our minds.

In many churches that emphasize God's love, God's holiness seems to be all but forgotten. Yet many scholars agree that holiness is a kind of synonym for God. It "embraces every distinctive attribute" and is "the outshining of all that God is," according to R. A. Finlayson.

> As the sun's rays, combining all the colors of the spectrum, come together in the sun's shining and blend into light, so in His self-manifestation all the attributes of God come together and blend into holiness.[6]

One reason why holiness seldom appears in our song lyrics is that it has become a foreign concept to us. God's holiness both repels and attracts. It gives us tremors and yet fascinates us.[7] A primary meaning of the term is "to separate." It tends to bring out the contrast between the pure God and His impure creatures, and it particularly emphasizes the awe-inspiring side of His character. He is transcendentally separate from us (*transcendence* basically means "beyond or without limits"). The Old Testament has a particularly strong emphasis on holiness, as does the Book of Revelation. Significantly, the threefold repetition "Holy, holy, holy," a literary device used for emphasis in Scripture, occurs only with the word *holy*. Nowhere do we find the expression "God is love, love, love."[8]

Young people in particular seem to be attracted to intimacy in worship, but they have little concept of God's transcendence. Our culture knows little of it. The only thing that comes close is the wonder inspired in us by celebrities. We say a certain athlete or musician is "AWE-SOME!" That seems to be about all we have to work with. Sadly, our family relationships don't help much. When a teenager refers to his father as "my old man," is he likely to view his heavenly Father with respect and reverence? Putting it more strongly, when the young in our society are not taught to respect their elders (the fifth commandment), we suffer a corresponding loss of transcendence in our worship.

I recently heard of a church in Greater Los Angeles that has a Coke machine at the back of the sanctuary. Whenever people feel thirsty during the morning service, they can wander out for a Coke and bring it back with them to the worship space. The church has grown rapidly. Many unchurched young adults have found there a church culture that feels comfortable to them. In permitting practices of this sort, however, there are definitely trade-offs.[9] What they gain in accessibility, they lose in transcendency.

Our worship needs more balance. We need to experience both God's transcendence and His immanence ("indwelling the universe and time, etc."), both His holiness and His love. Given the loss of a sense of transcendence in our culture generally, we will have to work harder to make sure it is present in our worship.

Those who select the songs and Scripture passages should try to help people feel transcendence by looking for materials that express it. David's recollection of his experience in the tabernacle stresses transcendence: "I have seen you in the sanctuary and beheld your power and your glory" (Ps. 63:2). He *felt* it.

HOLINESS: WHAT IS IT?

Holiness, such a foreign concept to many of us, was central to tabernacle worship. Engraved on the plate of pure gold on the front of the high priest's turban were the words "HOLY TO THE LORD" (Exod. 28:36). Until recently it was commonly believed that the extensive rules about holiness in the Pentateuch mainly had to do with hygiene or maintaining Israel's moral integrity. But scholars have come to realize that these rules formed the core of a comprehensive theological perspective that made no distinction between immorality and pollution (Ezek. 18:5–9), no forced dichotomy (as we are inclined to make) between the ceremonial and moral law, and between the spiritual and the physical.

It has become fashionable in evangelical circles to acknowledge the continuing importance of the moral law of the Old Testament while dismissing the ceremonial law. But Gordon J. Wenham, a noted Old Testament scholar, says that the Old Testament makes no such distinction between ceremonial, civil, and moral law.[10] The Ten Commandments, for example, form a part of the moral law, but is the commandment to keep the Sabbath day holy a part of the moral law or the ceremonial law?

In studying the Scriptures, it is valuable to try to understand how the people at that time perceived the Word spoken. In our Western way of thinking we tend to see the spiritual and the physical as opposites—roughly analogous to the inward versus the outward—but the true opposite of the spiritual is the nonspiritual or unspiritual, not the physical. No doubt the New Testament Jews erred in placing too much emphasis on the outward. Yet may we not err in giving the outward insufficient significance? Our objective should be to encourage a response that involves the total person in worship.

Both the Old and New Testaments raise a demand for holiness. The apostle Peter quotes the Leviticus refrain, "Be holy, because I am holy" (Lev. 11:44–45; 19:2; 20:26), and urges it on his readers (1 Peter 1:16). Our Lord also echoed the Leviticus passage when He said, "Be perfect, therefore, as your heavenly Father is perfect" (Matt. 5:48).

When we think about the holiness laws we tend to focus on the negative prohibitions. But every negative prohibition implied a corresponding, deeper positive meaning.[11] Mary Douglas, a social anthropologist who has provided a comprehensive reading of all the holiness laws, argues that the deeper, underlying qualities of holiness are wholeness, completeness, light, and purity—qualities consistent with the character of God.[12] The unblemished bodies of the priests and the animal sacrifices, for example, demonstrated outward projections of wholeness and completeness. As he came down from the mountain, Moses' face shone with reflected light. Purity and cleanliness in all their dimensions positively attract.

Try this outrageous idea and see if it does not help you. Meditate on the purity of holiness when you are taking a shower. Try to obtain a tactile sense of the attractiveness of cleanliness. Intone the hymn "Holy, Holy, Holy" as you shower. (At the least, it will give new meaning to the saying, Cleanliness is next to godliness.)

GRADUATED TABOO

According to Menahem Haran, "Any impurity that clung to man would tend to pollute the sanctuary and in the end would lead to the Divine vacating the temple because of its uncleanness."[13] Holy things were sanctified and set apart from the common things, the clean from the unclean, the blemished from the unblemished.

The particular application of the principle of holiness demanded by God resulted in a graduated taboo as one came closer to His dwelling place. There was a prohibition of touch, sight, and approach.[14] The people could approach no further than the altar. The Holy Place and the Holy of Holies constituted a domain inaccessible to all but the priests. A Levite who was not a priest could not touch even the most trivial piece of tabernacle furniture, for all the pieces were endowed with a "contagious holiness" that was transmittable. A person or object that came into contact with the altar, for example, "became" holy (Exod. 29:37).

This holiness was "conceived as almost a tangible holiness, material in quality," and according to Hebrew scholar Menahem Haran, we "are told of no activity or rite" by which it could be "shed from a person or object."[15] Aaronic priests, while officiating, could not come into contact with others who were not priests. Numbers 4:15 specifically warns those who were not priests (the Kohathites) that "they must not touch the holy things or they will die." They were even forbidden "to look at the holy things, even for a moment, or they will die" (Num. 4:20).

No idle threats! Strict protocol had to be observed. When Aaron's sons offered strange, unauthorized fire before the Lord, they fell dead (Num. 3:4). When Uzzah touched the ark as it was being transported to Jerusalem, God struck him down (2 Sam. 6:7). The prohibition on sight extended even to the high priest on the Day of Atonement, the one day in the year he was permitted to enter the Holy of Holies. He did not get to see much, for he was instructed to make a cloud of incense that would "conceal the atonement cover" lest he see it and die (Lev. 16:13). Nothing is to be taken for granted when people are in the presence of God.

RADICAL IMPLICATIONS IN THE TEARING OF THE VEIL

The veil was a veritable blockade to the Holy of Holies. To the Hebrews it was an impassable barrier to an area strictly out of bounds. Only the high priest was allowed to enter, and then only one day in the year. With this state of affairs in force for more than a thousand years, the tearing of the veil (Matt. 27:51) during Jesus' crucifixion effected a radical change that has radical (and glorious) implications for the New Testament believer. Believers now enjoy a new access anticipated in the Lord's Supper, where symbolically Jesus called His followers to a new level of community. Gone are the prohibitions on touching, seeing, and approaching liturgical furniture or the elements of Communion. The Lord's Supper is portrayed in the Gospels as a meal shared by friends.

New Testament believers not only have new access, but also have been given a new status. The New Testament extends the concept of the priesthood to include every believer.

> But you are a chosen people, a royal priesthood, a holy nation, a people belonging to God, that you may declare the praises of him who called you out of darkness into his wonderful light (1 Peter 2:9).

We call this the priesthood of believers. While members of the priesthood in the Old Testament commanded "offices" of authority, the concept of offices finds no parallel in the New Testament. Christ holds the only office, that of high priest (Heb. 4:14ff.). The body in its totality forms a priesthood: "In Christ we who are many form one body, and each member belongs to all the others" (Rom. 12:5). All are servants. There is no dichotomy of clergy and laity. Giftedness, not the possession of some office, becomes central to the question of ministry.

Further, Jesus foreshadowed in His life and ministry the coming of a new age by doing something unthinkable in the Old Testament— reaching out to touch the unclean, the outcasts, the lepers, the blind, and the maimed. He did it as well by eating with "sinners." Jesus calls us to both inward purity and involvement in all of life.

HOLINESS IN PAUL'S WRITINGS

Wenham says of his research, "It came as a surprise to discover how pervasive are Levitical ideas in the New Testament."[16] The Old Testament idea of purity extends into the writings of Paul. While we tend to treat the idea of the believer being "the temple of God" somewhat casually as merely metaphorical, a useful image for teaching purposes,[17] to Paul it was central to his teaching. "Don't you know you are God's temple," he wrote, "and that God's spirit lives in you?" (1 Cor. 3:16).

What Paul said in 1 Corinthians, he reiterates in 2 Corinthians:

> For we are the temple of the living God. As God has said: "I will live with them and walk among them, and I will be their God, and they will be my people" (2 Cor. 6:16).

Paul is concerned that a standard of purity be maintained within each person so that the church as a whole will continue to enjoy God's presence.

Newton says, "Just as conditions were laid down for the maintenance of the divine presence in the Holy of Holies in Jerusalem, so Paul sets out stringent conditions for the Christian community to preserve purity and thus maintain God's presence."[18] In 1 Corinthians 5–6 we find specific instances of church discipline with the unmistakable ring of accountability. The important point is that the character of God motivates this kind of disciplinary action. The character of God requires accountability.

WINDOWS TO TRANSCENDENCE

I was walking along the Welland Canal locks on the St. Lawrence Seaway in eastern Canada when it began to rain and thunder furiously. I stopped and pulled my full-length coat over my head, covering up my eyes. I could not see anything. Then a bolt of lightning struck about thirty yards from me and lit up the entire sky with such an intensity and brightness that right through the fabric of my coat I could plainly see the ship in the canal. What an awesome display of God's power! It set me thinking. My concept of God was enlarged!

How can we bring that kind of experience to our worship? One thing we can do is select Scripture texts that remind us of the greatness of our God and contain the words of transcendence—words like *glory, holy, grace, power, majesty, mountains, crown,* and *exalt.* We can read and meditate on verses like the following and share them with the people:

> Worship the LORD with reverence, and rejoice with trembling (Ps. 2:11 NASB).

> Let us show gratitude . . . with reverence and awe; for our God is a consuming fire (Heb. 12:28–29 NASB).

> . . . a God greatly feared in the council of the holy ones, and awesome above all those who are around Him? (Ps. 89:7 NASB).

Sometimes it takes the right combination of text and melody to convey a sense of greatness. A photographer-friend of mine had spent a week shooting pictures in Death Valley and had experienced a sense of God's transcendence there. He was in the parking lot about to head home when he felt led to stop and offer worship to God. He told me he tried to express his feelings in words, but the language of his prayer seemed flat and inadequate—he felt totally frustrated. Then a thought occurred to him—something risky, since there were other people mulling around in the lot. Sitting on the back bumper of his car, he decided (even though he can hardly keep a tune) to sing out the hymn "Immortal, Invisible God Only Wise." It worked. "Suddenly," he told me, "my praise was completely transformed. It came alive."

Another song in which the interaction of tune and poetry captures a sense of transcendence is "My Tribute" by Andrae Crouch. The refrain to the melody has a stretching quality to it. Notice that the notes are held on the word *God* and that the pitch is a note higher on each repetition. The melody itself encourages the people to "open up," stretch for the higher notes, and sing from the heart. When this refrain is played with a "triplet feel" (12/8 time), the effect is even more intense.

The same is true of the gospel song "What If It Were Today." On the words "Glory, Glory," the melody has a surge—a grand sweep to it— as each repetition stretches to a higher pitch. The "Coronation" and "Diadem" tunes to "All Hail the Power of Jesus' Name" as well as the hymn "Great God of Wonders" also have a sense of transcendency about them. So do the choruses "We Exalt Thee" and "Majesty." All these tunes provide vehicles for experiencing God's transcendence.[19]

Andrae Crouch

In performing songs and Scripture passages that accent transcendence, worship leaders need to pay more attention to the range of dynamics. On Mount Sinai God spoke to Moses in the thunder (Exod. 19:19), but on Mount Horeb He spoke to Elijah in the gentleness of a wispy wind (1 Kings 19:12). The extremes of loudness and softness can be windows to transcendence, and we can exploit these in our worship.

This phenomenon has been recognized by secular musicians. Fans of Chick Corea, outstanding jazz-rock musician, have reported that the most transcendent moments in his concerts have not been the loud, wailing sections, but the pianissimo moments that immediately follow them. It took sustained loudness to make the softness memorable. Corea sensed this and wrote about it, with the kind of insight—"wisdom"—worship leaders need as well.

In congregational singing, we need to explore the extreme boundaries of loudness and softness. Singing that lacks dramatic affect, that remains stuck in middle-ground dynamics, is deadly. It communicates indifference and unbelief. How can we hear that God is a consuming fire and then respond by singing listlessly? What does that communicate to our children? Are we not telling them in a powerful way that we don't really believe in this God? Or, that this God we serve is a middle-of-the-road God, flat and bland—nothing to be reckoned with? How false! Our God lives! He is a God of surprise and unimaginable gentleness, but let us not forget—above all—that He is a God to be feared and respected, a God of power. Our worship should reflect that.

Try exploiting the sudden shift from loudness to softness. Sing "Is It the Crowning Day" (robustly in the key of C), and follow it immediately without a break with the chorus "Majesty" (pianissimo in the key of F). The high-pitch ending of "Crowning Day" will provide a dynamic contrast with the low opening pitch of "Majesty." So sing the beginning of "Majesty" very softly and slowly. Let the sudden softness open a window to transcendence. Or have the people sing a rousing last stanza of "And Can It Be." Then allow them to meditate as the instrumentalists repeat the refrain pianissimo. If there is time, have the people hum it an octave lower at a slower tempo. The variations are endless.

Alternatively, you can use loudness. At the end of a Scripture reading, have the people repeat a refrain like "Glory to God," a little louder each time until it reaches a great shout. The leader could say "Glory to God" three times, with the people echoing it each time. Boldface or capital letters in the bulletin will reinforce the idea visually. You can even rehearse it with enthusiasm before the service begins. Inform the people of your intent. Let them know that by participating in varying the dynamics in these ways they can help to project to fellow worshipers a faithful image of the character of God and rekindle their own sense of God's transcendence.

Church architecture, artwork, and drama can also be windows to transcendence. With our largest numbers present and all the forces we can muster, let us stretch to project a greatness we have yet to imagine.

WHY LEARN FROM OLD TESTAMENT WORSHIP?

There are solid reasons why we can and should learn from Old Testament worship, the tabernacle model in particular. First, all Scripture is profitable.

> All Scripture is God-breathed and is useful for teaching, rebuking, correcting and training in righteousness, so that the man of God may be thoroughly equipped for every good work (2 Tim. 3:16).

"Every good work" includes the work of worship. For example, the tabernacle model has continuing significance because it points beyond itself to a timeless worship. It remains "a copy and shadow of what is in heaven" (Heb. 8:5).

Second, North Americans tend to forget that many people around the world continue to identify culturally with the Old Testament more than the New. Nomadic and tribal peoples are today where the Old Testament people were then. This suggests that the Old Testament can enrich and enlarge our own vision of worship. We can learn something, for example, about the selection of worship leaders and the function of drama, symbolism, and art in worship. If we have a strong sense of the biblical traditions of worship, we will be better able to make good decisions about worship and will be less likely to adopt new practices unthinkingly.

Third, tabernacle worship has value because, as we have seen, it points to the *underlying principles*. Particular outworkings of the principles may trigger fruitful lines of inquiry. Wenham is right when he says of the tabernacle system that the underlying principles "should bind the Christian, not the specific applications."[20] These principles include the ideas that the character of God is central to a proper theology of worship, that God is present as His people worship, and that costly worship is appropriate. In later chapters we will consider in more detail the Old Testament principles of drama, symbolism, and Davidic praise, the use of the arts, and the concept of celebration—all important elements of worship expression.

QUESTIONS FOR THOUGHT AND DISCUSSION

1. Why do you attend church on Sunday morning?
2. When does worship become more than a spectator sport?
3. How do we enter into God's presence? What actions can we take to prepare ourselves to "meet with God" during the Sunday morning worship service?
4. What can we do to make our worship more costly? Can you describe an occasion when you offered costly worship?
5. What is God like? List some characteristics.
6. Is holiness a difficult concept for you? In what way? Is holiness personally attractive to you? How can we make it more attractive?
7. Do we leave the time of worship with an enlarged sense of who God is and what He can do? How can we experience an enlarged concept of God? Have you had an experience (similar to mine on the Welland Canal) that broadened your concept of God?

RECOMMENDED READING

Leafblad, Bruce. *Music, Worship, and the Ministry of the Church*. Lectureship presented in January 1978 at Western Conservative Baptist Seminary. Portland, Oreg.: Western Conservative Baptist Seminary, Department of Information Resource Services.

Otto, Rudolf. *The Idea of the Holy*. Trans. John W. Harvey. New York: Oxford University Press, 1923.

Packer, J. I. *Knowing God*. Downers Grove, Ill.: InterVarsity Press, 1973.

Rayburn, Robert G. *Let Us Worship: Corporate Worship in the Evangelical Church*. Grand Rapids: Baker, 1980.

Tozer, A. W. *The Knowledge of the Holy*. Harrisburg: Christian Publications, 1961.

CHAPTER TWO

New Testament Principles

"Sir," the woman said, *"I can see that you are a prophet. Our fathers worshiped on this mountain, but you Jews claim that the place where we must worship is in Jerusalem."*

Jesus declared, "Believe me, woman, a time is coming when you will worship the Father neither on this mountain nor in Jerusalem. You Samaritans worship what you do not know; we worship what we do know, for salvation is from the Jews. Yet a time is coming and has now come when the true worshipers will worship the Father in spirit and truth, *for they are the kind of worshipers the Father seeks. God is spirit, and his worshipers must worship in spirit and in truth"* (John 4:19–24).

WHAT IS TRUE WORSHIP?

Many Christians consider the dialogue between Jesus and the woman of Samaria to be the critical passage on worship in the New Testament. Here Jesus communicates authoritatively a number of essential principles about true worship. We want to hear Him! We want to be receptive to all He has to say! Yet it is equally important not to overburden the text by making it into an endorsement for the way we happen to worship.

Jesus affirms five central principles of true worship in this passage:

1. True worship is not tied to a particular place.
2. True worship must be intelligent.
3. True worship must be spiritual.
4. True worship must be directed to God.
5. God seeks true worshipers.

Jesus deals in essentials. The first principle is essential because true worship is concerned more with a Person than a place. Christ knows that the Gentiles are about to be grafted into the plan of salvation, which will eventually embrace all the peoples of the earth. A sacred mountain or city for worshipers would be detrimental to the spread of this supranational faith. Christian worship can be celebrated with equal authenticity in a mud hut or a cathedral.

The second principle teaches that worship must be intelligent. The true worshiper needs to have a basic understanding of who God is and what He has done for our salvation. Interestingly, Jesus here identifies Himself with the children of Israel and their worship ("we worship what we know"), though His teaching supersedes Old Testament worship. He seems to be saying, "We Jews have a solid basis for our worship."

Third, true worship is spiritual in nature: "God is spirit, and his worshipers must worship in spirit and in truth."[1] Since God's essential nature is spirit, spirit must meet spirit and kind must meet kind for there to be a spiritual connection. That God is "spirit" means that He is invisible, immaterial, imperceptible to our senses, and "absolutely free from limitations of space and time."[2] Worship "in spirit" probably means worship that engages the human spirit.[3] Worship "in truth" probably means worship from the heart "without pretense."[4]

Fourth, true worship is worship of the Father. It is worship directed *to* the Father-God, as discussed in the previous chapter.

Finally, God actively desires our worship. This alone should inspire confidence in us to come before Him.

WHAT ABOUT EXTERNALS?

Note that Jesus is silent about the outward manifestations of worship. This suggests that He neither condemned them nor considered them essential.[5] Paul mentions them in his letter to the Philippians and warns believers not to trust in externals like circumcision for their salvation.

> Watch out for those dogs, those men who do evil, those mutilators of the flesh. For it is we who are the circumcision, we who worship by the Spirit of God, who glory in Christ Jesus, and who put no confidence in the flesh (Phil. 3:2–3).

The point seems to be that external religious observances and ceremonies cannot secure salvation, and Paul has harsh words for those who try to claim otherwise. But can we go beyond that and say, as some do, that all external forms of religion are illegitimate? Some have held this view in the past, and others perhaps unknowingly hold it today. Arthur W. Pink, writing in the early twentieth century, expresses this view in his commentary on this passage. He uses terms that sound strange to our ears because of their intemperateness.

Much of that which is termed "worship" today is fleshly rather than spiritual, and is external and spectacular, rather than internal and reverential. What are all the ornate decorations in our church-houses for? the stained glass windows, the costly hangings and fittings, the expensive organs! . . . "Yes," people reply, "but look at Solomon's temple!" Ah, *Solomon's*, truly. But look at it, and what do we see? Not one stone left upon another! Ah, dear reader, have you ever stopped to think what the future holds for this world and all its imposing structures? The world, and all that is therein, will be burned up! Not only the saloons and picture shows, but also its magnificent cathedrals and stately churches, erected at enormous expense. . . .

Worship, then, is the occupation of the heart with a *known* God; and everything which *attracts* the flesh and its sense, *detracts* from real worship. . . . Worship is not by the eyes or the ears, but "in spirit," that is, from the *new nature*. O how far astray we have gone! Modern "worship" is chiefly designed to render it pleasing to the flesh: a "bright and attractive service," with beautiful surroundings, sensuous music, and entertaining talks. What a mockery and a blasphemy! . . . *to whom* do the choirs sing—to God, or to the people? . . . The attractiveness of singing has been substituted for the "foolishness of preaching." . . . But is music wrong? Has not God Himself bestowed the gift? Surely, but what we are now complaining about is church-singing that is professional and spectacular, that which is of the flesh, and rendered to please the ear of man. . . .

We must worship "in spirit," and not merely with the physical senses. We cannot worship by admiring grand architecture, by listening to the peals of a costly organ or the anthems of a highly trained choir. We cannot worship by gazing at pictures, smelling of incense, counting of beads. We cannot worship with our eyes or ears, noses or hands, for they are all "flesh," and *not* "spirit." . . . Much, very much of our modern so-called worship is soulical, that is, emotional. . . . True worship, spiritual worship, is decorous, quiet, reverential, occupying the worshipper with God Himself.[6]

In this book we will challenge many of Pink's assertions, and let's begin with a couple of them here. Does Scripture indicate that true worship is always "quiet"? What about this statement: "The more spiritual is our worship the less formal and the less attractive to the flesh it will be."[7] Or what about the dichotomy Pink sets forth between so-called true and false worship: spiritual versus formal; spiritual versus physical; the spiritual versus the sensory; the spiritual versus the use of incense; spiritual versus emotional; spiritual versus professional; spiritual versus architectural; spiritual worship versus temple worship; known versus mysterious; internal versus external?[8]

I must respond to Pink on behalf of artists. Perhaps he, and preachers like him, do not cause grief intentionally, but they do it nevertheless. Upon hearing such preaching, artists of all kinds—especially recent, unchurched converts—are devastated. They pick up a "hidden message" that the body is bad and the arts are suspect.[9] After all, if the body is bad, then the things the body does—like hearing (music), seeing (banners, paintings), and smelling (incense)—are bad too. Artists, however, keenly recognize that their bodies, emotions, and senses are essential to their humanity and absolutely fundamental to their craft. Though attracted to the Jesus of the Gospels, they begin to sense inner tensions with church cultures like Pink's, and it hampers their development as artists. In our zeal to convert people to Jesus, we sometimes coerce them to buy into our particular church culture. Ironically, artists in this situation who should be finding new freedom in Christ instead are restrained from exercising their gifts within the church environment.[10]

Consequently people inclined toward the arts feel driven to decide between several unwholesome options. Those with strong identities eventually leave for other churches. Other, weaker artists—and this is tragic—drop their artistic endeavors altogether and stay. Still others, having grown up within these churches, tend to live a lonely, uneasy, schizophrenic existence, divorcing their professional artistic life from their church experience.

In his book *Jubilate!* Don Hustad, formerly an organist with the Billy Graham Evangelistic Association, speaks painfully of his own musical split personality.[11] I appeal to church leaders to show more sensitivity to those inclined toward the arts. Talk to them, encourage them, and learn of their inner struggles.

Fortunately, as a result of the work of Francis Schaeffer and others, anti-aesthetic attitudes seem to be receding among evangelicals.

> *I received in the mail from a pastor a package with a tape and a note inside. There was a person in his congregation contemplating a full-time music ministry, and the pastor asked, "Would you listen to this tape and assist us in advising our dear brother." I was moved by this pastor's obvious concern.*

But let's face it. All of us are bound by our own cultures, and often we're also blind to its faults. Because Pink writes in an earlier time, it's easy for us to dismiss his comments as a reflection of his own church culture and preaching style more than a careful exposition of Scripture. We can see *his* blind spots, but not our own! But if we are honest we will recognize some truth in his paragraphs! All too often our worship *does* border on entertainment. We *are* sometimes guilty of turning acts of worship into performances that appeal to our desire for spectacle.

In one sense genuine worship is, humanly speaking, very tenuous.

Leaders can determine ahead of time that a given worship service will have good content, be coherent and integrated, and have variety and interest. They can determine (if they have good performers) that they will make emotional contact with the people, even predict with good probability that there will be tears. Yet the result may not be spiritual worship! People can be taught to fall flat on their faces or raise their hands high in worship, yet even these gestures cannot ensure genuine worship.

Leaders simply cannot guarantee that true worship will occur each Sunday for each person. At best, they can prepare diligently, honestly try to model true worship, and strive to follow the leading of the Holy Spirit. True worship occurs when people offer their worship in faith, when they reach out to God and He comes to them, where spirit meets spirit.[12] Where such a spiritual connection takes place, there is true worship.

Thus, when Pink attacks the external trappings of worship he misses a basic issue. We can strip away all the externals—stained-glass windows, banners, organs, orchestral instruments, powerful tunes and lyrics, candles—and worship may not be any better, any purer, any more real, or any more acceptable to God. Bereft of ceremony, planning, and beauty, worship may still not be any better.

For true worship to occur, genuine faith, knowledge, and intelligent action is required. Yet if true worship is based in part on knowledge, then we who have a high view of Scripture have a definite chance for good worship. We, too, are in the running!

DISTINCTIVES OF NEW TESTAMENT WORSHIP

William Temple offers a definition of worship that speaks experientially of bringing the total person before God.

> What worship means is the submission of the whole being to the object of worship . . . the opening of the heart to receive the love of God . . . the subjection of conscience to be directed by him . . . the declaration of the need to be filled by him . . . the subjection of desire to be controlled by him; and as a result of all these together, it is the surrender of will to be used by him. It is the total giving of self.[13]

Elsewhere he conveys this idea in different terms:

> To worship is to quicken the conscience by the holiness of God, to feed the mind with the truth of God, to purge the imagination by the beauty of God, to devote the will to the purpose of God.[14]

Christian worship has so many aspects to it that it is futile to expect a single definition to embrace the subject adequately. As good as it is, Temple's definition is still so general that it could conceivably be applied to worship in other religions. What are some of the distinctive characteristics of Christian worship?

Christian Worship Is Trinitarian

Ralph P. Martin casts one of his definitions of worship in a Trinitarian form: "Christian worship is the adoration and service of God the Father through the mediation of the Son and prompted by the Holy Spirit."[15] The doctrine of the Trinity is expressed in benedictory statements in Scripture[16] and furnishes the structure of the three basic Christian creeds: the Apostles', the Nicene, and the Athanasian. It is "an inescapable frame within which all thought about worship must move."[17] Within that framework theologians use prepositions to stress the dynamics of Christian worship. We direct our worship *to* the Father, *through* the Son, *by* (or in) the Holy Spirit.[18]

Christian Worship Is Christocentric

At the very center of the Christian faith are the birth, life, death, burial, and resurrection of Jesus Christ. The apostle Paul says:

> For what I received I passed on to you as of *first importance:* that Christ died for our sins according to the Scriptures, that he was buried, that he was raised on the third day, . . . and that he appeared to Peter, and then to the Twelve. After that he appeared to more than five hundred of the brothers at the same time, most of whom are still living (1 Cor. 15:3–6).

Christ set Himself at the heart of Christian worship by instituting the Lord's Supper.

> Jesus took bread, gave thanks and broke it, and gave it to his disciples, saying, "Take and eat; this is my body." Then he took the cup, gave thanks and offered it to them, saying, "Drink from it, all of you. This is my blood of the covenant, which is poured out for many for the forgiveness of sins" (Matt. 26:26–28).

> "Whoever eats my flesh and drinks my blood has eternal life, and I will raise him up at the last day. For my flesh is real food and my blood is real drink. Whoever eats my flesh and drinks my blood remains in me, and I in him" (John 6:54–56).

> "Do this in remembrance of me" (Luke 22:19).

We do not appreciate the degree to which Jesus Himself permanently changed the face of Christian worship from synagogue worship. Social and cultural changes are difficult to sustain. We tend to slip back into former practices. Kenneth Tollefson contends that the process of change is never complete until "changes become institutionalized."[19]

When Jesus inaugurated the Lord's Supper and charged His disciples to "do this in remembrance of me," He effected a permanent change. It was a watershed statement for Christian worship. The Lord's Supper separates Christian worship from Judaism, from Hinduism, and from all the other major religions. The act of Communion is a true distinctive of Christian worship.[20] Keeping the Lord's Supper, therefore, is one way of ensuring the centrality of Christ in Christian worship.

In addition, Christ authoritatively reinterpreted Jewish worship customs. For example, He told the Pharisees, "The Sabbath was made for man, not man for the Sabbath. So the Son of Man is Lord even of the Sabbath" (Mark 2:27–28). Moreover, Jesus proclaimed Himself "greater than the temple" (Matt. 12:6) and sounded a new note of intimacy in worship. He taught His disciples to address God in prayer as *Abba* ("Dear Father"). Addressing Jehovah-God intimately as Father was foreign to Jewish thinking.[21] That intimacy is further extended in the New Testament in the person of Jesus Christ for He is with us in worship: "Where two or three come together in my name, there am I with them" (Matt. 18:20).

Christian Worship Is Energized by the Holy Spirit

As enlightener, enabler, energizer, inspirer, helper, interceder, transformer, convicter, and refiner, the Holy Spirit gives worship its source of immediacy and vitality. J. I. Packer compares the Holy Spirit to a powerful floodlight. We find something like this emphasis in the Gospel of John, where the Spirit enlightens, guides, and convicts.

> "But the Counselor, the Holy Spirit, whom the Father will send in my name, will teach you all things and will remind you of everything I have said to you" (John 14:26).

> "He will guide you into all truth" (John 16:13).

> "He will convict the world of guilt in regard to sin and righteousness and judgment" (John 16:8).

But in the Book of Revelation and elsewhere the Holy Spirit is symbolized by a yet stronger image: fire! He is called the seven "blazing" lamps. "Tongues of fire" marked the coming of the Holy Spirit on the Day of Pentecost.

> They were all together in one place. Suddenly a sound like the blowing of a violent wind came from heaven and filled the whole house where they were sitting. They saw what seemed to be tongues of fire that separated and came to rest on each of them (Acts 2:1–3).

This symbol associates the Holy Spirit with proclamation. Paul ties personal confession of Christ as Lord directly to the Holy Spirit, and he links the Spirit to boldness in preaching.

> You know that when you were pagans, somehow or other you were influenced and led astray to mute idols. Therefore I tell you that no one who is speaking by the Spirit of God says, "Jesus be cursed," and *no one can say, "Jesus is Lord,"* except by the Holy Spirit (1 Cor. 12:2–3).[22]

> After they prayed, the place where they were meeting was shaken. And they were all filled with the Holy Spirit and *spoke the word of God boldly* (Acts 4:31).

Likewise, prayers are made effective by the Spirit.

> The Spirit *helps* us in our weakness. We do not know what we ought to pray for, but the Spirit himself *intercedes* for us with groans that words cannot express (Rom. 8:26).

Moreover, the Spirit labors to see gifts manifested in the church body. Paul writes, "All these [gifts] are the work of one and the same Spirit, and he gives them each one, just as he determines" (1 Cor. 12:11).

Scripture says further, "Do not put out the Spirit's fire" (1 Thess. 5:19). The context of this passage seems to suggest that the Thessalonians were inclined to squelch the expression of the gifts of the Spirit.

On reflection we can see how crucial a role the Spirit plays in worship. The Spirit inspires public confessions of faith, the proclamation of the Word, prayer, and service—all basic aspects of worship.

The image of fire expresses well the living quality of the Spirit. Additionally, fire can be disturbing! And it can spread. Fire has energy and transforms, purges, and refines. *Frankly, I would like to see more fire in our worship.*

What are the results of the Spirit's fire? Joy. Liberation. The transformation of believers into Christ's likeness.

> And the disciples were filled with joy and with the Holy Spirit (Acts 13:52).

> For the kingdom of God is not a matter of eating and drinking, but of righteousness, peace and joy in the Holy Spirit (Rom. 14:17).

> For the letter kills, but the Spirit gives life (2 Cor. 3:6).

> Now the Lord is the Spirit, and where the Spirit of the Lord is, there is freedom. And we, who with unveiled faces all reflect the Lord's glory, are being transformed into his likeness with ever-increasing glory, which comes from the Lord, who is the Spirit (2 Cor. 3:17–18).

Nowhere do we find Scripture encouraging people to be gullible or involved in excesses, exaggerations, or a love for sensationalism (1 Thess.

5:19–21). On the one hand, God's people today, like the Bereans, should subject teaching and experience to the scrutiny of Scripture (Acts 17:11). On the other hand, Scripture encourages believers to trust the leading of the Holy Spirit and let Him work. When God's people let this happen, they can have a balanced worship that is reverent yet exuberant, free yet disciplined.

The Priesthood of Believers

The priesthood of believers is a concept whose time has come. Of all the doctrines and reforms that received impetus from the Reformation, the priesthood of believers has had much less impact on the church than might have been expected. Kenneth Haugk writes:

> For centuries, church people have talked, reflected, cogitated, preached, taught, and established committees and commissions to thrash out the meaning and practices inherent in the priesthood of all. But while Christians have thumbed their scripts until they are dog-eared, they haven't been given their cue to walk on the stage to play their part in the work of the church.[23]

Yet the New Testament gives prominence to the principle.

> Now to each one the manifestation of the Spirit is given for the common good (1 Cor. 12:7).

> God has arranged the parts in the body, every one of them, just as he wanted them to be. If they were all one part, where would the body be? (1 Cor. 12:18–19).

> You also, like living stones, are being built into a spiritual house to be *a holy priesthood, offering spiritual sacrifices* acceptable to God through Christ Jesus (1 Peter 2:5).

> But you are a chosen people, *a royal priesthood*, a holy nation, a people belonging to God, *that you may declare the praises* of him who called you out of darkness into his wonderful light (1 Peter 2:9).

The concept of the priesthood of believers derived from the Old Testament suggests worship "to the Lord." The Pauline concept of the church as a "body," though it includes a ministry of praise, focuses more directly on ministry to one another. And the Book of Revelation, which has a strong worship dimension, draws on the concept (1:6; 5:10; 20:6). The sum total is a holistic view of priesthood in worship.

One of my goals in writing this book is to contribute to a more complete realization of the priesthood of believers in our churches. Pastors can promote this by providing leadership training in all aspects of church life. Training people to lead in public prayer is one example; that in itself can become a form of discipling. One can start by preparing a one-page instruction sheet, similar to Ray Ortlund's in appendix 2, and spending time praying with prayer leaders. Similarly, some congregations have formed a Bible reading group to prepare those who read Scripture publicly.

WORSHIP IN PERSPECTIVE: PRIMARY, EQUAL, OR SECONDARY?

What place should worship have in the overall ministry of a church? An increasing number of evangelical pastors, musicians, theologians, and researchers of worship are taking the view that worship should receive priority over teaching, fellowship, or evangelism.[24] This seems to be a relatively new emphasis for Evangelicals.

Bruce Leafblad writes, "If God is to be first in our lives and first in our churches, then worship must come ahead of everything else we do. Worship is that process in which we make God first in our lives. . . . The worship comes first; then the work and the works follow."[25] He reasons as follows:

1. The great commandment—"Love the Lord your God with all your soul" and "your neighbor as yourself" (Luke 10:27)—puts the love of God first.
2. Our referents for God describe Him in terms of worship. The biblical words for God—both the Hebrew word *Elohim* and the Greek word *Theos* —mean "an object of worship."
3. Worship is a priority in the Old Testament. The first four commandments of the Decalogue have to do with worship (Exodus 20), and one of the chief struggles of the Old Testament prophets was to keep Israel's worship uncorrupted from foreign gods.
4. The Westminster Shorter Catechism answers the question "What is the chief end of man?" with the answer "to glorify God and to enjoy Him forever."
5. Worship is the central issue in the Book of Revelation. When teaching and evangelism are ended in heaven, worship continues.[26]

Jack Hayford also places worship before fellowship and evangelism. At the risk of sounding iconoclastic he says, "The idol of evangelism *has* distracted us from the worship of the living God, in more ways than many dedicated leaders and sincere believers realize. . . . our first sacrifice ought to be the sacrifice of praise. . . . our first work ought to be the humbling of ourselves in His presence."[27] He sees evangelism as the "by-product of spiritual life flowing from a healthy Body nourished through worship and fellowship." Furthermore, he views worship as "a key to the release of the Church's power."[28]

> God's revealed will in calling His people together [in worship] is that they might experience His presence and power—not as a spectacle or sensation, but in a discovery of His will through encounter and impact. . . .
>
> Worship is the means by which a place is prepared for God to meet with and move among His people. . . .
>
> I am troubled because, for the most part, believers gathering for worship generally do not expect God to: (1) be present in a distinct and profound way; or (2) do anything especially discernible. He [God] wants a place to display His presence, His love, His power and *Himself.*
>
> We present ourselves in worship purposing to provide a place for God to make an entrance among us, to shape us, to work among and through us.[29]

In Hayford's church the priorities for ministry are clear. Ministry to the Lord comes first, then ministry to the saints, and finally ministry to the world.[30] Other churches have set similar priorities.[31]

Wayne Peterson, a layman, echoes these ideas. He asked me, "Barry, has anyone put forward the thought that perhaps worship was intended not only to bless God, but to be the means by which the Holy Spirit is to empower us for ministry? Doesn't true worship direct our focus and center our lives in the Father? If true worship is so chronically absent in the evangelical church, could this be the root of our failure to live holy lives, to serve, and to evangelize? If contact with God energizes us, should not worship be our primary energizing contact?"[32]

On the other hand, Ronald Allen and Gordon Borror place the stress on balance—parity rather than priority. Noting that balance is not easily achieved, they suggest three primary areas for church ministry: worship, edification, and evangelism.[33]

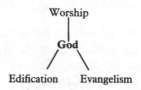

In visualizing their model, they say it is "essential to have God exactly in the center. All the ministry must revolve around Him. If we get the idea that He is interested in our concentrating in only one area, we will fall out of balance!"[34]

Donald Hustad adopts a somewhat similar view, but widens the definition of worship:

> Worship is any and every worthy response to God. There is no point to a question raised by some evangelicals, whether it is more important to "express adoration of God" or to "witness and evangelize" in our communal gatherings. One act gives corporate voice to our inner commitment; the other is our outward expression of our love in obedience to Christ's second great command, ". . . You shall love your neighbor as yourself" (Mark 12:31).[35]

Emphasizing the positive value of allowing for a variety of ministry approaches, church growth consultants Daniel Reeves and Ronald Jenson list five typologies of church ministry that lend themselves to church growth:

1. Soul-winning churches
2. Classroom churches with at least forty minutes of expository preaching
3. Life-situation churches concentrating on fellowship and meeting the needs of individuals
4. Special-purpose churches with programming around a single issue, style of ministry, or charismatic leader
5. General practitioner churches that give equal attention to evangelism, teaching, relationships, and social action[36]

The latter, according to Reeves and Jenson, is regarded by many churches as the ideal. Interestingly, worship as an emphasis does not appear on their list, even though worship seems to be a dominant factor in the rapid growth of many young congregations in Southern California. They do conclude, however, that one reason why charismatic churches are growing rapidly is that "they have learned how to praise. Praise unlocks all sorts of potential in people and churches" by building into congregations "a positive attitude toward God."[37]

Clearly God's blessing has attended a variety of church models. In soul-winning and classroom models, worship often receives a secondary emphasis. While appreciating the variety, this book seeks to make the point that the response of people in a worship service merits attention.

As our culture continues to diversify, we will see even more diversity in the church. But every church must have worship. My experience has confirmed again and again that good worship blends with and enhances the life of any church no matter what its philosophy of ministry. My greatest concern is that worship not be *neglected*. I would like to see worship receive parity with other emphases of ministry. Yet worship leaders who show concern *only* for worship and undervalue other church ministries are not helping a congregation.

Whatever weight worship is given, however, worship committees and worship leaders should understand and support the philosophy of ministry adopted in their local church. Worship needs to be integrated into the larger context of each church's mission.

QUESTIONS FOR THOUGHT AND DISCUSSION

1. How could the "priesthood of believers" be implemented more completely in your service?
2. What is the role of the Holy Spirit in your worship?
3. In what way is the image of the Spirit as fire valuable?
4. Why is the Trinity an important concept for Christian worship?
5. Has evangelism distracted us from worship? Need this be the case?
6. In what ways can worship become excessively entertaining? Illustrate.
7. "Everything which *attracts* the flesh and its sense *detracts* from real worship." Is this statement true? Why or why not?
8. "We can strip away all the external trappings of worship . . . and worship may not be any better, any purer, any more real, or any more acceptable to God." Is this true? Why or why not?
9. What are the priorities of ministry in your church? Should worship be the first priority?

RECOMMENDED READING

Hoon, Paul Waitman. *The Integrity of Worship*. Nashville: Abingdon Press, 1971.
Martin, Ralph P. *The Worship of God: Some Theological, Pastoral, and Practical Reflections*. Grand Rapids: Wm. B. Eerdmans, 1982.

PART II

Family Worship

CHAPTER THREE

Learning From the Patriarchs: Parents Leading Families

"No, Dad, that's not the way you do it! You have to get down on your hands and knees."

CONNECTING WITH CHILDREN

I remember coming home from work one day to be greeted by my son Jesse, then four years old, wanting to play with me. I tried, but my mind was off somewhere in the "ozone layer." Hovering over him, I interacted here and there absent-mindedly. Finally Jesse became frustrated with me. *"No, Dad,"* he said, *"that's not the way you do it! You have to get down on your hands and knees! Get down, Dad! Get down!"*

He took my hand and towed me underneath the grand piano. Having gotten me down on all fours—my white shirt, tie, and jacket still on—and feeling self-satisfied with this accomplishment, he gave me a choice of two toys. "Now, Dad," he said, "which one are *you* going to be?"

I'm so glad Jesse insisted! He helped me connect.

This chapter is intended to help you *connect* with your children in the area of family worship. You'll learn about recent research on how children learn, and you'll find practical suggestions of things you can try in your own family worship. I hope you find them realistic. We parents often feel guilt-ridden and inadequate in our parenting roles. Let's stimulate ourselves to have some small successes. We do need a starting point!

GUILT: MAJOR ROADBLOCK FOR PARENTS

The North American family has undergone significant change in the past several decades and now has assumed highly variegated forms. The traditional family—father working, mother homemaking—presently comprises only 7 percent of the households in the United States.[1] The typical contemporary family—both mother and father working—accounts for another 34 percent, while single persons head more than 38 percent of the nation's households.[2]

These are difficult days for families! Larry Richards reports that 98 percent of parents from conservative, evangelical backgrounds think it is "very important" that their children receive a Christian upbringing, yet only 4 percent say they are "very satisfied" with their efforts.[3] Church leaders need to be aware that an acute sense of failure leads parents to "draw back from programs that purport to offer them help."

> For many Christian parents, repeated failure to meet their own idealized expectations has made it too costly to make any fresh effort. Offers of training that promise new skills also carry the expectation of performance. And the price of additional failures—fresh guilt—has become so high that many are unwilling to try again.[4]

Leaders find that trying to help parents is not easy. Despite well-meaning efforts, weekend parent-training seminars, printed materials, and the like haven't proven effective in changing the way we parent. Some efforts may even have had negative side effects. Robert Hess advises beleaguered parents to avoid training emphases that increase self-doubt and uncertainty in their role and rob them of spontaneity. Attention should be focused on the child, not "Am I doing it right?"[5] Moreover, leaders can help parents by stressing the complexity of child raising: "If the task is difficult, failure can be accepted; if it is perceived as easy, failure is a serious threat to confidence and self-esteem."[6] Educators have discovered from experience that self-help, mutual support, and discussion among parents may be the most promising avenue to constructive change.

> The wisdom and experience of other parents may be the major resource available. . . . There is an authenticity that comes from having shared an experience; to realize that another parent has been through the problem gives a sense of confidence in their judgment and advice. . . . [That] other parents have problems they find difficult to solve carries a unique assurance. . . . [Parents] experience a great sense of relief when they discover these feelings are shared by other parents. The fear that one is uniquely incompetent is dissipated.[7]

Parents need one another. An interactive, caring church environment is ideally suited to helping parents and their families. The key is "not the training of parents, but involvement of parents in vital faith-community relationships with other adults."[8]

> Community is relational, and demands belonging and participation in a fellowship where personal relationships deepen and loving mutual ministry takes place. . . . two-parent, one-parent, or reconstituted families . . . must have roots sunk deep in supportive faith community relationships. . . . this kind of group can give specific support and help.[9]

LINKING CHURCH WORSHIP TO FAMILY WORSHIP

Churches are in a good position to offer leadership to parents by providing them with encouragement, ideas, and support for family worship. The best way to give it is to have the church worship committee lend a hand.

Unfortunately, when churches consider meeting their needs for worship, they often focus too narrowly on music and the Sunday morning worship service.[10] Typically, they form a *music committee* consisting of the church accompanists, the choir director, and maybe the songleader. This group limits itself to coordinating the weekly "special music" and planning the major events in the year—Christmas and Easter cantatas and the like. It usually doesn't even get involved in the weekly planning of the order of service. But if the group thought of itself as a *worship committee*, it could find other areas of ministry that a music committee might overlook. Specifically, *worship committees can offer support for family and small group worship.*

In carrying out this broader mandate, committee members should begin by devoting time together to study worship. After all, we expect Sunday school teachers to study for their lessons. Shouldn't we expect our worship leaders to become informed too? As a result of their study, committee members could actively seek to have a ripple effect on the entire congregation by sharing their insights and ideas with the church community (1) one-on-one, (2) in the church bulletin, (3) in a Sunday school class devoted to worship, (4) and by designing a variety of experiences that encourage family worship.

More parents would take an active role in the spiritual leadership of their families if they were given some specific ideas and if they knew other parents in the church were presently using these ideas.

WHAT ABOUT THE FAMILY ALTAR?

The family altar—the practice of reading the Bible and praying together as a family—was once central to American Christian culture and family life. Charles Sell writes that "before the American Revolution the family altar was the means of giving Christian nurture to the children."[11] Today, however, only 5 percent of professing contemporary Christian families have any kind of regular family worship,[12] and evangelical educators are divided on the question "Should we have daily family devotions?"[13]

"Not necessarily," says Sell. Family members can become bored, even hardened by the daily routine of family devotions. Some parents have "little gift for reading out loud or for creative planning and are primarily prompted by nagging guilt." He advises parents to "do what fits their family best" and to "avoid heaping oppressive guilt on themselves if they miss devotions from time to time."[14]

> *In my childhood, our family had its best times of heart-felt worship when we were singing duets and quartets and playing instruments together. As we sought to blend our voices and spirits together, the Lord used these times to create a bond between us and with Him. This was a very natural outcome of our music-making together.*

When families do have devotions together, Hess suggests, they should make them personal, simple, and short and allow for participation and spontaneity. Our desire is for children to catch "who we are," not just "what we do." If family worship springs from a healthy, happy relationship with a loving God, children can find worship to be special.

We should strongly encourage spiritual discipline in the home, including the family altar. But it is worth remembering that the family altar is not a practice expressly commanded anywhere in Scripture. There is a passage of Scripture that contains express instructions. More general in character than the family altar, its ramifications are wider, its injunctions never abrogated; as such it deserves our careful attention.

MOSES: "TEACH THEM WHEN YOU SIT DOWN AND WHEN YOU WALK"

While the Bible gives us no look inside someone's head, no "biblical psychology of learning," it does describe "the personal and social environment that stimulates growth in faith."[15]

> "You shall love the LORD your God with all your heart and with all your soul and with all your might. And these words, which I am commanding you today, shall be on your heart; and you shall teach them diligently to your sons and shall talk of them when you sit in

your house and when you walk by the way and when you lie down and when you rise up. And you shall bind them as a sign on your hand and they shall be as frontals on your forehead. And you shall write them on the doorposts of your house and on your gates" (Deut. 6:5–9 NASB).[16]

In the Old Testament, instruction is not isolated from life experience. Religious instruction is to be woven through the entire day— as family members sit together, walk along the road, lie down at night, or rise in the morning. "The underlying assumption seems to be that as life is lived together, godly parents will explain their actions by pointing out the words of God that are guiding their responses. . . . instruction is to infuse all of life."[17] The Deuteronomy model is not formal, structured, compartmentalized classroom learning, but informal, spontaneous, irregular, situation-specific learning. Deuteronomy learning is meant to encompass the whole range of life's activities, link attitudes with motives, and present to children the parent's outlook and perspective. It is to be a life-sharing interaction, an interpretation for children of the way we live.

FITTED TO THE WAY CHILDREN LEARN

The genius of Deuteronomy 6 is that it is fitted to the way children learn. We can derive several principles from the Deuteronomy instructional model.

Deuteronomy Learning Is Situational

Children don't learn by taking abstract concepts like forgiveness and applying them to a variety of situations. They do it the other way around. They gradually come to understand the meaning of forgiveness (for example) from numerous concrete situations in which they see forgiveness demonstrated. Long before they can articulate the principles, they grasp them intuitively. So the secret to teaching children the Christian life is to link biblical principles to concrete situations that will serve to guide their response.[18]

Deuteronomy Learning Is Affective (Emotional)

Deuteronomy learning occurs in the peaks and valleys of everyday living, amid life's joys and calamities. Part of the genius of this model is that when God's words are spoken of in everyday situations, "the emotional and affective components of the experience are immediately associated with the concepts, a linkage of concept and affect is immediately achieved!"[19] Classroom teaching, by contrast, tends to divorce concepts from emotions.

Larry Richards writes:

> It is in fact our emotional responses to situations that trigger our thoughts and shape our perceptions, rather than our analysis of a situation triggering our emotions. As long as our understanding of the Bible and its teachings is not linked to our emotions, it is unlikely that we will remember and apply appropriate Bible truths. . . . whenever we teach a core truth we must attempt to link that core truth to emotions associated with situations in which it is to be applied.[20]

He calls this tying a truth to a child's "emotional map." Feelings can serve as cues that recall a truth and guide the child's response.

To take full advantage of this principle, parents need to feel comfortable sharing their feelings with their children. Many of us have trouble with that. In our culture, men particularly find self-disclosure difficult. What can we do to encourage intimacy in sharing? One thing fathers can do is talk about situations and feelings they had when they were young. Talking about childhood experiences is less threatening, yet it gives children valuable insight into parents. Leafing through a family photo album can also stimulate this process. As Mom or Dad tell what they remember about the day a particular picture was taken, feelings can surface naturally.

Deuteronomy Learning Involves Parental Modeling

Young children are not always capable of moral reasoning. They trust the judgment of parents who point out to them what is right. In fact, says Richards, children will imitate the cues and models parents have given them, "without necessarily being aware of the moral nature of their actions!"[21] Factors that enhance the impact of modeling are

1. Frequent, long-term contact with the model
2. A warm, loving relationship with the model
3. Exposure to the inner states of the model
4. Observation of the model in a variety of life settings
5. Consistency and clarity in the model
6. Correspondence between the behavior of the model and the beliefs and ideals of the community
7. Explanation of the lifestyle chosen by the model with accompanying shared experiences and stories[22]

INTERVENTIONS

How can we apply this model from Deuteronomy to family life today? Christian educators are suggesting that we use carefully designed experiences called "interventions" to foster change. Richards defines the concept of intervention this way:

> [Intervention] seeks to touch each parent as a person and affect family lifestyle. . . . [Interventions] deal with *specific, small units of behavior.* Rather than dealing with the total patterns of a family's life, interventions use a series of *tiny, apparently insignificant experiences* to change patterns of lifestyle gradually over a long period of time. . . . Interventions *expect no radical or immediate changes.* Instead interventions are designed to *provide a variety of simple, repeated family experiences* that come in different forms time after time after time. . . . [they are] *ineffective when used in isolation* (italics added).[23]

We can look to the Old Testament patriarchs for clues to the kinds of family worship "interventions" we might try in our twentieth-century setting. The patriarchs were no different from you and me. They experienced their fair share of peak experiences and valleys. Yet it is significant that in their times of celebration and crisis, they gathered their families around them.

Naturally we will have to adapt their examples to fit our contemporary situation. Surveys show that parents are looking for short learning experiences (five-to-fifteen minutes long), fun-sharing family times, ideas that fit the flow of family life, and projects children can do on their own.[24] Not every suggestion below meets all these conditions, but some of them do so.

Noah: Marking Milestones With Thanksgiving

After disembarking from the ark, Noah, man of beginnings, built an altar and offered clean animals as a burnt sacrifice before the Lord (Gen. 8:20). For him and his family this was a memorable thanksgiving event marking the beginning of a new life together.

Idea: Worship During Peak Experiences

The milestones in our lives can become opportunities for worship and thanksgiving. A new birth in the family,[25] someone coming home from the hospital, a job promotion, a good report card, graduation, an award, victories in soccer or baseball—all these can be real reasons to feel thankful and celebrate. Highlight the good things that happen to your family with impromptu prayers of thanksgiving. If you plan a structured celebration, candles can add elegance to the occasion.

Abraham: Abraham and Isaac on the Trail Together

Abraham and the lad Isaac trekked to Mount Moriah, where Abraham's faith would be severely tested (Gen. 22). It's interesting that they *journeyed together* to the place of worship. They had ample time to converse (three days), knowing all the while that the purpose of their trip was to worship. They were on a kind of "worship hike."

Idea: Worship Hike

We tried this at the church I attend! Our worship committee did the research and planning and spearheaded the event. Five fathers with sons four-to-eight years old participated. Actually one daughter also got in on it! The event could have involved mothers only or entire families or singles.

At the hiking site, we formed a circle and explained our purpose: "This is going to be a worship hike. God made everything we are about to see. Every time we see something beautiful today, we want to thank God who made it."

Soon our kids were busy finding walking sticks and collecting rocks, leaves, and cones. For them worship seemed to be a natural thing. "Dad, I'm thankful for this!" one would say, bringing us some object. For us fathers it was a time to slow down and let our adult hearts be captivated once again by the playful movement of butterflies and the scent of pine trees.

On reaching our destination we had a short time of "show and tell." Each father paired off and asked his children what they were most thankful for. Then we each shared, sang a song, had a prayer, and ate our sack lunches, savoring the fresh air on a mountain peak.

It was a great time in every way. Later it struck me that families could do something like this as a natural part of their vacation, or even when taking a stroll around the block in the early morning or at night. For older children, another possibility might be to hike to a cabin and have Communion there, using wheat and grapes.

Jacob: Crisis Motivates Worship

Jacob was a man who learned to worship in times of extremity. When he was fleeing for his life, God came to him in a dream at Bethel and assured him of His faithfulness (Gen. 28:7). In response to this theophany, this powerful manifestation of God's presence, Jacob built an altar there.

Later one of Jacob's daughters was raped (Gen. 34:2). His sons retaliated by murdering not only the culprit, but all the males who lived in that town. As a result of his son's untempered vengeance, Jacob greatly feared for his family's safety. "You have brought trouble on me by making me a stench," he told them (Gen. 34:30).

During this time of acute crisis, Jacob rid his household of idols, then he gathered and led his family back to Bethel, where he had originally erected the altar. It was a journey back to repentance and renewal (35:1–7). Perhaps as his family sojourned, Jacob had opportunity to recount to his sons the many twists his life had taken—the seamy parts as well as the good. In the throes of calamity, the patriarch led his family back to his spiritual roots. You have to admire the man.

Idea: Walk Children Through Significant Crossroads in Your Life

If we can believe reports that families experience a crisis of some kind about every six months, parents need a strategy for turning even these calamities into times of worship. Such troubles can be a catalyst to develop faith.

We parents also have had our spiritual theophanies! Have you walked your children back through those significant crossroads in your spiritual life? Tell your story! If possible, take a journey, show them the very place where it happened. Express your thanksgiving to God before them: "Here I met the Lord. . . . Here I met my wife. . . . Here God provided a job for me when I didn't know where to turn. . . . Here God provided our first home."

Idea: Photo Album

We can use also life experience as a catalyst for worship by leafing through a photo album. Have Dad or Mom tell where they first lived, when they were married, where each child was born. Then have each child relate some memory about the family. Keep each person's turn short. After a few sentences let another family member continue. Each person may have more than one turn. Bring the family's story up to date by including something that has happened recently. After the last person shares, have a prayer of thanksgiving and then conclude by saying, "To be continued." After all, family stories don't end![26]

Idea: Bible Predicaments

Have one family member volunteer to be "it" and leave the room. While the person is gone, have the others decide on a Bible predicament—for example, David facing Goliath, Paul and Silas in jail, or Daniel in the lion's den. Then the person is brought back into the room and asks each family member, "What would you do?" Family members answer honestly what they would do in this predicament. They might say,

"I would pray a lot!" or "I would try to climb out." From the clues in the answers, the person who is "it" tries to guess the predicament. When that is accomplished, talk about how the people trusted God in the predicament. Also try to imagine the kind of prayer each person might have prayed when it was over.[27]

Job: Partying and Feasting Prompts Worship

Job's concern for his children extended into their adulthood. The Book of Job tells of their partying:

> His [Job's] sons used to take turns holding feasts in their homes, and they would invite their three sisters to eat and drink with them. When a period of feasting had run its course, Job would send and have them purified. Early in the morning he would sacrifice a burnt offering for each of them, thinking, "Perhaps my children have sinned and cursed God in their hearts." This was Job's custom (Job 1:4–5).

Some scholars believe a birthday celebration could have been the occasion for the festivity. Whatever the case, it is clear that Job regularly involved himself in intercessory action on behalf of his family.

Idea: "Remember When" Birthday Party

At prayer meetings many of us have heard grandparents not only request prayer for their children but also report feeling burdened or urged by God to intercede for them at particular times. We need to encourage more of that. Seniors and grandparents, how about instigating a "Remember When" birthday party!

If your children or grandchildren live far away, don't let that fact stop you! Invite over some friends and have a birthday party in your children's honor—even in their absence. Retell and relive all those prankish stories! Toward the end of your time together, offer thanksgiving and intercessory prayers for the children of all the seniors present.[28]

SHORT, EASY FAMILY WORSHIP EXPERIENCES

Family Praise Prayer

Gather in a family circle. Provide or have each family member offer a word that can be worked into a family prayer for the day. The words could be *God, beautiful, thank you, people, wonderful, big, small.* Repeat this idea on other occasions, soliciting different sets of words. The prayer can be improvised or written out, read, and tacked to the refrigerator.[29]

It's a good way to instill a sense of belonging and participation. This idea also works nicely while traveling in a car.

ABC Praise

Read aloud Psalm 113:1. Tell family members they will be given ten minutes to prepare an ABC praise list. Think of something to praise God for that starts with each letter of the alphabet: A—*Answer to prayer;* B—*Bananas;* C—*Christ;* D—*Daylight,* E *Eyes to see;* F—*Friends,* etc. Read your lists to one another. Have a circle of prayer with each person giving thanks. Sing a song of praise together (e.g., "God is so good").[30]

Compliments and Thanksgiving

Compliments can encourage a general attitude of thanksgiving in the home. Send one person from the room. Have each person write a compliment about him on a piece of paper. Recall the person and have a family member read each compliment while the person being complimented tries to guess who wrote it. Redistribute sheets of paper and repeat the procedure until each person has been complimented. Conclude with each person offering one compliment to God.[31]

Acrostic of Praise

Make an acrostic of praise to a family member. Beside each letter of the family member's name (listed vertically) write a word starting with that letter:

> Jolly
> Open
> Honest
> Neat

Cooperate collectively in this task or do it individually. Then do an acrostic on the name "God," or "Father."[32]

MORE INVOLVED, EXTENDED WORSHIP EXPERIENCES

Advent Candlelighting Ceremony

This ceremony is an effective way to keep Christmas in proper focus. It's easy to do, although with children participating you never can be sure just what will happen! As Sally Jarvis found out:

> A few years ago, our church gave us a pamphlet describing a typical home Advent ceremony. This is usually a simple ceremony in which the whole family participates. A candle is lit on a wreath on each of

four Sundays before Christmas. The family may say a prayer, read a passage of Scripture, or sometimes sing a hymn. The pamphlet was full of good ideas on how to conduct this ceremony, but we couldn't help wondering what kind of family the writer had in mind. I don't think it could have been ours.

The cover picture showed a mother and father, both looking peppy, and a boy and girl, both smiling. All were looking at the Advent wreath in the center of the picture. The boy and girls were (a) neatly dressed, (b) had their hair combed, and (c) were not fighting over their turn to light the candle. . . .

In our family the pamphlet children, two in number, would be replaced by four—all messy. The boy would be in jeans, the girls in slacks. The baby would still be in her pretty Sunday dress, but because she'd spent the day sleeping and eating in it, it would stick to her fat tummy in comfortable wrinkles.

The pamphlet had the first child say, "I light this candle on the first Sunday in Advent."

In our house the first child said, "It's my turn to light the candle." The second child said, "You did it first last year; it's my turn!" Third child: "Daddy, you promised me last year that I could do it first this year. . . ."

Finally Father had the inspiration of having one child strike the match, one child light the candle, and one child blow it out. He was lucky the baby was too young to speak out. . . .

On one occasion as we lit the candles, a magical hush came. . . . someone noticed that the candlelight from below was casting shadows on the ceiling from the chandelier. Because the chandelier was swaying slightly, so were the shadows, and the brother decided that this looked just like Superman. "It's a bird. It's a plane!" went the cry, and the six-year-old was so carried away that she leaped up from the table and ran around the house turning out lights so that we could see the shadows better. We were plunged into darkness, with everybody shouting "Superman!" . . . The next year the two older sisters fought over whose turn it was to light the first candle and one finally shouted, "Go on: light the candle of love, dummy!"

Five years has passed since our church introduced to us the Advent wreath. . . . Our Advent ceremonies would never make the typical-family pamphlet yet I feel the baby Jesus would have enjoyed every one.[33]

Family Bible Reading Project

Tim Stafford reports that well under 10 percent of our evangelical young people read the Bible regularly. He thinks the percentage for adults is probably no higher.

Because they believe in the Bible, many evangelical Christians make an attempt to read it every day. But most end the experiment in failure. That breeds a sense of guilt. . . . We must find ways to help lay people have feelings of success rather than failure.[34]

Many sincere Christians lack the discipline to follow through with long-term commitments. They make New Year's resolutions to read the Bible through in one year, but fail to read for several days and then give up entirely. An alternative approach might be to propose a less formidable goal of a one- or two-week, short-term, church-wide, Bible reading program. Motivate your people toward a small yet significant success.

At our church, the pastor was about to launch into a verse-by-verse series of sermons on 1 Thessalonians. Our worship committee decided to coordinate a one-week Bible reading program with him. Our idea was to have the entire church read the five chapters of Thessalonians—one chapter a day, Monday through Friday. We proposed that on the following Sunday the congregation would read the entire book in the morning service to initiate the series of sermons. By linking the home readings to the congregational reading on Sunday and stressing that the pastor was about to begin his new series, we hoped to reinforce all three.

It worked out reasonably well—although in retrospect I think we could have done even better with a two-week program. Reading the entire Book of Thessalonians during the service was wonderful! You can find the creative liturgy we fashioned in appendix 3.

The Rigsby Family All-Day Retreat

For parents with teenagers this experience is a good way to study a book of the Bible together intensively and to use that as a springboard for challenging each other to greater faithfulness. If the right spirit prevails, it can be a way of drawing the family closer to each other and to God. Our example uses Philippians, but any other New Testament letter can be used. Here's what the day's schedule could look like:

Breakfast

Prayer

Family members go separate ways

Each reads Philippians

Family members reconvene

Each person in turn reads part of Philippians from a different translation until entire book is read

Each shares insights from the book

Prepare lunch

Afternoon activity

Family members go separate ways

Each person reads Philippians a second time with the added perspective of the shared comments

Family members reconvene

Each responds to "What is God saying to me?"

More sharing, confronting, and communicating

"What is God saying to Dad?"

> Everyone contributes to discussion:

> Is Dad doing it?

Continue pattern for each person in turn

Prayer

NO DICHOTOMY

In considering worship in everyday life within the family setting, a very important principle is at stake. We want no dichotomy or inconsistency between public and private worship. We want to be in the privacy of our homes what we appear to be publicly at church on Sundays—i.e., a worshiping people.

In the time of Amos, the people appeared to be one thing in worship but were another in everyday life. Because of this, God administered a stinging rebuke through the prophet: "I hate, I despise your religious feasts; I cannot stand your assemblies" (Amos 5:21). Worship is not just what we do on Sunday morning; it needs to become a part of the rest of our lives too.

> I urge you, brothers, in view of God's mercy, to offer your bodies as living sacrifices, holy and pleasing to God—this is your spiritual act of worship. Do not conform any longer to the pattern of this world, but be transformed by the renewing of your mind (Rom. 12:1–2).

Charles Sell confronts us with the challenge that both church and home face in this regard:

> Among evangelical churches, awareness of the family's strategic role is expanding rapidly, if for no reason than that the family's struggles and problems are spilling like raw sewage into the life of the congregation. Everywhere I see church leaders with a growing realization that the church is located nearest to the scene of the accident and has the responsibility to aid the victims.[35]

Think about that.

VESPERS INCOGNITO

In concluding this chapter, I come back to the guilt mothers and fathers often feel over parenting inadequacies. Here's an idea to try out in secret that can help break down the public-private dichotomy and relieve parental guilt.[36] It's intended for younger children, but it can even work with older children or a spouse.

Just before retiring for the evening, Father or Mother can steal into the bedroom, kneel, lay hands on the children, and offer prayers of thanksgiving or intercession while they sleep unawares. Or the parent can do this when awakened during the night hours with a concern. There is something *very special* about the laying on of hands, about doing this at night in secret, and about entering into the room to pray without any distractions while a child is peacefully asleep. It certainly beats tossing and turning on your bed without taking action! Why not give it a try!

In trying this and other suggestions in this chapter, you will be following in the train of the patriarchs—Job, Noah, Abraham, and Jacob—who modeled worship for their families privately and publicly in everyday life.

QUESTIONS FOR THOUGHT AND DISCUSSION

1. Explore the following question with a panel of parents: "Should all Christian families have regular devotions together?" Have members take different sides of the question (yes, not necessarily, no).
2. Do you think adults have guilt feelings about their inadequacy as parents? What about you?
3. Do you think you better understand the Deuteronomy 6 learning model? Can you think of an instance when you were successful in applying it to a situation that happened in your family? Can you think of a situation when you lost an opportunity for Deuteronomy learning?
4. What kinds of "interventions" do you think would be successful in your church? your home?
5. Do you have any ideas about ways to foster interaction between adults over parenting and family worship?
6. What do you think of the idea of having a worship committee rather than a music committee?

RECOMMENDED READING

Dads Only. Edited by Paul Lewis. Box 340, Julian, CA 92036. Monthly magazine dedicated to Christian parenting.

Becker, Palmer, and Ardys Becker. *Creative Family Worship*. Worship Series, no. 15. Newton, Kans.: Faith and Life Press, and Scottdale, Pa.: Mennonite Publishing House, 1984.

Bock Lois, and Migi Working. *Happiness Is a Family Walk with God*. Old Tappan, N.J.: Fleming H. Revell, 1977.

Foster, Richard J. *Celebration of Discipline: The Paths to Spiritual Growth*. San Francisco: Harper & Row, 1978.

Griggs, Patricia, and Donald Griggs. *Teaching and Celebrating Advent*, rev. ed. Nashville: Abingdon Press, 1980.

LeBar, Lois. *Family Devotions With School-Age Children*. Old Tappan, N.J.: Fleming H. Revell, 1980.

Mattson, Lloyd, and Elsie Mattson. *Rediscover Your Family Outdoors*. Wheaton, Ill.: Victor Books, 1980.

Merrell, Jo Ann. *Tree of Life*. Minneapolis: Bethany Fellowship, 1980.

Rickerson, Wayne. *Family Fun and Togetherness*. Wheaton, Ill.: Victor Books, 1973.

Zimmerman, Martha. *Celebrate the Feasts*. Minneapolis: Bethany House, 1981.

CHAPTER FOUR

Pauline Worship: Balance or Chaos?

[In comparison with Pauline worship] the Protestant Churches of our own era are very much poorer, not only in respect of the free working of the spirit, but also of what is liturgical. . . . [Paul] has preserved everything which can contribute to the "building up" of the body of Christ.[1]

THE FIRST FELLOWSHIP

A sound of a violent wind breaks the air and fills the house where they are assembled. Tongues of fire come to rest on each of them, and they begin to speak. Jews from different parts of the world hear the wonders of God being spoken in their native languages. Peter explains to them what is happening. The response is overwhelming: three thousand come to faith in Christ. This is the sudden birth of the New Testament church.

What ingredients marked that first fellowship? A healthy balance of elements stands out:

> They devoted themselves to the apostles' teaching and to the fellowship, to the breaking of bread and to prayer. Everyone was filled with awe, and many wonders and miraculous signs were done by the apostles. All the believers were together and had everything in common. Selling their possessions and goods, they gave to anyone as he had need. Every day they continued to meet together in the temple courts. They broke bread in their homes and ate together with glad and sincere hearts, praising God and enjoying the favor of all the people. And the Lord added to their number daily those who were being saved (Acts 2:42–47).

We see here a blend of worship, nurture, community, and outreach.

Worship . . . they broke bread, prayed, and were filled with awe and
    praise

Nurture . . . they devoted themselves to the apostles' teaching

Community . . . all believers were together and had everything in
    common

Outreach . . . the Lord added to their number daily[2]

From this fountainhead event the church sprang, spreading
outward first to Jewish and non-Jewish peoples in nearby areas, then later
crossing the sea to cities like Corinth and Rome.

During these days the church was being transformed from a Jewish
"cult" into a supranational faith. This adjustment did not take place
without acute tensions. In fact, we learn from Acts and Galatians that
Jewish traditions remained so strong that some of the Jewish believers
who "belonged to the party of the Pharisees" desired to impose
circumcision and other ceremonial requirements on all the emerging
gentile congregations. Paul vehemently resisted these "Judaizers," but
late in his ministry he was persuaded to observe the temple purification
rites in Jerusalem (Acts 21:24). From this we know Paul continued to
keep in touch with his Jewish heritage.

In light of all this it is interesting that 1 Corinthians 14 takes a real
"position" on worship, the only New Testament text to do so.[3] The key
distinctives appear to be full participation of all members in the service
(e.g., "*everyone* has a hymn") and free rein given to the Holy Spirit.

It is reasonable to think that the Jerusalem and Corinthian churches
form the extreme edges of a continuum of worship styles in New
Testament times, the Jewish church in Jerusalem being most influenced
by the institution of the synagogue, the Corinthian church the least. The
Jerusalem church, you will recall, comprised Jews; the Corinthian
church, Gentiles. Jerusalem was the citadel of conservative tradition and
authority in an essentially rural setting, while Corinth was an urbane,
progressive city of trade and commerce.[4] Toward the center of this
continuum were those churches outside of Israel with a mix of Jews and
Gentiles.[5]

Some have claimed that Pauline worship in the Corinthian church
was "primitive" and undeveloped in its form, a chaotic "free for all." On
careful examination, however, the Pauline concept of Corinthian worship
appears to have been neither chaotic nor simplistic. It exhibited a balance
of liturgical and free-form elements.[6] Its richness of forms and its variety
are amazing, given the constraints and resources of small-group worship.

Keep in mind that both the early church of Acts 2 and the
Corinthian church were house churches, as were many gentile congrega-

tions during this time. In spite of these limitations, the Pauline conception is breathtaking. It is body-life worship in action.[7] Paul, the "master builder," provided all that was necessary for worship and edification. He tapped into the traditions of temple and synagogue worship and passed on the traditions that Jesus established. Perhaps most importantly, he taught the church to take itself seriously as a living body. In a unique way, the shape of Pauline worship as practiced in the Corinthian church gave expression to that "body theology" that many even today find immensely attractive. The church as a body became his dominating, overarching metaphor.[8]

BALANCE OF LITURGY AND FREEDOM

Liturgical Elements

All nonliturgical churches should consider the fact that Paul's letters are imbued with a liturgical flavor derived from worship in the synagogue and temple. There is a reason for this. As he writes, Paul imagines the people gathered in worship. He is consciously modeling worship for them. He knows his letters will be read at congregational gatherings, and he has a sense of propriety for the occasion.

> After this letter has been read to you, see that it is also read in the church of the Laodiceans (Col. 4:16).

> I charge you before the Lord to have this letter read to all the brothers (1 Thess. 5:27).

So we can get a feel for Pauline worship from his letters. Out of this sense for what is fitting and appropriate he writes benedictions at the beginning and end and prayers that have a liturgical ring. For the same reason he sprinkles acclamations, doxologies, and congregational "amens" throughout his texts. Limiting our attention to just 1 and 2 Corinthians, here are some examples:

Salutations and Benedictions

Grace and peace to you from God our Father and the Lord Jesus Christ (1 Cor. 1:3; 2 Cor. 1:2).

The grace of the Lord Jesus be with you (1 Cor. 16:23).

May the grace of the Lord Jesus Christ, and the love of God, and the fellowship of the Holy Spirit be with you all (2 Cor. 13:14).

Liturgical Prayer

Blessed be the God and Father of our Lord Jesus Christ, the Father of mercies and God of all comfort, who comforts us in all our affliction (2 Cor. 1:3–4 NASB).

Acclamations and Doxologies

But thanks be to God! He gives us the victory through our Lord Jesus Christ (1 Cor. 15:57).

But thanks be to God (2 Cor. 2:14).

Thanks be to God for his indescribable gift! (2 Cor. 9:15).

The God and Father of the Lord Jesus, who is to be praised forever, knows that I am not lying (2 Cor. 11:31).

Phrases like "thanks be to God" are not just the "sincere words" of Paul. They are stylized, fixed phrases that come out of the temple and synagogue worship traditions or early church practice.[9] They are similar in character to our formalized Trinitarian phrase "in the name of the Father, the Son, and the Holy Spirit."

Notice the buildup that occurs on the name of God, particularly in the liturgical prayer above, "Blessed be the God and Father of our Lord Jesus Christ, the Father of mercies and God of all consolation." It is highly reminiscent of the language style of the Eighteen Benedictions found in the synagogue liturgy (see ch. 7 for examples). Notice also the liturgical formula "Jesus is Lord" and the Aramaic form of one of the earliest Christian phrases, the ancient *maranatha* ("Come, Lord Jesus").[10] Of even greater antiquity is the congregational "amen," which can be traced to temple days.[11]

All of us, whatever our liturgical style, can strike a healthier balance in our services if we include disciplining elements similar in function to these. Oscar Cullmann remarks, "It is precisely in this harmonious combination of freedom and restriction that there lies the greatness and uniqueness of the early Christian service."[12]

Finally, while Paul defends the exercise of spiritual gifts, his overriding concern is that worship be intelligent and intelligible for everyone present.

So what shall I do? I will pray with my spirit, but I will also pray with my mind; I will sing with my spirit, but I will also sing with my mind (1 Cor. 14:15).

Free Working of the Spirit

If liturgical elements can be discovered in Paul's letters, we can assume that they do not in themselves hinder the free working of the Spirit. The first Christians stood within the "magnetic field of the Holy Spirit."[13] Paul says, "Where the Spirit of the Lord is, there is freedom" (2 Cor. 3:17).

As the large floodlights that arc the sky draw crowds to county fairs, so the Spirit draws us to the Father and the Son. The Holy Spirit then frees us to see God in His glory and to be changed.

And we, who with unveiled faces all reflect the Lord's glory, are being transformed into his likeness with an ever-increasing glory, which comes from the Lord, who is the Spirit (2 Cor. 3:18).

Graham Kendrick calls this "transformation through adoration."[14]

Elements of Freedom

The free elements of Corinthian worship include spontaneous prayer, praise, singing, prophecy and discernment, tongues and interpretations, healing, words of instruction, and revelation. Notice that the idea of balance extends beyond the liturgical elements to the free elements. Paul advocates checks and balances wherein the exercise of tongues is coupled with interpretation, prophecy with discernment. When these provisos are followed, he seems essentially satisfied. The same sort of balance is found in 1 Thessalonians:

Do not put out the Spirit's fire; do not treat prophecies with contempt. Test everything. Hold on to the good (5:19–21).

Paul says, "Do not squelch the Spirit," at the same time he says, "Test everything—do not accept uncritically everyone who claims to have a word from the Lord."

MAXIMUM PARTICIPATION

Concerning the outward structuring of worship, the repeated use of words like *everyone, anyone, someone,* and *all* bring the Pauline approach into sharp focus.[15] Each person is a full participant, ministering and receiving ministry. Guided by the Spirit, everyone in the body is encouraged to make a contribution, according to 1 Corinthians 14:[16]

Everyone has a hymn, a word of instruction, a revelation, a tongue, or an interpretation. All these must be done for the strengthening of the church (v. 26).

If *anyone* speaks in a tongue, *someone* must interpret (v. 27).

You can *all* prophesy in turn (v. 31).

To take a broader look for just a moment, Paul applies the same principle of participation to the leadership and governance of the Corinthian church. Paul is aware that as an "expert builder" he laid the foundation of the Corinthian church. Yet a plurality of leaders within in the church are now building on that foundation, as we see in 1 Corinthians 3:

Each one should be careful how he builds (v. 10).

If *any* man builds on this foundation . . . (v. 12).

In the Corinthian church, discipline was decided before the full assembly, not the elders: "When you are assembled, . . . hand this man over to Satan" (1 Cor. 5:4). The Corinthian church appears to have had a congregational form of government, the synagogue a representative form. Here are some additional examples that show that the accent of Corinthian worship and governance was thoroughly congregational:

Judge for *yourselves* (1 Cor. 10:15; 11:13).

Every man . . . who prays or prophesies . . . (11:4).

[If] *everyone* speaks in tongues . . . (14:23).

If an unbeliever . . . comes in while *everybody* is prophesying, he will be convinced by *all* . . . and . . . judged by *all* (14:24).

Two or three prophets should speak, and the *others* should weigh carefully what is said (14:29).

The punishment inflicted on him by the *majority* (2 Cor. 2:6).

Alexander MacDonald makes the point that the Corinthians had nothing tangible beyond their worship assemblies—no creed, no building, no rule. Assembly was the center of everything.[17]

What is envisioned here is obviously small-assembly worship, a point often overlooked. If, for example, you have a fellowship of under fifty people, this sort of structure may be highly meaningful. But it is just not practical for larger groups of several hundred people, *unless adjustments are made.* When three hundred people have assembled, "everyone" cannot contribute "in turn."[18]

MULTIPLE LEVELS OF WORSHIP

As a church grows, it becomes important that it find new ways to foster the intimate interaction between people that existed when it was small. One way to do this is to encourage worship at levels other than the large Sunday morning service. Body-life worship can especially flourish in smaller groups.

It is possible to identify four different levels of interaction in church groups, and worship can occur at each of these levels: (1) the *friendship* level, where the deepest relationships can form, usually involves two or three people; (2) the *cell* or *support group* level works well with six-to-fourteen people; (3) the *subcongregational* level can involve between forty and eighty people; and (4) the *general assembly* level (morning worship service) seems to have no numerical limits. Membership at the the Full Gospel Church in Seoul, Korea, had surpassed the 300,000 mark by 1984, yet "its complex, highly personalized structure provides all the benefits of a smaller church."[19]

The small cell or support group level (six to fourteen people) is ideal for maintaining intimacy, encouraging participation, and grooming emerging leadership.[20] Small groups can be on the cutting edge of your worship. Introduce new worship choruses and other unfamiliar practices there first. Then at the Sunday morning service a core of believers will be knowledgeable. For worship at this level, you don't necessarily need highly specialized and skilled singers and instrumentalists, just committed ones who come prepared.[21]

In home settings, errors are smaller and more correctable, and people find it easier to open up because they are among friends.[22] Small groups are forgiving. Even if the group is small, however, individuals who lead worship in this context will still need training and insight. Make sure you provide them with it.

Unfortunately, Evangelicals often fail to consider integrating worship into the activities of small groups.[23] This is a great loss. We need to learn that time spent in worship (even if brief) is time well spent, whether that be in Sunday school, membership classes, or any of the other church groups. Even choirs and church committees could benefit from it. The authors of *Good Things Come in Small Groups* make some insightful observations:

> A group which has experienced fifteen minutes of genuine worship together cannot move easily into petty argument about church business. Worship unites like nothing else. If your small group is dull, disunified or disintegrating, encourage true worship as part of the agenda. Even a church board might benefit from a few moments of praising and adoring God. Try it next time before jumping into a hard issue and see how the rest of the meeting goes.[24]

Worship enhances and blends with other emphases. The authors suggest that small groups should maintain a balance of nurture, worship, community, and outreach so as to mirror the early church of Acts 2. These factors "need not all be given equal time in each meeting, but all should be included to a significant degree on a regular basis."[25] Otherwise the cells may become ingrown.

> *I participated in a cell group that met weekly for worship and prayer in a house setting. We had a brief opening meditation, worshiped in uninterrupted song for thirty minutes, and continued with a season of sustained corporate prayer for forty-five minutes. It was a time of becoming quiet before the Lord, and He used the body-life interaction (which at times was amazingly complex and varied) to bring much healing and well-being to those present. During the prayer time, those with a particular need*

were encouraged to come to the center. We sometimes laid hands on them and offered concerted prayers on their behalf.

MINISTRY TIME

The dynamics of maximum participation can also be incorporated into larger worship assemblies of several hundred people. Some churches are achieving this through a segment in their morning worship called "ministry time." During the period of congregational praise, an announcement invites anyone with a need—mental, emotional, physical, financial, or spiritual—to come forward. People may also come to intercede for someone else they know is hurting. There is no great emotional appeal, no coaxing, pleading, or hype of any kind. When the announcement is completed, the ministry team goes to the front and faces the pulpit.[26] As the congregation continues its worship in song, people from the congregation are free to come forward, stand with the team, and then share their need with a team member.[27] Everyone is prayed for. After several minutes, a time of general congregational prayer takes place, followed by more praise, during which those who have come forward can take their seats.

Five years ago Pastor Allon Hornby of the Broadway Tabernacle in Vancouver, British Columbia, adopted the ministry-time concept in his worship service. He strongly endorses the idea.

> Apart from the sermon, it is the single most significant thing that happens in our morning worship service. We have seen people saved and God answer prayer. People have been healed. Ministry time is different from an "altar call." There is a process that goes on. There is a sharing of the need—a finding out of the need, before the praying and laying on of hands by the team member(s). The ministry team becomes *involved*. There are other benefits to our service from "ministry time." On the pastor's side, it breaks down the "Thou-I" distinction between the pulpit and the people. It allows for a body-feeling in the service. On the people's side it allows an opportunity for a one-on-one encounter. Most importantly, it has strengthened the faith of our entire congregation as our people have seen God work in answer to prayer.[28]

How does a church begin to move in this direction without making guests or members feel uncomfortable? For an inoffensive first step, the worship leader may gather prayer requests from the entire congregation and include these in a corporate prayer. Such a time could also involve sentence prayer responses from the people.[29]

Second, the whole church can divide up into groups of three to five. Each group can choose someone to give a small-group offertory prayer of thanksgiving for home and shelter and other material provisions God has given and for the privilege of giving back to Him. The worship leader may then conclude these prayers with one of his own.

Third, the whole church may divide into groups of three to five, introducing themselves to one another as part of a "welcome time" and sharing a need (if they have one). Then the pastor or worship leader could lead in a public prayer, including a period of silent prayer in which the needs shared in the cells could be prayed for by each person. The people could be encouraged to follow up on these needs during a coffee time after church. In some churches, the small groups of people spontaneously follow up needs after the service, praying and ministering to one another.

For a slightly more demanding fourth step, the congregation could break up into small groups, and the small groups *themselves* can pray sentence prayers for the needs collected, or offer sentence praises if no needs were shared.[30] Toward the close of this prayer time, the worship leader can start a worship chorus and follow this with a public prayer.[31] Exercises like this could be used periodically to acclimate the people to ministry.

Then for a fifth and final step, Pastor Hornby's idea could be considered, since it requires the greater commitment of actually organizing a ministry team. In all the suggestions, the key element is sharing needs. It tends to cut through shallow talk and socializing. Other body-life possibilities include congregational responses to the sermon, using a roving mike, and working spontaneous sentence prayers by the people into the benediction or other prayer-oriented parts of the service. In these ways the very structure of the worship service can be employed "for the equipping of the saints for the work of service, to the building up of the body of Christ" (Eph. 4:12 NASB).

BODY-LIFE DYNAMIC IN BLACK WORSHIP SERVICES

Arthur Paris describes the body-life dynamic of a black Pentecostal church. The majority of black churches are not Pentecostal, but many have a similar dynamic. Notice the occurrence of the word *everyone* and the fact that the performers sit in the congregation:

> The congregational singing is clearly a group effort. The testimonies, prayer requests, shouting, speaking in tongues, though performed individually, are available to everyone in the congregation, and everyone has the opportunity to partake in the serial performance of them. It is the total of such activities, not an individual performance such as a single testimony, that constitutes a unit of service. . . .
>
> At many services, individuals and/or choirs are called upon to "give us a selection or two." . . . The people who perform them are

primarily congregation members, and they sit in the congregation except when performing as singers.[32]

In actual practice, this Corinthian kind of dynamic is not "simple." Although people may be drawn to the *apparent* spontaneity, freedom, and flexibility resulting from an improvised kind of worship, they *often overlook the critical support roles* performed by various persons. The larger the congregation, the more vital these support roles become. In black churches, says Paris, the function of accompanists and other persons can be compared to the support roles found in jazz bands.

> The band, like the congregation, creates its performance as a collective enterprise. . . . The band has performers who function at times as stage managers, controlling the pace and flow of action. Bands also have performers of maintenance function, for example, rhythm sections, whose roles directly parallel those of musicians at church services. They provide the accompanying rhythmic patterns by which the creative effort moves. . . . Their roles as supporting players are too involved in the maintenance of the ongoing performance to allow them much solo role prominence.
>
> A band's efforts collectively and sectionally interlock around the composition, integrating the individual solos into a unified whole. At their most vital, these efforts transcend the limits of the score and the shortcoming of individual players, and the performance as a collective creation soars. Such a performance, like the church service, is a collaboration of all the participants: composer, soloists, sidemen, all melding their efforts into a complex unity.[33]

J. I. Packer, who is a clarinetist and a 1920s New Orleans jazz buff, takes a similar view. Students at Regent College once begged me to ask him to talk about jazz in our worship class. His opening words went something like this: "The best representation of New Testament *koinonia* I know of is New Orleans jazz. Everybody gets a chance to solo, and when they come together—it's magic, a real oneness. Unity-in-diversity. No one person predominates."

"No one person predominates." That's one of the keys. For a Corinthian dynamic to work in a local church situation, you can't have people trying to outperform or impress one another and "putting down" others.[34] This seems to have been the problem in Corinth. Immature Christians in their pride were putting their gifts on display rather than seeking to edify the whole assembly and focus attention on the Lord. One suspects that *adequate, superintending leadership was lacking* in overseeing the richness of expression in Corinth while Paul was absent.[35]

It is really remarkable that Paul did not put an end to it all in his second letter to the Corinthians and say something to this effect: "Okay, now you've completely botched it. I'm tired of your ego trips. This structure will never work here." He understandably could have opted for a more restricted format.

However, as Alexander MacDonald has observed, "he [Paul] seems to never have wavered in his confidence that the Spirit's leading was to be wholly trusted, and that it would be wrong to seek ease and safety with some lesser but more calculable guide."[36]

Paul trusted the Holy Spirit, and he trusted the people. It is a choice lesson for all of us. He rejected the poverty that would have ensued in favor of freedom with its attendant demands.

QUESTIONS FOR THOUGHT AND DISCUSSION

1. Is it important to incorporate elements of spontaneous worship in our services? How could this be done in your church?
2. What do you think of the worship described in 1 Corinthians 14? Is the Pauline concept of worship chaotic? Is our worship "very much poorer" than Pauline worship? If so, in what ways?
3. The early gentile church service has been termed as a "harmonious combination of freedom and restriction." Explain.
4. Can "everyone" participate in the manner Paul describes in 1 Corinthians 14:26, 31 when three hundred or more people meet at one time? Could there be some opportunity for people to have worship of this kind? How? Where? When?
5. How does "ministry time" differ from an altar call?
6. What roles in a jazz band are also present in "body-life" worship?

RECOMMENDED READING

Good Things Come in Small Groups: The Dynamics of Good Group Life. Downers Grove, Ill.: InterVarsity Press, 1985.

Cullmann, Oscar. *Early Christian Worship*. Translated by A. Stewart Todd and James B. Torrance. Naperville, Ill.: Alec R. Allenson, 1956.

CHAPTER FIVE

Extraordinary Variety!

[The elements of worship in the early Gentile church] are extraordinarily numerous, and it is astonishing how many forms the life of worship in these first Christian communities has assumed.[1]

ASTONISHING REPERTOIRE OF WORSHIP ELEMENTS

The sheer number of elements involved in Pauline worship is extraordinary. As you read through the list below, pause and try to imagine what the total picture of worship would be like with all these elements in operation in a "Spirit-led" meeting:

Opening and closing benedictions (1 Cor. 1:3; 16:23)

Doxology and acclamation (1 Cor. 15:57)

Liturgical prayer (2 Cor. 1:3)

Spontaneous prayer (1 Cor. 14:14ff.)

Hymns, psalms, and spiritual songs (1 Cor. 14:2; Eph. 5:19; Col. 3:16)

Praise, singing, and thanksgiving (1 Cor. 14:15)

Responsive *amen*s (1 Cor. 14:16)

Physical prostration (1 Cor. 14:25)

Holy kisses (1 Cor. 16:20; 2 Cor. 13:12)

Public reading of Paul's letters (Col. 4:16; 1 Thess. 5:27)

Prophecy, revelation, and discernment (1 Cor. 14:6; 12:10)

Tongues and interpreters (1 Cor. 14:23)

Instruction, preaching, and edification (1 Cor. 1:17; 14:26; 15:14)

Healing (1 Cor. 12:9, 28, 30)

Breaking of bread (Rom. 16:16; 1 Cor. 11:20ff.; 1 Thess. 5:26; 1 Peter 5:14)

Baptism (1 Cor. 1:14)

Use of *Maranatha,* an Aramaic liturgical form (1 Cor. 16:22)
Collection (1 Cor. 16:1)

VARIETY OF MUSIC EXPRESSION

We learn from this list that a multiplicity of forms existed for music expression. Although it may be impossible to pinpoint the exact musical form meant by the terms "psalms, hymns and spiritual songs," the central impression conveyed is that variety flourished in the selection of the materials employed.

> Let the word of Christ dwell in you richly as you teach and admonish one another with all wisdom, and as you sing *psalms, hymns and spiritual songs* with gratitude in your hearts to God (Col. 3:16).

In this verse "psalms" suggests using the words and tunes of the Hebrew psalter, that is, old, traditional materials.[2] "Hymns" may refer to more recent materials generated in either a Jewish or Christian setting (like the Incarnation canticles and hymnic passages with a Christological emphasis that we find throughout the New Testament).[3] It is very likely that 1 Timothy 3:16 is from such a hymn of the early church.

> He appeared in a body,
>   was vindicated by the Spirit,
> was seen by angels,
>   was preached among the nations,
> was believed on in the world,
>   was taken up in glory.

"Spiritual songs" may refer to shorter materials such as improvised one-line statements (1 Cor. 12:3) or confessional chants (Eph. 5:14), the result of "immediate inspiration."[4]

Twentieth-century analogies illustrating the same kind of variety might include settings on the Psalms, established hymns, and worship choruses. Balance is crucial. Each congregation will want to determine its own weighting of these variables—hymns versus choruses, for example—depending on the age groups and cultural orientation of the church. Congregations with a predominance of worshipers in their twenties and early thirties, however, would do well to include at least one hymn. Young people, particularly in our rootless, West Coast culture, *need* a sense of historical perspective.

This is my rationale. The Psalms themselves set a biblical *precedent.* They demonstrate a respect for history. Some psalms date all the way back to Moses while others were written after the Babylonian captivity. The Psalms also call for "new" songs. Therefore the older people should be willing to stretch and accept contemporary worship choruses, while the younger should be taught historic hymns. When both old and young stretch to accommodate one another, God is pleased.

Notice also that Paul encourages the people to be aware that in their worship they are addressing not only God but also one another and themselves:[5]

> *Speak to one another* with psalms, hymns and spiritual songs. Sing and make music *in your heart* to the Lord (Eph. 5:19).

This emphasis on edification (to others and oneself) seems to be more dominant in Paul's writing than in the Old Testament, where the focus is more exclusively on worship directed "to" the Lord. Why is this? We can only speculate. Perhaps one reason may be that on many occasions the Old Testament priests and musicians offered worship to God in the temple precincts or in their levitical towns without an "audience" present.

WAS CORINTHIAN WORSHIP NORMATIVE OR UNIQUE?

We have already taken the view that Corinthian worship probably contrasted with Jewish Christian worship in Jerusalem. Now we need to ask another question: Was the worship in Corinth fairly representative of gentile churches of the New Testament? We can't be certain, but it is the case that virtually every element of Corinthian worship in the long list above can be found in other parts of the New Testament. The only characteristic not explicitly associated with any other church is maximum participation (1 Cor. 14:26).

Paul makes it abundantly clear in 1 Corinthians that the teachings he imparted to them are the same as he has taught elsewhere:

> Therefore I urge you to imitate me. . . . [Timothy] will remind you of my way of life in Christ Jesus, which agrees with what I teach everywhere in every church (1 Cor. 4:14–17).

> Be imitators of me. . . . I praise you because you remember me in everything, and hold to the traditions [teachings], just as I delivered them to you (1 Cor. 11:1–2).

> For what I received I passed on to you as of first importance: that Christ died for our sins according to the Scriptures, that he was buried, that he was raised on the third day (1 Cor. 15:3).

Many of these teachings were doctrinal, but they also included numerous practical rules for Christian living.

> This is the rule I lay down in all the churches [Those recently converted to Christianity should retain their present jobs and social status] (1 Cor. 7:17).

> If anyone wants to be contentious about this, we have no other practice—nor do the churches of God [concerning the issue of women praying with their heads uncovered] (1 Cor. 11:16).

> For I received from the Lord what I passed on to you: The Lord Jesus, on the night he was betrayed, took bread (1 Cor. 11:23).

Was, then, the Corinthian style of worship, where each person brought a contribution to the whole, also normative? We cannot be sure. It may have been practiced elsewhere. Alexander MacDonald, for example, believes that Romans 12:3–8 has the body-dynamic and atmosphere of 1 Corinthians 14. He believes Paul is visualizing the Roman church at worship as he writes.[6] This is possible, since it is likely that Paul wrote the Book of Romans while in Corinth (Acts 20:2–3).

We also know that in the Montanist movement (A.D. 160–220) a Corinthian-type atmosphere blossomed in Asia Minor, and it seems probable that this large movement must have had some first-century foundation similar to Corinthian worship.[7]

Lastly, the Corinthian style of worship was consistent with Paul's concept of the church as a living body, and we do not find alternative worship models in the other Pauline epistles.

Nevertheless, it seems clear that different gentile churches had different *temperaments*. For example, the Thessalonians had a cooler disposition than the Corinthians, judging by Paul's exhortation to them: "Do not put out the Spirit's fire; do not treat prophecies with contempt" (1 Thess. 5:19–20). Furthermore, whereas rule by elders is not mentioned in Corinthians—though the argument from silence does not conclusively preempt its existence—it appears to be an established practice of Paul in other gentile places like Crete. Paul sent Titus on the specific mission of "appointing elders in every town" (Titus 1:5).[8]

The Pauline House Church: Rich and Poor Together

When the New Testament reports the conversion of a man "and all his house," the meaning seems broader than our idea of a nuclear family. In Paul's days, households could be quite large. A substantial householder was responsible for "slaves, former slaves who were now clients, and sometimes business associates (like craftsmen) and tenants."[9] Excavated floor plans of some large households show apartments for slaves, rented rooms, sometimes a tavern, even a connecting hotel.

To be a part of such a house, according to Wayne Meeks, was to be "part of a larger network of relations."[10] Servants would share the religion of their master. In short, some households were a community somewhat like the extended households of the Old Testament patriarchs.

Gaius may have had such a household big enough to accommodate the entire Corinthian church.[11] We know he provided housing for Paul.[12]

The social level of Paul and his congregations was "a good bit higher" than has been commonly assumed. "Until recently," says Meeks, "the prevailing viewpoint was that Pauline congregations came from the poor and dispossessed."[13] More likely, Pauline congregations reflected a fair cross section of urban society including slaves, slave owners, a few wellborn people, and upwardly mobile entrepreneurs.[14] Some scholars believe that when Paul refers to the "divisions" in the Corinthian church, social stratification was partly to blame. In other words, when members of the Corinthian church called each other "brothers and sisters," a profound resocialization was going on.

Gerd Thiessen suggests that the shaping of social relations in Pauline churches had far-reaching ramifications for Greco-Roman society as a whole.

> Hellenistic primitive Christianity [e.g., the Corinthian church] mastered the task of shaping social relations within a community which, on the one hand, demanded of its members a high degree of solidarity and togetherliness and, on the other, encompassed various social strata. . . . It produced the church's fundamental norms and fashioned lasting institutions. It solved problems of organization and prepared Christianity to receive the great masses. Its historical effectiveness is rooted not least of all in its ability to integrate members of different strata. . . . they [the upper and lower strata] found a fundamental equality of status before God. . . . It offered a new pattern for directing and shaping social relationships in contrast to that of Greco-Roman antiquity.[15]

The shaping of social relationships was accomplished in part through Paul's handling of problems related to worship. Thiessen believes that social stratification was behind the problems relating to the "*agape* meal" that occurred just prior to the Lord's Supper (1 Cor. 11:17–22). Paul settled the matter by confining this "private meal" to private homes. "Within their own four walls they are to behave according to the norms of their social class," says Thiessen, but "while at the Lord's supper the norms of the congregation have absolute priority."[16] He continues:

> . . . the Lord's supper is a symbolic accomplishment of social integration. The fellowship here achieves embodiment. . . . Paul moves the sacrament to the center to achieve a greater social integration. "Because there is one bread, we who are many are one body." . . . Because all have eaten portions of the same element, they have become a unity . . . as if the bodily boundaries between and among people had been transcended. . . . From a plurality of people emerges a unity.[17]

No doubt Donald McGavran correctly assumes that people—if there is a choice—"like to become Christians without crossing racial, linguistic, or class barriers."[18] Social homogeneity—similarity of education, income, lifestyle, and cultural upbringing—within and between congregations makes unity easier to achieve.

The Corinthian church, however, did not appear to have social homogeneity, and it was plagued by divisiveness and cliques. Barriers due to social stratification seemed to be in evidence. Paul took positive steps in planning worship to deal with the nitty gritty details that hindered unity of spirit. A decision was made. Slaves and slave owners were to eat at home in the manner befitting their social standing, but when they came to church they took Communion as one body and called each other "brothers and sisters." Paul warned them of dire consequences if they did not leave their prejudices at home: "That is why many of you are weak and sick, and a number of you have fallen asleep" (1 Cor. 11:30).

CONCLUSION

A rich balance of fixed and free elements characterized Pauline worship. Maximum participation, the Corinthian distinctive, is most naturally practiced in a small-group setting, but large groups can work at having a body-life dynamic too. The experience of worship in both large-group and small-group settings within local churches should be encouraged. The ministry-time option offers an equipping, relational emphasis within the structure of the worship service.

We have seen that cultural pluralism—not only doctrinal differences— hindered unity between the Jewish and gentile churches, and that the New Testament church was able to allow for cultural differences yet maintain unity. This remarkable achievement should encourage us to appreciate differences in worship style today even though, from a personal standpoint, we may think our way is best. An increasing diversity of worship expression is likely in North America, given the increasing pluralism of the social environment.

QUESTIONS FOR THOUGHT AND DISCUSSION

1. Should young people be willing to learn hymns and older people be willing to learn choruses? Explain.
2. Do you think the Corinthian worship style was normative for gentile churches in the New Testament? Why or why not?
3. "When members of the Corinthian church called each other 'brothers and sisters' a profound socialization was going on." Explain.

CHAPTER SIX

Back to the Fountainhead

If we increase our knowledge of the various options available to us in worship, we are in a better position to adopt those that seem valuable for us and make more informed decisions.

RENEWAL

In periods of decline we tend to look back to an earlier era when a sense of purpose was clearer and things seemed to be working. We look back to the fountainhead, the source. We look back hoping to recover what was lost in the passage of time.

That happens with institutions too, and it happens in the church. Throughout church history there have periodically been calls for a return to the simplicity and purity of the New Testament church. We see that happening again in our own time.

According to Joyce Thurman, it is happening today in the house-church movement in Great Britain that is said to number more than fifty thousand members.[1] "Its ranks," she says, "have been swelled by disillusioned members of churches who have become impatient waiting for the denominational structures to experience revival."[2] The majority of the members of the house movement are not "illiterates," but university graduates, doctors, executives, and middle-class families "at the peak of their life."[3]

Reports of similar manifestations of growth and/or renewal connected with house meetings come from other parts of the globe. In China and Korea an immense network of small prayer groups have been a central component in multiplied church growth.[4] On the West Coast of the United States young contemporary churches like Calvary Chapel and the Vineyard are springing up everywhere and growing rapidly. Many groups incorporate elements of Pauline organization and worship.

People in the renewal movement seem to be saying that it is vital for every Christian to realize the full potential of the Holy Spirit, that every person "make it a matter of conscious concern to release the Holy Spirit for the fulfilling of the whole of his/her ministry." Their desire is to give the Spirit, so to speak, "a free run."[5]

Church "Deregulation"

Though they may not be charismatic in orientation, many evangelical and fundamentalist pastors sense it is time to do some honest evaluation. They have heard that Charismatics have a greater delight in worship, and they want to know more about it. In North America there is every sign that the standard cleavage between Bible church and classical pentecostal worship styles is breaking down. Churches are splitting the difference, finding points of comfort between the two poles of the spectrum. Others are finding midpoints between free and liturgical worship formats and traditions. As someone put it, "We are going through a period of *church deregulation,* just as we've been going through deregulation in the airline industry, in business, and in government." After the initial chaos, the church's worship will be better for it.

Of course each church will have to find its own way during this period of "deregulation." A wise church leader will approach the matter of change in worship styles with a sensitivity to the congregation's needs. A pastor I know had sensed in his congregation a readiness for some change in regard to worship, so he put the chart below on the overhead one Sunday morning.

Charismatic Tradition	Fundamentalist Tradition
Sermons repetitious, reinforcing	Sermons content-oriented
More emotional than scholastic	More scholastic than emotional
Emphasis on responding (Hallelujahs)	Emphasis on listening
Physical responses (lifting hands, etc.)	Restrained physical reinforcements
Comparatively "warm"	Comparatively "cool"
Time flexible (i.e., long)	Time restrained, disciplined
Entertaining	Boring
Contemporary appeal	Traditional appeal

As you can see, the chart wasn't highly flattering to either Fundamentalists or Charismatics. Your own experience may not accord with the chart, but it was an honest attempt to compare the strengths and weaknesses of two very different worship styles. It was one of *several* means the pastor used to broach the subject and to help his congregation work through gradual change.

After he led them through the chart, sprinkling in some jokes that drew laughter along the way, he waited during the week for more in-depth responses from them. Over the years he had developed a sense of trust with his people. He knew he had earned the right to lead them. The people in turn were certain he would be sensitive to their needs and background. He told me later, "They were more ready for change than I had anticipated."

What to Make of the Charismatics

Many fundamentalist pastors wonder what to make of the charismatic movement. They may find in it both attractive elements and aspects that trouble them. How should they evaluate it?

In thinking about the charismatic movement, it is helpful at the outset to distinguish a *movement* from a *school*. A *school* passes on a relatively fixed, formal body of organized thought. For example, in American Evangelicalism there is the dispensationalist school of thought and the school of church growth. *Scholasticism,* a stronger, but related term, can refer to thinking that has become pedantic, ossified, resistant to any kind of change, even positive change. A *movement,* however, relates more to a group of people than a body of thought. Particularly in its incipient stages, it consists more of trends and currents and is more flexible, dynamic, and open to change.

The point is that the charismatic renewal is more a movement than a school and is likely to continue to experience change. Eventually it may even be absorbed into existing church institutions. Thus it may be unwise, especially while it is still in its nascent stages, to attempt to categorize it and write it off.[6]

J. I. Packer has some pertinent thoughts along these lines.[7] He says that the charismatic movement can be evaluated in two ways: (1) by examining its theology, and (2) by experiencing it. We can experience it by seeing firsthand what is happening in a charismatic fellowship and by getting to know charismatic individuals. And what of the theology?

Packer suggests that more has been experienced by Charismatics than they have been able to articulate theologically. Their experience is ahead of their theology. He maintains that the charismatic movement is "still looking for the theology it needs in order to be understood in a fully Scriptural way—in order to understand itself in a fully Scriptural way, and in order to be biblically understood by the rest of us."[8] He adds, "It is the Spirit's way to bless folk from time to time in advance of their theological rectitude and to take them further on than their understanding would have led you to expect they could go."

He finds instances of this pattern in Scripture. He says his particular experience of the charismatic movement and its people—which may be different from yours or mine—has been generally positive. (I personally would like to see more solid teaching of the Scriptures emerge in charismatic circles. Strong pulpit teaching and Christian education ministries seem to be lacking.)

LEARNING FROM CHARISMATICS

Packer lists some positive characteristics of Charismatics: (1) devotion to Jesus Christ, (2) concern to be filled with the Spirit, (3) concern for the emotional and feeling side of worship, (4) concern for a spirit of prayer, (5) concern to experience joy in Christ, (6) concern that all be involved in worship, (7) ministry "to each person through each person," (8) missionary zeal, and (9) willingness to be different (a measure of integrity). All these he takes to be positive.[9]

We could add other characteristics. For example, I have found that many charismatic churches have an accepting attitude to the unchurched. They take people as they are and are good at easing them into their church environment and helping them feel comfortable. Their informal dress code puts people at ease, and younger people also relate well to their contemporary music styles and sound sources. But it's not just the external characteristics of charismatic worship that make people feel welcome; Charismatics are also willing to be open, vulnerable, and intimate in individual relationships.[10]

Five Steps Toward Worship Enrichment

Five other characteristics may have value for your church situation and deserve an extended look.

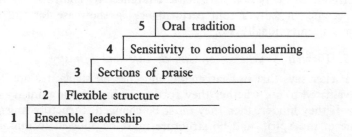

5	Oral tradition
4	Sensitivity to emotional learning
3	Sections of praise
2	Flexible structure
1	Ensemble leadership

1. Ensemble Style of Leadership

It appears that many churches in the charismatic renewal movement have links with itinerant ministers or leaders who lead workshops and conferences and who periodically visit and counsel churches on their direction and goals. Walter Hollenweger says that in England, "This hardly visible subterranean network explains why suddenly and apparently spontaneously house churches are mushrooming in different parts of the country and following the same pattern."[11]

The links between the churches and these itinerant leaders are not formal or hierarchical; they're based on personal relationships. But they're not casual either, and the leaders often wield a powerful influence in the life of the churches.[12]

The apostle Paul seems to have worked in a similar way. He and a coterie worked in concert as itinerant church planters and cultivators for a network of churches that could count on their invaluable expertise. His leadership style seems especially unique to the New Testament and is evident in many of his epistles, including the following passage from 1 Corinthians 16:10–11, 17:

> If Timothy comes, see to it that he has nothing to fear while he is with you, for he is carrying on the work of the Lord just as I am. . . . [Later, send him to me] along with the brothers. . . . I was glad when Stephanas, Fortunatus and Achaicus arrived.[13]

By way of contrast, many Protestant pastors seem to have lonely jobs. They tend to be relatively isolated from fellow believers in their own churches, from pastors in the area, and from the encouragement of pastoral consultants.

Often charismatic churches conduct their worship services in ensemble style. The worship leader and the pastor tend to share more equally the leadership of the Sunday morning services, and in general more participants are involved in the leadership of the service. This sharing stems in part from charismatic churches' giving more importance to praise in their worship. Praise no longer serves as a "preliminary" to the sermon. In many noncharismatic churches, by contrast, the service may become virtually a solo performance, a showcase for the pastor (perhaps unintentionally so).

2. Flexible Structuring of Church Life and Ministry

Packer says that in charismatic churches all structures are "tested and evaluated to see whether they further or hinder the ministry of the Spirit. If they hinder, then they must be changed. Structure must serve the life of the Spirit, and no structure must be allowed to inhibit that life."[14] In practical terms this means that if someone has something to share, time is made available. If congregational praise needs more time in order to flower, more time is given.

3. Sections of Free-flowing Praise

Sustained sections of praise are now being used with success by young congregations in California. Instead of organizing their services into a series of discrete events—a single hymn followed by a prayer, another hymn, the choir, the offering, a solo, a Scripture reading, and then the sermon—they have a time of sustained, unbroken, flowing praise that often lasts anywhere from ten to fifty minutes.

Using a section of praise can sometimes result in greater depth and richness of expression for the people experientially, since the rhythm is longer and more sustained. Eddie Espinosa of the Vineyard in Anaheim, California, offers a rationale for the long rhythm. He likens it to a physical workout. He says it has been demonstrated that long, sustained periods of exercise are better for the cardiovascular system than a series of short bursts. Analogously, sustained exercise in worship benefits the soul. He sees the forty-five minutes of congregational singing as a chance to give worshipers sustained, uninterrupted time with the Lord, an experience that they can take with them into their private worship. Then when they're stuck in a traffic jam on the freeway, they may be more inclined to use that time worshiping the Lord than listening to the radio.

To use another analogy, sustained worship is like sitting down to a leisurely meal and lingering and enjoying fellowship with one another around the family table. Longer sections of praise allow time to offer the whole person (mind, will, and emotions) to the Lord. Humanly speaking, we need a longer frame of time to prepare ourselves psychologically to offer genuine adoration.

The Psychological Dimension. The psychological shape of worship has primary importance in planning the order of service. The psychological dynamics of worship operate much like the dynamics of love-making.[15] It is unwise to expect people to come to church and plunge immediately into adoration. Time is required before the people are ready to express adoration and intimacy in worship. Psychologically, adoration will often flow naturally from a period of exaltation leading to an experience of transcendence.

The Five-Phase Worship Pattern. John Wimber and Eddie Espinosa discovered a five-phase pattern for guiding their long worship song service, or as they term it, "worship set." Evangelical churches may find aspects of it useful for their Sunday morning or evening services, as well as weekday, small-group meetings.

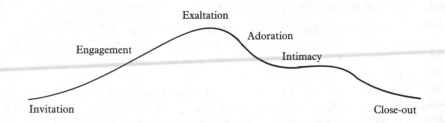

Wimber and Espinosa have used this pattern for several years in leading both groups of a thousand people and small, home praise groups. The idea for this pattern evolved from their experience, practice, and Bible reading.[16] Only later did it crystallize in their thinking. They became aware that there are different types of choruses and that these can be categorized in a sequence. The five phases are (1) invitation, (2) engagement, (3) exaltation, (4) adoration, and (5) intimacy (plus a close-out).

The *invitation phase* is like a call to worship. The lyrics used in this phase should address the people and draw their attention to worship, as in the choruses "I just came to praise the Lord" or "Don't you know it's time to praise the Lord." They may be accompanied with hand clapping where appropriate. For a vigorous call to worship with hand clapping, the Hebrew chorus "The Celebration Song" (Chambers) is excellent. A mellower opener could be "Let's forget about ourselves and magnify the Lord and worship Him." More traditional churches might wish to have a mix of speaking, reading, and singing. They might include Scripture readings in the call and substitute hymns for choruses.

The key is that the lyrics of the song can now do the inviting and focusing without the song leader having to resort to verbal exhortation. The leader can continue with hymns and choruses until he has made contact with the people and they with him and everyone is focused.

In the *engagement phase* the people begin to draw near to God, and the lyrics should reflect that. They are now singing to God, not encouraging one another. Espinosa likens it to the engagement period before marriage (e.g., "Praise Song").

In the *exaltation phase* the people sing out with power in response to key words in these choruses like *great, majestic, worthy, reigns, Lord, mountains,* and so on (e.g., "Our God Reigns"). The pitch spans of the melodies are generally greater than in the other phases.

In the *adoration phase* the dynamics may gradually subside and melody may have a smaller range. The key words may be *you, Jesus* (e.g., "Father, I adore you").

The last phase before the close, the *intimacy phase,* is the quietest and most personal. It's like addressing God as *Abba* or "Daddy" (e.g., "In Moments Like These" or "O Lord, You're Beautiful"). This is the "kiss." One meaning of the Greek word for worship, *proskuneō,* is "to turn toward to kiss," as in kissing the feet, the hands, or the lips. Closeness is required for kissing; this closeness can happen in worship only if it is properly prepared for in the phases that precede it.

It all ends with a close-out chorus or hymn that leads out of intimacy and helps the people to adjust to the next event in the service.

Using the Five-Phase Model. The five-phase progression has a beautifully balanced and graduated arch shape with the high point in the middle. Use it as a handy frame to guide your own worship practice, but *feel free to be flexible with it.*

You can be flexible about time; the same progression can be used in either long or short worship sets. You can also be flexible about content; use all choruses, all hymns, or a mixture of hymns and choruses (or even humming and prayers).

You can even rearrange the phases. For example, you can give a single phase like adoration more weight than the others, or limit a set to one or two of the phases. I've experimented successfully with short sets (ten to fifteen minutes) toward the middle of the morning service that focus on adoration pieces exclusively. It works especially well when the set emerges out of a time of prayer. I've also tried moving from *exaltation to adoration and vice versa* —or even *from exaltation to adoration and back to exaltation.*

One benefit of the model is that it encourages us not to jump around between categories in a worship set when we select choruses and hymns. This jerking about tends to be confusing and results in a lack of direction. It's like a home decorated without cohesive colors, furniture, and paintings.

Another advantage of the progression is that if a group is leading the song service, group members don't need to know the exact sequencing of the individual tunes. They can identify the phase they are in from the lyrics and the progression of songs over time and know how they should be functioning musically to achieve an ensemble effect.

Here is one more thought on linking choruses. Try to find key words and similar thoughts. Many choruses have only one key thought. Two choruses back-to-back that reiterate the key word *love*, for example, will promote a sense of continuity rather than patchiness. "You" or "Jesus" are other examples of key words.

4. Sensitivity to the Emotional Aspect of Learning

Charismatic services often last two hours. The first hour may be devoted to praise, the second to preaching the Word. Whereas noncharismatic churches follow a brisk pace, the pacing in charismatic churches may be slow and repetitious. For example, they may sing the same song over and over. This is not, Packer contends, because Charismatics are "sluggish of mind." Rather, it reflects, says Packer.

> part of a strategy for ensuring that everything that is said and expressed is also felt—that you don't move on from any thought about our relationship with God until time has been given for everyone to feel it. This isn't necessarily emotionalism of a bad sort. It is an attempt to call into expression in worship, genuine responses, and joyful emotion on the part of God's people. And since our emotional makeup is part of the image of God in us one cannot say it is improper or inappropriate.[17]

We often mistakenly think of repetition in an oversimplistic way. Repetition, however, may function as accumulation. For example, the praise offered to the Lamb in Revelation is *intensified* by the sevenfold repetition: "power and wealth, wisdom and might, honor and glory and praise" (5:12). This is in effect a listing of the attributes of God in nontechnical terms; it has an extolling function. The language is not *merely* repetitive. It has a cumulative, rhythmic, climactic effect to it similar to the kind of language we use in human emotion. For example, if you tell your wife, "I love you," that means something. But if you say to her, "I love you! I love you! I love you!"—that's something far more than simple repetition. It imparts to her a sense of intense, genuine feeling.

The Lord's Prayer in the musical setting by Malotte provides another example of accumulation. Here the "list" idea and the soaring tune combine in a powerful way in the final words of the prayer: "For thine is the kingdom, and the power, and the glory, forever and ever, Amen." Note the heightening, intensifying effect that results.

Still, repetition *can* become boring! Good leaders introduce variation into repetitions. They assist the intensification by altering the tempo, the rhythmic accentuation, or the volume. This not only relieves boredom, but also makes the expression more emotional and increases the richness, depth, and penetration of the congregational response.

In all this, a very real danger exists that leaders may use these techniques to manipulate people. *Worship leaders have an obligation to refrain from manipulating the people. They must earn and never betray the trust people place in them.*

5. Emphasis on Oral Tradition

Most charismatic churches use oral tradition more extensively than the typical evangelical or fundamentalist church. In the written tradition people learn by *reading.* But in the oral tradition people learn through repetition—through repeated hearings—without a printed medium. They *listen* and *memorize.* The new material is "caught." In contrast to churches that rely on written material, churches that use oral methods emphasize memorization.

In the deep South, church leaders often "line out" the words and music of new songs. The leader sings one line of text at a time and the congregation repeats it back until in the end everything is memorized without using printed materials. There is a rhythm of demonstration followed by immediate congregational response.

Learning of this kind is going on now in many of the younger churches in California that teach choruses without having the words in print. (If overheads are used, an attempt is made to put them to the side rather than the center of the platform, so they don't distract from worship.) Over a period of time, a congregation may memorize hundreds of choruses this way. They even sing hymns from memory; hymnbooks, if present in pew racks, are seldom used.

There are some obvious advantages to using oral methods. First, people commit the words to memory—*and they stay there!* Once learned, Scripture set to music tends to remain fixed in the memory. Second, the learning process requires greater attentiveness and more active participation and involvement than in the written tradition. Third, numerous repetitions encourage people to internalize the piece. Fourth, people are freed up to focus on worship when they are no longer distracted by fumbling with a book or looking at words. Fifth, not having to announce hymn numbers removes a distraction to the flow of worship.

It is also true that oral methods take more time. After all, it's far easier to sing a new hymn by reading it. It takes time for the congregation to build a repertoire of songs that they know by heart. *Worship leaders should probably consider using a mix of both methods* when learning new material or reinforcing the old.[18]

I believe we should work (as much as possible) toward the long-term goal of having people memorize hymns and choruses—especially those that are easily memorized. We should at least attempt to memorize the first stanza of hymns; this helps the congregation get off to a good start, and that part of the piece then becomes available in impromptu situations. A leader could use it in any segment of the service, and people could sing it at home, at work, or while driving on the freeway. In this way people can make melody in their hearts to the Lord at any time or place. The oral tradition, therefore, can be a means of spurring congregations toward an integrated lifestyle of worship.

Most of the charismatic worship leaders I've met usually tote guitars, but I have not found them to be frothy or mentally vacuous. Rather, they are active students of worship. Their style of leading may appear to be natural and spontaneous, but after talking with many skilled ones, I have found they are often working with definite, guiding ideas. Their leadership just *looks* effortless because it is well thought out. They work strenuously at what they do and tend to be well prepared. The churches they lead seem to have the services efficiently organized and show a complete absence of "pentecostal disorder." Most importantly, many have expressed to me the vital importance of taking time out to worship in private before stepping up to the podium to lead publicly.[19] Surely we can all agree that's a good practice.

WHERE DOES MUSIC FIT INTO THE SPIRITUAL GIFTS?

Many worship leaders wonder how the music ministry relates to Paul's lists of spiritual gifts. Donald Hustad tells of receiving a letter from a former student, now serving as a church music director, who asked this question: "In Ephesians 4:11–12 Paul lists the ministries God has given the church. Where does music fit in?"[20]

Here is the Ephesians passage in question:

> It was he who gave some to be apostles, some to be prophets, some to be evangelists, and some to be pastors and teachers, to prepare God's people for works of service, so that the body of Christ may be built up until we all reach unity in the faith and in the knowledge of the Son of God and become mature, attaining to the whole measure of the fullness of Christ.

While music doesn't appear on Paul's list, Hustad believes that music can be used to fulfill each of these roles for ministry. He speaks of the church musician's possible role as a prophet, evangelist, pastor, teacher, and apostle. Although he answers the question from the perspective of a full-time minister of music, the principles offered are equally valid for a part-time music director or a lay worship leader:

In the general New Testament sense, a *prophet* is not a foreteller—a divine Jeanne Dixon!—but rather a "forth-teller," one who brings the Word of God to others. . . . this means that musicians should consider themselves to be "musical prophets" who are as concerned with the words of hymns and anthems as they are with their music. To be true to their calling, they must choose texts that bring the whole Word to the whole person, and they will equip themselves theologically to do this. . . . they will occasionally "break the bread of life" in the anthem text, explaining it verbally in the choir rehearsal (sometimes even in the corporate worship service), or in writing in the church bulletin. . . .

Thoughtful musical prophets will also understand that music, like speech, is a language; it should be intelligible. . . . if they feel that the hymn texts common to their fellowship do not provide a healthy singing diet or that their musical settings do not really help to make the words more meaningful, they will speak to their people as prophets, and help them find alternatives.

Today's ministers of music in the local church should also see themselves as evangelists. They should be prepared to address another person with a simple, personal witness to "the old, old story." . . . the graded choir program, too, contributes to evangelism and church growth. Young children are attracted by the musical activity, learn to sing the truth of God, and often come rather easily and naturally to personal faith. . . .

Every Christian is in a sense a *pastor*. . . . Ministers of music have a responsibility to show love and special concern for the members of their musical groups, giving counsel when needed, visiting them in their homes or in the hospital, and standing by them in the occasions of celebration as well as in the times of crisis and sorrow. . . .

A central role for today's ministers of music is that of a *teacher*. They are involved in Christian education . . . when they teach worship and churchmanship. In choosing music with strong scriptural texts, they teach theology and discipleship. . . .

There are some [church musicians] in our day who serve musically in foreign lands, and they may be said to "follow in the train" of the *apostles*, the first missionaries![21]

APPLY WITH DISCERNMENT

In summary, each church must evaluate its own situation. Churches eager to try new styles of worship do well to move slowly, taking "baby steps" in adapting to contemporary culture.

One way to begin is to work toward an ensemble style that involves more individuals in leading worship and does not treat praise as merely part of the "preliminaries." Church leaders should also consider ways of structuring the life and ministry of the church that allow the Spirit to work more freely. Other possibilities include introducing sections of continuous praise into the service, using the oral method for learning choruses and hymns, and maintaining a sensitivity to the emotional aspect of the learning process.

Keep in mind that the intent of this chapter is not to communicate that charismatic worship on the whole is better or preferable, but to examine and increase understanding of some of the ideas that underlie it. Then, given a broader range of options, we are free to adapt whatever elements seem appropriate to our church culture as we attempt to discern the leading of the Lord for our particular body of believers.

QUESTIONS FOR THOUGHT AND DISCUSSION

1. Do you think churches are presently going through a period of "deregulation"? Explain your answer.
2. What about the length of the worship service in your church? Do longer services require that the people take a less passive role?
3. Is your worship service a solo performance by the pastor? If so, what are the consequences?
4. "Structure must serve the life of the Spirit." If this idea were acted on in your church, how would that change your worship?
5. Do you desire to give the Holy Spirit a "free run" in your life? How might that be done?
6. Is institutionalism necessarily a bad thing? Explain your answer.
7. Do you agree that the psychological shape of worship is of primary importance? Does adoration more naturally follow exaltation psychologically?
8. What are the pros and cons of starting a service with an organ prelude instead of an "invitation phase"?
9. "Their leadership just looks effortless." Comment.
10. Is it really possible for worship leaders absorbed in the task of leading to worship along with the people? Why or why not?

RECOMMENDED READING

Buchanan, Colin. *Encountering Charismatic Worship.* Bamcote: Grove Books, 1977.

Cornwall, Judson. *Let Us Worship.* South Plainfield, N.J.: Bridge Publishing, 1983.

Gibbs, Eddie, ed. *Ten Growing Churches.* N.p.: Marc Europe, the British Church Growth Association, 1984.

Hayford, Jack W. *Church on the Way.* Grand Rapids: Chosen Books, 1983.

Kendrick, Graham. *Learning to Worship as a Way of Life.* Minneapolis: Bethany House, 1984.

Smith, Chuck. *Charisma Vs. Charismania.* Eugene, Oreg.: Harvest House, 1983.

Thurman, Joyce V. *New Wineskins: A Study of the House Church Movement.* Bern: Verlag Peter Lang, 1982.

CHAPTER SEVEN

Synagogue Worship: Patterns for Protestants

Synagogues were widespread during the time of Christ. Jesus grew up in a synagogue environment and later read and taught in the synagogue. Synagogue worship has strongly influenced the direction of Protestant worship. To this day Protestant worship is indebted to its emphasis on prayer, Scripture reading, teaching, lay involvement, and elder rule. What were synagogue services like? Who led them? How? Was synagogue worship uniform from one place to another? What functions did the synagogue serve? What was the role of women? These and others questions are dealt with in this chapter.[1]

Bear in mind that long after Paul wrote his first letter to the Corinthians and until the destruction of the temple (A.D. 70), Christian Jews continued to worship at the synagogue and the temple in addition to churches.[2] Both of these institutions, though they had contrasting worship styles, continued to function in a complementary and mutually supportive fashion. Not until A.D. 100 were Christian Jews finally forced out of the synagogues. Church history shows that after that time, the gentile churches tended to revert to aspects of the synagogue model, particularly the catechistic tone of the synagogue.

SHABBY ROOM, OR SEVENTY-ONE SEATS OF GOLD?

The origin of the Jewish synagogue remains shrouded in uncertainty. Some researchers believe it evolved during the Babylonian captivity when the Jews had no temple.[3] By the time of Christ, the institution was already well established. Meeting places were generally buildings designated for worship rather than homes. Ten males were required in order to form a synagogue. If we assume that each had a wife and two children, the minimum size must have been about forty people. One early source estimated there were more than four hundred synagogues in Jerusalem alone at the time of Christ. Some were physically large and attractive, but most were no more than a single—sometimes shabby—room.[4]

The Basilica-Synagogue of Alexandria in Egypt (destroyed about A.D. 90–117), for example, was so huge it had several colonnades and seventy-one elders. Members were seated according to their trade guilds. Because the voice of the worship leader could not be heard, flags had to be waved to signal the people when to perform their responsive *amens*.

> Now there were seventy-one golden thrones set up there, one for each of the seventy-one elders, each one worth twenty-five talents of gold, with a wooden platform in the middle. The minister [attendant] of the synagogue stands on it, with flags in his hands. When one began to read, the other would wave the flags so the people would answer, "Amen," for each and every blessing. . . . They did not sit in a jumble, but the goldsmiths sat by themselves, the silversmiths by themselves, the weavers by themselves, bronze-workers by themselves, and the blacksmiths by themselves. All this why? So that when a traveller came along, [he could find his fellow craftsmen] and on that basis could gain a living.[5]

It is interesting to observe the principle of subcongregations present in this large group, a principle that church growth leaders have only recently rediscovered. Also observe that innovation (the flags) serves the purpose of preserving the congregational *amens*. This shows the great importance accorded congregational involvement in synagogue liturgy.

THE SYNAGOGUE IN THE GOSPELS AND ACTS

The small, rural synagogue like the one in Nazareth described by Luke, however, is more typical than the one in Alexandria.

> On the Sabbath day he [Jesus] went into the synagogue, as was his custom. And he stood up to read. The scroll of the prophet Isaiah was handed to him. Unrolling it, he found the place where it was written: "The Spirit of the Lord is on me. . . ." Then he rolled up the scroll, gave it back to the attendant and sat down. The eyes of everyone in the synagogue were fastened on him, and he began by saying to them, "Today this scripture is fulfilled in your hearing." All spoke well of him and were amazed at the gracious words that came from his lips (Luke 4:16–22).

From this passage we learn that Jesus regularly attended synagogue worship on the Sabbath ("as was his custom"). It seems that in His hometown a building was especially designated for worship and a formalized office existed: an "attendant" performed the ritual of taking the scroll from the cabinet located up front (a type of the Old Testament ark of the covenant) and handing it to the reader.[6] This act effectively elevated the place accorded the reading of Scripture.[7] Notice the reading preceded the teaching. Leaders stood when reading and sat when preaching.

That teaching was an important aspect of the service becomes clear in Mark's Gospel. "Jesus went into the synagogue and began to teach" (Mark 1:21). Any competent person was allowed to teach. This practice later gave Paul and his companions opportunity to speak in synagogues outside Israel.

> After the reading from the Law and the Prophets, the synagogue rulers sent word to them, "Brothers, if you have a message of encouragement for the people, please speak" (Acts 13:15).

Notice that *multiple* passages of Scripture were read. It was the practice in the synagogue service to read from both the Law and the Prophets. Usually more than one layperson performed these readings.

Note also that the invitation to speak was issued to Paul by the synagogue leaders (plural). This instance appears to be somewhat exceptional. Extrabiblical evidence indicates a "president" (singular) was usually appointed to make the reading and speaking arrangements, supervise the order of service, and see to it that nothing improper took place.[8] The invitation issued in Acts also seems to have been impromptu; it was given during the course of the service.

Usually the sermon was a short homily, the readings and prayers being regarded as the more important parts of the service.[9] Though the homily did not dominate their service as it sometimes does ours, it constituted a highly distinctive aspect of the synagogue service compared with worship in the temple.[10] As far as we can discover, there was never any preaching in the temple service during its thousand-year history, but teaching occurred in the temple porticos, which were separated from the worship area proper.

Although He supported the synagogue institution by His regular attendance, Jesus harshly criticized the conduct and underlying motivation of the Pharisees, the leaders in the synagogue. The elders customarily took the front seats. Our Lord said of the Pharisees, "You love the front seats in the synagogue" (Luke 11:43 NASB). Their worship, He declared, stemmed from a desire to be "seen" (Matt. 6:1–6). The gold-plated seats of the Alexandrian synagogue help us understand how well this criticism applied! Moreover, the officers' love for titles ran squarely against the grain of Jesus' teaching:

"They love to be greeted in the market places and have men call them 'Rabbi.' But you are not to be called 'Rabbi,' for you have only one Master and you are all brothers. . . . Nor are you to be called 'teacher,' for you have one Teacher, the Christ" (Matt. 23:7–10).

Titles can be detrimental to ministry. It is right to respect positions of authority and to value learning and degrees, but in the church they should not be allowed to engender social stratification. After I received my Ph.D., I agreed to serve in a small, blue-collar church. The pastor asked if I wanted to be called "Dr. Liesch." I said it was okay with me, but later I regretted it. Too much was made of the title, and I found that it came between me and the people. It became a barrier to ministry.

Making much ado in the church bulletin and in public announcements about who does what in the service can also be counterproductive, though it's sometimes necessary. It is amazing how much can be done when the people involved are not concerned about who gets the credit.

There are some definite advantages to leaders' adopting a low profile. When people are not told who did what, it minimizes the potential for jealousy among leaders and makes it easier to work with various individuals on subsequent occasions and to take better advantage of future opportunities. We find that Jesus' criticisms were directed at the Pharisees, not the institution of the synagogue as such. But He also said that new wine needs new wineskins, and this has often been interpreted to mean that the newness He was inaugurating could not be contained in old forms.

"No one sews a patch of unshrunk cloth on an old garment, for the patch will pull away from the garment, making the tear worse. Neither do men pour new wine into old wineskins. If they do, the skins will burst, the wine will run out and the wineskins will be ruined. No, they pour new wine into new wineskins, and both are preserved" (Matt. 9:16–17).

The parable may also give general advice relating to the capacity of old, established churches to change and adapt. New churches often have more freedom to innovate. In old churches with long-time members still living and active, history and traditions need to be respected. Try to build upon and add to the positives in the foundation already laid. Patience and sensitivity must accompany the introduction of change.

VARIETY

Just as today's churches on America's west coast have a different flavor from those of the Midwest and the east coast, so too the synagogues of Jerusalem, Galilee, the coastal cities, and the Diaspora all had their differences. Scholarship and archaeology have led to the conclusion that greater differences of local color existed among synagogues than had been imagined previously. Joseph Gutman maintains that "a monolithic, homogeneous Judaism is no longer tenable."[11]

The culture, politics, presence or absence of persecution, and socioeconomic conditions of a given locality all had a profound effect on the worship occurring in the synagogues. Because of persecution, some synagogues were severely restricted in every way. Others, though located outside Palestine, enjoyed wide public support from the Gentiles and had wealthy patrons. This allowed for unique developments. For example, archaeologists have unearthed the presence of spectacular artwork in the wealthy synagogue of Dura (third century A.D.). Elaborate murals, paintings, and frescoes depicting biblical scenes decorated its walls.

But there was also diversity in the mid-first century, for the synagogue provided a place for a great variety of activities and functions. It was primarily a place for prayer and study, but it was also used as a dining hall for sacred meals, a repository for communal funds and charities, a place for communal law courts, a hostel for travelers, a residence for synagogue officials, and even a general assembly hall (e.g., a place to gather and decide whether to join the war effort against Rome in A.D. 66).[12]

THE SYNAGOGUE SERVICE

The main object of the synagogue service was not religious worship in the narrow sense, but instruction in the Torah.[13] The emphasis, in contrast to temple worship, centered more on teaching than praise. In this sense it may be likened to many evangelical churches that have teaching services and Sunday schools. It was a place for reading the Law, learning its meaning, and instilling its precepts in young and old alike.[14] Four main parts to the synagogue service occurred in this order: (1) the Shema, a kind of synagogal creed, (2) the Eighteen Benedictions, fixed prayers with congregational responses, (3) the reading of Scripture, and (4) the sermon. We will examine the first three in some detail and discuss their consequent adaptation to Christian worship.

Reciting Creeds

A rationale for employing creeds in Christian worship services can be found in Scripture and in the synagogue service. Creeds are like manifestoes. The Shema of the synagogue service eventually took on the function of censoring Judaism *in* and rival groups like Christianity *out*. It was a kind of manifesto of the Jewish faith. A form of the Shema had been recited by priests in the temple long before A.D. 70.[15] But by the early second century it was recited at each synagogue service and supposedly twice a day by each adult at home.[16]

Old Testament Precedent

The idea for a "credo" in the synagogue service did not emerge from a vacuum. A powerful historical precedent for it exists in Old Testament worship. A "historical" credo that reinforced the identity of each Israelite as he brought his offering was part of a regular ritual drama:

> "And you shall go to the priest who is in office at that time, and say to him, '*I declare this day to the* LORD *my God* that I have entered the land which the LORD swore to our fathers to give us.' Then the priest shall take the basket from your hand and set it down before the altar of the LORD your God. *And you shall answer and say before the* LORD *your God*, 'My father was a wandering Aramean, and he went down to Egypt and sojourned there, few in number; but there he became a great, mighty and populous nation. And the Egyptians treated us harshly. . . . Then we cried to the LORD . . . and the LORD brought us out of Egypt with a mighty hand . . . and He has brought us to this place, and has given us this land, a land flowing with milk and honey. And now behold, I have brought the first of the produce of the ground which Thou, O LORD hast given me.' And you shall set it down before the LORD your God, and worship" (Deut. 26:3–10 NASB).

The passage is confessional in nature and speaks of personal identity. The language has an obvious catechistic emphasis, a question-answer format that is very much part of both the Old Testament and synagogal worship styles.[17] Notice how active a role Israelites had in their worship! They came forward and responded to the question with an individually recited "speech."

The Shema had roots in this cultural environment. People recited it near the beginning of the synagogue service. A couple of prayer benedictions preceded and followed it. The following excerpt (about one-fourth of the Shema) shows its monotheistic emphasis and general character. Worshipers recited it in unison at every Sabbath service.

> *Hear, O Israel! The* LORD *is our God, the* LORD *is one!* And you shall love the LORD your God with all your heart and with all your soul and with all your might. And these words, which I am commanding you today, shall be on your heart; and you shall teach them diligently to your sons and shall talk of them when you sit in your house and when you walk by the way and when you lie down and when you rise up. And you shall bind them as a sign on your hand and they shall be as frontals on your forehead. And you shall write them on the doorposts of your house and on your gates (Deut. 6:4–9 NASB).[18]

Constantly reciting the Shema burned into the psyche of parents their responsibility to involve themselves in the religious training of their children. The Shema consolidated, preserved, and affirmed individuals in the Jewish faith.

New Testament Precedent

A number of historical Christological confessions function in the same way in the New Testament. Consider this passage:

> Great indeed, we confess, is the mystery of our religion:
>
> He was manifested in the flesh,
> vindicated in the Spirit,
>   seen by angels,
> preached among the nations,
> believed on in the world,
>   taken up in glory (1 Tim. 3:16 RSV).[19]

We do not find full-blown creedal statements in the New Testament, for official church creeds did not appear until the third and fourth centuries. We do have, however, the seeds of creeds in compact statements like the above or "Jesus is Lord" or "Jesus is the Christ."

The early church possessed a body of teaching that was beginning to become fixed into formulae.

> For what I received I passed on to you as of first importance: that Christ *died* for our sins according to the Scriptures, that he was *buried,* that he was *raised* on the third day according to the Scriptures, and that he appeared to Peter, and then to the Twelve (1 Cor. 15:3–5).

The hymnic passage from Philippians that follows has both a creed-like theological emphasis and a soaring quality admirably suited to worship recitation:

> Your attitude should be the same as that of Christ Jesus:
>
> Who, being in the very nature of God,
>   did not consider equality with God something to be grasped,
>   but made himself nothing,
>   taking the very nature of a servant,
>   being made in human likeness.
>
> And being found in appearance as a man,
>   he humbled himself and became obedient to death—
>   even death on a cross!
>
> Therefore God exalted him to the highest place
>   and gave him the name that is above every name,
>   that at the name of Jesus every knee should bow,

in heaven and on earth and under the earth,
and every tongue confess that Jesus Christ is Lord,
to the glory of God the Father (Phil. 2:5–11).

Purpose

The great credos of the Christian church, such as the Nicene and Apostles' creeds, focus on basic affirmation with no intention of being sectarian, exclusive, or overly intellectual. They arose out of practical needs when the church was beleaguered by foes of basic doctrine from within and without. Creeds also serve both to preserve purity in the church and to release joy in corporate worship. Christians embrace a positive belief system. They of all people can rejoice in what God has achieved for them, and there is therefore great joy in declaring and affirming this publicly and unashamedly. The outward act of reciting a creed does not make one a Christian, yet John Leith well says that creeds can be affirmed, not just ritualistically, but by the whole person.

> The confession of faith is an essential moment in the life of a Christian. In confession the believer speaks out before men the silent thought and affirmation of his heart and mind. He makes outward what is inward. In confession the believer takes his stand, commits his life, declares what he believes to be true, affirms his ultimate loyalty, and defies every false claim upon his life.[20]

Creeds can provide balance for church services that center on an almost exclusively emotional kind of worship. Creeds are also helpful in imparting to children and young Christians the basics of difficult concepts like the Trinity and the deity and humanity of Christ. As we witness the building of temples of other religions and cults in North America, creeds may become more valuable in serving to clarify the essentials in an increasingly pluralistic society.

Implementation

Churches that have not practiced reading or reciting creeds as a part of their church culture, but would like to, could ease into it in a series of steps.

Pastors could begin by first involving their people in affirming their faith using biblical texts like those cited from Philippians 2 or 1 Timothy 3. They can put these passages in the bulletin or on an overhead. The congregation can even memorize them. During the pre-service, the congregational act could be explained and rehearsed, and then performed in the service for a few Sundays in a row.

Alternatively, the Ten Commandments could be read. There are a number of inventive ways of doing this. For example, one side of the congregation could declare the commandments as "shalt nots" (such as "Thou shalt not commit adultery") and the other could respond with positive affirmations (such as "We choose to show respect for each person's sexuality").

Older hymns like Luther's "A Mighty Fortress" or newer ones like Bryan Leeche's "We Are God's People" can also be used to convey a manifesto-like quality.

If these efforts are successful, the Nicene Creed might be read for the first time congregationally on a Sunday in which a baptism is performed. A baptismal service is essentially a "confessional service." Some pastors require those being baptized to verbalize their faith publicly during a series of short questions and answers. In this ceremonial environment, the reading of a creed by the entire congregation may be especially meaningful and appropriate. Communion Sunday may be another time when the reading of a creed is appropriate since that service tends to have a more liturgical flavor anyway.

Here is the Nicene Creed.[21] Some churches replace the words "I believe" with "We believe."

The Nicene Creed

I believe in one God, the Father Almighty, creator of heaven and earth, of all things visible and invisible;

And in one Lord Jesus Christ, the only-begotten Son of God, begotten from the Father before all time, Light from Light, true God from true God, begotten not made, of the same essence as the Father, through Whom all things came into being, Who for us men and for our salvation came down from heaven, and was incarnate by the Holy Spirit and the Virgin Mary and became human. He was crucified for us under Pontius Pilate, and suffered and was buried, and rose on the third day, according to the Scriptures, and ascended to heaven, and sits on the right hand of the Father, and will come again with glory to judge the living and the dead. His kingdom shall have no end.

And I believe in the Holy Spirit, the Lord and giver of life, Who proceeds from the Father, Who is worshiped and glorified together with the Father and Son, Who spoke through the prophets.

And I believe in one universal and apostolic Church. I confess one baptism for the remission of sins. I look forward to the resurrection of the dead and the life of the world to come. Amen.

Some churches might prefer to sing a creed rather than read it. A paraphrased version of the Apostles' Creed can be sung to the hymn tune of "Glorious Things of Thee Are Spoken" (Austrian Hymn). This text is excellent for Easter. Sing it in the key of E-flat major.

The Apostles' Creed (Paraphrased)

I believe in God the Father, Maker of the heaven and earth,
And in Jesus Christ, our Savior, God's own Son of matchless worth;
By the Holy Ghost conceivéd, Virgin Mary bore God's Son,
He in whom I have believéd, God Almighty, Three in One.

Suffered under Pontius Pilate, crucified for me He died
Laid within the grave so silent, gates of Hell He opened wide.
And the stone-sealed tomb was empty, on the third day He arose,
Into heaven made His entry, Mighty Conqueror of His foes.

At God's right hand He is seated, till His coming, as He said,
Final judgment will be meted to the living and the dead,
I confess the Holy Spirit has been sent through Christ the Son,
To apply salvation's merit, God the Spirit—Three in One.

I believe that all believers form one body as a whole.
We are one throughout the ages, with the saints I lift my soul.
I believe sins are forgiven, that our bodies will be raised,
Everlasting life in heaven, Amen, let His name be praised!

Reading and Responding to Fixed Prayers

When Jesus drove the money changers from the temple, He said, "Is it not written: 'My house will be called a house of prayer for all nations?' But you have made it a 'den of robbers'" (Mark 11:17). The synagogue had a strong tradition of prayer and became known as a house of prayer. Eighteen fixed benedictions collectively formed the structure for what they termed their "prayer." Not only were the benedictions read during the service, but the people were also required to recite them three times each day. So they became exceedingly well known.

The wording of the benedictions has come down to us in at least two versions so it must have been somewhat elastic.[22] The set number of eighteen and the wording of the congregational responses are thought to have crystallized around A.D. 70–100, but the "underlying foundation" and framework of the prayer is considered much older. Benedictions 1–3 praise God's greatness; 4–9 ask for knowledge, repentance, forgiveness, deliverance, healing, and prosperity; 10–16 pray for the reunion of Jews, the coming of the Messiah, and the return of the sacrificial system; 17–18 offer thanksgiving to God for His goodness.

The language, which is formal and at times transcendent in tone (see example 1), is set in a disciplined liturgical environment. Each benediction closes with a doxological refrain. Note that the congregational participation in the refrain (in italics) is often cued by a key word (in boldface). They were read or recited at a brisk, rhythmic pace.[23] Here are some examples as they appear numerically in the Palestinian version:

1. Blessed art thou, Lord, God of our fathers, God of **Abraham,** God of Isaac and God of Jacob, great, mighty and fearful God, most high God who createst heaven and earth, our shield and the shield of our fathers, our trust in every generation. *Blessed art thou, Lord, shield of* **Abraham.**

3. Thou art **holy** and thy Name is awesome, and besides thee there is no God. *Blessed art thou, Lord, the* **holy** *God.*

6. **Forgive** us, our Father, for we have sinned against thee. Wipe out and remove our evil deeds from before thine eyes. For thy mercies are many. *Blessed art thou, Lord, rich in* **forgiveness.**

15. Hear, Lord our God, the voice of our **prayer,** and be merciful to us; for thou art a gracious and merciful God. *Blessed art thou, Lord, who hearest* **prayer.**

18. Bring thy **peace** over Israel, thy people, and over thy city and over thine inheritance; and bless all of us together. *Blessed art thou, Lord, who makest* **peace.**[24]

Fixed, written prayers like the Eighteen Benedictions are standard today in many liturgically oriented churches. It is important to understand that from a historical viewpoint, the synagogue provided the initial model for this material. The style of synagogue and temple prayer during the New Testament times was influential (as far as we can tell) in all churches—even in the Pauline churches—but probably more strongly in churches in the Jerusalem area than in those outside Israel. As mentioned previously, in Jerusalem some Jewish Christians continued to attend temple and synagogue services, and "official separation between Judaism and Christianity did not take place until the end of the first century, and was then instigated primarily by Judaism."[25] Tradition says the Eighteen Benedictions were reformulated into nineteen around A.D. 90 with a new special petition aimed against Christian heretics and other supposed "enemies" of Judaism.[26]

There were also some differences in nuance between the New Testament prayers and their synagogue counterparts. In Judaism (and in the Eighteen Benedictions) confession of sin and petition occupy a considerable place, but the New Testament shows relatively little trace of them.[27] Praise and thanks predominate. Also free prayers—as opposed to fixed prayers—prevailed in the early church until the third century, but by the fifth century prescribed, fixed ordinances were everywhere.[28]

In many evangelical churches today, spontaneous, improvised prayer is the *only* form of prayer employed. Many have an *aversion* to fixed, written prayers. They consider them insincere compared with spontaneous prayers that "come from the heart."

We need to overcome this artificial distinction. I have been in fundamentalist churches where a layman comes to the front and reads a prayer he has written for the first half and then improvises the last half. Shall we view the first half—written at home with the added benefit of being able to revise, reflect, and improve upon the wording—less genuine? As Evangelicals we can learn to be open to more variety in the way we offer prayer without sacrificing anything in genuineness of expression.

In our concept of prayer, furthermore, another inconsistency must be addressed: while fixed, written prayers are not spoken in our tradition, they may be sung! A case in point would be a hymn like "O God Our Help in Ages Past." Its text, a paraphrase of Psalm 90, is a straightforward, "fixed" prayer. We need to understand that some of the best praying in our services could be occurring while the people are offering their worship in song. Some hymns are, simply put, prescribed prayers. Yet we do not think of our singing in this way!

Seven Readers Reading Scripture

In synagogue services in Palestine, the reading of Scripture was accorded unusual prominence. Not only was the taking of the scroll from the scroll case a high point in their ceremony, but also many lay readers were invited by the president to take part in multiple Scripture readings. On the morning Sabbath services the Mishnah ruling was that at least seven readers should always participate:

> The first and the last were to pronounce a benediction at the beginning and the end. Each had to read at least three verses of the Torah, and was not to repeat them by memory.[29]

The afternoon Sabbath service required only three readers since no reading from the prophets took place. Minors were allowed to read. Boys' schools existed for the almost exclusive purpose of teaching the "reading and memorizing" of the Torah, not for general education.[30] Nicholas de Lange, rabbi and lecturer in Rabbinics at Cambridge University, says:

> Unfortunately, the biblical command to teach children Torah (Deut. 6:7) was interpreted narrowly by some authorities so as to apply to sons but not to daughters. Accord to one rabbi, "to teach a daughter Torah is tantamount to teaching her lechery" (Mishnah *Sotah* iii, 4). Fortunately there were other rabbis who disagreed with this opinion, and gave their daughters the same education as their sons. There are even recorded cases of women scholars, whose opinions were respected by men. Such cases, however, are rare, and are outnumbered by the instances of women who worked, like the "worthy wife" of Proverbs, so that their husbands would have the leisure to study.[31]

Though women "could not be counted in the quorum for public worship, which was ten adult males, they were permitted to read the lesson" in the synagogue.[32] In synagogue services outside Palestine (where persons may not have been as fluent in Hebrew?) the Scriptures could be read in Hebrew by one person and translated by another.

The first five books of the Bible received priority in the public reading program. Even as early as the time of Christ, the Torah (Pentateuch) may have been read through in a three-year cycle. A custom was established somewhat later to divide the Torah variously into 161, 167, or 175 sections to make a triennial lectionary cycle, or in 54 sections to make a one-year cycle.[33] The "lectionary" Scripture readings (that is, planned, systematic reading) used in many mainline Protestant churches today flows from this practice.

I go into such detail on the manner of the reading of Scripture in the synagogue service to show how important and developed a ritual it had become. By strange contrast, Evangelicals, who hold firmly to a high view of Scripture, sometimes fail in actual practice to have even a single reading of the Scriptures (let alone *multiple* readings or systematic reading) in their services.[34] Such an omission would have been unthinkable in a synagogue Sabbath service! Paul's admonition to Timothy echoes to us as well:

> Until I come, devote yourself to the public reading of Scripture, to preaching and to teaching (1 Tim. 4:13).[35]

Reader's Theater

An innovation on the idea of multiple readers is the concept of "reader's theater." It is especially useful for heightening interest on festive or special occasions. Two or more readers participate in reading a passage of Scripture. The readers may be located together at the front or in the audience or in any other configuration in the worship space that seems appropriate. Reader's theater can be an exciting way to read Old and New Testament stories and miracles, such as the account of the Incarnation, the Easter story, or the descent of the Holy Spirit in Acts. Each reader takes a part: one could be the narrator, for example. By having everyone read at the same time, you can achieve a choric effect for emphasis. It's a very versatile technique, and you can do it in different ways. It can take from three to thirty minutes of the service and from two to twenty people. You can use it with a variety of narrative passages with a number of different spacial arrangements.[36]

SYNAGOGUE PRACTICES

Elder Rule

The Scriptures suggest that in Jerusalem the elders exerted both religious and civic authority.[37] Apparently they didn't have "separation of church and state." Extrabiblical evidence corroborates that in purely Jewish districts both city administration and religious matters lay entirely in the hands of the elders of the synagogue.[38] In localities of Gentiles or a mixed Jewish and gentile population, the elders controlled synagogue affairs only. Schurer maintains:

> There is . . . no trace in Jewish congregations of anything resembling the way in which the full assembly of the Christian church at Corinth (1 Cor. 5) . . . discussed and decided on individual cases of discipline and administration. Instead this was done by the appropriate bodies, i.e., the elders of the congregation.[39]

Offices, Titles, and Seats of Honor

There are marked differences between the Corinthian church and the synagogue in the attitudes toward offices, titles, and seats of honor. In the Corinthian church Paul makes the point that the most "presentable parts" should receive "no special treatment . . . so that there should be no division in the body, but that its parts should have equal concern for each other" (1 Cor. 12:24–25). In the synagogue, however, the distinguished members sat at the front and the younger ones behind.[40] Moreover, according to Wayne Meeks, synagogues in gentile cities

> depended on benefactions of patrons, including non-Jewish sympathizers as well, whom they rewarded by inscriptions, special seats in the assembly room, and honorary titles like "Father" or "Mother" of the Synagogue.[41]

The synagogue, as we saw earlier, had formal officers, a president and an attendant. As far as we can tell, the Corinthian church had none. Meeks holds that even the term "apostle" represented no office, though persons so designated were invested with substantial authority in missionary activities. The Pauline mission band was a "collective enterprise with something that loosely could be called a staff."[42] What impresses Meeks most is the "complexity and fluidity of the network of leaders" working with Paul.[43] He says that leadership roles in early Pauline congregations focused more in terms of "laboring, admonishing, and presiding over" than in terms of offices (1 Thess. 5:12). The variety among the ministry lists in Corinthians, Romans, and Ephesians, he feels, indicates local variation and freedom for charismatic leadership and shows that Paul is trying to "play down differences of status in order to stress group cohesion," while allowing a diversity of gifts to operate.[44]

This kind of thinking can be helpful in creating "body flow" among the worship leaders of a local church and is worth striving for. I have felt it at work, and it is wonderful! This fluid network of leadership is quite different from the importance attached to fixed offices of elders, presidents, attendants, and so forth in the synagogal organization who exercised power both in local religious and formal civic affairs.

"What Shall We Do With the Women?"

The role of women was more extensive and more nearly equal to that of men in the Corinthian church than in Judaism. In Corinth, women prayed and exercised the charismatic gift of prophecy in the congregation (1 Cor. 11:5). Meeks says, "in terms of their position in the larger society and in terms of their participation in the Christian communities, . . . a number of women broke through the normal expectation of female roles. . . . this produced tensions within the groups."[45]

In regard to the status of women in Judaism, Allen Ross of Dallas Theological Seminary says, "It is easy to find statements in the Mishnah (and Talmud) that display a very low view of women or a very high view. Probably a balance between the extremes was more commonly the position."[46]

De Lange says, "Her presence certainly was welcome at services, and was necessary at most family celebrations, but her religious role was glorified and her involvement greatest in the seclusion of her home." The Jewish home has been called "the other sanctuary":

[at the Friday evening meal at home] On a spotless white tablecloth stand a pair of candles in silver candlesticks, a silver goblet of wine, a loaf of bread baked in the traditional plaited shape. The mother lights the candles and says a Hebrew blessing, and this act is the formal inauguration of the Sabbath. The father lays his hands on his children's heads and pronounces the ancient priestly blessing (Num. 6:24–26). Then after a song welcoming the angelic visitors who are supposed to enter the home on the Sabbath, he turns to his wife and recites the Hebrew poem which ends the Book of Proverbs. . . . This biblical poem, and its honoured place in the Sabbath ritual, highlights at once the great respect traditionally accorded to the Jewish wife and mother, and also her distinct role in society.[47]

De Lange continues on the subject of segregation in the synagogue:

Although women came to be segregated from men in the temple, and later in the synagogue too, there is no evidence that the sexes were separated in synagogues in Gospel times. We read in Acts (1:14) how Mary and a group of women joined the apostles in prayer in their lodging-house in Jerusalem, and there are many references in Acts to women being present in synagogues in the Diaspora [i.e., synagogues located outside Palestine].[48]

It is not uncommon in the literature on this topic, however, to find assertions like the following by A. C. Bouquet: "in all synagogues the sexes were separated and the women put behind a screen."[49]

One reference in the Babylonian Talmud maintains a woman's voice was "a sexual incitement." In Christian churches the reference that women should "keep silent" (1 Cor. 14:34) was applied to the singing of married women in church.

> The mixing of men's and women's voices was seen as a symbol of sexual union and forbidden. Nevertheless, Christianity approved the singing of virgins.[50]

All this seems confusing and highly culture laden![51] Not many readers of Scripture today would imagine that to "keep silent" would be interpreted by some to mean that married women should not participate in congregational singing! That has ceased to be an issue for us.

Music and worship often lie on the cutting edge of social change. Donald Hustad comments penetratingly: "It is interesting to note that some pastors have no problem working with a part-time 'director of music' who is a woman, but they would not consider her as a candidate for a full-time position as 'minister of music.' "[52]

Like Hustad I would like to see anyone, male or female, who deeply senses the spiritual significance of the calling and who is dedicated and equipped for the task, to be allowed to serve in this capacity. "Minister of Music" could be replaced by some other designation ("Worship Leader" or "Worship Director") in churches where it would be inappropriate for a woman to hold such a title.

SUMMARY

We have seen that the synagogue with its emphasis on prayer, the reading of Scriptures, teaching, lay involvement, and elder rulership has provided a basic model for many Protestant churches. Liturgical ideas such as recited creeds, congregational responses, multiple readings of Scripture, and the use of a lectionary also flow from synagogue practice.

QUESTIONS FOR THOUGHT AND DISCUSSION

1. Can titles be detrimental to ministry? Explain your answer.
2. "A church's history and traditions need to be respected." Discuss.
3. Is a diversity of worship practices between churches a positive thing? Why, or why not?
4. What are the pros and cons of reciting creeds? Do you think Scripture gives support for the idea?

5. Are fixed prayers or written prayers less genuine than spontaneous prayers? Explain.
6. "Some of the best praying occurs when people worship in song." Is this true of your service?
7. Should women be allowed to lead the choir? Lead the song service? Read Scripture or pray? Why, or why not?
8. What are the advantages and disadvantages of using lectionaries?
9. When are we praying?
10. Does your church accord the public reading of Scripture a high-enough place? How can the public reading of Scripture be made more interesting?

RECOMMENDED READING

Leith, John H. *Creeds of the Churches*. 3d ed. Atlanta: John Knox Press, 1982.

Martin, Ralph P. *Worship in the Early Church*. Grand Rapids: Wm. B. Eerdmans, 1975.

Schaller, Lyle E. *The Middle-sized Church: Problems and Prescriptions*. Nashville: Abingdon Press, 1985.

_____. *The Small Church Is Different!* Nashville: Abingdon Press, 1982.

CHAPTER EIGHT

The Legacy: Corinth, Synagogue, Church Fathers, Puritans

In this chapter we will keep close to our purpose to learn about the biblical models of worship, but we will also look at the post-biblical influences that helped shape the Protestant heritage. With the background of the four previous chapters, we will compare the elements of the synagogue and Pauline worship cultures. We will learn why musical instruments are not mentioned in the Gospels and Epistles. We will inquire into what happened between the years A.D. 60–100. We will also look at an order of worship reported around A.D. 100 by an early church father, then further widen our lens to take in Puritan decisions about worship after the Protestant Reformation that have deeply affected Evangelicals ever since.[1] With this historical perspective we will be better equipped to deal with tabernacle worship in chapter 9.

SYNAGOGUE AND CORINTHIAN WORSHIP CULTURES COMPARED

The chart below reviews some of the contrasts between synagogue and Corinthian worship.

The chart should by no means be construed to represent a complete picture of what actually happened in Corinthian or synagogue worship. Our information is incomplete. Paul's treatment of worship in 1 Corinthians, for example, is neither systematic nor comprehensive. He focuses primarily on problems related to worship. For instance, it might be assumed that a Scripture reading from the Old Testament was a regular occurrence in a Corinthian service, but we cannot be sure because Paul writes nothing about it. Silence in this case may simply mean that the reading of Scripture was nonproblematic.

Synagogue	Corinthian (Early Gentile)
Met (mostly) in worship buildings	Met in homes
On Sabbath	On first day of week
Presence of ten males	Where two or three are gathered
Membership by birth	Membership by faith
Elder rulership	Assembly rulership
Offices of president, attendant	No apparent offices
Regulated by president	Gift of discernment
Representative participation	Maximum participation
One homily	Prophesying in turns
No counterpart	Teaching on spiritual gifts
Circumcision	Baptism
Torah/scroll ceremony	Lord's Table
Torah lectionary	No weekly Torah
Prayers of confession	Prayers of praise and thanks[2]
Transcendent prayer language	Both transcendent and intimate prayer
Fixed prayers	Predominantly improvised prayers
Men wear skullcaps (yarmulkes)	Men bare-headed, women covered
Women silent, separated	Women tend not to be silent and separated?
Women could not sing	Virgins could, married couldn't
Teach sitting down	Teach standing up
People facing forward	Circle/relational?

Some newness appears in early Christian worship as compared with the synagogue. There is no real counterpart in the synagogue service to the symbolic communication found in baptism and the Lord's Supper.[3] Circumcision and bar mitzvah, for example, do function as rites of initiation, but they do not have the symbolic aspect of baptism. To find symbolic communication of that kind we must look to the temple ceremonies. Thus, in a sense Christian worship has built into it a more comprehensive model of communication. It weds the verbal communication of the synagogue with the symbolical communication of the temple.

THE TUNNEL YEARS

The years A.D. 65–100 are mystery years. Documents from that period are scarce. Not until about A.D. 110 do we begin to get a trickle of extrabiblical sources on the early church. We know the church was going through a time of severe persecution, but we don't know what was going on internally. Alexander MacDonald suggests this synopsis:

> By about the year A.D. 65 the three great apostolic leaders, Peter, Paul, and James were dead; and from that time till the end of the

century is one of the darkest periods of Christian history, "illuminated by no great name, and by any scarcely recorded incident." To
pass from the year 65 to the year 100 has been compared to passing
through a tunnel; but, we might add, it is the kind of tunnel that
pierces a frontier range of mountains; when we emerge from it we
find ourselves in another climate; the air is cooler and the landscape
more ordinary. . . . We have passed from the region of creative
Enthusiasm into a region of growing ecclesiastical system and order.[4]

Some students of worship would agree with MacDonald's assessment. They see this dark period as one in which the church lost its early
enthusiasm and became more institutionalized, putting more emphasis on
"duly appointed officers." Others may find MacDonald's assessment
overdrawn.

There is an alternative view. During this period Roman leaders
viewed the growth of the church as a threat to their power and regarded it
with alarm. The long arm of the state seized many apostolic leaders for
their faith. Around A.D. 90 the apostle John, who had taken oversight of
the Pauline churches in Asia Minor, was banished to the Isle of Patmos.
The letters of evaluation that he wrote concerning the condition of these
churches in the Book of Revelation show highly variegated conditions and
responses. One church is dead; another has an open door of opportunity.
One is lukewarm; another is improving. Yet another, though grievously
afflicted, has through persecution become rich in spirit. It is possible that
overall an institutional "tightening up" took place, not out of apathy but
in response to widespread persecution and the steady onslaught of an
active, heathen environment. Church leadership may have been more
ordinary, lacking the apostolic fire of a Paul, but the church as a whole
was rooted and very much alive.[5]

If an institutional "tightening up" took place, did it affect the form
of worship during this period? Again, we really do not know. We search
in vain to find a detailed order of worship in the New Testament or
extrabiblical sources for any synagogue or church service that dates back
to the first century. For that sort of information we must look to early
church fathers who lived in the second century or later.

THE WORD AND THE TABLE

One of the oldest Christian documents containing an order of
worship is Justin Martyr's *First Apology,* written about 125 years after
Christ's death. Justin Martyr is representative of the early church fathers
whose writings on worship have been influential in Western history. The
order of service in *The First Apology* seems to have been typical for
churches of that time and has furnished support for a time-honored order

of service employed in some Protestant circles. The elements, in order of occurrence, are (1) Scripture reading, (2) discourse, (3) prayers, and (4) Communion.

Notice that the Lord's Table follows the discourse. Robert Webber, an evangelical Episcopalian, says Justin Martyr's order of worship is of historic importance in being the first clear statement of the two-part structure commonly called, among liturgical churches, "The Word and the Table."[6] First the Word is read and taught; then it is followed by the Lord's Supper. This is a pattern for *every* Sunday, as described in *The First Apology:*

> And on the day called Sunday there is a meeting in one place of those who live in cities or the country, and the memoirs of the apostles or the writings of the prophets are read as long as time permits. When the reader has finished, the president in a *discourse* urges and invites [us] to the imitation of these noble things. Then we all stand up together and offer prayers. And, as said before, when we have finished the prayer, *bread* is brought and wine and water, and the president similarly sends up prayers and thanksgivings to the best of his ability, and the congregation assents, saying the Amen; the distribution, and reception of the consecrated [elements] by each one, takes place and they are sent to the absent by the deacons [italics added].[7]

Observe that prayers are offered up in both parts. The first part of the service centers on verbal communication, the second on symbolic communication. Since Communion followed the sermon, it well may have been the climactic event of the service. A single reader reads from either the Old or New Testament. Whereas we do not find synagogue terminology in the New Testament, we find here that the word *president* is used. The excerpt reveals a blend of synagogue and New Testament church elements.

Synagogue Elements	Christian Elements
President	Sunday service
Reading from prophets	Reading from memoirs of apostles (N.T. substitute for Torah?)
Congregational amen	Spontaneous prayer ("to the best of his ability")
Discourse	Lord's Table
	Deacons

Here is a more detailed description of the Lord's Table after a baptism in the church service. Again, it is from Justin Martyr's *Apology:*

> Our prayers being ended, we salute one another with a kiss. Then bread, and a cup of wine mixed with water, are brought to him who

presides over the brethren. He, taking them, offers praise and glory to the Father of all through the Name of the Son and the Holy Spirit, and gives thanks at great length for that we have been counted worthy to receive these gifts from God; and when he finishes the prayers and thanksgivings all the people present cry aloud, Amen. Amen in the Hebrew tongue means, So be it.

After the president has given thanks and all the people have said Amen, those among us who are called deacons give to all present, sharing it among them, the bread and wine mixed with water over which thanks have been given, and carry it also to those who are absent. And this food is called eucharist by us, of which it is not right for any one to partake save only he who believes that the things taught by us are true, and is washed with the washing that is for the forgiveness of sins and regeneration, and so lives as Christ commanded us.[8]

Churches that place a high value on the authority of the early church fathers (the first six centuries A.D.) are inclined to view worship practices like the above as normative for the contemporary church.[9]

WHY WERE INSTRUMENTS BANNED IN SYNAGOGUES AND CHURCHES?

A number of Evangelicals are troubled that musical instruments do not appear to be mentioned in connection with worship in the New Testament. But this is not quite the case. They are both mentioned and used in worship in the Book of Revelation.[10] Also, extrabiblical sources from the time of Christ record that instrumentalists from the temple orchestra, after performing in the temple service, left to perform at the synagogue service in Jerusalem attended by the the high priest and the Sadducees. So did the temple choristers.[11] Thus we have at least one instance recorded where instruments performed with regularity in a synagogue. And, of course, instruments continued to be used in the temple services until the temple was destroyed by the Romans in A.D. 70.

Yet the question remains: "Why were instruments in general banned in synagogues and churches?" Eric Werner, an authoritative Jewish scholar, offers a response that is the chief source of the following discussion.[12]

According to Werner, Greek music culture was exerting a powerful influence on Jewish culture in the time of Christ. We know that the culture of Hellenism "had penetrated the daily life of Palestine" because the Jews there were using Greek musical terms almost exclusively "for instruments, their parts, their tuning."[13] Jewish musicians were using Greek instruments, the same kinds of instruments that the Greeks used in their temple orgies. Most rabbis associated both the music and the instruments with immorality and banned them from the synagogues. It was similar to the situation today in which rock and jazz music and instruments are considered by some to be unfit for church use because of their association with frenzied performances, drugs, and alcohol.

Werner says rabbis referred to Isaiah 24:9 and Hosea 9:1 for biblical support in banning the use of instrumental music after A.D. 70.[14] But these passages do not make any clear connection between instrumental music and *worship* and are of doubtful value for settling this question. What they do is link *revelry* to musical instruments and consequently show what rabbis thought of musical instruments.

> Woe to those who rise early in the morning
>   to run after their drinks,
> who stay up late at night
>   till they are inflamed with wine.
> They have harps and lyres at their banquets,
>   tambourines and flutes and wine,
> but they have no regard for the deeds of the LORD.
>   (Isa. 5:11–12)

God's judgment falls on these revelers:

> The gaiety of the tambourines is stilled,
>   the noise of the revelers has stopped,
>   the joyful harp is silent.
> No longer do they drink wine with a song;
>   the beer is bitter to its drinkers (Isa. 24:8–9).

Similarly God speaks in judgment through Hosea.

> Do not rejoice, O Israel;
>   do not be jubilant like the other nations.
> For you have been unfaithful to your God (Hos. 9:1).

Apparently the rabbis contended that instrumental music was stylistically "like the other nations" and therefore unfit for the synagogue. They considered the aulos, a pipelike instrument with "many holes," to be "full of frenzied tones." When they pictured an aulos in their minds they imagined someone with a Pan's pipe "imitating" a serpent song. When they saw a trumpet, they imagined men being called to war "in wild terms."

Werner says that instruments that had played a considerable role in the psalter (aulos, tympanon, and cymbals) were now held in low regard. The rabbis felt horror and contempt for them. He says, "Instruments— very popular and used frequently in the temple—were considered suspicious and unclean through their use in syncretistic religions, so that the rabbis frowned even on the kinnor (the noblest of them)." What a classic case of overreaction!

Christian sources, according to Werner, reflected the same attitude of horror for the flute, tympanon, and cymbal up to the third century. For example, he quotes Clement of Alexandria as saying:

> One makes noise with cymbols and tympana, one rages and rants with instruments of frenzy. . . . the flute belongs to those superstitious men who run to idolatry.

Like Werner, *The New Grove Dictionary of Music* explains the ban on instruments as a reaction against Greek culture.[15] It also describes the practice of unaccompanied chanting or singing in the synagogue.

> Instead of the chorus of Levites, the synagogue had an honorary elected lay precentor . . . [who was] responsible for the core of the synagogue service. . . . [The fixed prayers] had to be memorized because their writing was forbidden. These were chanted psalmodically, whereas scripture had to be recited in a special recitative that was regulated by oral tradition. To recite scripture without chant was considered a minor sacrilege according to the Talmudic saying: "He who reads the Torah without chant . . . of him it can be said as it is written [Ezekiel 20:25] 'the laws that I gave you were not good.' "[16]

Notice that the practice of not chanting Scripture and fixed prayers was termed a *minor* sacrilege. Presumably those synagogues without gifted musical leadership employed chant less extensively.

We need to make a broader point about the ban on instruments in the early church. It can be dangerous to focus too narrowly on only the Gospels and the Epistles for the last authoritative word on worship. The whole Bible needs to be considered in the context of the culture; otherwise we may draw misleading conclusions. That is exactly what the Puritans did. They considered the unaccompanied vocal music of the Epistles the only legitimate kind of music for worship even though God Himself instituted instrumental praise in the Old Testament temple and the elders held harps in their hands in the Book of Revelation.

THE PURITAN REACTION

The Puritans of sixteenth-and-seventeenth-century England, reacting against the theological and liturgical excesses of Roman Catholicism, banned from worship all use of images, all musical instruments, and even all hymns. Their worship was characterized by a severe simplicity, and they sang—or rather chanted—only unaccompanied psalms.

Many Christians in the arts believe that the Puritan reaction was a mistake, that in their zeal for purity the movement severely restricted the legitimate uses of the arts in worship, a practice that had its precedents in the Old Testament.

Ralph P. Martin summarizes the outstanding features of the Puritan tradition this way:

> a) The sole criterion was the written Word, found almost exclusively in the New Testament. The Old Testament was treated as belonging to the Jewish people whose worship, centered in the tabernacle and temple, had given way to a more spiritualized mode. Moreover, only those items of worship that were specifically mentioned in the New Testament could claim authority. Musical instruments, for example, which are not explicitly referred to in the New Testament church, were treated as distracting from "pure" worship. No room was given to innovation or to a sense of a developing tradition. Indeed, on the contrary, a stifling literalism effectively blocked any notion of creative spontaneity in the forms of worship to be employed.
>
> b) The sermon was made the climax and culmination of the service. This led inevitably to a devaluing of other forms of worship, for example, the eucharistic [the Lord's Table]. Even those parts of the service that were not strictly "preaching" or exposition were made the vehicle of instruction. Pulpit prayers were chiefly didactic in content and tone; and Scripture readings were interspersed with the preacher's homiletical comments on the text. Congregational participation was reduced to a minimum, especially to the ministry of hymns or psalms singing.
>
> c) The freedom of the Spirit was seen in the cultivating of worship from the heart and the stress on personal religion. Written prayers were frowned on if not roundly condemned, since it appears that the Puritan objection was to the exclusive use of the Prayer Book, thus denying free prayer. Sole reliance on prearranged orders of service was regarded as a quenching of the Holy Spirit. . . .
>
> d) By strange quirk, while the priesthood of all believers was cherished as a theological conviction and the concept of the church as a "gathered community" prevailed in theory, a Protestant clericalism developed, with the minister occupying a central and determinative role as leader and chief performer in the service. The preaching of one man in a raised pulpit took pride of place, and this arrangement reduced the worshipers to the level of an inert body of passive auditors.[17]

Martin adds:

> The preacher's rostrum became the church's sounding board and the minister's throne. This led to a style of worship that was heavily intellectualized and notional. . . . When worship became excessively devoted to the ministry of the word, thus ignoring the human being's many-sided personality which includes appreciation of visual art in architecture, painting, sculpture, and drama, something was lost.[18]

What Martin catalogs is zealotry gone awry. Roughly speaking, in the Reformation the Catholics took art and the Protestants took music. That is, Protestants removed art and embraced a participatory form of musical expression while the Catholic Counter-Reformation embraced the art the Protestants negated. We even see signs of overreaction in the way the Protestants responded to music; in the Cromwellian era in England, the reformers took axes to organs!

What are we to make of all this? Is it wrong to value a preaching ministry as the Puritans did? Absolutely not! Many churches sorely need a solid pulpit ministry with expositional teaching. In fairness to those who trace their roots to the Puritan tradition (or feel close to it, as I do), we want to express appreciation for their immense contribution to many aspects of church life and society—their intellectual vitality and sense of the transcendent in their sermons, and their outstanding efforts in systematic theology, for example. We would not want to fix blame for all that is "bad" about traditional evangelical worship on them or on the other Reformation movements. But we do want to encourage a strong congregational response. It should stand on a more equal footing with the preaching of the Word.

And what about the removal of art from worship? In the Puritans' desire for a New Testament purity in worship did they not also throw out a rich heritage of Old Testament worship patterns? It seems so. What we are fundamentally questioning here is the Puritans' position that simple worship (without the accoutrements of art) is necessarily better or more scriptural rather than a heartfelt option using the arts. Moreover we applaud our contemporaries, like Nicholas Wolterstorff of Calvin College, who demonstrate a profound understanding and appreciation for the legitimate place of the arts in the church and in all of life.

If we are to develop a complete philosophy of worship we must consult *all* of Scripture.

Some Evangelicals tend to dismiss Old Testament worship outright. What, they wonder, could the Old Testament possibly have to say to us now about worship? Hasn't Christ's sacrifice negated all those sacrifices and ceremonies?

Ironically the same people who utter such sentiments often go to the Psalms—the hymns of the Old Testament worship—for help in times of deepest need and greatest spiritual staleness. They find there again and again the cry of a heart hungering for God and are renewed.

There is more to Old Testament worship than the mere slaughtering of animals. There is genuine worship! There is more *continuity* in the *underlying principles* of biblical worship from Genesis to Revelation, more of a sense of a *developing tradition* than we Evangelicals in particular have previously appreciated.[19]

QUESTIONS FOR THOUGHT AND DISCUSSION

1. Do you think God had a reason for not giving us an order of service in the New Testament? Explain your answer.
2. Which does the worship format in your church resemble more—Pauline or synagogue worship? In what ways?
3. Would you say that "guilt by association" (as in the early church and synagogue) is a major roadblock to the use of new instruments and styles in the church today? Why, or why not?
4. Is it possible for a church to be on the cutting edge and set new trends in the arts? What factors or conditions would tend to encourage or discourage this possibility (age of congregation, etc.)?
5. What aspects of Puritan worship can be found in your church service?
6. Do people at your church look at Old Testament worship as outmoded and unuseful? What aspects of your worship reveal a valuable "continuity" between the Old and New Testament worship? If this question is difficult to answer, you might want to come back to it after you have finished reading this book.

RECOMMENDED READING

Bailey, Robert W. *New Ways in Christian Worship*. Nashville: Broadman Press, 1981.

Dix, G. *The Shape of Our Liturgy*. London: Dacre Press, 1945.

Martin, Ralph P. *The Worship of God: Some Theological, Pastoral, and Practical Reflections*. Grand Rapids: Wm B. Eerdmans, 1982.

Maxwell, William D. *A History of Christian Worship: An Outline of Its Development and Forms*. Grand Rapids: Baker Book House, 1982.

Michener, James A. *The Source*. New York: Fawcett Books, 1965.

Schaper, Robert N. *In His Presence: Appreciating Your Worship Tradition*. New York: Thomas Nelson, 1984.

Webber, Robert E. *Worship: Old and New*. Grand Rapids: Zondervan, 1982.

Wolterstorff, Nicholas. *Art in Action: Toward a Christian Aesthetic*. Grand Rapids: Wm. B. Eerdmans, 1980.

PART IV

Large-Group Worship

A. Tabernacle Worship
B. Temple Worship

CHAPTER NINE

Tabernacle Worship: Drama

THE PEOPLE'S DRAMA

Worship as practiced in many of our churches today appears passive, dull, and tame compared with the moving account in Leviticus 1:1–9:

> The LORD called to Moses and spoke to him from the Tent of Meeting. He said, "Speak to the Israelites and say to them: 'When any of you brings an offering to the LORD, bring as your offering an animal from either the herd or the flock.

> "'If the offering is a burnt offering from the herd, he is to offer a male without defect. He must **present** it at the entrance to the Tent of Meeting so that it will be acceptable to the LORD. He is to **lay his hand on** the head of the burnt offering, and it will be accepted on his behalf to make atonement for him. He is to **slaughter** the young bull before the LORD, and then Aaron's sons the priests shall bring the blood and sprinkle it against the altar on all sides at the entrance to the Tent of Meeting. He is to **skin** the burnt offering and cut it into pieces. The sons of Aaron the priest are to put fire on the altar and arrange wood on the fire. Then Aaron's sons the priests shall arrange the pieces, including the head and the fat, on the burning wood that is on the altar. He is to **wash** the inner parts and the legs with water, and the priest is to burn all of it on the altar. It is a burnt offering, an offering made by fire, an aroma pleasing to the LORD.'"

The drama of tabernacle worship involved the heart as well as the hands and feet of the worshiper. It must have indelibly impressed the Hebrew imagination. Imagine, for example, a child seeing his father select a costly, unblemished lamb as he prepares to appear before the Lord. Imagine as he hears from the lips of his mother what will take place inside the tent of meeting. He can see the cloud of God's presence overhead and hear the trumpet call for the morning sacrifice. And she tells him:

> Father will take the lamb to the tent of meeting. Before he goes in he will fall down and pray outside. The priest will be standing in the door dressed all in white. Father will present the lamb to him there in the entrance. The priest will motion for him to lay his hands on the lamb's head.[1] Father will hold tight to the lamb and seek the Lord's forgiveness. For the lamb is dying for him, for his sins and for ours, and Father is offering himself to God through the animal.
>
> When the sacrifice is accepted, father will slit the lamb's throat, and the lamb will struggle and scream. He is dying for us! The blood will splatter everywhere, but the priest will catch some and sprinkle it on the sides of the altar. When the blood has all drained out, Father will skin it and chop it into pieces and wash the parts, and then the priest will place the cut-up pieces on the altar.
>
> The fire will sizzle and crackle, and there will be smoke. The smell of burning flesh will mix with the smell of the incense. The fire will consume everything. Nothing will be left. That is how God wants it. He wants us to be totally dedicated to Him. He will be pleased with the smell of burning flesh. It will be soothing to Him.

What poignancy arises from these actions of prostrating, advancing to the altar, placing one's hand on the head of the victim, putting a knife to its throat, and then cutting the animal into parts! We see costly drama performed here—not entertainment, but liturgical drama.

DRAMA: VISIBLE OR MENTAL?

Many Evangelicals don't seem to realize that worship *is drama no matter what format we choose*.[2] What, you may ask, does drama have to do with worship? The essence of drama is action,[3] and there are elements of drama present in any public gathering. The issue is not *whether or not* to have drama in worship, but *what kind* of drama we're going to have. We can either have *visible drama* with external action and movement or *mental drama* in which action takes place internally, in the hearts and minds of the hearers as they listen to the sermon or hear a story told.

In the Leviticus account we have the first type, an enacted, visible drama. The form the drama takes here resembles baseball. Each "player" appear at the plate for his turn, so to speak. In this case, the lamb is presented, slaughtered, skinned, cut into pieces, washed, and burnt as a sweet aroma to the Lord. In our churches today we too have visible dramas: altar calls for prayer or salvation, dedications of babies, baptisms, footwashing ceremonies, the lighting of an Advent candle. In each case someone comes forward, or some kind of dramatic-symbolic movement takes place.

The Drama of the Lord's Supper

The Lord's Supper is another example of a visible drama. In Communion we enact a drama that consists of one extended action: the elements are taken, blessed, broken, distributed, and consumed. Drama of this kind stresses personal involvement and participation, something many churches are presently seeking to inject into their services. In most evangelical churches, however, the people remain passively in their seats during Communion.

A church can heighten the dramatic elements in the Communion service in a number of ways by introducing more congregational movement and participation. One idea is to invite the people to come forward to receive the elements. Another is to choose a family to walk the aisle with the elements and present them to the minister. In small-group meetings, people can stand in a circle and receive the elements from each other.[4]

Some churches may be reluctant to make changes in the way Communion is administered in the Sunday morning service, but they might be willing to try a different format in the evening service first or in a small-group worship setting. You could even try alternating between a traditional format in the morning service one month and a nontraditional one in the evening service the next.

And what about the mood of Communion? Have you observed that the mood is generally somber and introspective, and the emphasis is on our unworthiness? We can learn to balance solemnity with joy as we remember not only Christ's death for us but experience His presence with us and celebrate with thanksgiving His resurrection power. We can bring that joy into the service by singing uplifting hymns in thankful response such as "Marvelous Grace," "Because He Lives," and "One Day." *But remember, the object isn't to make changes just to be different. The point is to infuse fresh meaning into the act. Make sure the meaning is clear, and that the people can see the changes as contributing to that.*

The Chest of Joash Day: A Contemporary Drama

The First Baptist Church of Jacksonville, Florida, has an unusual tradition that further exemplifies the kind of dramatic action we are talking about. Each year on the first Sunday in November the church has been pledging its yearly budget. The service is a family event. Each adult brings the regular weekly tithes and offerings and a pledge card for the coming year's financial gifts and places them into the chest located in front of the auditorium. One of the members says, "There is no sight on earth any more thrilling, nor is there any single service more exciting than this Chest of Joash Day." Pastor Homer Lindsay, Jr., relates how it started:

> The Chest of Joash idea comes from the Old Testament where King Joash had a chest made and placed it in the temple. The people then placed their offering in the chest and the money was used to repair the temple. When I was a young boy, this chest was in my room, and I kept my toys and different things in the chest. Once a year, Dad would come in and empty this chest and carry it to the church where it would be used for this service. When the church was small the chest was large enough. Now the chest is filled many times and has to be emptied several times during the service.[5]

Laying on hands and anointing with oil are also examples of visible drama. In the New Testament the laying on of hands occurred when Ananias restored Paul's sight (Acts 9:17), when Paul and Silas were commissioned as missionaries (Acts 13:3), and when the elders affirmed Timothy's spiritual gift (1 Tim. 4:14). This practice seems appropriate for today, as does the practice of elders anointing the sick with oil (James 5:14).[6]

Some churches have a "ministry time" in the middle or at the end of the service when those with needs can come forward (see ch. 4). A ministry team consisting of mature believers circulates and discovers each individual's kind of need while the congregation continues in song or prayer. A few of the team members may pray for each person, perhaps also laying on hands. If a member requests it, the elders may anoint the sick person with oil. Alternatively, the entire church may divide into small cells and minister to one another in a similar way.

TRANSFORMING PAST EVENTS INTO THE PRESENT

Ben Patterson and Robert Webber suggest a still broader conception of liturgical drama that retains elements of visible action. In this approach, readings from Scripture, prayers, hymns, and the sermon serve "not only to recite past events, but to bring them into the present."[7] It weds the synagogal and tabernacle styles of worship. The emphasis falls on storytelling and symbolic action.[8] Corporate worship becomes a dramatic representation or reenactment. We see that kind of worship throughout the Psalms, where what had been explained and taught by fathers was "seen" (reenacted) in the liturgical experience at Jerusalem.

> As we have heard,
>   so have we seen
> in the city of the LORD Almighty,
>   in the city of our God (Ps. 48:8).

Churches can introduce elements of dramatic reenactment into a worship service through readings and recitations. Such recitations remind us in a fresh way of what we believe, and they involve the whole congregation in the process. The retelling of the story of Christ's death and resurrection, for example, reminds us again of all He did for us. Done as a dramatic reading, it could involve several readers as characters in the story. The congregation can respond as the crowd.

Implicit here also is the idea of giving the reading of Scripture back to the people (see appendix 3). In some churches where Scripture reading receives high priority, a designated person brings the Bible to the pulpit, opens it to the desired passage, and arranges the bookmark properly as a signal for the service to begin. It serves as a nonverbal way of communicating the importance of the Bible. The act of standing for the reading of Scripture is another means of expressing reverence.

Unfortunately, in many services, nobody moves—neither the pastor nor the congregation. There are no processionals. The people just sit. How regrettable! In such services where there is little visible movement and the main event is the sermon, the second type of drama occurs, what Eric Routley calls the "drama of the mind." The pastor serves as the chief actor, using rhetoric and eloquence to involve the audience and trying to obtain from them a "supreme mental effort."[9] In this model the pastor (and possibly a choir) do the major performing. The people do the listening—we hope active listening.

WORSHIP IS RESPONSE

Many contemporary students of worship feel a need for change. They want people to assume more responsibility for carrying out public worship. They would like to shift the dramatic focus around. All too often the congregation sees itself as an audience for the performing pastor and choir. The proponents of change would rather view the pastor and choir as the prompters of worship, the people as the performers, and God as the audience.[10]

To visualize this idea, think of a football stadium. We normally think of ourselves as the audience in the stands. But in worship we should think of ourselves more as the players on the field and God as the audience. For many people this concept presents worship in an entirely new and exciting perspective! Presbyterian minister Ben Patterson goes so far as to say:

> For many evangelicals worship has degenerated into convocations for the teaching of the Bible. If we have forty-five minutes of teaching and no worship, we have a lot of cause and no effect. The teaching

itself is not the worship. It is the response—*that* is the worship. The history of the early Church shows that it included teaching in its worship as a very important part, but it relegated its major efforts in instruction to another time in the week.[11]

Please do not misunderstand. As an Evangelical I too want strong teaching. I think, however, that Patterson makes a good point. Teaching from the pulpit is often little integrated with the worship. The teaching is just that; the service becomes a class. The preacher lectures, and the people take notes, but they are not given opportunity to respond to the Lord. In contrast, in 1 Thessalonians 3—a letter written to be read in church—Paul works a worship response into his presentation. He incorporates a prayer that becomes a release point for worship.

I also agree with Patterson that we need to focus more on the response of the people, for many good reasons. Our present culture can offer more teaching to thirsty Christians than was possible in early church times. Our people can supplement the teaching they receive from local pulpits with excellent cassette tapes, books, and radio programs. What they *can't* get from tapes or television is a corporate experience of worship. They can only get that by being at church and offering their worship publicly in the company of God's people. Corporate worship at the local church level that involves the people in active response fills a unique and irreplaceable function. That makes it even more important in our culture, and we need to protect it.

We should evaluate how we spend our time in the morning services. Time the parts of the service for a month and see what you find out. How much time do you devote to the reading of Scripture, to prayer, to praise, to the sermon? If the pastor regularly preaches for two-thirds of the service (especially if the total length is only seventy or seventy-five minutes), can we honestly call it a "worship service"? Can we say that we are genuinely interested in worship if the *proportions* of our services favor a long sermon and a short time of congregational response? I cannot conclude that we are if we do not provide sufficient time for worship by the people to blossom.

We minimize the importance of congregational response in worship in a number of ways. We do it when we cut worship items if there are too many announcements or the pastor's sermon runs too long. We do it when we make the sermon the "main event" by putting it last and letting it take up the largest part of the service.[12] We do it by not allowing time for the congregation to respond after the sermon.

I am not advocating abandoning sermons. It's just that we need to redress an imbalance in our current worship practices. If worship is response—our response to God—we need to provide more time and opportunity for that to happen in our services.

Congregational response played an important part in Old Testament worship. On one occasion the Israelites devoted three hours to reading Scripture and three to praise:

> On the twenty-fourth day of the same month, the Israelites gathered together, fasting and wearing sackcloth and having dust on their heads. . . . They stood in their places and confessed their sins and the wickedness of their fathers. They stood where they were and read from the Book of the Law of the LORD their God for a quarter of the day, *and spent another quarter in confession and in worshiping the LORD their God.* . . . The Levites . . . said: "Stand up and praise the LORD your God, who is from everlasting to everlasting" (Neh. 9:1–6).

Notice that the corporate worship response followed the teaching of the Word.

DRAMATIC ENACTMENT

An example of congregational dramatic "enactment" on an awesome scale occurred in the recitation of blessings and cursings on Mounts Gerizim and Ebal by the whole nation of Israel just before they entered the Promised Land (Deut. 27–28). The two mountains faced each other and a valley lay between them. Moses ordered half the people to shout from Gerizim the blessings that would be theirs if they obeyed the law and the other half to respond from Ebal with the curses should they disobey the law. With possibly millions of people participating and trumpets sounding to prompt the congregational response, it must have been a memorable event, especially for the children. A touch of symbolism further illuminated this worship event: the landscape of Ebal was desolate, but Gerizim was a lush green.[13] When our people meet for an Easter sunrise service at daybreak at a high, outdoor location, they experience some of the quality of this event.

Solomon also perceived that worship is drama. For the temple dedication ceremony, he had a raised platform especially built for the occasion to his dedicatory prayer, which was the centerpiece of the event. It reaffirmed the Mosaic covenant between God and His people. The Scriptures indicate Solomon was positioned on a raised platform, so all the people could all see him, and had his back to the people and his hands raised to God.

> Then Solomon stood before the altar of the LORD in front of the whole assembly of Israel and spread out his hands. Now he had made a bronze platform, five cubits long, five cubits wide and three cubits high, and had placed it in the center of the outer court. He stood on

the platform and then knelt down before the whole assembly of Israel and spread out his hands toward heaven. He said: "O LORD God of Israel, there is no God like you in heaven or on earth—you who keep your covenant of love with your servants who continue wholeheartedly in your way" (2 Chron. 6:12–14).

Some may be inclined to respond, "Wasn't Solomon creating a 'show' for himself?" No. Solomon, in his wisdom, did what was proper and fitting for the occasion. This occasion was a pivotal event. The covenantal promise was to David and his seed, and it was important for the people see Solomon, as David's successor, personally assent to the terms of the covenant (that is why "he knelt" and "spread out his hands toward heaven") and take the reins in leading the people to do the same.

LARGE GROUPS VERSUS SMALL GROUPS

Solomon performed the action before a large group. Large-group worship requires more "vision," more drama, more symbolism. Drama relates to size. In a small Bible study or church group, visible drama may not be essential; in large assemblies, the elements of drama and symbolism become more important. For example, if a person stands to speak before ten people, that action is hardly dramatic. If, however, a person stands to speak before ten thousand people, the very act of standing with the intent of speaking is dramatic. The same dynamics apply to the time Elijah brought down fire on the altar at Mount Carmel. If a handful of people had watched the event, that would have been one thing. But the fact that a great crowd looked on as one solitary man, Elijah, opposed 850 prophets of Baal and Asherah—that was dramatic! It had dramatic scale.

Large-group worship became a central component early in Israel's experience and remained so for more than a thousand years. Worship was the stated purpose that originally initiated the Exodus: "Let my people go," said Moses to Pharaoh, "so that they may hold a festival to me in the desert" (Exod. 5:1).

Large groups offer many possibilities for drama. I participated in a dramatic vignette on Pentecost Sunday in a small church. We had "Peter," dressed in flowing garments, come down the aisle and quote from memory his great address (Acts 2:14) that God used to bring many to a saving knowledge of Jesus Christ.

Small groups are inherently different from large groups. Small groups in general accent intimacy; large groups, power. To a certain extent, when any small church group grows and becomes large, a change takes place. There is an inevitable loss of intimacy, but a gain in the ability to project power, greatness, and transcendence in worship. This should not be taken to suggest that either large- or small-group worship is better. Both "cathedral" and "chapel" experiences are needed. The chapel lets us bask in the warmth of God's gracious intimacy; the cathedral causes us to stand in awe of His majesty. Our God is both personal and infinite.

QUESTIONS FOR THOUGHT AND DISCUSSION

1. What can we do to encourage parents who have children who don't want to come to church because it's boring?
2. "The pastor and the choir are prompters, the people are performers, and God is the audience." Discuss.
3. Scripture readings, prayers, hymns, and the sermon can serve "not only to recite past events, but to bring them into the present." Comment. How can this be done?
4. What is meant by the statement "worship is drama no matter what format we choose"?
5. Can you think of some examples of visible, enacted drama that might be appropriate for your church setting?
6. "For many evangelicals worship has degenerated into convocations for the teaching of the Bible. . . . we have forty-five minutes of teaching and no worship." What do you think of the idea of having the major teaching some other time besides Sunday?
7. "People cannot obtain a corporate worship experience by listening to tapes or watching television." Does this statement clarify a need that can be met in your church? Explain. Are you meeting it? How?
8. Should worship be one of the "preliminaries" on Sunday morning? Is worship a preliminary at your church? By what criteria do you evaluate whether it is?
9. Is small group worship different from large group worship? How?
10. How can we get more drama into our services?

RECOMMENDED READING

Routley, Eric. *Words, Music, and the Church.* Nashville: Abingdon Press, 1966.

CHAPTER TEN

Symbolism

THE MOABITE AND THE GATEKEEPER

A Moabite gazes down on the tents and tabernacle of Israel from a lofty height. Attracted by what he sees, he descends to the plain and makes his way toward the sacred enclosure surrounding the tabernacle—a high wall of dazzling linen reaching over his head. He walks around it until he comes to the gate, where he see a man.

"May I go in there?" he asks, pointing through the gate to the bustle of activity in the tabernacle's outer court.

"Who are you?" demands the man suspiciously. Any Israelite would know he could go in there.

"I am a man from Moab," the stranger replies.

"Well," says the man at the gate, "I'm very sorry, but you cannot go in there. It's not for you. The law of Moses has barred the Moabites from any part in the worship of Israel until his tenth generation."

The Moabite looks sad. "What would I have to do to go in there?" he pleads.

"You would have to be born again," replies the gatekeeper. "You would have to be born an Israelite. You would need to be born of the tribe of Judah, perhaps, or of the tribe of Benjamin or Dan."

Says the Moabite, "I wish I had been born an Israelite of one of the tribes of Israel." As he looks more closely, he sees one of the priests, having offered a sacrifice at the brazen altar and cleansed himself at the brazen laver, go into the tabernacle's interior.

"What's in there?" asks the Moabite. "Inside the main building, I mean."

"Oh," says the gatekeeper, "that's the tabernacle proper. Inside there is a room containing a lampstand, a table, and an altar of gold. The man you saw is a priest. He will trim the lamp, eat of the bread on the table, and burn incense to the living God on the golden altar."

"Ah," sighs the man of Moab. "I wish I were an Israelite so that I could do that. I should love to worship God in that holy place and help to trim the lamp, to offer Him some incense, and to eat at that table."

"Oh, no," says the man at the gate, "even I could not do that. To worship in the holy place one must not only be born an Israelite, but be born of the tribe of Levi and of the family of Aaron."

The man from Moab sighs again. "I wish," he says, "I wish I had been born of Israel of the tribe of Levi of the family of Aaron." Gazing wistfully at the closed tabernacle door, he says, "What else is in there?"

"There's a veil," replies his informant. "It's beautiful, I'm told. It divides the tabernacle in two. Beyond the veil is what we call 'the most holy place,' the Holy of Holies."

The Moabite shows more interest than ever. "What's in the Holy of Holies?" he asks.

"A sacred chest called the Ark of the Covenant," answers the gatekeeper. "It contains certain holy memorials of our past. Its top is made of gold, and we call that the Mercy Seat because God sits there between the golden cherubim. You see that pillar of cloud hovering over the tabernacle? That's the *shekina* glory cloud. It comes to rest over the mercy seat."

Again a look of longing shadows the face of the man from Moab. "Oh," he says, "if only I were a priest! I would love to go into the Holy of Holies and there gaze upon God and worship Him there in the beauty of holiness."

"Oh, no!" says the man at the gate. "You couldn't do that even if you were a priest! To enter into the most holy place you would have to be the high priest of Israel. Only he can go in there, nobody else, only he."

The Moabite's heart yearns once more. "Oh," he cries, "if only I had been born an Israelite, of the tribe of Levi of the family of Aaron. If only I had been born the high priest. I would go in there, into the Holy of Holies. I would go in there every day. I would go in three times a day. I would worship continually in the Holy of Holies."

The gatekeeper looks at him again and once more shakes his head. "Oh, no!" he says, "You couldn't do that. Even the high priests of Israel can go in there only once a year, and then only after the most elaborate preparations, and even then only for a very little while."

Sadly the Moabite turns away. He has no hope in all the world of ever entering there.[1]

JOURNEY INTO THE HOLY OF HOLIES

To the Moabite the tabernacle was extraordinarily enchanting. It invoked in him the mysterious. The tabernacle remains important for us too. Although the sacrificial system is abolished in the New Testament, we learn in the Book of Revelation that the tabernacle furniture has enduring significance in the worship in heaven and its symbolic meanings provide us with insights into many aspects of our own worship.

The complex design of the tabernacle and the sheer number of furniture articles should serve to remind us that Judeo-Christian worship is not simplistic. In the exposition of the tabernacle furniture that follows, I have freely borrowed from Graham Kendrick's *Learning to Worship as a Way of Life,* in which the furniture is viewed from a New Testament perspective.[2] Other explanations may be equally valid. I offer these to prompt your thinking.

When Christ died, the *curtain* veiling the Holy of Holies in the temple was supernaturally torn in two from top to bottom. This act made possible a radically new access to God. To the Jew the curtain had been a barrier and symbolized a disqualification from God's presence in the Holy of Holies. As Kendrick has put it, in the New Testament the *curtain* "no longer became a symbol of exclusion but of entrance, as the tearing of Christ's body on the cross and the shedding of his blood became a way into the very presence of a Holy God."[3] Now, by faith believers are invited to journey into that holy place to meet with God.

From the New Testament perspective, the offerings that worshipers bring to the tent for sacrifice are themselves as "living sacrifices" (Rom. 12:1). And we come not empty handed, but "offer to God a sacrifice of praise—the fruit of lips that confess his name" (Heb. 13:15). At the *altar* inside the door of the tent, the offering is wholly consumed and goes up in smoke to heaven, illustrating the need for total consecration. The *laver,* the washing basin for the priests, speaks of our need for cleansing before a holy God. Psalm 24:3 reads: "Who may ascend the hill of the LORD? Who may stand in his holy place? He who has clean hands and a pure heart."

Advancing into the holy place, we see the *table of shewbread,* which foreshadows the Lord's Supper and reminds us that we come as members of one body. In the enclosed space, the seven-branched *golden candlestick* burns continually, replenished by a continuous supply of oil (Zech. 4). It typifies the Holy Spirit, who enlightens the Word of God and enables us to perceive spiritual things (1 Cor. 2:14). In front of the veil, "now torn and open wide," stands *the altar of incense,* symbol of prayer, the gateway into the Holy of Holies. It symbolizes the risen Christ offering prayers on

The Tabernacle

Most Holy Place with the ark of the covenant 10 cubits square (*15 ft. square*)

Curtain

Holy Place, with the golden table for the bread of the Presence, golden lampstand, and altar of incense.
length: 20 cubits (*30 ft.*)
width: 10 cubits (*15 ft.*)

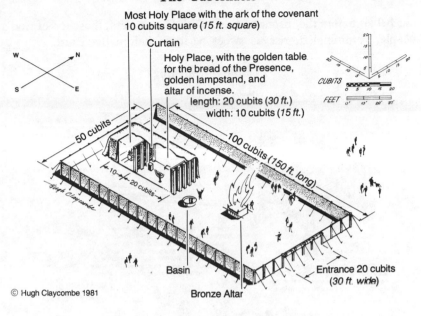

50 cubits

100 cubits (150 ft. long)

10 — 20 cubits

Hugh Claycombe

CUBITS 0 5 10 15 20

FEET 10' 10' 100' 200'

Basin

Bronze Altar

Entrance 20 cubits (*30 ft. wide*)

© Hugh Claycombe 1981

Solomon's Temple

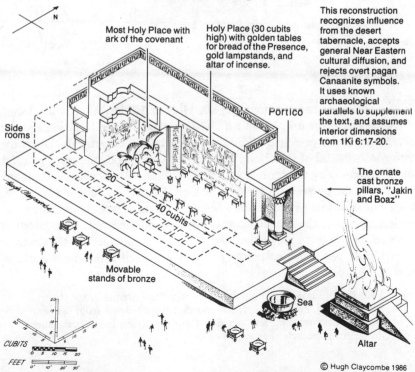

Most Holy Place with ark of the covenant

Holy Place (30 cubits high) with golden tables for bread of the Presence, gold lampstands, and altar of incense.

Portico

This reconstruction recognizes influence from the desert tabernacle, accepts general Near Eastern cultural diffusion, and rejects overt pagan Canaanite symbols. It uses known archaeological parallels to supplement the text, and assumes interior dimensions from 1Ki 6:17-20.

Side rooms

The ornate cast bronze pillars, "Jakin and Boaz"

Hugh Claycombe

20

40 cubits

Movable stands of bronze

Sea

CUBITS 0 5 10 15 20

FEET 0' 10' 20' 30'

Altar

© Hugh Claycombe 1986

our behalf before the throne of God. With His prayers, those too of God's people, commingled, rise as sweet perfume before the Lord.

Temple Furnishings

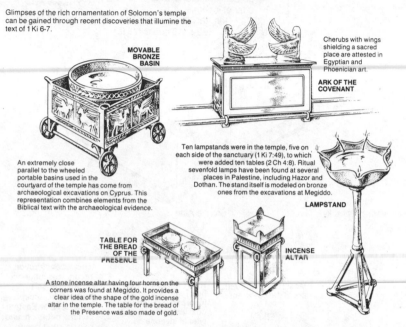

Glimpses of the rich ornamentation of Solomon's temple can be gained through recent discoveries that illumine the text of 1 Ki 6-7.

MOVABLE BRONZE BASIN

Cherubs with wings shielding a sacred place are attested in Egyptian and Phoenician art.

ARK OF THE COVENANT

An extremely close parallel to the wheeled portable basins used in the courtyard of the temple has come from archaeological excavations on Cyprus. This representation combines elements from the Biblical text with the archaeological evidence.

Ten lampstands were in the temple, five on each side of the sanctuary (1 Ki 7:49), to which were added ten tables (2 Ch 4:8). Ritual sevenfold lamps have been found at several places in Palestine, including Hazor and Dothan. The stand itself is modeled on bronze ones from the excavations at Megiddo.

LAMPSTAND

TABLE FOR THE BREAD OF THE PRESENCE

INCENSE ALTAR

A stone incense altar having four horns on the corners was found at Megiddo. It provides a clear idea of the shape of the gold incense altar in the temple. The table for the bread of the Presence was also made of gold.

In stillness and awe we enter the Holy of Holies, where the adoring *cherubim* guard the *ark,* a wooden chest overlaid with gold inside and out representing the presence of God dwelling in the desert tent. Upon the *mercy seat,* the lid of the chest, we see sprinkled blood, the price paid for our forgiveness by the completed work of Christ. We now cease from any effort to make ourselves acceptable to God. Christ has done it all, and we are clothed in His righteousness. Inside the ark we see three things: the tablets of stone, the pot of manna, and the budded rod. The *tablets of stone* tell of the demands of the Law, now totally satisfied by the death of Christ. The *pot of manna* points to Christ, the self-proclaimed bread of life:

> I am the bread of life. Your forefathers ate the manna in the desert, yet they died. But here is the bread that comes down from heaven, which a man may eat and not die. I am the living bread that came down from heaven (John 6:48-51).

When Aaron's *budded rod* comes into view, we understand that as this dead stick flowered and bore fruit, so also Christ arose and lives forever and has obtained "a permanent priesthood" (Heb. 7:24). Because we are "in Christ" and partake in the power of His resurrection, we too have become a "royal priesthood" and shall one day become a kingdom of "priests" (Rev. 5:10).

SYMBOLS AS COMMUNICATION VEHICLES

Curiously the Old Testament does not give a verbal explanation of the meaning of the tabernacle furniture even when it has such an enormous symbolical function. The Scriptures focus on how the liturgical action should be performed, not the meaning of the action. One result of this lack of verbal closure may be to intensify contemplation and to provoke faith on the intuitive level.

Symbols tend to communicate truth on the intuitive level. Perhaps this is one reason why many of us today find the verbal medium safer and the nonverbal medium more threatening. We can analyze and control words in a way that we can't control symbols. They're harder to pin down, and we're not sure where they will lead us. But God, who is bigger than the boxes we may want to put Him in, has chosen throughout history to communicate through symbols.

Symbolism functions best within a context, and the tabernacle provides such a context. Because all the symbols there are contained within a circumscribed space, they tend to be related one to the other. Similarly, where the written Word is powerfully proclaimed in our churches, symbols can function with added precision. The clarity of the Lord's Supper, for example, is strengthened by Paul's verbal explanation of its meaning in 1 Corinthians 11.

Symbols are good for arousing the curiosity of children and can lead to "teachable moments." It is interesting that Moses specifically commanded the Israelites to verbally explain the meaning of the Passover ceremony to their children: "When your children ask you, 'What does this mean?' then tell them, 'It is the Passover sacrifice to the LORD, who passed over the houses of the Israelites in Egypt and spared our homes when he struck down the Egyptians' " (Exod. 12:26–27). In all likelihood parents were asked similar questions concerning the unusual furnishings of the tabernacle.

Since the Old Testament does not specifically fix the symbolic meaning of the tabernacle furniture, it eases the way for us to spiritualize it through New Testament eyes. For example, in the tabernacle the blood of animals was sprinkled by the priest on the mercy seat on the day of atonement, but now the blood of Christ (not the blood of animals) covers our sins:

> When Christ came as high priest . . . he went through the greater and more perfect tabernacle that is not man-made, that is to say, not a part of this creation. He did not enter by means of the blood of goats and calves; but he entered the Most Holy Place once for all by his own blood, having obtained eternal redemption (Heb. 9:11–12).

Metaphorically the depicted cherubim, if they existed now, would look down and see the provision for atonement, the blood of Christ.[4]

IS TABERNACLE SYMBOLISM RIGHT-BRAINED?

A growing body of information is becoming available about the hemispheric organization of the human brain. Apparently, the right hemisphere is especially involved in "the perception and expression of emotionality" and the left hemisphere in the "perception and expression of speech."[5] Of course, we must not press this distinction too hard. One side of the brain may perform a dominant function, but both sides are involved.

When a person reads a story the specialized abilities of each side of the brain contribute to the total understanding. The *right* hemisphere plays "a special role in decoding visual information, maintaining an integrated story structure, appreciating humor and emotional content, deriving meaning from past associations and understanding metaphor." The *left* hemisphere plays "a special role in understanding syntax, translating written words into their phonetic representation and deriving meaning from complex relations among word concepts and syntax."[6]

Impairment of the right hemisphere can result in a diminished capacity to identify the emotional expressions on people's faces or to transmit emotions in one's voice. A thirty-four-year-old schoolteacher, after suffering right hemisphere damage, could no longer communicate "firmness or anger" in her voice. It remained "flat and expressionless" so that none of her students paid attention to her, and as a result she could no longer control her classroom.[7]

There is also evidence that people "vary in the relative balance of activation of the two hemispheres." While people are not purely "left-brained" or "right-brained," there is evidence of a continuum in which some people may be more oriented to one hemisphere.[8] Some people may be more emotionally/spacially oriented in their mode of perception. Others may be more verbal/analytic in their mode of perception.

This has important ramifications for worship leaders. Tabernacle worship, in emphasizing a visual, spacial, symbolic orientation to worship, tends to engage the right brain in worship, while most evangelical worship accents the verbal/analytic left side. Therefore, when individuals convey a suspicious attitude toward a worship style that has a strong spacial, visual, or symbolic orientation, their criticism may fly in the face of those who rely on and are especially keyed to a right hemispheric mode of learning and expression.

Interestingly, Evangelicals in the past have tended to value verbal, propositional communication and to depreciate symbolic communication. By contrast, Japanese culture appears to value symbolic communication. For example, in Japan the act of baptism (not verbal confession) is the sign of a serious commitment to Christianity. Just as preferred orientations exist between individuals, so there may be a preferred *valuing* of one brain hemisphere within congregations—even within cultures.[9]

In *Pastoral Psychology* David A. Miller reports an apparent link between physiology and religious experience that has important implications for worship. Four patients whom he encountered at a rehabilitation center, and who suffered a loss of emotionality as a result of right hemisphere lesions, were struggling with the reality of their faith. He says, "These individuals were continuing to act in accordance with well-ingrained patterns of belief, but without the same *quality* as before their injuries." One of these people said, "My faith has left me." Another said, "I can't pray any more, but I can say the words."

What an evocative statement! In God's sight that person's worship was just as genuine as it had been before, but it didn't *feel* authentic. Something akin to this may be going on in churches where the feeling element in worship is muted or suppressed. Miller relates, "Those closest to the patients reported that they showed a diminished interest and zest in religious activities." Miller concludes that "gross damage to the right hemisphere appeared to disrupt the emotional component of their faith and belief systems."[10]

What this means in regard to worship is that it may not be enough to provide people with an intellectual faith and an intellectual worship that centers on verbal expression. Our worship must be holistic, involving both the intellect and the emotions. Feelings and emotions are as important to worship as thinking and speaking. The spacial and symbolical may be as crucial as the verbal and analytic.

Moreover, the *quality* of our worship and our *motivation to worship* may depend on the richness and variety of expression found in our churches. Until we engage both the emotions and the intellect, commitment may be incomplete. In achieving this full-bodied worship, the arts may well be a vital means of providing a more holistic, life-changing, worship experience.

COMPREHENSIVE CONFESSION OF JESUS AS LORD

Does Scripture encourage holistic worship involving both sides of the brain? I leave you to ponder that question as you work through the chapters of this book. But consider this: When the Scriptures insist that all people will someday make a public acknowledgment of the one true God, biblical language indicates that the form this confession takes will be unmistakable and comprehensive and will involve the total person in both verbal and symbolic communication. The Scriptures say every knee shall bow and every tongue shall make confession:

> "By myself I have sworn,
>   my mouth has uttered in all integrity
>   a word that will not be revoked:
> Before me every knee will bow;
>   by me every tongue will swear.
> They will say of me, 'In the LORD alone
>   are righteousness and strength.'"
>   (Isa. 45:23–24)

It is written:

> " 'As surely as I live,' says the Lord,
> 'every knee will bow before me;
> every tongue will confess to God.' "
>   (Rom. 14:11)

> . . . that at the name of Jesus every knee should bow,
>   in heaven and on earth and under the earth,
> and every tongue confess that Jesus Christ is Lord,
>   to the glory of God the Father.
>   (Phil. 2:10–11)

Bowing is spacial, symbolic communication. It conveys a sense of reverence and submission through bodily movement.

THE LAMP WITH THE EVERLASTING FLAME

The menorah (the golden candlestick) formed a part of the symbolic tabernacle furniture. Candles are still a part of synagogue and Jewish home worship today. For example, Jews celebrate Hanukkah, the Feast of Lights, and families light candles in their homes.

Light is also an important symbol in the New Testament. Jesus declared that He is the "light of the world." Candles can be an effective means to communicate such a message. Candlelight with its flickering flame and deep shadows conveys—in a way that electric lights can't—a sense of life and of mystery. It also carries with it an element of dramatic uncertainty. The flame could go out or be snuffed or stamped out.

Candles can signify that a life has died. Some candles relight themselves and can signify resurrection.

I would like to suggest some ways that candles can enrich the experience of worship in a variety of contexts. They're good for Thanksgiving, Christmas, New Year, or Easter services, and they also have a place in services with a special missions or evangelism emphasis.

Consider having a candlelighting service as part of a worship-missions or worship-evangelism emphasis. During the lighting ceremony have the pastor or people from the congregation read verses that picture God and Christ as light and that emphasize that we are to be light. These verses can be read in a particular order to develop a point, or randomly, letting the images build on each other.

Have a *Jesus Candle* burning at the front of the church, or if you are meeting in the round (perhaps in the church gym or some all-purpose room), in the center. Then at the end of the service light candles for the whole congregation to symbolize the spread of the gospel.

You can light the congregation's candles in a number of ways.

1. Ushers can light theirs from the Jesus Candle and then go down the aisles lighting for the person on the end of each row, who in turn can pass the light until everyone has a lighted candle.
2. People can come forward row by row, light their candles, and return to their seats.
3. People can come forward and light their candles "when they feel ready" throughout the service. This is my favorite procedure. It allows people freedom. If this option is chosen, people should be instructed not to come all at once, but several at a time at most. Allow for an extended time of quiet reflection (silence interspersed with readings) as the worship environment gradually fills up with light.
4. If the space is circular or semi-circular, let the light spread out to four corners of the space like the winding roots of a tree, as selected persons (each with a candle) pass the light to its final destination. When the destination is reached, there could come from that location in the audience a planned testimony, an unaccompanied solo, and a choir response, each representing a different country.
5. Candles can be lit in the church vestibule as the people gather outside before processioning into the church while singing a hymn or carol. When the Jesus Candle at the front is lit in the church, the people can extinguish their candles.
6. At the conclusion of the service the people can come to the front and light their candles from the Jesus Candle and recess.
7. Ideas 5 and 6 can be combined with a processional and recessional.

ARE CANDLES VALID IN WORSHIP?

As we have noted, oil lamps were used in the Holy Place in tabernacle worship. Their use recurs in Revelation worship. This is an important point. For today, we can take their use as *suggestive* rather than *required* and by this means highlight worship on special occasions rather than regular worship. This is the way candles are generally used in our culture.

The New Testament allows Christians enormous freedom for innovation in worship as long as the underlying principles are strictly adhered to. In Peter's vision, the voice of God spoke to him three times in order to shake him loose from cultural chains that would have impeded the propagation of a supranational gospel.

Do not call anything impure that God has made clean (Acts 10:14).

This verse has fundamentally to do with culture, and it releases Christians from the restrictive dietary laws of the Old Testament. But the basic principle seems to have broader implications. Paul's writings also contain a strong call to freedom within guidelines:

"Everything is permissible"—but not everything is beneficial. . . .
"The earth is the Lord's and everything in it" (1 Cor. 10:23–25)

"Everything is permissible for me"—but I will not be mastered by anything (1 Cor. 6:12).

In keeping with the tenor of these passages, the texts suggest to me that symbols such as candles are also "clean." Evangelicals are sometimes reluctant to use symbolic communication like candles. We fear and distrust anything that looks and smells too "Catholic" or "high church." But symbolic communication deserves a second look. Just because Catholics use candles is not in itself a good reason for Evangelicals not to. Instead of rejecting candles outright—and this goes for other symbols too—we would be better off evaluating each symbol's appropriateness for worship. Will it help communicate something important? Will it stimulate the spirit? Then use it.

We already use symbols at the Lord's Table. Paul says, "Whenever you eat this bread and drink this cup, you *proclaim* the Lord's death until he comes" (1 Cor. 11:26). As symbols the elements of Communion engage us deeply. At the Lord's Table we do more than *think* about Christ's death. We *eat and drink* symbols of His body and blood, and that involves our whole being.

Ironically we have no trouble using candles at wedding ceremonies. When a couple take the two side candles and together light the single one in the center, we consider it an elegant symbol of two people becoming one. With weddings we seem to understand that few events of beauty and power just happen and that symbolic acts can have great meaning and power. How curious that we lavish more care on our wedding ceremonies than our worship services!

Fortunately this negative attitude toward symbolic communication and worship planning seems to be changing. In the past Protestants have used their own distinctive brand of symbolism—the open Bible on the Communion table, the thanksgiving horn of plenty. More recently symbols like the fish, dove, and menorah have also gained wide acceptance in churches.

OTHER CANDLELIGHTING VARIATIONS

Have a candlelighting *testimony time* as part of a Thanksgiving service. Place six-to-twelve candles in the configuration of a cross, and invite people to come forward, light a candle, and give a testimony.

Have an *Advent wreath* and a candlelighting ceremony for four Sundays prior to Christmas. One candle could be lit on the Sunday four weeks before Christmas, two candles three weeks before Christmas, and so on. On Christmas Eve light the fifth candle (the white Jesus Candle in the middle). A family can be appointed to light a candle on each Sunday, with the father reading a short explanation of the ceremony while a child does the lighting. It could also be done by fathers and sons, mothers and daughters, or young couples, elderly couples, or single adults. This can be an effective means of anticipating the Incarnation (small children will be asking "How many weeks to Christmas now, Mom?" anyway), of countering the commercialization of Christmas, and of maintaining a Christian focus with elegance.

At the Sunday school Christmas program, have a *Jesus birthday cake* with one candle. Line up the children, youngest to oldest. The youngest child to blow out the candle gets the cake. The action of little tikes blowing on the candles will draw a lot of oohs and aahs from the congregation. It will be great family fun for old and young alike because so much drama is inherent in the event. And in the course of events like these you will have opportunity to bring home the true meaning of Christmas!

CONCLUSION

I have tried in this chapter to select ideas for using candles that will be particularly memorable for small churches. Large churches can use them too, of course, but candlelighting ceremonies can be an effective alternative for churches that lack the resources to mount choir cantatas at Christmas and Easter.

Small churches should not try to duplicate what large churches do more effectively. Instead they should learn to take advantage of their uniqueness and provide intimate experiences. The Robert Schuller "Crystal Cathedral Christmas Pageant" (1986) involved fifty-two performances and required a production budget in excess of $1 million. Yet a tastefully done candlelighting service may be just as meaningful in its own way in an intimate, small church setting. Too many small churches compare themselves unfairly and unfavorably with large churches. Let's do everything possible to improve the self-esteem of small churches!

I hope I have been successful in whetting your appetite.[11] Evangelicals can enjoy learning to respond in worship with hands, feet, nose, and mouth. It can do us good to break—if only occasionally—from a service format that is too exclusively verbal, mind-oriented, and passive.

QUESTIONS FOR THOUGHT AND DISCUSSION

1. What is symbolism? How do we use symbolism in our services at present?
2. Why is symbolism important?
3. "Symbols tend to communicate on the intuitive level." Explain.
4. Does your church's style of worship favor one side of the brain?
5. "I can't pray any more, but I can say the words." Discuss the implications.
6. "The quality of our worship and our motivation to worship may depend on the richness and variety of expression found in our churches." Discuss.
7. Does symbolism function best within a context? Explain.
8. The nonverbal level is "more threatening. We are afraid to trust it." Discuss.
9. Why are candles a more effective worship symbol than electric lights?
10. "Evangelicals are reluctant to use symbolic communication like candles. We fear and distrust anything that looks and smells too 'Catholic' or 'high church.'" How might this be true or not true of your church?
11. Do we lavish more effort on our wedding ceremonies than our worship services? Explain.

RECOMMENDED READING

Griggs, Patricia, and Donald Griggs. *Teaching and Celebrating Advent.* Rev. ed. Nashville: Abingdon Press, 1980.

————. *Teaching and Celebrating Lent–Easter.* Rev. ed. Nashville: Abingdon Press, 1980.

Marshall, Michael. *Renewal in Worship.* London: Marshall Paperbacks, 1982. Especially chapter 6, "Signs, Symbols, and Ceremonies."

CHAPTER ELEVEN

Fine Arts

"This professor of yours—does he talk about God?"

ARTWORK AND THE SECOND COMMANDMENT

The Ten Commandments have exerted an enormous influence on the artwork of Hebrew, Islamic, and Christian people. The second commandment reads:

> "You shall not make for yourself an *idol in the form of anything* in heaven above or on the earth beneath or in the waters below. You shall not bow down to them or worship them; for I, the LORD your God, am a jealous God, punishing the children for the sin of the fathers to the third and fourth generation of those who hate me, but showing love to a thousand generations of those who love me and keep my commandments" (Exod. 20:4-6).

Some translations substitute the words *graven image* for *idol*.

In interpreting these verses, some Christians have placed the emphasis on the images as *pictures or representations* and have prohibited all pictures or representations of God. Others have placed the emphasis on the images as *objects of worship* and have prohibited only those images that would be used for worship, like idols and icons. In this view the issue has more to do with false worship than "the attempt to reflect God in images."[1]

Different religious traditions have interpreted these verses differently too. Islam—which also accepts the Ten Commandments—has always rejected *all* representational art. As a result of this narrow interpretation, Islamic artistic energy has been channeled into abstract, decorative art. The ancient Hebrews reacted similarly by focusing on nonrepresentational art. For example, Pontius Pilate's introduction of Roman coins that depicted a bust of Caesar occasioned an uproar in Jerusalem; a representational human face on a coin was considered scandalous. However, the Roman Catholic and the Eastern Orthodox churches have interpreted the commandment less narrowly and have therefore permitted representational art, including images, frescoes, and large sculptures.

The Protestant Reformers reacted (and rightly so) to abuses within the Roman Catholic Church. Like the Hebrews and Muslims, they held to a more narrow interpretation. They reacted against the practice of honoring, adoring, and praying to images and the use of images to promote false doctrine and the sale of indulgences. Yet even the responses of the Reformers varied. Luther removed the images of Mary and canonized saints, but retained crucifixes because he felt they did not obstruct faith. Zwingli and Calvin forbade all paintings and sculptures in the church, but permitted representational paintings of Christ to be in Christian homes as long as they were not used as objects of veneration.

By driving art out of the church, these Reformers played a key role in secularizing art. Now, after four hundred years, the situation has remained relatively unchanged. Art has remained secularized. Francis Schaeffer believed that the Reformers overreacted.

So the question remains, How is the second commandment to be interpreted? To find an adequate answer we must consider the second commandment in the context of tabernacle worship, which prevailed at the time the Ten Commandments were delivered. Was representational art permitted? Interestingly, Francis Schaeffer has observed that "almost every form of representational art that men have ever known" was involved in making the tabernacle furnishings.[2] For example, representations of the angelic cherubim were woven into ten curtains and the veil of the Holy of Holies (Exod. 26:1, 31), and statues of cherubim were sculpted (Exod. 25:18). Shapes of almond flowers with buds and blossoms were hammered into the cups of the lampstand (Exod. 25:33). Blue pomegranates were woven around the hems of priestly garments.[3] The guiding principle in the tabernacle was that the closer to the ark the furnishings were positioned, the more ornate in figuration and costly in material they were.[4]

In Solomon's temple, pomegranates and lilies were fashioned on two freestanding pillars in the outer court (1 Kings 7:18–19). Figures of bulls were formed on the washing basin reserved for the priests. Lions, bulls, and palms trees were engraved on ten movable bronze stands (1 Kings 7:36). In the the Holy of Holies, the gold cherubim statues were imposing in size, each wing extending seven feet (2 Chron. 3:13). In short, the skills of weaving, embroidering, engraving, sculpting, working with precious stone, and woodcarving were all represented.

GOD, THE ORIGINAL ABSTRACT ARTIST

Even if the second commandment is taken in its narrowest sense of prohibiting representational art, however, it still leaves room for abstract art, including the symbolic and the fictional. This is an important point. By "abstract" we mean art consisting of pure design, as in the complex tapestry of a Persian rug, the highly ordered and intricate margins of a medieval manuscript, or the "floral patterns, geometric designs, and symbols like the menorah" found on native Jewish coins.[5] In many evangelical circles today, abstract art in general is suspect and abstract artists are considered spiritually "lost."

> *I heard the story of a custodian at a Christian college who was cleaning the office of an art instructor. The professor had several of his abstract paintings on the wall and others in progress scattered in different parts of his office. As the custodian cast his eyes at the paintings, he was overheard asking a student incredulously, "This professor of yours—does he talk about God?"*

We fail to realize that God is the original abstract artist, the maker of the structure of the DNA molecule, snowflakes, the Spiral Nebula—indeed, the maker of a creation that in both its macro- and micro-structures reveals dazzling intricacy, infinite variation, and sublime abstractionism on every level.[6] In the presence of this abstractness, Gene Veith insightfully says, "Representational art should be the style that makes those who believe in the Scriptures the most uneasy."[7]

Veith contends that the nonrepresentational art of Islam has in many ways extended the heritage of radical monotheism. Of the mosaics in their mosques and the illuminated manuscripts and tapestries, he writes:

> Islamic art presents a riot of colors and interlocking forms. The tiniest details, considered separately, seem anarchic in their bold colors and dynamic shapes, yet viewed from a distance those details are seen as contributing to a larger design that is harmonious, symmetrical and beautiful. There can be no better evocation of human life, with its freedom, variety, and occasional appearance of random meaninglessness, all subsumed under the providence of God, who orchestrates all the seemingly contingent, accidental events of a person's life according to his saving design.[8]

For Veith, the multiple and abundant designs of a Persian carpet reflect the aesthetic rejoicings of the psalmist: "O LORD, how manifold are thy works!" (Ps. 104:24 KJV).

SUGGESTIONS FOR WORSHIP-ENHANCING ARTWORK

What a shame that many of our evangelical churches overwork those with musical gifts when planning worship services and totally ignore those in the congregation who are equally gifted in the nonmusical arts. Gene and Mary Lou Totten, directors of FACE (Fellowship of Artists for Cultural Evangelism), offer the following worship-enhancing ideas that have met with great success in their local church.

Banners

Banners, according to the Tottens, are a good place to begin. They make excellent vehicles for praise. Take advantage of color, shape, and texture. Avoid stretchy material; felt or burlap is better. Make them abstract, and use a minimum of text. Spring is an excellent time of the year to start. Bring the feeling of spring into the sanctuary with flowers in pastels. Express springlike feelings of renewal and rebirth. Work with the pastor to coordinate a series of messages so the banner will be on target for several Sundays.

Communion Cloth

A Communion cloth can be embroidered by a women's group.

Easter

A cross draped in black can be effective. So can plants and environmental pieces. Large, found objects—a gnarled tree or thorny plants artfully placed—can arouse interest and cause people to wonder, "What does this have to do with the sermon?"

Real-Time Overhead Drawing

During the singing of a solo or duet that speaks of nature, draw a picture on the overhead projector with color. Frame the overhead area so it is smaller and more focused. Practice drawing at home so you can perform it within the time constraints—three-to-five minutes. Try to capture a holistic feeling of the music piece. Sign the drawing with the name of Jesus. If you can't get live performers, use a cassette.

IDEAS FOR WORSHIP AND SERMON-ENHANCING DRAMA

Picture-Frame Idea 1

Build a six-by-five-foot oversized picture frame and raise it from the floor. Have someone dressed as the apostle Paul sitting in a frozen posture at a desk at the front as the people enter for worship. For the Bible reading of the day, tape "Paul's" voice on a cassette with a quill sound scratching away. (We have used this idea in my own church. See appendix 3.)

If an oversized picture frame near the pulpit area of the church would be too traumatic a change, place it successively in the foyer area, then in the middle of the congregation, and finally up front in the pulpit or choir area. This will allow the people to adjust to it gradually.

Picture-Frame Idea 2

Drama can be an effective means of provoking interest. Rather than give answers, raise questions. Perhaps consider confronting (voicing) the negative side of an issue. Make a recording of a dramatic dialogue on a cassette tape and pantomime the tape. The incident in the Scriptures where Peter denied Christ three times offers a possibility; the characters could come down the aisle and enter the picture frame while the tape plays. Or the account of the Spirit coming at Pentecost could be taped; Peter and his friends can come down the aisle and enter the picture frame for the duration of Peter's speech.

Stream-of-Consciousness Idea

Have a tape or a live voice come over the sound system and express the private feelings and straying thoughts of people in the audience ("The lawn needs mowing" . . . "remember the groceries" . . . and so on) during the service. If the pastor is concerned his topic may be tedious, he can prepare a recording to interrupt himself throughout the sermon in dialogue fashion. This technique has resulted in memorable sermons!

LITERATURE: THE HEBRAIC IMAGINATION

Contemporary congregational readings, responses, prayers, and poems can all be part of the offering of worship to the Lord too, and we can call upon those in our congregations with a talent for writing to compose them.

Consider for a moment the nature of Hebrew poetry. The Hebraic imagination of the Old Testament differs from the Western imagination. Our Western imagination has been dominated by Greek forms of thought and styles of art. The Greeks preferred representational art, logic, and analysis in their forms, and visual and spacial descriptions of setting, atmosphere, and background in their literature. Hebrew poetry, however, is not primarily visual or spacial. It appeals to a wide range of associations and senses, especially in terms of sound.

This passage from the Song of Songs mixes extravagant and dissimilar metaphors:

> Behold, you are beautiful, my love,
>   behold, you are beautiful!
> Your eyes are doves
>   behind your veil.
> Your hair is like a flock of goats,
>   moving down the slopes of Gilead.
> Your teeth are like a flock of shorn ewes
>   that have come up from the washing,
> all of which bear twins,
>   and not one among them is bereaved.
> Your lips are like a scarlet thread,
>   and your mouth is lovely.
> Your cheeks are like halves of a pomegranate
>   behind your veil.
> Your neck is like the tower of David,
>   built for an arsenal,
> whereon hang a thousand bucklers,
>   all of them shields of warriors.
> Your two breasts are like two fawns,
>   twins of a gazelle,
>   that feed among the lilies (4:1–5 RSV).

Veith explains the imagery:

When we read "your two breasts are like two fawns," we think of a visual picture, in this case a jarring absurdity. When we realize that the image is not visual but *tactile*, the sensuousness of the description is nearly overwhelming. The woman's cheeks do not *look* like pomegranates (what a horrible complexion that would be!) but rather the poet has made an image of fragrance, and even more sensuously, of taste. . . . The eyes-like-doves metaphor seems to refer to the timorousness but liveliness of the dove, to the woman's reticence and modesty, a sense also conveyed in the metaphor of the fawns. The hair like goats is another tactile image, with also the associations of richness and the pastoral life. . . . The description of the neck refers to the way she stands, tall and aloof, proud, in a sense, and inaccessible. Throughout are allusions not only to her physical desireability but also to her overpowering attractiveness, nearly forgotten in the West but still present in other cultures, of chastity.[9]

Veith concludes, "The lover is attracted not only by what she looks like but by what she feels like when he touches her, what she tastes like, the associations of sheepfields and battle that she calls to mind."[10]

What can this passage teach us about Hebraic worship? We find in the Bible a sensitivity to aesthetics. The use of symbolism in the Scriptures goes far beyond the furnishings of the tabernacle and temple. It is a vital element in Hebrew poetry also.

Previously we have spoken of the holiness of God and the transcendent severity of tabernacle worship. The passage quoted from the Song of Songs reveals the other side of the coin. It reveals a culture open to the richness of human feelings, of intimacy and closeness. In our worship the severity of transcendency can be matched with an adoration of rich and varied feelings and associations, one that is spiritual, yet profoundly and unashamedly human. As a musician I strive to bring into my worship leadership both the sounds of majesty and evocative chord touches, shadings, and intertwining musical phrases that speak of the language of love.

THE SELECTION OF ARTISTS

What were the qualifications of the artisans who crafted the liturgical furnishings in the tabernacle? This may come as a surprise, but the first person described in the Scriptures as being "filled with the spirit" was an artist: Bezalel. (Bezalel means "in the shadow and protection of God.") He was chosen and empowered by God to head the team of artisans who were to make all the furnishings for the tabernacle.

> Then Moses said to the sons of Israel, "See, the LORD has called by name Bezalel the son of Uri, the son of Hur, of the tribe of Judah. And He has filled him with the spirit of God, in wisdom, in understanding and in knowledge and in all craftsmanship; to make designs for working in gold and in silver and in bronze, and in the cutting of stones for settings, and in the carving of wood, so as to perform in every inventive work. He also has put in his heart to teach, both he and Oholiab, the son of Ahisamach, of the tribe of Dan. He has filled them with skill [lit., 'wisdom of heart'] to perform every work of an engraver and of a designer and of an embroiderer, in blue and in purple and in scarlet material, and in fine linen, and of a weaver, as performers of every work and makers of designs. Now Bezalel and Oholiab, and every skillful person in whom the LORD has put skill and understanding to know how to perform all the work in the construction of the sanctuary, shall perform in accordance with all that the Lord commanded."
>
> Then Moses called Bezalel and Oholiab and every skillful person in whom the LORD has put skill, everyone whose heart stirred him, to come to the work to perform it (Exod. 35:30–36:2 NASB).

Veith says this passage is "incisive in its analysis of what artistry involves—indeed, it is the most comprehensive analysis of the issue I have ever found."[11] He says whereas human theories about art tend to be partial and narrow—some emphasizing talent, some training, some technique—it is characteristic of Scripture to be comprehensive.

Hebrew scholar Tom Finley sees in the Hebrew words translated

(1) wisdom, (2) understanding, (3) knowledge, and (4) craftsmanship a progression from the general to the specific.[12] The first word *wisdom* relates more to envisioning, while the last quality relates more to embodiment in a product. The qualities that Bezalel possessed are generalizable and could apply equally to a musician or a worship leader, and they can be helpful in establishing criteria for the selection of worship personnel in a local church setting. Let's examine these words in more detail.

Wisdom

If worship is fundamentally the responsibility of the people, then the worship leaders—including committee members, musicians, etc., not just the church staff—need wisdom to carry out their task. The Hebrew word translated "wisdom" here occurs three more times in this brief passage. In the context, the Hebrew word for wisdom means to have insight or perspective into the overall plan, to see how everything fits together. The word for wisdom is used in Jeremiah in connection with the creation of the earth:

> But God made the earth by his power;
> he founded the world by his *wisdom*
> and stretched out the heavens by his *understanding*.
> (Jer. 10:12)

This word is rendered in other translations as "ability" or "skill." Musicians, thinking of the translation "skill" in musical terms, are likely to get a wrong connotation. It means having the big picture and understanding the philosophy or rationale of the whole. This is a quality much needed today by those involved in leading worship.

The word *wisdom,* in terms of the passage itself, also relates well to the idea of *conceiving,* as in conceiving the designs and *innovating* the settings of particular abstract, decorative art pieces. The actual design of the cherubim, of the stone settings on the high priest's ephod, of the weaving of the figures on the curtains was left by God to human imagination. In the same way, the worship leader gleans general scriptural principles for the design of the order of service, yet the details are left to human invention.

Understanding

The word *understanding* is often linked with *wisdom* in Scripture. In the context of worship, *understanding* further suggests the attribute of intelligence or ability in practical problem solving. The worship leader needs both vision and an analytic mind.

I have had the privilege of studying for extended periods of time at five universities. In doing so I have had the opportunity to become acquainted with some remarkable people who have reached the zenith of their profession. A characteristic of all of these exceptional individuals has been their openness to new knowledge—even knowledge outside their given discipline. They have developed the ability to make insightful connections. If you penetrate far enough into any subject, you will begin to discover interrelationships. Your understanding will grow.

Knowledge

The knowledge meant here, in the context of art, has to do with "know-how" knowledge, the knowledge of particular crafts. Bezalel had to know his materials. He needed to know how to prepare acacia wood, cast bronze, beat gold, and make dyes. In the same way keyboard musicians need to have technical knowledge on how to manage transitions between songs or choruses and how to modulate between verses. Choir directors need conducting and rehearsal techniques. Song leaders need to know not only their hymnals, but also techniques for linking choruses and hymns together and teaching new songs to the congregation. What strikes me about the Exodus passage is Bezalel's expertise in so many fields—truly a "Renaissance man." Similarly, a worship leader who has a broad range of skills and knowledge is invaluable. Are you interested in improving your knowledge?

Craftsmanship

The root of the word translated "craftsmanship" has to do with work. It appears in Genesis 2:2: "So on the seventh day he [God] rested from all his work." An alternative for "craftsmanship" is "workmanship." Craftsmanship involves working in a specific medium. It requires the mastery of technique in the act of embodying an idea. The emphasis is on the quality of the product.

The Scriptures have a comprehensive, practical concept of creativity. They place the focus for judging something creative on the outcome. That is, we have to see (or be told about) the results of the work. The *process* of creativity, or even the *original flash of insight* if it does not result in tangible results, is not in itself sufficient to be judged creative. Ideas have to work. In the biblical view, ideas conceived and envisioned have to be fleshed out into some feasible form of expression.[13]

Ability to Teach

Worship leaders should measure up to the same character qualities required of elders and have as well the traits discovered in Bezalel: wisdom, understanding, knowledge, and craftsmanship. Additionally leaders must have the ability to teach. This quality, evident in Bezalel, is also required of elders (2 Tim. 2:24). Teaching is basic to leadership. The Scriptures say that God had put in Bezalel's heart the desire to teach.

Many artists today, it seems, if they had the choice, would choose not to teach. The nature of Bezalel's assignment, however, required him to engage other workers in completing the task. I find that it is simpler and requires less effort to lead worship myself completely from the piano (and I like to do this occasionally since it is a skill in itself); however, it is wise to involve others in leadership for the ripple effect alone. Involvement stimulates interest. Furthermore, a worship leader should engage others so they can develop their gifts.

> It was he who gave some to be apostles, some to be prophets, some to be evangelists, and some to be pastors and teachers, to prepare God's people for works of service, so that the body of Christ may be built up (Eph. 4:11–12).

If a given leader should leave at some future date, the personnel trained will then be available to carry on the work.

A Heart Stirred

In selecting worship leaders, look for a worshiper who is spiritually stirred to do the work. Fire, intensity, and enthusiasm are essential. Try to hear the cry of these words of matchless power and eloquence by Jeremiah. Here is a man who is divinely impelled, motivated. He tells of his compulsion to speak God's message to the people.

> But if I say, "I will not remember Him
> Or speak any more in His name,"
> Then in my heart it becomes like a burning fire
> Shut up in my bones;
> And I am weary of holding it in,
> And I cannot endure it (Jer. 20:9 NASB).

QUESTIONS FOR THOUGHT AND DISCUSSION

1. How do you interpret the second commandment?
2. The first note in this chapter includes the statement "The prohibition in the second commandment has primarily to do with false worship

and not with the attempt to reflect God in images. The line is drawn between God and idols but not between God and images." Discuss.

3. What implications do you draw from this statement: "The guiding principle in the tabernacle was that the closer to the ark the furnishings were positioned, the more ornate in figuration and costly in material they were."

4. "Even if the second commandment is taken in its narrowest sense of prohibiting representational art, however, it still leaves room for abstract art, including the symbolic and the fictional." Discuss.

5. "We fail to realize that God is the original abstract artist." Discuss.

6. "Representational art should be the style that makes those who believe in the Scriptures the most uneasy." Discuss.

7. Should worship leaders have the same character qualities as elders? Explain.

RECOMMENDED READING

Gaebelein, Frank E. *The Christian, the Arts, and Truth: Regaining the Vision of Greatness.* Portland, Oreg.: Multnomah, 1985.

Ryken, Leland. *Culture in Christian Perspective: A Door to Understanding and Enjoying the Arts.* Portland, Oreg.: Multnomah, 1986.

Veith, Gene E., Jr. *The Gift of Art.* Downers Grove, Ill.: InterVarsity, 1983.

White, James F. *New Forms of Worship.* Nashville: Abingdon Press, 1971.

Wolterstorff, Nicholas. *Art in Action: Toward a Christian Aesthetic.* Grand Rapids: Wm. B. Eerdmans, 1980.

CHAPTER TWELVE

Temple Worship: What Is Davidic Praise?

One does not have to engage in a manipulative, high-pressure determined campaign to convince people of the worth of praise. The preaching of the truth will do the job (introduction). . . . When a congregation begins to accept the biblical truth about praise, there begins to be freedom in the exercise of praise. . . . ignorance on the subject abounds. The subject is not marginal or peripheral—it is central.[1]

Our culture is in transition. Our entire North American culture is becoming, in some respects, more Hebraic. Have you noticed how people applaud at rock and country concerts on television these days? They clap with their hands over their heads. At classical concerts, the bastions of older European culture, listeners clap more sedately at the waist level. This is just one indication of a many-faceted transformation occurring in our culture.

I am particularly concerned that people in conservative, Bible-believing churches may have great difficulty adapting to this change. Many of us would rather not talk about it, or we don't even see a need to talk about it. After all, it's not basic theology. When we do talk about it, we feel we must apologize for bringing it up. Is this a healthy attitude?

I believe this is a big mistake! "Cultural fit" was a central issue for the early church. In the Book of Acts the church wrestled with cultural problems very early on. It even had a major church council on the matter. It rightly perceived that success in the expansion of the church from a Jewish into a supranational entity rested in part on not requiring Gentiles to practice particularistic Jewish dietary laws codes and circumcision (Acts 10 and 15).

How are we going to find a style of worship that fits our

contemporary culture? We can start by taking a fresh look at the model of Davidic praise.

By the term "Davidic praise" we do not mean a particular style of praise invented by David, but rather we take David, the recipient of God's plan for praise in the temple, to be a representative of the Old Testament praise tradition and a man with a true heart for worship. We're not interested in imposing specific aspects of Hebrew culture on a local church today—the specific outworking of these ideas in temple worship are for us suggestive, not mandatory—but we want to look at the principles that undergird Davidic praise and see how we can apply them today. We'll find a lot to look at, and we cannot fail to be enriched and stretched by the exercise.

DAVIDIC PRAISE: WHAT IS IT?

Jack Taylor, a leader in the Southern Baptist Convention, defines Davidic praise as "always active, assertive, demonstrative, and open. It is not passive, presumptuous, undemonstrative, or secretive. Whenever it is mentioned, movement, action, and songs are seen and heard."[2] Doesn't that sound oddly contemporary?

Perhaps the most extravagant Old Testament image of utter abandonment in worship is the picture of David leaping and dancing as the ark was carried in procession to its permanent site in Jerusalem. Before we (like his wife Michal) become too critical of David's expression of praise, we ought to take a second look at the biblical evidence for praise that has a strong physical dimension. Does the Bible support or permit a more physical kind of worship than we, in our upbringing, may have been used to?

TO WORSHIP MEANS TO BOW DOWN

> Come, let us worship and bow down;
> Let us kneel before the Lord our Maker.
> (Ps. 95:6 NASB)

The primary word for worship in the Old Testament means literally to "bow" (politely or respectfully), to "prostrate oneself," to "make obeisance," or to "bend low" (in worship as a mark of respect).[3] It has a definite physical dimension to it in Hebrew culture. Ralph Martin says it "emphasizes the way in which an Israelite fittingly thought of his approach to the holy presence of God. He bows himself down in lowly reverence and prostration."[4] Used in combination with another verb so as to mean that one's "nose" touched the "ground" (Gen. 42:6), it is a gesture that reflects absolute submission.[5]

The gesture, in the Old Testament, may be performed before persons, before Yahweh, or before other gods. Used as a greeting between persons, bowing means to acknowledge a higher rank. Ruth bows to Boaz, David to Saul, Saul to Samuel. One bows when begging. You will recall that the story of Joseph begins with a dream about who will bow to whom; six chapters later, the dream becomes a reality (Gen. 37:5; 43:28). The gesture can also express an inner attitude; when God provides a bride for Isaac, the servant of Abraham bows and worships God out of gratitude (Gen. 24:48).

Interestingly, the word for worship in the Old Testament is not a propositional word. It is visual, gestural, attitudinal, and public, and it often involves the relinquishing of rights. *Proskuneō,* the primary Greek counterpart for worship in the New Testament, has the same basic meaning with the same overtones of "submissive lowliness and deep respect."[6] To worship God is to fall down before Him and to serve Him. We simply cannot do better than to meditate on these words. Prostration is particularly frequent in the Book of Revelation and can have intense overtones.

> And when I turned I saw seven golden lampstands, and among the lampstands was someone "like a son of man," dressed in a robe reaching down to his feet and with a golden sash around his chest. His head and hair were white like wool, as white as snow, and his eyes were like blazing fire. . . . When I saw him, I fell at his feet as though dead (Rev. 1:12–17).

OLD TESTAMENT WORDS FOR PRAISE

Ron Allen, a scholar of the Psalms, finds that the Old Testament terms for praise also emphasize intensity. Observe the verbs in his translation of Psalm 142:1:

> Aloud to Yahweh I scream out;
> Aloud to Yahweh I implore favor!
> I pour out before him my trouble.

Thanksgiving Versus Praise

Allen points out that thanksgiving differs from praise. *Thanksgiving,* he maintains, is a New Testament word; *praise,* an Old Testament word. The New Testament speaks of thanksgiving that can be done in one's heart, in private, or in a closet, but all the Hebrew terms for praise have about them "a public and vocal nature."[7] To us the word *meditate* means to cast over in the mind silently, but to the Hebrew in the Old Testament it had more of the meaning to intone or chant. Consider this point in reading Psalm 1:2:

> But his delight is in the law of the LORD,
> and on his law he meditates [intones] day and night.

Similarly, for us thanksgiving occurs when one inwardly "breathes a prayer of thanks"; for them, praise occurs when one "tells someone else about it." Allen says:

> One of the most startling and surprising observations of recent studies of the Book of Psalms is that in the Hebrew language there appears to be no word meaning "thank you." Modern Israeli Hebrew has taken a word from the Old Testament and now uses it for the meaning of "thanks," but that word did not not seem to mean "thanks" in the biblical period. This is hard for us to believe, so deeply ingrained in our culture is the word "to thank." . . . In the Old Testament culture, the word used in place of thanks was praise. That is, one would tell another what God had done, rather than merely saying "Thank you, Lord."[8]

Application. A church musician told me that his pastor insists that all Sunday morning hymns should be addressed to God. His idea is that if the song does not specifically address God or (worse yet) is addressed to the people, it is not a worship hymn and therefore should have absolutely no place in the Sunday morning service. "By being this doctrinaire he is excluding one-half of our hymnbook," the music director complained.

Though the main emphasis in worship should be on God and His character and on singing directly to His person, nonetheless, the above emphasis in Davidic praise which tells of boasting to others about what God has done indicates there is a place for testimony hymns in worship.

Sound Versus Silence

All the Hebrew words of praise are words that call for sound, not silence. When the Old Testament prophets call for silence (Hab. 2:20; Zech. 2:13; Zeph. 1:7), it is the silence of fear in lieu of God's impending judgment.[9] Moreover, when David says "Before the 'gods' I will sing your praise" (Ps. 138:1), he is combatively asserting, against the pagan environment surrounding him, a "frontal attack" of emboldened praise in the midst of "enemy territory."[10]

Application. Graham Kendrick has an interesting concept of "taking praise to the streets." He has recently been organizing praise marches of a hundred people or more through the streets of ill-repute in London. He speaks of not being civilly disobedient, but obedient to bring the commands of Christ to the streets. The marchers have guitars and tambourines. They wave banners and flags, play wind and brass instruments, and sing joyous, exhilarating songs. It is an excellent idea especially for churches located in the inner city.

Praise at the Center

In David's perception, praise was not at all a peripheral issue. David was used by God to establish praise at the center of his nation's life. For him praise was an imperative, not an option or elective. The absence of praise, Taylor says, means someone "has an inadequate view of God."[11] Davidic praise has a strong physical dimension that may include, besides bowing and prostrating, the actions of kneeling, lifting the eyes and hands, clapping, dancing, shouting, and processioning. Davidic praise is far removed from the comfortable pew of noninvolvement.

PRAYER POSTURES

Hudson Taylor, missionary to China, relates the experience of a Chinese person endeavoring to comprehend the Christian form of worship. He misperceived the intent of Christians at worship. Observing them with their heads bowed at their seats, the Chinese man asked, "Why do you pray to a chair?" He thought he at least bowed before something of significance, a Buddha.

Some evangelical worship traditions, when analyzed, stem more from European than biblical tradition. For example, many of us have seen displayed in homes the painting of "praying hands." *This hallowed image we have of hands folded in prayer with eyes closed is found nowhere in Scripture.* Yet we do not discount it as an appropriate form of worship expression.

It's interesting, though, that forms of worship expression that *are* modeled in Scriptures raise eyebrows and even create tremendous controversy among the very people who are the staunchest supporters of the Bible as "the guide for faith and practice." Take, for example, the repertoire of prayer postures found in the Bible. It is broader than typical evangelical practice. The chart below adapted from William Hendriksen indicates the kinds of prayer postures found in the Bible, their probable meaning, and frequency of occurrence.[12]

The chart communicates a significant aspect of Hebrew culture. Note that the greater the body movement, the greater the frequency of occurrence. This is virtually the converse of evangelical tradition. We mostly bow the head and seldom become prostrate. In the Book of Revelation, however, prostration does not even seem to be cultural; it seems to be an inevitable response to the presence of God (1:17; 11:16). Similarly, it appears that bowing, at a future time in heaven, will not be a suggestive, but a *mandatory* form of public confession.

Posture	Meaning	Frequency
Bowing the head	Reverent submission	4
Standing	Reverence, respect	6
Lifting the eye	Looking to the source of blessing	9
Kneeling	Humility and adoration	12
Hands spread or lifted with palms up	Expectancy, servitude	14
Prostration	Awe in the divine presence	28

> Therefore God exalted him to the highest place and gave him the name that is above every name, that at the name of Jesus every knee should bow, in heaven and on earth and under the earth, and every tongue confess that Jesus Christ is Lord, to the glory of God the Father (Phil. 2:9–11).

I personally consider these practices only suggested for the church today. These postures are *modeled not mandated, suggestive not required, and should be permitted not coerced*. It is interesting, however, that the First Baptist Church of Dallas has installed kneeling pews in its sanctuary— that's a form of permission. When we suppress and mute the Davidic elements of praise in our worship, it is like having a marriage with excellent verbal communication but no sex.

RESPONSES OF JOY

In Old Testament Davidic praise, responses of joy include clapping, shouting, raising the hands, and dancing—responses that reflect an intensity of feeling in worship. We cannot charge the Hebrew people with irreverence because they did this. These actions were an appropriate human response to the great things God had done for His people.

Some people may think this kind of expression extreme—"too emotional." These same people come home hoarse after football games. It reminds me of a conversation between a pastor and a church member:

> *Member:* It seems that our churches don't have any emotion. Why are we so cold, Pastor?
>
> *Pastor:* Now that's where you're wrong. We have LOTS of emotion. Lots of anger!

Clapping

Clapping can take on a variety of meanings in the Hebrew culture. In the following verses the Hebrew imagination envisions mighty choruses of clapping by the peoples of whole nations, by whitecaps on fast-flowing rivers, and by swaying branches of trees clapping in the wind their praise to God. For the Hebrews, clapping and joy go together:

Clap your hands, all you nations; shout to God with cries of joy (Ps. 47:1).

Let the rivers clap their hands, let the mountains sing together for joy (Ps. 98:8).

You will go out in joy and be led forth in peace; the mountains and hills will burst into song before you, and all the trees of the field will clap their hands (Isa. 55:12).

But clapping has other meanings also. God commands Ezekiel to clap (even stomp his feet) in response to God's revelation of judgment on Israel and Babylon (Ezek. 6:11; 21:14). *Even God (metaphorically) claps His hands.* "I too will strike my hands together, and my wrath will subside" (Ezek. 21:17).

In our culture, too, we find different kinds of clapping and different meanings and purposes for it. Black congregations sometimes clap for musical emphasis. They clap selectively, only at certain places, or on certain beats and accents, and it often enhances the clarity of their music expression. Through this kind of clapping, when artfully done, the hand can become a kind of percussion instrument. By contrast, clapping in white congregations often projects a sense of power; once the people start, they generally clap right through to the end of a piece.

At the Billy Graham Greater Los Angeles Crusade of 1985, tens of thousands in the crowd began to applaud as people came forward to profess salvation. Billy Graham was taken aback. He tried to stop the audience from applauding but could not. He seemingly did not know what to make of it. Then he said something to the effect, "You

The Celebration Song

Psalm 22:3

Words and Music By
BRENT CHAMBERS

In the pres-ence of your peo-ple I will praise Your name,

For a-lone You are ho-ly, en-throned on the prais-es of Is-ra-el.

Let us cel-e-brate Your good-ness and Your stead-fast love.

May Your name be ex-alt-ed here on_earth and in heav'n a-bove.

Californians are different." To the Californians their clapping was a means of affirming those making a decision for Christ, a way of praising God for answered prayer.

In the worship services of many charismatic churches, applause routinely expresses praise to God. In noncharismatic evangelical churches, however, clapping seldom expresses a worship response; it is more often an expression of delight in being entertained by a special musical number. For others, applause may even seem to cheapen worship to the level of performance. All these differing reactions make up part of our cultural baggage.

Application. If you are interested in introducing clapping that contributes to corporate praise into your worship, consider clapping to sturdy Hebrew choruses with great texts like "The Celebration Song," "Sing to the Lord," or "King of Kings and Lord of Lords."[13]

The Celebration Song

[x = clap at the end of the line]

In the presence of your people, x
I will praise your name. xx
For alone you are holy,
Enthroned on the praises of Israel. xx
Let us celebrate your goodness x
and your steadfast love xx
May your name be exalted
here on earth and in heav'n above. xx

The double claps occur on beats 4 and 1. Introducing clapping as an accompaniment will more likely be better received with Hebrew choruses than with other choruses.

Shouting

God proved Himself to be such a great God on behalf of His people that at times their praise could not be restrained—it erupted in shouting. Scriptures record more than sixty references to shouts of joy in Davidic worship. (The term "shouts of joy" is rendered "songs of joy" in some translations.) Ezra 3:11–13 provides an interesting, moving example:

> With praise and thanksgiving they sang to the LORD: "He is good; his
> love to Israel endures forever." And all the people gave a great shout
> of praise to the LORD, because the foundation of the house of the
> LORD [the second temple] was laid. But many of the older priests and
> Levites and family heads, who had seen the former temple, wept
> aloud when they saw the foundation of this temple being laid, while
> many others shouted for joy. No one could distinguish the sound of

the shouts of joy from the sound of weeping, because the people
made so much noise. And the sound was heard far away.

The Psalms picture not only people, but also *God* shouting.

> God has spoken from his sanctuary: . . .
> "Moab is my washbasin,
>   upon Edom I toss my sandal;
>   over Philistia I *shout* in triumph."
>   (Ps. 108:7–9)

Jeremiah depicts God as roaring and shouting in judgment:

> The Lord will *roar* from on high; he will *thunder* from his holy
> dwelling and roar mightily against his land. He will *shout* like those
> who tread the grapes, shout against all who live on the earth. The
> tumult will *resound* to the ends of the earth (Jer. 25:30–31).

These pictures of God certainly don't reveal Him as an introvert! I
hope I am not overstating this, but in one sense I think it is fair to say the
people shout because God has set the precedents and dimensions in His
own shoutings and thunderings. The character of God even here can
inform our style of worship. At the Jotabeche Methodist Pentecostal
Church in Santiago, Chile, the people (fifteen thousand strong) conclude
their congregational praise by standing and crying out "Glory to God"
three times in a mighty "thunder of praise."

Interestingly, some Evangelicals accept shouts of "Amen," but view
"Hallelujahs" as taboo because the Pentecostals use them.[14] Yet it is a
wonderful word. But should non-Charismatics allow the practices of
Charismatics to confine and limit their praise vocabulary? "Hallelujah" is
a combination of three Hebrew words: *hallel* ("praise"), *u* ("ye"), and *yah*
(Yahweh). *Hallelujah!* "Praise Ye God" or "Praise God." *Hallelujah* is
the premium word for praise. It is pronounced the same way "in every
major language on earth," and therefore it is an invaluable resource.[15]

Application. I have not seen many occasions where all the people in
an evangelical church came close to shouting. But I remember one
instance with unusual circumstances that came close to it. We were a
rapidly growing young church and had been meeting in a small school
when the pastor and elders of a nearby church asked to speak with our
pastor and elders. "We want to make you an offer we don't think you will
be able to turn down," they said. Out of the blue they offered us the title
deed of their church property and building. "You are growing rapidly
and will need a larger space; we have only thirty-five people." Their
pastor was very much behind this idea and offered to resign: "We'd like
to join you and become part of you." When asked by our elders what

spiritual gifts they thought they could add to our fellowship, they answered, "We think we are good tithers."

The congregations courted each other for a couple of months and decided to make a marriage of it. The week before we were to worship as one for the first time in the facility, we received a call from a man who was not a part of our church. He said he would donate the organ in his home, provided that we pay an appraisal fee so he could get his tax exemption. To our astonishment, the organ was appraised at more than forty thousand dollars!

The day before our first Sunday in the sanctuary, everyone came out in full force to give the church a thorough cleaning from top to bottom. People everywhere sang and talked as they worked. One could feel a certain amount of apprehension in some ("Will the feeling in our church change?"), but over and beyond this an overriding sense of joy and wonderment was welling up in everybody. Certainly God was at work! I entered the sanctuary that morning to rehearse for Sunday and could feel all this crackling in the air. I found myself saying things like "I can't wait for Sunday" . . . "This is going to be a once-in-a-lifetime experience" . . . "I'm just so glad to be a part of this and to see it happening before my eyes" . . . "You won't be able to hold these people back from singing on Sunday." I was excited.

Sunday arrived, the people arrived early, and the place was jammed. The atmosphere was electric. I've never found it so easy or so much fun to lead people in worship. There was so much joy in the place! As the people sang with happy, shining faces, it felt like a tidal wave of sound coming at me. The people were so responsive! After the service I was talking to one of the elders, Bryan Jones. He told me, "I never in my life heard singing like that before. Barry, there was so much noise! You know I can't sing for anything . . . but it was so loud, I knew they'd never hear me. So,"—and he was laughing—"I just shouted too!"

When Jones said that, it almost brought tears to my eyes, because I have many times wished that nonmusical people could be in the kind of environment where they too would feel comfortable voicing their praise strongly. Upon reflection, this incident has taught me that God is the creator of the conditions that make for true praise.

> I [God] will heal him; I will guide him and restore comfort to him,
> creating praise on the lips of the mourners in Israel (Isa. 57:18–19).

When we think it through all the way, God is the cause, the initiator of praise.

Recovering the Shout

What value lies in "shouting"? How am I using the term? Let me explain with another illustration. One summer I attended a morning service at the stately Hollywood Presbyterian Church. On entering the sanctuary I must confess I was a little skeptical of these people who seemed to possess great material wealth. I wondered if their faith was really genuine. My family had been poor as I was growing up.

I took a seat in the middle section about two-thirds back and became aware that I was surrounded by a group of older people. They seemed to be quite cohesive. When the service began, I could feel their participation. I became particularly conscious of an old man's voice directly behind me. His voice was shot (what was left of it was mainly air), but he pronounced his consonants crisply, his rhythms lively. Whenever any response from the people was required, he was right there on time, every time. As I focused on him more and more, I could hear that the force of his whole body was behind the sound. I sensed a tremendous vitality in the man. I could feel the "shout" in his voice. I started asking myself, "Who is this man?" and was about to turn around and look at him, but I couldn't bring myself to do it. His voice had been such a great gift to me, I just wanted to remember it without a face. I would like to meet this man in heaven someday. The incident leads me to say, "Let's recover the shout!"

Raising Hands

The raising of hands—until recently a phenomenon limited to charismatic churches—is now becoming an issue among Evangelicals.[16] Evangelical Christians appear to be divided over it. Some term themselves "closet Charismatics": they may not endorse all aspects of charismatic theology, but they are drawn to the freedom and spontaneity that characterizes charismatic worship. For many it comes down to a choice between good doctrine and good worship. Some couples have told me they are now attending a charismatic church because they like the worship even though they are uncomfortable with aspects of the theology. Others have told me they decided not to attend a charismatic church because of doctrine, even though they were deeply attracted to the worship.

One of the strongest endorsements for raising hands comes from Jack Taylor in his book *The Hallelujah Factor*. Taylor says of the raising of hands: "This exercise is one of the most explosive and meaningful expressions of praise. I believe that God loves it, the flesh hates it, and the devil is devastated by it. I believe that with its exercise faith stands firm, fear takes flight, and joy takes hold."[17] To Taylor, the symbolic act means "Father I want you, I receive you, I yield to you. . . . take me."[18] He calls it "an international sign of surrender."[19] These are evocative meanings! He also sees it as a means of "extending our emotions, as well as expressing our personalities."

Chuck Smith of Calvary Chapel in Costa Mesa, California, also endorses it, but adds a caution.[20] He says it should not be abused as a vehicle for show by people who, like the Pharisees, desire to be seen:

> And when you pray, do not be like the hypocrites, for they love to pray standing in the synagogues and on the street corners to be seen (Matt. 6:5).

One objection I often hear about raising hands is that it will make non-Christians uncomfortable. In certain sectors of North America that may be true. On the one hand, both the churched and nonchurched may be culturally uncomfortable with the raising of hands, and for that reason it may not be wise to encourage its practice. On the other hand, many southern California churches that raise hands have learned to practice it in a way that seems to be culturally acceptable to a wide range of people. In fact, these churches seem to have the nonchurched present in larger numbers than the churches that do not raise hands.

We may be wise to look at our own North American culture the way a missionary looks at a culture in a foreign land: "When in Rome, do as the Romans do." We should show some willingness to be flexible, adapt, and grow with the given culture or subculture as long as we don't compromise biblical morality or our theology. Pastors will need to do some teaching on this to make its meaning clear and dispel possible tensions.

What Does the Bible Say?

You will recall from the prayer postures chart that there are fourteen references in the Bible to raising hands. Consider these four representative examples, the first two occurring in the context of public worship, the second two in private worship:

> Ezra praised the LORD, the great God; and all the people lifted their hands and responded, "Amen! Amen!" Then they bowed down and worshiped the LORD with their faces to the ground (Neh. 8:6).

> Praise the LORD, all you servants of the LORD who minister by night in the house of the LORD. Lift up your hands in the sanctuary and praise the LORD (Ps. 134:1–2).

> May my prayer be set before you like incense; may the lifting up of my hands be like the evening sacrifice (Ps. 141:2).

I meditate on all your works and consider what your hands have done. I spread out my hands to you; my soul thirsts for you like a parched land (Ps. 143:5–6).

Lifting up hands was apparently culturally acceptable and comfortable to all the Hebrew people (Neh. 8:6). It was variously an outward expression of an attitude of praise (Ps. 134:2), or of offering oneself to God (Ps. 141:1–2), or of thirsting for more of God (Ps. 143:5–6).

In 1 Timothy, a book not noted for a charismatic emphasis, Paul says, "I want men everywhere to lift up holy hands in prayer, without anger or disputing" (2:8). No doubt Paul's main emphasis seems to be on holiness, but hands function as the visible symbol. The tone of Scripture does not suggest unsuitable emotionalism was connected with the raising of hands; it formed a part of the accepted tradition.

In the Scriptures, then, the raising of hands occurs frequently, is used in public and private prayer, and is an intertestamental phenomenon. Some people, however, believe raising hands is merely metaphorical in meaning. In light of Nehemiah 8:6, particularly, this seems unlikely. But let us explore this more.

Isn't Raising Hands Metaphorical?

Tom Finley cautions that in the study of words, not only the original meaning, but also the context of the particular passage and the cultural setting should be considered. He reasons that a narrow study of etymology without reference to the larger whole can lead to error, for the meaning of words can change over time. It is wise to see if cultural and historical clues reinforce a particular meaning.

Does the identification of the raising of hands with praise meet this test? Yes, it does.

First, the etymological evidence links praise and the raising of hands very closely. The Hebrew language uses more than fifty words in connection with praise.[21] The Hebrew word for the hand, *yad*, provides the root word for several praise words. *Yadah*, the lengthened form of *yad*, means "to throw, to cast, or to shoot." It means "to worship with extended hands, to throw out the hands, to give thanks to God."[22] *Yadah*, the second most frequently used word for praise, occurs ninety times and is translated in the King James Version as "praise" (fifty-three times), "give thanks" (thirty-two), "confess" (sixteen), and "thank" (five). The Hebrew word *todah* (from *yad*) is also translated "praise." And *hodayoth* (also from "hand") means "song of thanksgiving."

We also have cultural evidence. Archaeologists have found statues of men with hands upraised in prayer at several cites in the Middle East.[23] From extrabiblical sources we know that when the Hebrew people saw the smoke rise from the burning incense at the daily sacrifice, they prostrated themselves and spread their hands in silent prayer.[24] Furthermore, the practice of prostration and the spreading of hands has continued to this day in Judaism as well as Islam. It is a part of Middle East culture. Both the word meanings themselves and the cultural context support a literal interpretation to the raising of hands. We must inevitably conclude, therefore, that there is a strong case in the Bible for lifting hands. In fact, it's hard to make a case against it.

Implementation

How should a congregation introduce the practice of raising hands in praise?

First, recognize that this is a sensitive issue for many. In some ways Evangelicals express themselves in very physical ways in church practices. We encourage people to walk an aisle or raise a hand for salvation. We stand to give testimonies. Some immerse rather than sprinkle. But in other ways there is reluctance and even disdain for expressing emotions through actions. We tend to be quite selective about the kinds of physical reinforcement we will permit. We will raise one hand for salvation, but raising two hands in praise is taboo. Though it may seem like a silly inconsistency, it's a reality we must acknowledge.

Also, many Evangelicals associate raising hands with Pentecostals, and they have vivid memories of stories in which Pentecostals were castigated as "holy rollers." These memories can be very deep-seated. They have the power to paralyze. For such people the raising of hands has become so symbolically linked to that negative image of fervor gone wild that they cannot bring themselves to participate in it.

Second, bring good biblical teaching to bear on the issue. I think it is fair to say that we may have been unjustly critical of Pentecostals in the past because our memories were loaded with only the most extreme stories of abuse. Because we lacked adequate biblical teaching, we may have misunderstood the whole subject. It is time for Pentecostals to avoid abuses and for conservatives to look honestly at what the Scriptures say. The raising of hands is not really a Pentecostal phenomenon at all—it is an Old Testament phenomenon, and it needs to be seen within the context of Davidic praise.

All of us need to press on to a greater maturity. And we could benefit from balanced teaching that imparts a more comprehensive picture of the physical side of worship.

Third, be sensitive. Be patient with those who have bruised memories, tender consciences, or grave misgivings. They shouldn't be suddenly forced, pressured, or coerced into raising their hands in public.

Some people may never feel comfortable raising their hands. They too need to be respected. Their praise is no less valid.

Fourth, bring the people along slowly. Encourage them to experiment with new prayer postures, especially in private. In most cases praise should be practiced in private before it is performed in public. We can try raising hands at home and test its effect on our prayer life. We can allow ourselves time to become comfortable, to change. We can be patient with ourselves. Time is an important element here. Leaders in churches often try to implement change in this area too quickly. Conversely, we can learn to be tolerant and give permission to those who wish to raise their hands, even if we do not.

Jack Taylor says about implementation:

> Praise is new, revolutionary, and smacks of fanaticism. . . . If there is defense and counterattack, the plot thickens and the congregation polarizes. The results are division and confusion. The practice of *praise becomes the scapegoat and the culprit.* The church retreats, and the cause for the time in that particular congregation is lost. . . . The challenge is to plot a course of deliberate, scriptural education relating to the principles and practice of praise—and engage in plans to "steer the course" with guarded zeal (italics added).[25]

Wouldn't it be good if we could reduce the raising of hands to a nonissue and people could have the freedom to raise or not raise their hands without incurring the judgment of those present?

> *David Niquette, the pastor of a fundamentalist church that suffered a painful split over the charismatic issue several years ago, decided the time was appropriate to offer some teaching on the raising of hands. One Sunday evening he showed his people the prayer postures chart on the overhead. He reviewed the biblical references and reminded the people that they were a Bible-believing church. He stressed that raising hands was not mandatory, but that permission (on the basis of the modeling of Scripture) should be given to those who wished to raise their hands in worship.*
>
> *David caught me by surprise. "Barry," he said, "would you go to the piano and lead us in a chorus?" [I'm not that secure in leading this kind of thing myself!] "As we sing, I'd like us all to close our eyes. Those who wish to raise their hands are given permission, even encouraged, to do so. If you feel uncomfortable raising them high, you may raise them half-mast, or you may wish simply to turn your hands over with palms up on your lap and say to God by doing this, 'I look expectantly to you, Lord. Thank you for being my heavenly Father. I worship you.'" Many did one or the other. It was a pregnant and tender moment as many people lingered after the chorus in an extended season of silent prayer with outstretched arms.*
>
> *The worship committee met after the same service for its usual meeting and of course we talked about what had happened. The pastor stuck his head in for a few minutes. His transparency startled us. He said that as*

some of the people were raising their hands, he walked to the back of the church and raised his hands—"before the wall." He smiled, "That shows you something about my own public inhibitions in this area."

The pastor waited several days and then asked for feedback from the people about the Sunday night service. This time he was startled. Some of the more conservative people in the church said, "That was a gutsy thing you did!" They praised him. I have not yet observed a great change in the worship practice at the church in relation to the raising of hands. I don't see raised hands very often. But the people now know they have freedom. I personally think that is a step forward. The people have remained united; they are growing in their expression and understanding of worship and are maturing in many other areas as well. Recently I received a phone call from David: "Concern for outreach is increasing. We are very close to revival. Pray for us." It is exciting to see God working at many levels.

PRAISE EPILOGUE

An artist friend, Barry Krammes, told me about a moving service he and his wife had attended at the Hollywood Presbyterian Church. "My wife and I left with tears of joy," he said. "At the end of the morning Communion service, unannounced, the people began to sing the chorus 'Alleluia, Alleluia.' It started low and on each repetition of the tune, the pitch was raised a half step as they sang, 'He's my Savior,' and then 'I will serve Him,' and so on. At about the fifth repetition, I started to see a sprinkling of hands go up. On the last stanza, all the hands in the place went up as the people sang, 'I will praise him.'"

QUESTIONS FOR THOUGHT AND DISCUSSION

1. "The subject of praise is not marginal or peripheral—it is central." Discuss.
2. Is our North American culture becoming more Hebraic? Explain.
3. Do you think the "cultural fit" of your church in contemporary society is important to talk about? What can you say about it?
4. Is worship any better or any worse because people raise their hands? Explain.

RECOMMENDED READING

Allen, Ronald Barclay. *Praise! A Matter of Life and Breath.* Nashville: Thomas Nelson, 1980.
Taylor, Jack R. *The Hallelujah Factor.* Nashville: Broadman Press, 1983.

CHAPTER THIRTEEN

The Organization of Davidic Praise

> *The complaint which I hear from conductors of music is that there is no person in the congregation so indifferent to the cultivation of music as the minister. Now and then there is an exception; but generally the minister is glad to have a conductor who will take the whole responsibility from his shoulders; and then, so that there be quiet in the choir and no disturbance in the congregation, he does not trouble himself any more about the matter (Yale College, 1873).[1]*

Happily, times have changed since that was written. Today many pastors may not feel competent to deal with questions pertaining to music and worship, but there is at the very least greater interest in the subject. Common sense tells pastors that music is a vital component in today's worship. In Protestant churches with a traditional format, "20 to 25 percent of most general church meetings will be given over to music."[2] This percentage is likely to be even higher in young, less traditionally inclined churches. Paul Wohlgemuth, a Mennonite, reports that in churches recently influenced by the worship style of the charismatic movement, there tends to be a more equal sharing of the leadership of the service between the pastor and the worship leader. He says:

> It is important to be aware that this style of worship demands a new kind of song leader, choir director, keyboard performer, as well as instrumentalist. . . . No worship movement in recent years is so dependent upon music for the heart of its expression. . . . While the traditional Protestant church leans upon the pastor for the major leadership role in its worship service, the renewal calls for a dual leadership of pastor and Minister of Music, called the Worship Leader. . . . Currently, no seminary offers training or a graduate-degree program for a music leader that would be preparation for this new, emerging role as a worship leader. . . . Since this movement has

reached into most mainline church groups, e.g., Methodist, Presbyterian, Baptist, Mennonite, Episcopal, Lutheran, and Roman Catholic, it is imperative that persons responsible for church-music training
keep abreast of major worship movements and give leadership and
direction. . . . In particular, the need is for trained leaders of the
church's worship life who are at least informed about significant,
new, and even threatening worship music and practices.[3]

How sad that evangelical seminaries have failed and continue to fail
to exert a leadership role in the awakening interest in worship presently
occurring in evangelical churches! The person in the pew may not have
understood why Evangelicals in general have been so slow to recognize
the vital connection of worship to personal growth in the Christian life, to
the growth of churches at home and abroad, and to the educative function
of the local church. The long and short of it is that the issue of worship
has received scarcely any attention in most evangelical seminaries or
schools of theology for decades.[4]

A study by Norman W. Regier published in 1985 reported on 150
midwestern pastors who were asked what were the most significant
worship influences on them. Only 3 percent rated their seminary
experience as foremost. Rather, their childhood experiences (in church
and school) and post-educational studies were ranked highest. Regier's
conclusion was that "seminary training was not influential."[5]

The point is that seminaries could be doing a better job of teaching
and modeling worship. Somewhere in their studies prospective pastors
should learn at least to know the issues affecting church music. In a study
by J. W. Schwarz, responses from seminarians led him to conclude that
"students in the protestant seminaries of the United States are generally
aware of their need for training in church music and are desirous of
having more of such training available to them."[6] Once out in the field,
however, the typical minister, because of the heavy demands of his
vocation, is not in a position to acquire the training he needs.[7] For this
reason Carlton Young calls for "the reconstruction of basic theological
education so as to incorporate introductions to specialized ministries [like
music/worship] within the basic Minister of Divinity degree program."[8]

J. F. White concludes that the present state of teaching in the field
of music and worship at the seminary level "is where pastoral care was
about twenty years ago. Today it is unthinkable not to teach pastoral care,
someday it will be unthinkable not to teach worship."[9]

DIVORCED!

Not only have prospective ministers received scant training in
worship, but musicians and pastors have been divorced from each other

in their training.[10] Even today the great majority of people who become professional church musicians upon graduation receive a *different* education in a *different* location from seminarians.

Musicians receive their education at conservatories, colleges, or universities, while pastors and church educators receive theirs at seminaries and schools of theology. Musicians talk a different language from seminarians—and both languages can be highly technical! Musicians have no contact or communication with seminarians during their course of study, nor do they study theology or take courses that emphasize the pastoral dimension of ministry. The two groups do not share common-core classes. Musicians and seminarians do not have the privilege of rubbing shoulders and sharing ideas together in their practicums.[11] The professional musician "is usually the product of a private or state music school with attending high regard for performance at all levels, and minimal attention to educational models of music ministry and the basic theological disciplines."[12] When musicians and preachers are suddenly thrown together in a pastorate, no wonder there is often a lack of communication and trust!

It is not hard to see why seminaries have failed to provide leadership in worship. First, most evangelical seminaries have not given themselves seriously to the study of worship. Second, even though musicians and pastors have a joint responsibility in leading worship, these two groups have not been integrated into seminary life. Seminary structures are deficient in this regard! Third, seminarians tend to experience a very restricted modeling of worship in their chapel programs. Seminaries do not have the practical skills of musicians and artists present within their schools to help give concrete expression and modeling to the theological ideas of worship they may affirm.

The curriculum of many seminaries has accorded worship and music an exceedingly low priority. Of the 103 seminaries surveyed in M. R. W. Costen's study (1978), only eight offered degree programs in church music.[13] In theological institutions that *do* offer church music programs or degrees, Wohlgemuth's study (1983) found a "cloudy picture emerges" of nonuniform standards, of "courses taught only in interim sessions that may be cycled every second or third year with no assurance that they will actually be taught."[14]

The personal experience of Robert Webber of Wheaton College echoes Wohlgemuth's findings:

> Unfortunately our evangelical seminaries are not prepared to offer our churches adequate leadership in worship.
> I speak from experience. I graduated from three theological seminaries without taking a course in worship. Even though I was

planning to become a minister, no one ever sat down and said, "Look, worship is one of the most central aspects of your future ministry. Now is the time not only to learn all you can about the subject but also to become a worshiping person so you can offer mature leadership to your congregation." The simple fact is that my seminary professors themselves knew little about the subject. Unfortunately my seminary education left me with the impression that the only important matter in morning worship was the sermon. All else was preliminary. Pick out a couple of hymns. Say a few prayers. Get through the announcements. Let the choir sing. And now, here comes what we all come for—the sermon. I say heresy, bunk, shame! . . .

What is needed within seminary education is a recognition of worship as a legitimate discipline among other disciplines. . . . it is a field of study in its own right. Indeed it is an interdisciplinary study demanding expertise in biblical, historical, and systematic theology as well as the arts, practical expertise, and personal formation.[15]

Though there has been very little accommodation to the teaching and modeling of worship in evangelical seminaries, there seems to be increased interest among pastors in the field.[16] Clearly the hunger to experience integrity and reality in worship and the high value recently placed on it in a growing number of churches has come from pastors and congregations, not from the seminaries. Probably, it will take pressures from these pastors in the field acting as concerned alumni to bring about corrective changes in seminary curriculum and structuring. In the past this is how pastoral care, counseling, and Christian education emphases have found a place in seminaries.

If this analysis accurately describes the "divorce" between seminarians and musicians and the unsatisfactory state of worship instruction and modeling in seminaries today, what was the nature of the temple organization in Old Testament days?

WEDDED!

In the plan that David received from God, the priests and the musicians were wedded together. They were drawn exclusively from one family—the tribe of Levi. Both priests and musicians had prominent roles in the temple services. Both received tithes from the people.[17] They lived together in Levitical towns.[18] They shared a common education, and the structures of their organizations were very similar, as we shall see.

First, let us examine why and how the change from tabernacle to temple worship took place. The differences between temple and tabernacle worship were brought about, it seems, more for sociological than theological reasons. During the wilderness wanderings the Israelites had a semi-nomadic existence and worshiped in a portable sanctuary (the tent). Under David, Israel became a sedentary nation with might and wealth sufficient to erect a permanent temple in Jerusalem. Since Levites were no longer needed to carry the ark and its furnishings, manpower became available for selected Levitical families to devote themselves exclusively to music. Temple worship was similar to tabernacle worship. It retained the entire tabernacle symbolism but expanded and broadened into new areas.

It is interesting that music took on a formalized, institutionalized role in worship precisely when Israel became wealthy. (Institutionalized music and abundant financial resources generally go together.) The religious life of Israel also became centralized in Jerusalem. Three times each year the Israelites were required to attend a festival in that city.

The Scriptures are specific that innovations in the organization of the temple were not David's idea but the Lord's: "All this," David said, "I have in writing from the hand of the LORD upon me, and he gave me understanding in all the details of the plan" (1 Chron. 28:19).

Therefore music in the temple was God's idea. The regulated music and the pilgrimages to the Jerusalem feasts were the main innovations. To get a feeling for how temple worship worked, study 1 and 2 Chronicles, Ezra, and Nehemiah and connect that with the Psalms.[19] The writers of Chronicles, Ezra, and Nehemiah show particular interest in music.

MODULAR ORGANIZATION

If you have assumed that the temple music was performed by musicians living in the Jerusalem area, you are wrong! Only a fraction of the Levitical musicians remained there. The musicians (and priests) were divided into twenty-four groups, most of which resided outside Jerusalem in towns and hamlets scattered throughout Israel.[20] We might call this arrangement in contemporary terms a "modular organization."[21]

Each music group, comprising singers and instrumentalists, had the privilege of performing all week long for two separate weeks in Jerusalem each year. Lots were drawn for performance weeks so each group would be treated fairly and could plan ahead. This meant that on each Sabbath a new group would arrive and the group that had been performing for that week would depart. There was a lot of traffic to and from Jerusalem! There are about fifty weeks in the Jewish calendar year. With twenty-four groups reporting to Jerusalem for two weeks of duty (24 times 2 equals 48 weeks), that accounts for all but two weeks in their calendar year. For the remaining two weeks, all twenty-four groups reported for the three gala Jewish festivals, two of which—the Feast of the Passover and the Feast of Booths—lasted a full week.

It was worked out this way. At the time of Solomon's coronation David selected three extended Levitical families (Asaph, Heman, Jeduthun) to be the temple musicians. He then subdivided these three families into twenty-four courses or groups of singers-instrumentalists. Altogether these groups constituted a force of 4,000 musicians (1 Chron. 23:5), a number probably necessary given the magnitude of the crowds that converged on Jerusalem on festival days. Each group, then, may have numbered about 150 or more people. The heads of the three Levitical families resided (probably year-round) in rooms in the temple and were likely responsible for developing musical materials (liturgy, lyrics, and sound) and supervising and coordinating the entire organization:

> Those who were musicians, heads of Levite families, stayed in the rooms of the temple and were exempt from other duties because they were responsible for the work day and night (1 Chron. 9:33).

The Scriptures also refer to 288 master teachers who were dispersed among the twenty-four groups to tutor their pupils (1 Chron. 25:7–8).

Think for a moment about the Levitical modular structure. What were its assets and liabilities? The liabilities were that it was highly elaborate, expensive, and required much planning and coordination to maintain. A simpler organization could have had one efficient temple choir and orchestra residing in Jerusalem doing all the work. An asset was that since the groups were coming in and out from all Israel, every population sector of Israel had a stake in the music of the temple. The choirs were representative of the people; responsibility was shared.

If all the daily performing had been done by one group stationed in Jerusalem, the musicians might have become complacent, stale, or burned out. But this plan called for a fresh batch of well-rehearsed musicians to arrive each week just itching to have their opportunity to serve. And each group, since it had its own leadership personalities and roster of variously talented individuals, may have had a somewhat unique sound and personality. The people of Jerusalem must have been treated to a highly varied musical diet every week. Moreover, with twenty-four skilled groups available for use in various combinations or summed together for the festival holidays, the national celebrations must have been magnificent.

IDEAS FOR SMALL CHURCH CHOIRS

It's easy to see that it would require a very large church indeed— with a wealth of talent besides—to emulate the temple system. A small church has all it can do to keep one choir going. But small churches want to have an active ministry of music too. What can they do?

The first thing a small church should do is stop trying to imitate big churches. Small churches think, for example, that they *must* have a sanctuary choir that will perform each Sunday to be a bona fide church. Unfortunately many of the people who insist most on this have not sung regularly in a choir, nor have they experienced the effort required to get something of quality ready each week. They simply do not realize how difficult it is to prepare pieces for performance each Sunday, especially when there is only a small pool of musical people from which to draw. Choirs take lots of energy, skill, and human resources to maintain properly. I have met many discouraged, burned-out choir directors who now sit on the sidelines.

Think about it. Do you really want (or can you afford) a struggling choir? Take heart! A number of *options of opportunity* are available to stop you from ever again thinking you are a second-rate church!

Option 1: Make the Congregation Your Choir

The single most important step is to instill in the entire congregation the idea that *they* are your first and foremost choir! Some gigantic churches in California have not formed choirs at all and do well without them. These churches teach the congregation to sing and to understand *their* active role as performers in offering up praise.[22] If you choose this option, work as hard at this as you would a choir. Have the congregational choir practice during the pre-service, even consider teaching them to sing parts. Men and women can divide and sing the rounds, obbligatos, or echo parts found in worship choruses. Carefully select hymns with easy-to-learn alto, tenor, and bass parts and teach them to the choir. For a starter, spend several weeks teaching the men to sing the bass part in "All Hail the Power of Jesus Name" (Diadem tune) in your pre-service time. Start off with the descending passage halfway through and on to the end.

Taking positive steps like these will be a source of limitless blessing to you and your people. Develop your congregational choir whether or not you choose any of the options below.

Option 2: Have Rotating Groups and a Festival Choir

Develop individuals and small groups (duets, trios, quartets, men's and/or women's octet—singing even in unison) and, as in temple days, have these fresh groups perform at regular intervals. Obtain from them a commitment to be part of mounting a choir at festive seasons (Christmas and Easter) for a period of perhaps six weeks. Perform single numbers from your choir cantata or presentation in worship services immediately before and after your presentation date and get more mileage out of the total chorale effort. Then disband the choir and return to small groups (after Christmas and Easter most choirs want a break anyway).

In this manner you obtain some variety each week and yet are able to generate something special on festive occasions when it really counts. Moreover, the individuals in the small groups will be receiving regular training and can become the backbone of a regular choir when the time is ripe to form one.

Option 3: Have the Choir Lead the Congregation

If you now have a small, struggling choir, consider lightening the load for both your leader and choir. Have the choir that sings every Sunday morning be responsible for (1) aiding the congregation in learning new choruses and parts to hymns, and (2) singing anthems.

Prepare a new anthem only every other Sunday. On the alternate Sunday, have the choir help with the congregational response. In integrating the choir into your congregational praise, they will be perceived less as a performing group and more as a ministering and enabling group.

Option 4: Get Your Choir Focused

Here's another way to lighten the load of a small, struggling choir. *Be realistic.* Know your limitations and use them to advantage.

If your choir is small and inexperienced and you have limited practice time, prepare a few pieces well rather than lots of pieces poorly.

Select pieces that are realistically within the reach of your group to perform. If your choir is small, do music that will sound good performed by small groups.

Ron Clarke, a choir director in Vancouver, British Columbia, has been very successful with the following approach. First, he rehearses only one new piece each week and makes it an easy one. The choir works hard at learning that one piece well. He encourages them to "go all out" to have it ready for Sunday. Morale is high because choir members come away from practice with a sense of accomplishment, which the director underscores.

Second, as the Christmas or Easter season nears he repeats the numbers the choir already knows and devotes rehearsals totally to the upcoming special-season music.

Advice for When You Do Start Your Choir

Start an adult choir (which you expect to perform weekly) only when there is a strong call for it, you have good reasons for doing so, and there is a reasonable chance for success. Then go for it! Generally I think you need a congregation of at least 175 regular attenders to draw from, unless you have an abundance of talent or a strong choir tradition (as in Mennonite Brethren churches), but this is not always the case.[23] Be a leader who has an ear to the choristers' spiritual, personal, and social needs. Choir directors in general need to see themselves as functioning more in a pastoral role. Some Catholic churches term their music leaders "pastoral musicians." This name seems insightful. Groom your choir into a caring "subcongregation."

> *My father sang in a choir in a very large church, and he hardly missed a Sunday in thirty years! Choir was a continual inspiration to him, and he'd come home laughing about some incident that happened and humming and singing the songs they'd been rehearsing.*
>
> *Picture a tiny man just five-foot-three with a bald head, a long face, and a fourth-grade education. That was my Dad! He was a kind man with a sense of humor—not at all a pushy or assertive type of person. I can't remember him ever winning any awards or honors, but one day he came home with this "story." (He was in the habit of inventing stories on himself that would have our family howling with laughter.) Around the dinner table he told us that he asked if he could appear before our choir director and the music committee and say a word to them the next time they met.*
>
> *When the day came, my father said to the group, "As you know, I have been standing in our church choir for thirty years now. For thirty years! I wonder if some recognition might be in order—a word of commendation— a present, or something. Think it over—I have been standing in the choir for thirty years."*
>
> *Several weeks passed, Dad said, before the group called him into their meeting. "Mr. Liesch, we appreciate the fact that you have been standing in the choir for thirty years. You may sit down now."*

THE STATUS OF TEMPLE MUSICIANS

What was the status of musicians in the temple hierarchy? They were clearly ranked below the priests but above the ordinary Levites. Old Testament scholar H. L. Ellison has said, "It may be that many Christians do not rank music high enough in the service of God."[24] He said this because there was a close connection between the music function and the prophetic office throughout the Old Testament. For example, Samuel told Saul to go to the hill of God:

[There] you will meet a group of prophets coming down from the high place with harp, tambourine, flute, and a lyre before them, and they will be prophesying. Then the Spirit of the LORD will come upon you mightily, and you shall prophesy with them and be changed into another man (1 Sam. 10:5–6 NASB).[25]

The same book later records a link between music and mental health-therapy, as David assuaged Saul's evil spirit through music:

So Samuel took the horn of oil and anointed him [David] in the presence of his brothers, and from that day on the Spirit of the LORD came upon David in power. . . . Now the Spirit of the LORD had departed from Saul, and an evil spirit from the LORD tormented him. . . . Whenever the spirit from God came upon Saul, David would take his harp and play. Then relief would come to Saul; he would feel better, and the evil spirit would leave him (1 Sam. 16:13–14, 23).

With this background, it is noteworthy that the heads of the three music families appointed by David—Asaph, Heman, and Jeduthun—were all called "seers."[26] The emphasis of "seer" is on revelation by visions—i.e., on seeing.[27] Did musicians have visions? It seems they did. On at least one occasion a musician, Jahaziel, uttered an amazing, detailed prophecy "in the midst of the assembly" and it was fulfilled to the very letter (2 Chron. 20:14–30). Keep in mind also that eleven of the twenty-two occurrences of the word *seer* in the Old Testament are connected with the name of a particular person, indicating his office as a prophet.

Moreover, the Scriptures indicate that the divisions of the Levitical musicians were set apart "to *prophesy* with lyres, harps, and cymbals" (1 Chron. 25:1 NASB). How are the words *prophesy with* here to be interpreted? "Prophesy with lyres" can also be rendered as "prophesy *accompanied* by lyres" (NIV), suggesting that instruments accompanied vocal prophecy, or narrowly as "prophesy *by means of* lyres." Keil and Delitzsch interpret the word *prophesy* in the wider sense of performing in the "power of the Divine Spirit."[28] Curtis and Madsen maintain that in using the term *prophesy*, the writer gives the musician an elevated status: "the chronicler gives the service of song the same dignity as to the service of exhortation, i.e., he ranks the singers with the prophets of Israel, thus placing them above the ordinary serving Levites."[29]

Another reason why the heads of the temple musicians may have been called "seers" is because their inspired psalms were accepted as Scripture and had an exhorting function.

In the temple service the priests' role was nonverbal. For more than a thousand years there were no sermons. Teaching was done in the temple porticos. Even public prayer was at the periphery of the priests' activity. The priests basically led a "soundless worship" of precise liturgical actions related to the sacrificial system, lamplighting, incense offering, and so forth.[30]

The musicians, by contrast, performed both nonverbal (instrumental) and verbal (vocal) worship. The song of the musicians, proclaimed in words, reinforced and gave verbal meaning to the liturgical action of the priests. In short, while the priests did the flaying, the musicians did the playing.

Many of the psalms were composed by skilled poet-musicians under the inspiration of the Holy Spirit and show evidence of being ingeniously crafted. And in being involved in the high-level skills of playing, singing, and composing, musicians were the ones who performed the function of exhortation and praise in the temple service.

Tom Finley has some provocative thoughts in this vein:

> I don't think we pay enough attention to the form in which prophecy has been communicated to us in Scripture. Over half of the prophetic literature is the poetic form, not the narrative. Yet many pastors, it would seem, view the form as a kind of hindrance to meaning. They feel you have to analyze the words, strip away the form, and convert the passage into propositional statements in order to "really" understand it. This question needs more consideration. I also agree with Curtis and Madsen that the singers, according to 1 Chronicles 25:1, are ranked with prophets. And, it is interesting to me that their prophecy is accompanied by a nonverbal art form—instrumental music.

In our culture popular musicians generally have a low reputation— they are viewed as free spirits, drug abusers, and the like. In the Old Testament documents, the temple musicians are portrayed as responsible, conscientious, and intelligent. They were chosen as supervisors in the rebuilding of the walls of Jerusalem (2 Chron. 34:12–13). A son of Asaph was the one chosen to distribute the tithe money because he was "reliable."[31] Hezekiah complimented them for their "good insight" (intelligence) into the temple service (2 Chron. 30:22).[32] On another occasion the Scriptures say the Levites, in the festival preparations, "were more conscientious to consecrate themselves than the priests" (2 Chron. 29:34 NASB). Extrabiblical sources record that during the destruction of the temple of Jerusalem in A.D. 70, as the Roman soldiers scaled the temple walls and stormed the temple grounds, one unrelenting force met another. The musicians refused to abandon their stations; they continued sounding their instruments as soldiers hacked them to bits.[33]

As for the value placed on song in temple worship, Psalm 69:30–31 is provocative. Many of us are familiar with the phrase "to obey is better than to sacrifice," but the Old Testament also says that to praise is better than to sacrifice:

> I will praise God's name in song and glorify him with thanksgiving. This will please the LORD more than an ox, more than a bull with its horns and hoofs.

We who are musicians could well reflect on the excellent modeling set before us by the Levitical musicians.

QUESTIONS FOR THOUGHT AND DISCUSSION

1. Why have Evangelicals been so slow to recognize the importance of corporate worship?
2. What are the assets and liabilities of the Levitical modular structure? What aspects of the Levitical modular structure do you think have relevance today?
3. "Small churches often make the mistake of trying to emulate big churches." Discuss.
4. "The congregation should be the first and foremost choir." Discuss.
5. "Many Christians do not rank music high enough in the service of God." Discuss.
6. Do you think the concept of "instrumental praise" is legitimate? What is your understanding of instruments "prophesying" in the Old Testament?

RECOMMENDED READING

Leaver, Robin A., and James H. Litton, eds. *Duty and Delight: Routley Remembered.* Carol Stream, Ill.: Hope Publishing Co., 1985.

Fortunato, Connie. *Sing to the Lord: A Music Education Program for Adult Choirs.* Elgin, Ill.: David C. Cook, 1984.

Mitchell, R. H. *Ministry and Music.* Philadelphia: Westminster Press, 1978.

Nordin, Dayton W. *How to Organize and Direct the Church Choir.* West Nyack, N.Y.: Parker Publishing Company, 1973.

Schalk, Carl. *The Pastor and the Church Musician: Thoughts on Aspects of a Common Ministry.* St. Louis: Concordia, 1984.

Stapelton, Peter. *New Directions for a Musical Church.* Atlanta: John Knox Press, 1975.

CHAPTER FOURTEEN

Musical Style

OLD TESTAMENT INSTRUMENTATION

Old Testament passages reveal that a wide variety of sound sources were employed in Davidic praise, including the modern equivalent of string, wind, brass, and percussion instruments (2 Sam. 6:5). Nowhere do we find prohibitions on certain instruments. In fact, the emphasis is on inclusiveness: "Let everything that has breath praise the LORD." In the space of a few verses Psalm 150 lists the basic families of instruments found in a modern orchestra—brass (trumpet), wind (flute), strings (harp, lyre), and percussion (tambourine, cymbals).

> Praise him with the sounding of the trumpet,
>   praise him with the harp and lyre,
> praise him with tambourine and dancing,
>   praise him with the strings and flute,
> praise him with the clash of cymbals,
>   praise him with resounding cymbals.
> Let everything that has breath praise the LORD.
> Praise the LORD.

Archaeological evidence indicates that instruments of ancient cultures were similar from culture to culture. The Davidic instruments of praise such as those mentioned above were not culturally unique. Solomon's Egyptian wife included a thousand instruments in her dowry; there is every indication that Hebrew musicians used them and became highly skilled at playing them. In fact, Hebrew musicians acquired such an international reputation for their skill that they were desired in the courts of surrounding nations and were given as compensation in lieu of tribute money. Not until the time of Christ did extrabiblical writings call for restrictions on the composition of Levitical orchestras. For example, where the Old Testament speaks of using cymbals in the plural,[1] the Mishnah limits the temple orchestra to one percussion instrument.[2]

The Role of Choir Directors

How did the choir directors see their role in the temple service? The title of Psalm 39 is suggestive. The Hebrew word translated "for the choir director" (from the psalm's inscription) suggests the idea of a "master of ceremonies or a triumph maker."[3] The "triumph maker" side of the word has the meaning of "to make brilliant, to be illustrious, bright or victorious." It lends further support to an emphasis on transcendent worship. The "master of ceremonies" aspect seems to underline the director's function of not only leading the musicians, but also overseeing the order of service and of directing the congregational response.

Musical instruments seem to play a prominent role in pointing to transcendent worship. We noted in a previous chapter that the musicians were "to prophesy with lyres, harps, and cymbals" (1 Chron. 25:1 NASB). There is no specific mention here of prophesying with voices—with words—though that may be implied. The text may well be expressing that instrumentalists, in their own unique way, are capable of a revelatory function of a sort.[4] Inspired instrumental music is a "language" which can communicate insight. Other Scripture seems to support the idea of instrumental praise in and of itself—i.e., without the necessity for accompanying words (see Ps. 43:4; 147:7).

The Role of Instruments

How did the various instruments function? For one thing, they were used for making "announcements." They were also used by the Hebrews as elegant and evocative ways of communicating to large numbers of people without the intrusion of words that might detract from worship. In brief, the horns were used for signaling and announcing and for music of an exalting nature, the strings for blending with the human voice, and the percussion for signaling and the dance.

Brass Instruments

In the Psalms the trumpet (*chatsotsrah*) and the horn (*shophar*) are employed both separately and together for music of acclamation and praise.[5] The priests (exclusively) used the horn of a wild goat or ram for signaling and announcing new moons and the commencement of a new day, the Sabbath, and festivals. It was considered particularly sacred, had a foghorn-like quality of great carrying power, and also signaled revelations from God (Exod. 19:16–19).[6]

String Instruments

The lyre (*kinnor*) and harp (*nebel*) occur in the immediate context of singing. The lyre had a high, sweet tone (Ps. 81:2). Seven or more lyres were regularly used in accompanying choirs as a kind of guitar choir. The harp was lower in range and had a deeper, richer tone. Both instruments were often used in combination (Ps. 81:2) and were portable for processions.

Percussion Instruments

Percussion instruments attained prominence in Hebrew worship for signaling and for projecting joy in dance. The hand drum (*top, tuppim*) was tapped to movement and the dance.[7] Shakers and cymbals (the Hebrew means "to quiver, to tingle") were also used in worship (2 Sam. 6:5). It is noteworthy that when the Scriptures list cymbals, harps, and lyres together, the cymbals usually head the list.[8]

Percussionists occupied a high position in the Levitical music hierarchy. Asaph, a prominent percussionist, stood at David's "right hand."[9] The three founding fathers of the Levitical musicians were under the authority of the king, not the priests.[10] Of the three, Asaph's name is usually listed first when their names appear together, his family is listed first in the musicians' genealogies, and in the time of Hezekiah and Nehemiah it is his name that is linked in leadership with David's.[11] It is interesting that Asaph, "the chief," played the loud-sounding cymbals in the procession which brought the ark into Jerusalem (1 Chron. 16:5). Asaph may well have signaled and directed the event using the cymbals, and the cymbal player may have often had a prestigious role. Some scholars believe that the presence of the Hebrew word *selah* in some psalms probably originated as a direction for the conductor to sound a clash of the cymbals "to interrupt the chanting."[12]

A major point to bear in mind is that in the Hebrew culture percussion instruments were accepted as bona fide religious instruments. Similarly, in many non-Western cultures today percussion is considered the worship instrument *par excellence*.

Harps Were Like Guitars

Aspects of Hebrew orchestration are still current. For example, we continue to use brass to announce—at least at Easter services—and we still use strings to blend with voices. As for harps, they were a lot like our guitars. When we read about harps in the Scripture we imagine golden-haired women playing large nineteenth-century instruments. But Hebrew harps were relatively small portable instruments one could carry under the arm. In Revelation, too, the twenty-four elders hold harps in their hands.

When people object that guitars are not an appropriate medium for Sunday morning worship, they need to be aware that both the lyre and the harp in the Old Testament were the staples of temple worship and were something like our modern guitar. Actually a guitar often functions better than an acoustic keyboard in the intimacy of small-group worship. It can also serve well for leading large-group worship if it is properly amplified.

Objections to using other percussion instruments in worship appear to be diminishing today. A number of churches are presently using conventional instruments like hand bells effectively, and technical innovations in electronic percussion sounds among contemporary popular and serious musicians are also likely to find their way into worship as a more refined generation of electronic synthesizers gradually becomes commonplace in churches.[13]

THE ISSUE OF STYLE

Did you know that the piano, technically a percussion instrument, was banned by the pope in 1903 as a worship instrument! To many Evangelicals today this decision would doubtlessly seem highly arbitrary, even ludicrous. During the nineteenth century, however, the piano was a secular instrument and was not considered acceptable for church worship.

I think we should admit there is in many of us the same tendency toward rigid categorizing, and in many cases it does not serve us well. Over time, instruments and their uses change. They undergo further physical development and are used in new instrumental combinations and sound environments. Moreover, new playing techniques evolve, and different performers can obtain highly different sounds from the same instrument. A Stradivarius violin, for example, will sound quite different in the hands of a classically trained European virtuoso than in those of an accomplished American Indian musician. Our perception of what a good "Strad" sound should be like might then undergo change. All of which should lead us to be more cautious about condemning an instrument out of hand and make us more open to the worship possibilities of new instruments.

Discrimination in Reverse

Missionary-ethnomusicologist David Osterlund shares a true story that shows how relative and culture-bound our opinions about instrumentation are. He asked a Coptic priest in Ethiopia for permission to perform

Handel's Messiah *in his church with an Ethiopian orchestra of string, brass, and percussion musicians he had gathered together and trained. The priest replied that percussion and brass would be acceptable, "but strings," he said, "absolutely not! Don't you know strings belong in the beer halls, not the church?" David had to have his orchestra perform the oratorio in a theater.*

Isn't this a wonderful example of cultural prejudice in reverse? The saga continues! Students from Kenya tell me that churches there are presently divided over the use of instruments in worship. The younger generation (influenced by nationalism) desire to incorporate traditional African instruments in their worship, while the older generation (influenced by missionaries) view them as pagan and are pressing for singing accompanied by Western instruments or none at all. Similarly, in America I note that Don Hustad indicates he personally can tolerate just about any instrument in church except saxophones.[14] I presume he finds the association of saxophones with dance bands and/or its supposedly "sexy tone" inappropriate. Yet I heard a quartet of saxophones play a Mozart Divertimento for an offertory at the Pasadena Congregational Church that I think would have met with his approval.

The point is that with some imagination and in the right setting and circumstances, almost any objectionable sound can become acceptable. I once taped the baby sounds of our church nursery and let these cooing sounds serve as an accompaniment to the Scripture reading on the birth of Christ during the Christmas season. The effect was magical; the people listened.

I have also used a tape of sounds from a bird aviary as accompaniment for an offertory solo of "This Is My Father's World." I created some birdlike sounds at the piano as well, so the live piano accompaniment would interact with the tape as I sang. These are unconventional sound sources. *I am not saying that we should necessarily seek to dazzle the congregation with innovation at every service. That becomes boring. I believe, rather, we could encourage openness to a wider variety of sound sources in our churches* than the piano and organ—and, isn't it true, occasional surprises add spice to life!

Hebrew Style

The style of music in the Hebrew temple was dramatically different from Western music today in a number of significant ways.[15]

To begin with, there was no harmony in the sense we know it: heterophony (melodic embellishing of the tune) prevailed. Harmony developed in Western civilization gradually from A.D. 1000 to 1600.[16]

It is also likely that Hebrew scales were fundamentally different from ours.[17] There was no music notation as we now know it; that evolved somewhere around 1350 to 1500.

The Hebrew music tradition was probably more oral and less written than ours. Therefore memorization and internalization of the materials through repetition was a necessity.

The Hebrews did not have rhythmic meters like ours. Their rhythmic style was closely related to the natural pattern of constantly varying accents inherent in the Hebrew language. Our music tends toward regular pulses of either two or three beats, and our music lyrics are made to conform to this pattern.

But the parallelism of phrases is a pervasive feature of Hebrew poetry. Consequently, antiphonal responses and the stationing of choirs to enhance antiphonal responses seemed to have been basic developments.[18]

Tradition: An Ongoing, Ever-renewing Process

If the music style employed by the ancient Hebrews differed so greatly from ours and was acceptable to God, we must beware imposing or elevating any one style as intrinsically better for worship than that of a different age group or a different culture.

It is easy for tensions over the acceptability of various styles to develop, but we need to form bridges of understanding toward one another. One way to do that is to adopt the perspective of a missionary who attempts to understand, accommodate, and communicate within his adopted culture.[19]

We have many subcultures in North America today, one of which is Evangelicalism. And there are pronounced subcultures represented within Evangelicalism itself, even among age groups in local churches. If a music culture in a local church becomes ossified and impervious to change while the culture surrounding the church is in dynamic transition, the future of that church is in peril. The nonchurched (and probably the majority of the young people) will feel that their style of worship is not relevant or functional for them.

> *Noted missiologist Alan R. Tippett related to me a missionary experience from the Fiji Islands. He said that in the 1840s some missionaries who had real insight into the Fiji language paraphrased Wesley's hymn lyrics into Fijian and invited the people to chant them in their own pentatonic scales and idioms. He said the project met with success. Later on, in the 1880s another group of missionaries arrived on the scene and insisted that standard Western rhythms and tunes be sung with the Wesleyian lyrics. This change was never well received by the people— the tunes and rhythm felt strange to them.*

We live in a dynamic, changing culture. Styles change. What speaks to one generation may not readily speak to another. One way to solve this problem is to think of *tradition as an ongoing, ever-renewing process.* [20] That is, a local church has a history, a tradition that needs to be respected, yet those traditions need to be adapted and reevaluated in the light of present needs.

We have something of this emphasis in the Psalms. The various texts of the Psalms span approximately a thousand years. There are psalms from Mosaic, Davidic, and postexilic days, yet we find there a frequent call to sing a "new song" to the Lord.[21] Each generation is called to make its faith real and relevant. Musicians of all centuries have now set the Psalms to music, be it in Gregorian chant melody, Baroque harmonies, or Romantic chromaticism. The rub for us today comes when a young person plays our beloved hymn tune with a rock-style accompaniment. Ouch! Instead of cringing in horror, we could try to see in this response a valuable attempt at integration. And, it may happen that some hymns in fact lend themselves to this kind of accompaniment!

Jamaican Rumba

When I was about twenty years old, a friend, pianist Mel Bowker, taught me how to play the Jamaican rumba. My brother Don and I came up with a clarinet-piano arrangement that used this beat in the gospel song "There's a New Song in My Heart." We played it in an evening service during the offering—and it stunned our people. It hit them like a harpoon. There was life and movement in the piece. They were so mesmerized they ignored the offering plates. Our pastor, noticing this, said, "Pass the plates a second time!" Everyone laughed.

After the service an elderly lady expressed her appreciation to us: "Boys, that song of yours was just WONDERFUL! It was so lively! I could feel the joy of the Lord in you. You boys are a constant blessing to us." I am glad she felt this way, because there was joy in us. And her affirmation of us was genuinely appreciated. My brother and I have always felt greatly beloved by our people. Silently though, I said to myself, "Ma'am, a lot of that 'joy of the Lord' you are experiencing is the rumba." Fortunately I had enough sense to keep my mouth shut; I could have extinguished her joy. I used that rhythmic pattern a lot in the sixties, but kept mum about its source in Latin American dance. As a result, I encountered absolutely no problems.

The point I am trying to make is that it is often the *associations* people have with a certain musical style or sound that makes it unacceptable to them. It is something like the problem of personal conscience and meat sacrificed to idols described in 1 Corinthians 8. If people are unaware of the associations, they often have no problem. For another example, the earlier music of John W. Peterson can be traced back stylistically to jazz roots. But most Evangelicals don't recognize this relationship, so it doesn't bother them.

Look to the Lyrics

The issue of style is difficult and complex. For this reason I am disturbed when people sound off that a certain beat is "of the devil" or a particular rhythm is "satanic." It is not that simple. People who make general statements like this do not know what they are talking about. I like the basic approach of Al Menconi to questions concerned parents ask him about rock music.[22] Since the Bible does not say much about style, he counsels parents to sit down with their children and *examine together (line by line) the philosophy behind the lyrics.* Lyrics are easier to talk about. Passages can be identified that explicitly support or go against the Christian value system. *This way the issue is not so much the music style, but the philosophy of life advocated.* Using that standard, would Frank Sinatra's "I Did It My Way" be any better than the latest song on the hit parade? We must be careful of double standards.

Menconi advises parents to accept Christian contemporary music that has strong texts. This is an excellent start. To be sure, values are imbedded in music styles themselves, but this is an area most parents do not have the expertise to talk about coherently. We *are* more readily equipped to discuss the meaning of words.

Faith, Craftsmanship, Commitment

Consider the words of Harold Best, dean of the Wheaton Conservatory of Music, regarding music style in worship:

> I am no more impressed with group "x" preferring great music than I am appalled by group "y" preferring bad music, as long as both are stretching and yearning for the unexpected. Taste by itself, no matter the refinement of its preference, is useless. If God senses faith at work, faith which makes us creatively discontent and free of conditioned reflexes, He smiles, whatever the supposed level of achievement *at the time.* And the important words are *at the time,* because he ever expects us to be on the move. The question to us is not, "What have you achieved?" The question is, "What is your next move?" Only when we are in this restless attitude is the Spirit free to work a newness.[23]

Frank E. Gaebelein wrote:

> Where there is integrity, honest craftsmanship, and devoted cultivation of talent, there something of truth may break through.[24]

"Faith," "integrity," "honest craftsmanship," "devoted cultivation of talent"—these qualities, I believe, were offered on the day of the dedication of the temple:

> And when the priests came forth . . . and all the Levitical singers . . . with cymbals, harps, and lyres . . . and with them one hundred and twenty priests blowing the trumpets in unison, . . . they lifted up their voice accompanied by trumpets and cymbals and instruments of music, and when they praised the LORD saying, "He indeed is good for His lovingkindness is everlasting," then the house, the house of the LORD, was filled with a cloud, so that the priests could not stand to minister because of the cloud, for the glory of the LORD filled the house of God (2 Chron. 5:11–14 NASB).

There we have it! Faith, craftsmanship, commitment, and the crowning factor, the presence of the Lord.

QUESTIONS FOR THOUGHT AND DISCUSSION

1. What is your response to the fact that the piano was banned by the pope as a worship instrument in 1903, that harps in the Old Testament were similar in size and sound to guitars, and that in Ethiopia strings belong in the beer halls?
2. "Let everything that has breath praise the LORD"— platitude or operational directive for worship in the Old Testament? In what ways does Old Testament worship model inclusive praise?
3. The inscription to Psalm 39 can be interpreted "triumph maker." What does this term connote to you?
4. What do you think of the concept of instrumental praise?
5. What are your thoughts about using electronic instruments in worship? (Consider also the quality of these instruments and their cost effectiveness and flexibility.)
6. What was the style of music like in the Old Testament?
7. What is your concept of "tradition"? What is the Old Testament concept of tradition?
8. "If God senses faith at work, faith which makes us creatively discontent and free of conditioned reflexes, He smiles, whatever the supposed level of achievement *at the time*." Discuss.
9. "Where there is integrity, honest craftsmanship, and devoted cultivation of talent, there something of truth may break through." Discuss.

RECOMMENDED READING

Johansson, Calvin M. *Music and Ministry: A Biblical Counterpoint*. Peabody, Mass.: Hendrickson Publishers, 1984.

Lawhead, Steve. *Rock Reconsidered: A Christian Looks at Contemporary Music.* Downers Grove, Ill.: InterVarsity Press, 1981.
Leafblad, Bruce. *Music, Worship, and the Ministry of the Church.* Portland, Oreg.: Western Conservative Baptist Seminary, 1978.
Niebuhr, H. Richard. *Christ and Culture.* New York: Harper and Row, 1975.
Ryken, Leland. *Culture in Christian Perspective: A Door to Understanding and Enjoying the Arts.* Portland, Oreg.: Multnomah Press, 1986.
Werner, Eric. *The Sacred Bridge: The Interdependence of Liturgy and Music in Synagogue and Church During the First Millennium.* New York: Harper and Row, 1956.

CHAPTER FIFTEEN

Movement in Worship

It is abundantly clear . . . from the Bible, from Talmudic literature, and from historical and ethnic studies that sacred dance was a normal and intimate part of everyday Jewish life.[1]

"GLORY TRAIN"

How should a fundamentalist missionary couple respond when movement and dance form a natural part of the culture where they serve? Paul and Becky Warnock, graduates of the Biola University Music Department, recently received their assignment to Kenya with the Daystar missionary organization. In a letter back home Paul tells his parents what occurred while he and a group of Africans from three countries were selecting hymns for a songbook of indigenous music:[2]

There are about fifteen of us, mostly Africans. . . . Each group has an assignment to dig up songs. . . . The group looks at the songs, and if they're worth pursuing, they write out the words and the chords. Then all the groups get together for more weeding out. A group sings the songs with guitars. If there is applause, the song is approved. There is a lot of discussion about many of the songs. . . . It takes quite a bit of energy to listen to so many songs. [The group listened to literally hundreds of them.] When we get too tired, we have the glory train. That's when we get up and dance in a circle to a song called "Glory Train." . . . After a bit of that you feel refreshed again.

Dad, there's a little [Ugandan] dance I wanted to share with you. . . . It's not done to a song, but more of a chant. (You can insert it nicely between verses of a song though.) Here are the words and the rhythm:

```
   Q    E    E    E    E         E
||: MY FEET HAVE GOT A  MESS-  AGE,
   *    *         *          *
```

```
     E      E      E      E      E  E           Q
THEY ARE FILLED  WITH  JOY AND  PRAISE:‖
     *            *            *          *
```

[Q = quarter note; E = eighth note]

You can repeat it over and over. At the asterisks you do some kind of movement with your feet. You might jump up with both feet. You might kick one foot out. You can jump on one foot, or kick backwards. Or try jumping so that your body is turning in a circle. You can do all kinds of things with it. If you are leading a group, they watch and do whatever you do, and never know what to expect. You get a very free feeling doing this. I tried it once in a Daystar chapel. I felt very nervous about it. . . . After I taught it to them, I told them that any time during the song singing I might break into it, and they would have to follow whether it came between songs or not. I think people enjoyed it, and it got everyone involved.

A few weeks ago at church, they asked the people who were all visiting from one of the sister churches to come and sing a song. Their special song was sung to drum accompaniment and the whole group of them dancing together. We were right there on the front row and could have touched them.

From the letter we see that Paul and Becky are assimilating their new culture. One of the contact points is dance. Many Evangelicals need to understand that dance—perhaps better termed "movement"—is a natural means of expression, as normal for many people as breathing. As singing is sustained talking, so dancing is sustained movement. Was dance an acceptable form of expression in the Old and New Testaments?

DANCE IN HEBREW LIFE AND SOCIETY

A study of the Scriptures, the Talmud, and other historical and ethnic literature makes clear "that sacred dance was a normal and intimate part of everyday Jewish life."[3] The sort of religious-secular distinction common to Western society did not exist in Jewish culture. Dance and religion were intimately related. Dance was predominantly communal and was rarely an end in itself. It functioned variously as a means of expressing heartfelt praise and thanksgiving, of celebrating a visitor or commemorating a historic or religious event, of welcoming home a loved one, of celebrating a harvest or feast, or of wooing and courting.[4]

The chart below lists the references to dance in the Bible.[5]

As these examples indicate, dance (like music) was associated with *both godly and ungodly* activities. That being the case, Evangelicals—with a tradition of opposition to dance—would do well to explore further the *positive* uses of dance in Scripture.

Favorable References to Dance in Scripture

Exodus 15:20	Deliverance from the Red Sea
Judges 11:34	Jephthah's return
1 Samuel 18:6	David's victorious return
1 Samuel 21:11	David praised in music and dance
1 Samuel 29:5	David's victorious return
2 Samuel 6:14	David dances before the ark
1 Chronicles 15:29	David dances before the ark
Job 21:11	Children singing and dancing
Psalm 30:11	Weeping and wailing/dancing and rejoicing
Psalm 149:3	Praise Him in the dance
Psalm 150:4	Praise Him in the dance
Ecclesiastes 3:4	Time to dance
Song of Songs 6:13	Wedding dance
Jeremiah 31:4	Joyful dance
Jeremiah 31:13	Maidens will dance and be glad
Lamentations 5:15	Dancing turned to mourning
Luke 15:25	Dancing at return of Prodigal Son

Unfavorable References to Dance in Scripture

Exodus 32:19	Worship of the golden calf
Judges 21:21	Women of Shiloh (?)
1 Kings 18:26	Worship of Baal
Matthew 14:6, Mark 6:22	Dance of daughter of Herodias
Matthew 11:17, Luke 7:32	We played the flute for you (?)

OLD TESTAMENT DANCE ASSOCIATED WITH JOY

Old Testament dance offers an instinctive means of expressing joy. For example, when the pursuing Egyptian army was destroyed in the Red Sea, Miriam danced "to the Lord":

> Then Miriam the prophetess, Aaron's sister, took a tambourine in her hand, and all the women followed her, with tambourines and dancing. Miriam sang to them: "Sing to the LORD for he is highly exalted. The horse and its rider he has hurled into the sea" (Exod. 15:20–21).

Similarly, when David foresaw the potential of the ark to bring unity to the northern and southern kingdoms, he was overwhelmed with joy. As the ark was being carried in procession into Jerusalem, he began leaping and dancing (publicly) with all his might "before the Lord" (2 Sam. 6:14–16). As for dance in structured worship, the people in the temple were told that God "takes pleasure" in them. Accordingly, the order was given to dance to Him as if sacred dance were a normal feature of praise:

> Let them praise His name with dancing;
> Let them sing praises to Him with timbrel and lyre.
> For the LORD takes pleasure in His people.
> (Ps. 149:3–4 NASB)

> Praise Him with timbrel and dancing. . . .
> Let everything that has breath praise the LORD.
> (Ps. 150:4–6 NASB)

The reference in Psalm 149 comes close to being a "command" to dance. The same imperative connected with *singing* to the Lord is applied to *dancing* to the Lord! The inescapable inference is that God delights in His people as they dance to Him. Similarly, in the story of the Prodigal Son in the New Testament, Jesus does not depict the father as a "kill-joy." "Music and dancing" formed part and parcel of the party the father threw in celebration of his son's return. Joy and dancing go together in the Scriptures.

GREEK DUALISM: A FALSE DICHOTOMY

Apparently many Evangelicals today do not believe dance can in any way, shape, or form bring pleasure to God. Where did we get this notion? Certainly not from Scripture! How did this attitude toward dance become established?

Many of our ideas about dance and the human body today have roots in large measure in ancient Greek philosophy. One line of Greek philosophers—from Pythagoras (died 497 B.C.) and Plato (died 347 B.C.) to Plotinus (died A.D. 270)—thought of the body as bad and as having a negative impact on the soul. In their dualistic thinking, Greek philosophers viewed the body as separate and antithetical to the soul. The body was considered a "barrier or impediment to seeing the true world":

> Death was seen as the happy release from the *prison-house or tomb* of the body. Much of this disparagement—indeed almost hatred—of the body was absorbed into Christianity as it sought to come to terms with the thought world of the Graeco-Roman culture.[6]

Affirming this dualism with the greatest clarity, the Greek philosopher Plotinus spoke of the soul as "deeply infected with the taint of the body," as being immersed in "filth" and daubed with the "mud" of the body. He said:

The soul is *evil* by being interfused with the body and by coming to share the body's states and to think the body's thoughts.[7]

The nature of the body, in that it partakes of matter, is *an evil thing* . . . *a hindrance* to the soul in its proper act.[8]

Many early church fathers, including Augustine, resisted this idea intellectually, yet it still had a powerful hold on them emotionally. The reactions of the early fathers were absorbed by the Catholic church and the Reformers, who in turn passed them on to us. The disparagement of the body appears to be a uniquely Western phenomenon.

THE BIBLICAL VIEW OF THE BODY

What, however, is the biblical view of the body and the soul? Quite different! Scripture depicts the flesh as *yearning for God* and as *singing for joy* to God:

My soul thirsts for Thee, my flesh yearns for Thee, in a dry and weary land (Ps. 63:1 NASB).

My soul longed and even yearned for the courts of the LORD ; My heart and my flesh sing for joy to the living God (Ps. 84:2 NASB).

In the Old Testament the term *flesh* can be a synonym for *soul*. The Hebrew does not have a term for *body*, but rather speaks of the *flesh*.[9] There was no strict dividing line between flesh and soul, no distinct "bits" or "parts" that together made up the person.[10] The Old Testament affirms the following, according to J. G. Davies:

Life is one and allows of no separation between the material and the spiritual as basic forms of existence. One cannot speak of soul and body being united: body is soul in its outwardness and soul is body in its inwardness. . . . I do not have a soul and body: I am soul/body.[11]

The same divergence from Greek dualism is expressed in the New Testament. The terms *soul* and *flesh* continue to be interchangeable and can stand for the whole person.[12] The Greek word for "body" (*sōma*) signifies the spiritual as well as the material with no suggestion that the body is inferior:

Present your bodies as a living sacrifice (Rom. 12:1 RSV).

The body is not for immorality, but for the Lord; and the Lord is for the body (1 Cor. 6:13 NASB).

Your bodies are members of Christ (1 Cor. 6:15 NASB).

You are the body of Christ and individually members of it (1 Cor. 12:27 RSV).

It is sown a natural body, it is raised a spiritual body (1 Cor. 15:44).

The apostle Paul, however, does use the word for "flesh" (*sarx*) in a disparaging way. Because of this, some have mistakenly assumed that Christianity is "anti-body." This misunderstanding has resulted because people have taken verses in isolation (not in context) and have failed to appreciate that for Paul, *sarx* has more than one meaning.[13] Paul uses *sarx* to refer variously to the whole person, the material body, or the lower nature:[14]

Whole person:	"By the works of the Law shall no flesh be justified" (Gal. 2:16).
Human materiality:	". . . that the life of Jesus may be manifested in our mortal flesh" (2 Cor. 4:11).
Lower nature:	"Do not turn your freedom into an opportunity for the flesh" (Gal. 5:13).
	"For since there is jealousy and strife among you, are you not fleshly" (1 Cor. 3:3).

Notice that Paul uses *sarx* (flesh) for psychological sins such as jealousy and strife (1 Cor. 3:3). Clearly *sarx* is not equated here with literal flesh![15] When Paul links carnality with the flesh, he is characterizing the whole person as fallen—not the body as evil.

J. Hastings summarizes Paul's teaching on the flesh and the spirit:

St. Paul's doctrine of man is firmly rooted in the soul of the Old Testament teaching and anything like the great dualistic antithesis between body and soul was far from his thoughts. For him, as for other Old Testament writers, the psychophysical unit of the person was the fundamental feature in the conception of man.[16]

The clinching argument for the legitimacy of using the body in worship, however, must rest on the incarnation of Jesus Christ:

In all true worship there is a living link between heaven and earth, sacred and secular, spirit and flesh—the link is Jesus Christ.[17]

THE EARLY CHURCH FATHERS AND DANCE

J. G. Davies contends that the early church rejected dance "not so much of its own volition but because it endorsed the opinions of the educated class of the day."[18] He says, "It was not so much Christianity that turned people against dance; culturally it was already despised by the educated, Christian or not."[19]

Thus the negative approach to dance was "more a product of Western culture than of Christianity per se."[20] At root was the familiar problem of bad associations. On the one hand, "striptease" and indecency had become a "regular" feature of dance in pagan religions of the day and in society in general; on the other, asceticism was fast developing within the church. As a result of these two extremes, "the journey of the soul," Davies says, "was conceived as a never-ending war with the flesh."[21]

CRITERIA FOR INCLUDING DANCE IN WORSHIP

Out of this discussion the question arises, "If dance is to assume a place in public worship today, what criteria should it meet?" J. G. Davies answers, "Whether or not liturgical dance proves acceptable, despite its novelty, will depend upon an affirmative answer to two questions: first, is this new element intelligible to the Christian community? second, is it valuable for its life?"[22] In other words, like any other ministry in the church, sacred dance must have meaning to the people and be regarded by them as providing a valuable contribution. Moreover, it should not be an intrusion, a filler, or an external gimmick to enliven the service. Sacred dance performers must see themselves as offering an act of worship:

> . . . when dancing in a church, he or she must be aware that they are being invited to contribute to an event in which God is encountered. . . . a place where God can be met; if the dancing aids that meeting, its integration with worship has been achieved.[23]

Martin Blogg lists additional criteria for sacred dance performance, criteria that could be applied to other art forms as well:

> Does it glorify God?
> Is there due reverence, fear and awe at the root of the dance?
> Is the dance and dancing God-centered or man-centered?
> Does it build up the church body? Or is it foreign and unintelligible?
> Are the fruits of the Spirit in evidence?
> Are we behaving decently and orderly?
> Is the dancer in control of herself or himself?
> Does it involve a proper balance of mind, body and heart?
> Am I upstaging the Word?
> Does it submit to judgment?[24]

Of the last criterion, Blogg says:

> [The liturgical dance group] must be prepared to submit to the authority and responsibility of the church body . . . be answerable to some body outside itself. It must, above all, be looked after by a mature and committed group of Christians.[25]

Dancers must be willing to submit to church authority. But those in authority, such as the pastor and the elders, should also be open to hearing what Christians working in the arts have to say. I have known of a number of situations in which the artists whose ministries were affected were not even given a chance to make their case. It is important to keep the lines of communication open.

In our constantly changing culture, art involves some risk-taking, and Christian artists inevitably open themselves to criticism. At such times those lines of communications are invaluable. Church leaders who understand what their artists are trying to do can defend their artists and educate their people as to *why* they are taking those risks. I want to underscore the point that the church leadership needs to be an informed one if it is to be effective in supporting the artists.

WHAT SACRED DANCE CAN CONTRIBUTE TO THE CHURCH BODY

With all this in mind, I would like to give an expert in Christian dance an opportunity to tell us what contribution he believes sacred dance can make to the church body. (For those who have never been involved in any form of dance, it is very difficult to conceive what value dance might have.) Martin Blogg, senior lecturer in dance and the performing arts at Middlesex Polytechnic and a director of Christian Dance Ministries in Britain, offers this perspective.

1. *Sacred dance is therapeutic.*

> When dance and music are combined, we have a very special therapy for many of the ineffable sicknesses and tirednesses of the soul. . . . Time and time again, I have gone into the dance "sick" and come out "healed"—physically, intellectually, emotionally, and socially. . . . "Dance is like a swim, it refreshes and cleanses."[26]

> Dance has the power to renew, to enliven and to enable people to shake off disappointments. It is so because through movement spiritual energy may be released, emotional tensions eased, the rigidity of daily existence loosened.[27]

2. *Sacred dance effectively expresses the feeling side of worship.*

> Dance is probably at its most efficient and effective when concerned with the emotional/feeling aspect of reality.[28]

> All human feelings and emotions are valid legitimate concerns within worship. The performing arts generally, but dance and music specifically, can accommodate such heartfelt expressions.[29]

3. *Sacred dance is an integrative form of expression.*

> Dance . . . is an integrating factor; it enables the spiritual and physical aspects of human nature to interact, to become one, so that the spiritual is enfleshed and the fleshly is transfigured and we

become whole because we are involved as whole persons. The physical is not denied in favour of the spiritual nor vice versa.[30]

. . . is there any other form of expression which involves our whole self—intellectual, physical, social, emotional, and spiritual—in such a comprehensive way as dance? . . . Most expressive forms are based upon extensions of the body. The instrument of expression in dance *is* the body. We *are* the body.[31]

4. *Sacred dance is another "way of knowing."* Now Blogg touches the heart of his case. He suggests there are different ways of knowing:

Knowing "that"—is propositional knowledge; knowledge *about* the faith and *about* dance.

Knowing "how"—is practical or procedural knowledge in relation to the faith and dance.

Knowing "of"—is knowledge by acquaintance which refers to the existential, the inner, heartfelt and ineffable nature of knowledge.[32]

No one knowledge form is sufficient to cover all man's thinking and feeling. . . . no one knowledge form has exclusive right to truth.[33]

Dance relates most strongly to "knowing of":

. . . some kinds of truth have to be lived into and not just thought into. . . . You may read the Bible to know certain facts but this is only the beginning. Your real aim is to know Christ.[34]

[Dance functions and really comes into its own] by giving expression to the ineffable, the mystical and unutterable. Dance is essentially a language of the heart and the spirit. Through this non-verbal and non-rational (note: *not* rational) "language" we are able to come to know and express that which is beyond the everyday verbal and rational. Although dance is rooted in theoretical ("that") and practical ("how") knowledge, it is a unique means to knowledge "of" the inner psyche—the heart and spirit.[35]

Blogg quotes David Watson:

There are many forms of communication between the believer and God; silence, "sighs too deep for words," intelligible words, songs, shouts, movement, dance, and so on. When my spirit wants to worship God or pray to Him, a wide variety of meaningful expressions may be called upon.[36]

5. *Sacred dance is a visual art form to which non-churchgoers are receptive.* Having been extensively involved in presenting the gospel through the medium of dance in high school assemblies, Blogg speaks of the effectiveness of the dance medium as a form of communication:

The work by Christian performing arts groups within schools has been little less than spectacular in spreading the gospel.[37]

When I go into a comprehensive school in East London, my problem is not the Word, but how to express and communicate it. This can be done in a wide variety of ways, and in a society dominated by the visual media, it may be that visual communication has an important part to play.[38]

[Within the current media] there is less need to rely exclusively on verbal symbols to communicate the awareness of God.[39]

Dance may be categorized as a "low definition medium" that demands "a higher degree of audience participation," since more is left to the viewer's imagination. On the other hand, propositional communication may be regarded as a "high definition medium" where the audience is more a passive receptor of information that is stated explicitly.[40]

DANCE: CLEAN OR UNCLEAN?

The same insensitivity found in communication within churches afflicts relationships between churches. I often hear statements like this: "Have you heard what they're doing down the street? They're dancing in the aisles . . . hanging from the rafters!" Now that I'm older, I ask my informants whether they've seen any of this. If I have time, I try to visit these churches. Often I don't see anything approaching the rumors circulating. Why do you think there's sniping without hard evidence? Do you suppose we're putting others down to build ourselves up?

This practice is particularly destructive in our pluralistic culture. In the Greater Los Angeles area, for example, eighty-five languages are spoken.[41] Given this enormous cultural diversity, can we realistically expect every church to dot every *i* and cross every *t* the way we do? We face a tremendous challenge in the days ahead in learning to distinguish what is cultural and stylistic from what is fundamental and binding. People from a variety of religious and cultural backgrounds are joining evangelical ranks. Will we be able to assimilate them and keep them assimilated in our local church cultures? Will we have a kind word for the church down the road that is able to integrate into its body some people that we might not be able to retain? We face a tremendous challenge in learning to tolerate cultural diversity, yet hold firmly to the fundamentals.

Movement and dance in worship relate directly to church culture. Talk to recently converted Catholics and try to persuade them that dance is bad—they'll look at you as if you are from the moon! Talk to black people about movement and worship—they can't imagine worship without it! Talk to converted Jews about dance—they will tell you that structured circle dances and the like are a natural part of their culture.

We smile with easy approval upon hearing of Africans dancing to the Lord, but when it comes to granting someone permission to do the same in our own backyard, that's a different matter. Yet attitudes toward dance among Evangelicals are rapidly changing as large numbers of young couples are discovering their bodies in fitness classes involving dance aerobics. Also, the advent of modern dance, with its emphasis on abstract form and "pure" movement, has provided a model much more suited to liturgical assimilation than older forms such as ballet. Thus it has made Christian dance "much more of a feasible option than ever before."[42]

THE BIBLICAL CONCEPT: SOPHISTICATED!

Biblical concepts relating to cultural questions like dance are not at all simplistic. Scripture tolerates logical inconsistencies in people: dance and movement in worship might be "right" for some people and "wrong" for others. There is nothing in Scripture that indicates dance in worship is mandatory. Scripture wisely and sensitively considers factors such as "personal conscience" (1 Cor. 8:13; 10:25). The Bible cautions people against violating their conscience. Given this condition, Blogg properly stresses that education is vital (something the apostle Paul understood):

> As dance propagators, we have to recognize sensitively and lovingly that for many, dance is not helpful within the context of worship. We must accommodate this fact and also, educate our brothers and sisters. . . . When we have done this and have reached the point where all can be built up by the dance in worship, then we have a right and proper foundation from which to dance.[43]

> When today we accept or reject dance, let us consider carefully this point: nothing is unclean in itself; for the religious man, everything comes from God and is good. What makes dance unclean or clean is that which comes from our hearts. The New Testament particularly is very clear on this point.[44]

> . . . while it is true that nothing is unclean in itself, if it is unclean for a Christian brother or sister, then initially at least, we must carefully consider what we are doing. However right dance is in itself, and right for us Christian dancers, if it is a stumbling block for others, if it undermines the faith. . .the dance is wrong. . .out of respect for the faith and the fellowship, [we must] recognize that for some dance is "unclean." We must also recognize that dance within worship is never an end in itself, but always a means to worship. Worship must be our first priority.[45]

> Let me reiterate on what is "clean" and "unclean" in dance. The dance itself, its steps, postures and gestures, are neither clean nor unclean in themselves. I sometimes receive letters asking for "religious steps!" There is no such thing. . . . It is our hearts which make a dance clean or unclean (Matthew 15).[46]

The following story told by Blogg reveals much integrity under the most trying circumstances. Both the dancers and the church leadership are to be commended:

The sacred dance company Springs [a group Blogg founded and directed] grew out of a famous city church in London. The church loved us, prayed for us, taught us and looked after our general spiritual wellbeing. They gave us all that we needed as members of the church body and yet, during the four years that we were church members, we never once danced in worship. We were all fully trained, professional dancers with a unique commitment to propagating dance and the Christian faith within the Church generally, education and community, both in this country and abroad. And yet we never danced within our own church worship. It was out of that church's love and respect for us as members of the church body that they encouraged us in every possible way—except by allowing us to dance within worship. It was out of our love and respect for the church body that we accepted this decision of the elders. Both sides made every effort to keep the unity of the spirit in the bond of peace.[47]

TAKING BABY STEPS: CONGREGATIONAL MOVEMENT PIECES

As you may have realized, this chapter is really an extension of Davidic praise. If you desire to open up your congregation (and yourself!) to the idea of using some movement in worship, choruses with accompanying movement are a good place to begin.[48]

Choruses that appeal to both children and adults are especially helpful in easing the transition. Adults will join in heartily for the sake of their children. The truth is, however, that in doing so, adults themselves are learning to be childlike and free again. I've included four choruses that you can try with movements.

"He Loves Me"

In all my experiences the first tune, "He Loves Me," and its accompanying movements have been favorably received, even in the most conservative, fundamentalist churches. The song's simple but profound message poignantly ministers to adults. Introduce it at an evening service first, if your church has one, and then in the morning.

Teach the tune first, then perform the following actions whenever these words or syllables occur:

HE	Point up.
LOVES	Cross arms hugging chest.
ME	Point to chest.
JE-	Point right index finger in palm of left hand.
SUS	Same, but reverse hands.

(Pointing the index finger in the palm of the hand is sign language for the name "Jesus.")

For variation, substitute the word *me* with *you* and point to a person in the audience.

He loves me, He loves me; Je-sus loves me. He loves me, He loves me; Je-sus loves me.

"We Have Come Into His House"

(Words and music by Bruce Ballinger)
(Choreography by Dorie Mattson, June 1987)

Another worship chorus that has been used effectively with structured movement is "We Have Come Into His House."[49] This chorus and the two that follow it use more elaborate movements. Have the congregation learn the words and melody first (take at least two Sundays). Then introduce hand movements. The first time through, have the congregation sing the tune as someone demonstrates the hand movements. Then have the leader or choir sing the tune while the congregation imitates the movements. Finally, invite the congregation to sing and do movements at the same time. Allowing all to do structured movement together relieves apprehension over it.

Codes for Congregational Movement

(rt = right hand; lt = left hand; DSR = down stage right;
DSL = down stage left)

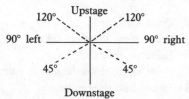

WE HAVE COME INTO HIS HOUSE AND GATHERED IN HIS NAME TO WORSHIP HIM	Slowly raise rt arm to 120°, palm facing up, focus up.
WE HAVE COME INTO HIS HOUSE AND GATHERED IN HIS NAME TO WORSHIP HIM	Slowly raise lt arm to 120°, palm up, focus up.
WE HAVE COME INTO HIS HOUSE AND GATHERED IN HIS NAME	Open arms to sides, palms facing forward.
TO WORSHIP CHRIST THE LORD	Raise both arms directly in front of body 120°, palms facing up, focus up.
WORSHIP HIM	Clasp hands in prayer position over head.
JESUS CHRIST THE LORD	Gently bring hands in front of heart, head bows.

"Holy, Holy, Holy Is the Lord of Hosts"

(Isaiah 6:3; tune by Nolene Prince)[50]
(Choreography by Dorie Mattson, October 1985)
(Copyright © 1976. All rights reserved. Used by permission.)

HOLY, HOLY, HOLY	Raise rt arm to 120°, palm upward.
IS THE LORD OF HOSTS	Bring rt hand over heart.
HOLY, HOLY, HOLY	Raise lt arm to 120°, palm upward.
IS THE LORD OF HOSTS	Bring lt hand over heart.
THE WHOLE EARTH IS FULL OF HIS	Circle arms to sides, then front, palms upward.
GLORY	Put hands in prayer position, bring them into chest.
THE WHOLE EARTH IS FULL OF HIS GLORY	Repeat above movement.
THE WHOLE EARTH IS FULL OF HIS GLORY	Repeat above movement.
HOLY IS THE LORD	Bring arms to second position, palms upward.

"I Will Bless the Lord"

(Words and music by Frank Hernandez)
(Choreography by Dorie Mattson, October 1985)
(Copyright © 1981 by Candle Co. BMI. Used by permission.)

Use the same procedure to introduce this chorus as the last one. Ask the congregation to try to imagine God's blessing raining down on them on the words "the Lord is gracious and merciful."

The tempo should be slow. A liberal use of sevenths in the music accompaniment will help convey a sense of softness and graciousness. (If the organist finds the sevenths "too thick," omit them). The key of F pitches the tune low and helps promote a restful feeling.

I   Extend rt arm front to 90°, palm upward.

WILL   Extend lt arm front to 90°, palm upward.

BLESS THE LORD	Clasp hands in prayer, but don't intertwine fingers.
AND GIVE HIM	Slowly bring arms to sides, palms forward, then raise to 90°.
GLORY	Raise arms to high V.
O	Swiftly lower arms to sides.
I	Extend lt arm front to 90°, palm upward.
WILL	Extend lt arm front 90°, palm upward.
BLESS HIS NAME	Bring hands together clasped in prayer, but fingers not intertwined
AND GIVE HIM	Slowly bring arms to sides, palms forward then raise to 90°.
GLORY	Raise hands to high V.
THE LORD IS GRACIOUS AND MERCIFUL	Slowly lower arms to sides, palms facing sides of body.
GREAT IN KINDNESS	Extend rt DSR arms to 90°, palms upward.
AND GOOD TO ALL	Extend lt DSL arms to 90°, palms upward.
THE LORD IS RIGHTEOUS	Bring arms parallel in front, palms upward.
ALL HIS WAYS	Bring palms in near chest, still facing upward.
BLESS THE LORD	Clasp hands in prayer.
AND GIVE HIM PRAISE	Bring arms to sides, palms upward.
(Repeat)	
(Ending)	
AND GIVE HIM	Raise arms to 90°, palms upward.
GLORY	Raise arms to high V.
AND GIVE HIM	Hands clasped in prayer.
GLORY	Look upward.

CHRISTIAN ARTIST TAKES A RISK

Having studied with the finest dance instructors in America, Jackie Coffey, a professional dancer and choreographer from a Catholic-Hispanic background, found Christ as Savior while intensely involved in performing-choreographing in the Los Angeles-Hollywood scene. While Jackie was still a new Christian, Kurt Kaiser, who was interested in having someone create dance choreography for a musical he had written, heard of her. Arrangements were made for them to meet. "When he arrived," she told me, "I had no idea who he was. He sat down at the piano and began playing to me as if I were the person next door. I was really impressed with the humility of the man."

The musical, Jackie learned, was to be premiered before several thousand people at the national convention of the Christian Booksellers Association in Anaheim, California. Jackie agreed to create the choreography and prepare the dancers for performance.

Work was proceeding nicely with twelve Christian dancers when she received a long-distance phone call. Kurt was on the line from Texas, and he sounded apprehensive. From the conversation she became aware for the first time of the tremendous risk he was taking in including dance with his musical to an audience consisting of a wide sampling of Christian denominations with a strong conservative element present—especially since he would be unable to review her work until a day before the performance. Sensing he was stepping out on a limb, she suggested, "Why don't we go ahead? But when you get here, I will give you complete authority to cut anything or everything." He agreed.

Jackie's troubles were just beginning. Her faith and that of the dancers was about to be severely tested. For most of the professional dancers it was their first involvement in a specifically Christian production. They wanted to do it, but it was also the summer of the Olympic Games in Los Angeles, and the strongest dancers were offered other jobs that were a real allurement—especially since they had no guarantee the sacred dance would take place. Everyone was forced to reevaluate their commitment. "We struggled for six weeks to hold to a strenuous rehearsal schedule," she told me, "and make each rehearsal an act of worship, knowing full well any or all of the dance could be cut."

The day preceding the premier performance arrived. In a prior rehearsal the group had experienced a wonderful sense of God's presence as they danced through the entire production. Now they met to read and meditate on the words of the musical, have a time of prayer, and hear Kurt's verdict. During the time of extensive prayer the dancers were greatly moved and expressed to one another that it no longer mattered to them whether they performed publicly or not. They had already offered their best privately to the Lord, and He had received it.

Jackie said, "After prayer we were all together waiting for Kurt to arrive and make a decision. He then appeared; he asked us to pray with him. While praying he began to weep. Then after a time he got up—'I don't need to see it,' he said. 'Let's go do it!' "

In introducing the musical to the large audience at the premiere,

Kurt read the dance passage from Psalm 150. The musical was a great success, and the dance was extremely well received. But very few people knew what had gone on behind the scenes.

I phoned Kurt to verify this story. "Are the details right?" I asked.

"You've told it accurately," he said. "I was tremendously moved. . . . The tragedy of Christian communication is that once these dancers become Christians, there is nothing for them to do. What they did at Anaheim enhanced my piece unbelievably! A one-dimensional work became three-dimensional. And they did it in such good taste—it was incredible. Everybody loved it. It opened my eyes! . . .

"I didn't realize the dancers were suffering so much. Their discipline really moved me. There is something to be said for discipline. I saw their flat bellies. They were doing stretching exercises a full hour-and-a-half before the choir arrived, and praying together, and reading over the text. . . . The experience was one of the highlights of my life. . . .

"I have another story that might interest you," Kurt went on. "Some time ago Word Records did an album with Carol Lawrence. She probably dances even better than she sings. On the album we wrote an arrangement of the Shaker tune, 'Simple Gift,' with thirty-two measures of music in the middle that she could dance to in concert. I saw her sing and dance it. Turning to Don Hustad at my side, I asked him, 'What do you think of that?' He said to me, 'Kurt, we may never see anything more beautiful this side of heaven.' "

QUESTIONS FOR THOUGHT AND DISCUSSION

1. What thoughts and feelings did this chapter generate in you?
2. If a skilled or professional dancer were to join your church, do you think that person would be allowed to contribute through dance to the worship at your church? If this were allowed, what kinds of questions and reactions would this act evoke? How would you respond then?
3. What have you learned from this chapter?
4. Have you personally seen any form of sacred dance? What was your reaction?
5. Do you agree that the biblical view in relation to culture is "sophisticated"? Why or why not?
6. Are all dance steps "neutral"?
7. Dance is a "low definition medium." Explain.

RECOMMENDED READING

Blogg, Martin. *Dance and the Christian Faith—Dance: a Form of Knowing.*
London: Hodder and Stoughton, 1985.
Davies, J. G. *Liturgical Dance: An Historical, Theological and Practical Handbook.*
London: SCM, 1984.
Edwards, Brian, H. *Shall We Dance? Dance and Drama in Worship.* Welwyn,
England: Evangelical Press, 1984.
Fisk, Margaret. *The Art of the Rhythmic Choir.* New York: Harper, 1950.

CHAPTER SIXTEEN

Celebrating Festivals

In the best of the churches, the leaders have created, over a period of several generations, a rich tapestry of symbols, parables, folk sayings, favorite expressions, beliefs, legends, stories, rituals, customs, and festivals which reinforce the feeling that indeed this is a unique congregation. By contrast, the weak churches are swathed in layers of gray cloth—ready for their funeral.[1]

Question. What do these have in common: Billy Graham crusades, denominational conferences, Christian conference grounds and family camps, interdenominational sunrise services and praise meetings, contemporary concerts, and choir festivals?

Answer. They are contemporary, Christian counterparts of the Hebrew festivals.

Question. What functions do they serve?

Answer. They serve a variety of needs and functions quite similar to Hebrew pilgrim festivals presented in the Old Testament.

For example, Christian camps and family conference grounds are vacation centers that foster family togetherness and personal sanctuary and retreat. They are places of inspiration, fellowship, teaching, and education. They also have a pilgrimage aspect to them: people leave their familiar surroundings, enjoy one another as they journey together in cars or buses, and experience a new environment for an extended period of time.

A church denomination, on the other hand, is like a tribe. The psalmist describes the Hebrew festivals as "where the tribes go up" (Ps. 122:4). Various regional and national denominational meetings are like tribal convocations where different strains of the church body are called back to their distinctives, reminded of their roots and history, and challenged toward new directions. They are times of refreshing, of renewing friendships, of celebration, of enlarging one's vision. These are important functions.

City-wide evangelistic crusades, Billy Graham crusades, and the like are a little different. They are times when tribes meet together, disregarding differences for the sake of witness to the world and focusing on what they have in common. All the tribes are briefly unified, the stadium becomes the "temple," and, viewing the assembled masses, they experience firsthand what it is like to be a part of the greater body of Christ. We are not alone but are partakers of something very big and important. We learn what it means to cooperate with other believers and see God work through that. We become conscious of being part of the ever-enlarging, swiftly flowing river of God.

CALENDAR HOLIDAY WORSHIP IN THE LOCAL CHURCH

Three annual pilgrim festivals shaped Hebrew life and gave it a distinctly spiritual cast: the Passover (April), the Feast of Weeks (late May/early June), and the Feast of Tabernacles (October). The festivals of our North American culture—both those with Christian origins and the secular ones—give shape to our lives too, and we have come to observe many of them in our churches. Often we don't even know why we observe one and not another. As Christians we should think about the festivals we observe and make conscious decisions about which ones are important for our church.

Several issues are involved. There is first of all the issue of how to handle secular holidays. Do we want to incorporate elements of the secular calendar like Memorial Day and Mother's Day, or do we want to keep only Christian holidays?

The answer to that question may be affected by the kind of church we are trying to be. For example, churches that see their Sunday morning services as a part of their evangelistic outreach often like to emphasize cultural holidays as a way of relating to the unchurched. Others, involved in "side door" rather than "front door" evangelism, limit special holiday emphases so that continuity can be given to systematic teaching of the Word from the pulpit. Missionary-minded churches elevate the importance of their missions conference. In the church in which I was reared, the greatest emphasis in the entire year was given to the missionary conference.

Bear in mind that you can have only a few prominent emphases in a church. You will be tempted to try to celebrate everything. Select the holidays and special observances that fit best with the church's vision for ministry.

During the Middle Ages the church calendar year became clogged with such a multitude of saint's days that the festivals capable of carrying the greatest theological weight—Christmas, Easter, Pentecost—were lost in the maze. Some of the Reformers reacted to this by dropping everything. John Calvin, for example, eliminated the entire church year. Other Protestants followed suit, and in the sixteenth century the Puritans rejected even Christmas as a festival day. As a result, evangelical churches today in the main tend to observe liturgical festival days with a minimum of pageantry.

In fact, in our time secular holidays like Independence Day and Mother's Day generally receive more emphasis in our churches than festival days like Pentecost, a day with momentous theological significance.[2] If I could encourage you to think about just one festival, however, this would be the one. The coming of the Holy Spirit must rank as the single most important historic event in the New Testament subsequent to Jesus' ascension (another neglected holiday).

It is possible to opt for a simplified church year that reinforces the events that really matter—the birth, death, and resurrection of Jesus, and the giving of the Holy Spirit—without becoming encumbered by a host of unessential occasions. A simplified liturgical year, an unfamiliar though valuable concept, deserves a second look by Evangelicals.

By observing the liturgical year people can feel the weight of the major events over a broader space of time.[3] Each year becomes a spiritual pilgrimage, and the historical reality of the events comes home with greater force.

During the Christmas season there is the cycle of light that comprises Advent, Christmas, and Epiphany. Advent (which begins four Sundays before Christmas) focuses on messianic prophecies, while Epiphany (in early January) marks the visitation of the wise men and represents Christ as the Light to the Gentiles. During the spring season there is the cycle of life (Lent, Easter, and Pentecost). Lent is a preparation period for Easter that begins on Ash Wednesday, forty days before Easter, while Pentecost, which occurs seven weeks after Easter, marks the ascension of Christ, the giving of the Holy Spirit, and the birthday of the Christian church. In November there is Thanksgiving.

If a full liturgical calendar is more than your church would want to take on, at least consider doing something special to mark four points in the year—Christmas, Easter, Pentecost, and Thanksgiving. These four days can be used to proclaim foundational theological truths and reinforce core values. In any case, we are not proposing an elaborate grid of special days of the kind Paul decries (Gal. 4:10).

HEBREW CALENDAR WORSHIP

On the three pilgrim festivals of the Hebrews, people came from far and near to present themselves at Jerusalem. These festivals were the Passover (our Easter), the Feast of Weeks (our Pentecost), and the Feast of Tabernacles (our Thanksgiving). In other words, there is a close link between a simplified Christian liturgical year and the Hebrew festivals that emphasizes continuity between the Old and New Testaments.

	April	Late May/ Early June	Oct/Nov
OT Festivals	Passover	Feast of Weeks	Feast of Tabernacles
Church Holidays	Easter Sunday	Pentecost Sunday	Thanksgiving Sunday

Of the three festivals, the Passover and the Feast of Tabernacles were family events that lasted seven days and functioned as a retreat, a vacation time, rest, and a time to refocus and regain perspective. They provided the people with a memorable, inspirational, celebratory, large-group worship experience. They also served an educational purpose: the Passover, for example, rehearsed the history of the Exodus, tapped children into their historical roots and identity, and reinforced values. They served to keep the people unified.

We now want to focus on one of these festivals, the Feast of Tabernacles. What can we learn from this Hebrew festival and the festivals in general? We can learn something about the importance of rejoicing.[4]

For a couple of years my family and I had the privilege of serving in a small, struggling church. It was going through a time of transition, and there were many difficult problems to address. Some of the older people who were wonderful, longtime supporters were very set in their ways. Consequently we did not have much flexibility. I can remember saying to myself, "My, this is really hard work." Having grown up in a large church, I had not realized how difficult life could be in a small church. We desperately needed a break. I found that our congregation benefited tremendously from participating in a large denominational conference. We had an opportunity there to gain a new perspective, to leave behind our own church culture and celebrate with other believers. It was health to our weary bones. These thoughts, therefore, are born out of my own personal experience.

There are times when it is right to celebrate. To celebrate requires three things:

First it demands that we know how to live—to act, to experience, to love. Next, it requires awareness—thinking back over an experience, assessing it, judging it, evaluating it. The third requirement is the foremost one—the ability to share, or to turn private reflections into public awareness of them.[5]

We need times of celebration, and we should participate whole-heartedly, confident of the Lord's approval. We read in Acts 20:16 that Paul made an effort to get to Jerusalem in time to celebrate the Feast of Pentecost. In the Old Testament the Hebrews were called (really "commanded") to celebrate the festivals by the Lord Himself—"you shall celebrate."[6] Since our culture is markedly different from theirs, we can also be stretched by pondering the ways in which they rejoiced.

THE FEAST OF TABERNACLES

The Feast of Tabernacles is often referred to under two other names: the Feast of Booths and the Feast of Ingathering. Moreover, when the Old Testament refers to just "the Feast" without specification, the Feast of Tabernacles is meant:

> When you have gathered in the crops of the land, you shall celebrate *the feast* of the LORD for seven days (Lev. 23:39 NASB).

The Feast of Tabernacles was the last feast of the year, the longest, the most joyous, and the best attended. At one time it was considered the greatest of the Jewish festivals. It was the culmination of the High Holy Days following shortly after the Day of Atonement. More Scriptures refer to it than to any other feast. The dedication of Solomon's temple and the second temple in Ezra and Nehemiah's era were timed to coincide with it. The feast is also uniquely distinctive in that an unfulfilled prophecy indicates it will again assume international significance in future days:

> Then the survivors from all the nations that have attacked Jerusalem will go up year after year to worship the King, the LORD Almighty, and to celebrate the Feast of Tabernacles. If any of the peoples of the earth do not go up to Jerusalem . . . they will have no rain (Zech. 14:16–17).

At the time of Christ thousands upon thousands of Jews from all parts of Palestine and Egypt and Asia Minor and across the sea in Greece made a pilgrimage to attend this festival at Jerusalem in October.

The Gathering People

Along the trails resound the songs of pilgrims wending their way to observe the great festival. One leads a goat, another an ox, a third a sheep to offer to God at the sanctuary. There they will recite prayers and sing hymns and dance in religious processions about the altar. Knowing robbers infest the countrysides, Jews from far-off countries travel in caravans, for they bring their tithes with them. Speaking many dialects, they come from many lands, but they are brethren and children of Abraham, and for all of them Jerusalem is the Holy City. Ascending to Jerusalem while singing the Hallel with ever-enlarging throngs ("that is where the tribes go up, the tribes of the Lord, to praise the name of the Lord"), the pilgrims catch first sight of the temple, its gold plates and white marble glistening in the sun. Some fathers with their sons tour the perimeter of the temple examining each gate. And in the swarming crowds and throbbing life in the city one can meet Jews from every corner of the earth, and on the streets learn firsthand their present lot and hopes for the future.[7]

Nothing But Joy

The Feast of Tabernacles *was* uniquely the feast of joy. Three times in the Law the people were enjoined to rejoice during this festival:

"You shall *rejoice* before the LORD your God for seven days" (Lev. 23:40 NASB).

"You shall *rejoice* in your feast" (Deut. 16:14 NASB).

"You shall have *nothing but joy*" (Deut. 16:15 Goodman).[8]

Why? Because the crops from the fields and orchards, especially the grapes from the vineyards, had been harvested and gathered indoors, and atonement for sin had already been made on the Day of Atonement just days earlier. So the people naturally had a mind to celebrate. It was the merriest time of the year.

According to the command of Moses they were to construct and dwell in booths for seven days and celebrate by waving branches:

Mark, on the fifteenth day of the seventh month, when you have gathered in the yield of your land, you shall observe the festival of the Lord [to last] seven days: a complete rest on the first day, and a complete rest on the eighth day [the days in between were semi-holidays]. On the first day you shall take the foliage of goodly trees, branches of palm trees, boughs of leafy trees, and willows of the brook, and you shall rejoice before the Lord your God for seven days. You shall observe it as a festival of the Lord for seven days in the year; you shall observe it in the seventh month as a law for all time, throughout the generations. You shall live in booths for seven days; all citizens in Israel [foreigners were invited] shall live in booths, in order that future generations may know that I made the Israelite people live in booths when I brought them out of the land of Egypt, I the Lord your God (Lev. 23:39–44 Goodman).[9]

The booths were to serve as a reminder that their forefathers were exposed to the elements and hardships of the wilderness for forty years. Eric Routley has termed this "the feast of insecurity." The Hebrews were not to become complacent in the security of their now well-furnished houses and say in their hearts, "My power and the strength of my hands have produced this wealth for me" (Deut. 8:17). Tradition says they were to construct booths with enough spaces in the thatches so they could feel the wind blowing through and see the stars shining at night.

They also had branch-waving ceremonies (symbolizing the fruits of the harvest) in which the entire family (especially children) were required to hold and wave—something like Palm Sunday. Psalm 118:19–29 suggests a procession that began outside the gates of Jerusalem and ended at the altar:

> The LORD is God, and he has made his light shine upon us. With boughs in hand, join in the festal procession up to the horns of the altar (v. 27).

The Mishnah says the people walked around the altar with willow branches seven times on the seventh day of the festival[10] and waved the branches when they recited, "Give thanks to the LORD" (v. 1) and "O LORD, save us" (v. 25). They used Psalm 118, one of the Hallel group (Pss. 113–18), at each of the three great festivals. Having memorized it in their educational studies, everyone knew it.

Torch Dancing in the Night

By the time of Christ the Feast of Tabernacles had developed and become rich in parades and ceremonies.[11] In addition to the trumpet blast at daybreak, the morning sacrifice, the special sacrifices offered all day long by the pilgrims, the Bible teaching in the temple porticos, and the water pouring ceremony, there was a torch dance in the evening that took place in the Court of Women. According to the Mishnah, this is what the torch dance was like:[12]

> *Three balconies were erected from which the women and children could witness the event. Arranged in a diamond configuration were four great golden menorahs (seven-branched candlesticks) set on bases that were seventy-five feet high. The branches terminated in huge cups into which oil was poured. Ladders were placed on each base, and children watched as priests mounted them, and poured in enough oil to last until daybreak. The light was of such intensity that all Jerusalem was lit up.*
>
> *As the light flared higher and higher, men gathered in the court bearing torches in their hands, and they danced, waving their torches, throwing them high into the air, and catching them again. On the fifteen steps that led from the Court of Women to the Court of Laymen stood Levites accompanying the dance with guitar-like lyres, cymbals, flutes, and trumpets and singing the Hallel psalms. Some of them sang, "Lift up your hands in the sanctuary and praise the LORD" (Ps. 134:2). It was said that "he who has not seen the rejoicing at this ceremony has never seen rejoicing in his life."[13]*

The four menorahs must have looked somewhat like the Olympic flame, and the whole event may have had something of the festive feeling of our Independence Day and fireworks shows. What is also striking about this happening, drawn from the Mishnah, is the combination of lamplighting, dancing, and juggling with Levitically endorsed instrumental and vocal music-making. It is an integrative art form that had the support of the temple leaders. I doubt, however, that many Evangelicals would have been comfortable with the combination of such disparate elements—especially as an accompaniment to Scripture texts! It gives us insight into their culture.

The primary point, nonetheless, is that celebration was a central feature of Hebrew culture and that it was a response to a call to celebrate that came directly from the Lord. Are Christmas, Easter, and Pentecost of any less significance? Of any less worth? Pastors, artists, musicians, worship leaders, let's do our part to see that Christian holidays are remembered!

FOUR CONTEMPORARY APPLICATIONS

Idea 1: A Christmas Parade. John F. White tells of a festival project in which God gives three men in Winnipeg, Canada, a vision of awakening their entire city to the true message of Christmas:

> They envisioned a parade in which floats would simultaneously portray the prophetic and historical incidents surrounding the birth of Christ, and the witness of Christians joyfully celebrating them. It would not be evangelism but *pre-evangelism*—a prior straightening of the facts. The floats would be professionally designed, and the parade would wind up with a mass celebration in the Winnipeg Convention Centre.[14]

White explains in some detail the hurdles they had to overcome to bring this vision to fruition. Not everyone is prepared to undertake something of this magnitude. An alternative might be to provide the impetus for a "carol" choir festival. Whether it involves a parade, a choir festival, one church, two churches, or tens of participating churches—if you are led to do it, do it!

Idea 2: A Thanksgiving Block Party. Did you know that the Pilgrim fathers got the idea of the American thanksgiving feast from the Feast of Tabernacles in the Scriptures? It's true! They too wanted to express their thankfulness to God after their crops had been gathered and safely stored in barns. In fact, the Puritans had the bold vision of creating a Christian theocracy on North American soil. That goal failed, but their idea of celebrating in thanksgiving caught on and has been retained to this day. Yet many Americans are not aware of this connection.

At our church we thought Thanksgiving Eve would be an excellent time to retell this story and to attempt at the same time a low-key outreach project in our neighborhoods using our home groups. We invited our neighbors to a "block party" at a home where we regularly meet for praise, prayer, and Bible study each week. Several people from the church dressed up as Pilgrims and "crashed" the party that was in progress for children and adults. They put on a short dramatic vignette that gave everyone the feeling of Pilgrim life. They then communicated to us that when the Pilgrims read in the Bible of people celebrating and expressing thankfulness to God after their crops were gathered, they wanted to do something similar. That was the beginning of the American Thanksgiving holiday.

After finishing their presentation, the drama troupe continued on their way, performing for the other small groups meeting that evening while our group sang, ate, and socialized.

Idea 3: A Small-Group Thanksgiving Ceremony. Divide the church into small groups that meet in several homes the evening before Thanksgiving. Have a sign-up sheet ahead of time. The committee can provide some music leadership and a simple format. Here are some possible ideas: (1) sing hymns and choruses, (2) have people light candles and share a thanksgiving blessing, (3) have a pouring ceremony (fill a glass with water until it overflows as a symbol of overflowing blessings), (4) take Communion together, or (5) have a collection bag at the door so that those who wish may give to World Vision, Food for the Hungry, or some other Christian relief agency. Through repeated experiences like this, fathers and mothers who feel inadequate in a leadership role might be encouraged as they see other parents model leadership in a family context. A father could close in a prayer of thanksgiving.

Idea 4: A Pentecost Reenactment. On Pentecost Sunday during the church service we had people representing Peter and two other disciples come down the aisle dressed in traditional garb and act out the the scene in Acts 2:5–42. The person playing Peter memorized the sermon (vv. 14–36), turned around, and preached (recited) it to the awe-struck congregation! The choir and other readers were involved in the preliminary narrative (vv. 1–13) before Peter came on the scene, and in the group responses at the end (vv. 40–47). A few Scripture lines here and there were cut to make the presentation flow better. Try it!

CONCLUSION

To conclude, we need to be reminded of the statement by Lyle E. Schaller:

> In the best of the churches, the leaders have created, over a period of several generations, a rich tapestry of symbols, parables, folk sayings, favorite expressions, beliefs, legends, stories, rituals, customs, and festivals which reinforce the feeling that indeed this is a unique congregation. By contrast, the weak churches are swathed in layers of gray cloth—ready for their funeral.[15]

QUESTIONS FOR THOUGHT AND DISCUSSION

1. Is it worth it to expend the effort required to mount something special on holidays at your church? Explain?
2. Where do you want to place your emphasis as a church? How much do you want to adapt to secular culture (secular calendar) or retain uniquely Christian distinctives (the church calendar)? What needs and functions are served by each for you?
3. What do you think of the analogy of church denominations to the "tribes" of Israel? Is it a good one? Why or why not?
4. Describe the range of activities the Hebrews performed in their festivals. How can this serve as a model for us today?
5. Do we often imagine God as a "kill-joy"? Do you have trouble accepting that God wants you to celebrate and experience joy?
6. If you were to apply one idea from this chapter, what would it be?

RECOMMENDED READING

Bailey, Robert W. *New Ways in Christian Worship*. Nashville: Broadman Press, 1981. See especially the worship formats toward the back of the book.

Goodman, Philip. *The Sukkot and Simhat Torah Anthology*. Philadelphia: Jewish Publication Society of America, 1973.

Zimmerman, Martha. *Celebrate the Feasts*. Minneapolis: Bethany House, 1981. (Excellent ideas for Christian, family celebrations.)

PART V

Revelation Worship

CHAPTER SEVENTEEN

Our Heaven on Earth

> You have not come to . . . darkness, gloom and storm. . . . You have come to thousands upon thousands of angels in joyful assembly (Heb. 12:18–22).

The model of worship in the Book of Revelation is my favorite, and it continues to give me much to think about. I see it as timeless, overarching, comprehensive, and "architectonic."[1] Revelation worship is the culminating model of worship. It boggles the mind. It is new, yet old; it is revolutionary, yet offers continuity with the past. It has none of the racial particularity of the Old Testament. Thoroughly Christian and inclusive, Revelation balances proclamation through words with proclamation through symbols. Revelation strikes for the jugular vein. In the compass of a short space, it penetrates to the root of things, to the elemental, central, and foundational. I believe it holds the key to all the models.

Revelation worship existed before the earth was formed and will continue into the future. Revelation worship serves as a review of all the previous chapters, yet develops beyond them. And Revelation is the only book in the New Testament where we get a picture of large-group, Christian worship in action.[2]

REVELATION GIVES US A MODEL FOR WORSHIP

Although the Book of Revelation has been studied avidly as a book of prophecy, what it says about worship has been widely neglected. Yet at least fourteen of the twenty-two chapters deal with worship. Worship is depicted as going on unceasingly before the throne. It is not an "interlude" between a sequence of dramatic scenes, as some have termed it.[3] The reverse is true.

In the deeper structure of the book, revelatory events themselves are the interludes that break up the practice of continuous worship before the throne of God. Moreover, worship in the last days becomes a strategic issue. The book unveils overall a cataclysmic conflict being waged across the expanse of heaven and earth as to *who* is to be worshiped, Satan the Deceiver or the Lord God. In addition, it contains pertinent information about *how* God is to be worshiped. Revelation 4 and 5, for example, provide the most detailed description in Scripture of the style, structure, and design of a single worship event.

The Book of Revelation is highly relevant to today's worship.[4] Indeed, it furnishes *a viable model* against which our own worship can be compared and challenged.[5] In this chapter we look at practical ways to duplicate the heavenly worship of Revelation in a contemporary church setting. As we seek to imitate what we find there, we will search for the underlying principles, which are binding. The particular details can only be suggestive, not mandatory.

In reality it would be impossible to model our corporate worship *in toto* on the worship in Revelation. First, we on earth have to attend to teaching and evangelism more than the heavenly company. Our teaching, though, could be the kind that leads to worship, the ultimate goal, as Revelation shows. More preachers could so lift up Christ and extol the person and acts of our heavenly Father that people feel cause to worship (respond) during the course of the sermon. Second, we do not have the visible presence of God and His throne to bow down before. This ensures that Revelation worship (with God at the center) will be unrivaled. Third, our new resurrected bodies may allow for a heightened perception and performance of worship. These are substantial, critical differences. For all this, we can still identify aspects of real correspondence.

This is possible partly because Revelation projects worship in ways that have precise meaning to our earthly frame of reference. Worship elements are cast in anthropomorphic terms with which we can identify. We read of God seated at His throne, of elders wearing crowns and falling prostrate, of white raiment and golden sashes, of palm branches, of a wedding supper, of thunder, lightning, hail, torches, trumpets, harps, of hair white as snow and eyes that burn like a blazing fire.

THE CONFIRMING FUNCTION OF REVELATION WORSHIP

Worship ideas in Revelation are not just for the future, because Revelation worship *confirms* that practices we employ now are biblical. Let me enlarge on this idea by citing several specific confirmations often overlooked.

1. Priesthood of Believers Confirmed

Revelation sets forth the concept of the priesthood of believers in both the letter to the churches (1:6) and in the body of the heavenly vision. The words of Peter that believers make up a "holy priesthood" (1 Peter 2:5, 9) are confirmed, for *all* the redeemed in heaven are priests:

> . . . with your blood you [Jesus] purchased men for God from every tribe and language and people and nation. You have made them to be a kingdom and priests to serve our God (Rev. 5:9–10)

In the heavenly temple no veil blocks us from God's presence; we are in (not outside) the worship space (5:9–13). Everyone offers praise. Worship in Revelation is thoroughly corporate and genuinely congregational and should be viewed against the New Testament backdrop of Pauline and synagogue worship, which is also thoroughly congregational.[6] What a difference this understanding could have made to the development of liturgy in the Roman Catholic Church from the fifth century through the Middle Ages if this principle had been observed! Unfortunately, the priests in large part did the work of praise while the people observed.[7]

Notice too that the people are "inside." In the temple at the time of Christ, worshipers were "outside": "When the time for the burning of incense came, all the assembled worshipers were praying outside" (Luke 1:10)—but in the heavenly temple of Revelation we see the altar with four horns not outside in the courtyard, but within the space "before God" (9:13).

2. Worship of Jesus Christ Confirmed

Gerhard Delling observes that "the giving of thanks" was never applied to Jesus in the Jewish or gentile church—only Revelation ascribes blessing to the Lamb (5:12).[8] Prayer is addressed to Jesus Christ in Revelation, in the custom followed in our churches today (22:17). Worship poems are directly addressed to Jesus Christ in Revelation (5:12; 7:10). And the two times John starts to worship some lesser being (19:10; 22:8), an angel tells him not to.

3. Vocal and Instrumental Music Confirmed

The Gospels and the Epistles make no reference to instrumental music in worship, but in Revelation the four creatures, the twenty-four elders, and those victorious over the beast receive harps to play. John hears the sound of their music (Rev. 5:8; 14:2).

4. Principle of Costly Worship Confirmed

Particularly noteworthy in the light of rewards granted is the value placed on costly worship. Worshipers who come out of the Great Tribulation have the privilege of being positioned nearer the throne and of serving day and night within the temple (7:14–15). ("Serving" here probably means "worshiping.")[9] Worship becomes their exalted and exclusive occupation. Similarly, the 144,000 have the honor of singing their unique song before the throne and of being in close relationship with the Lamb wherever He goes (14:1–4). Costly worship is specifically linked with the ultimate sacrifice of martyrdom (implied in 15:2).[10]

5. Worship as Response Confirmed

Revelation worship confirms with great clarity what students of worship have learned elsewhere from the Scriptures. *In the framework of worship, the pattern of action and response is basic.* God initiates action and the people respond. For example, the action of taking the scroll (5:9), breaking the seal (8:1), sounding the seventh trumpet (11:15), and throwing Satan to earth (12:10) are all followed by response. Also, as a direct result of the sealing of the 144,000 the response of worship occurs (7:10).

Further, the responses of the 144,000 (14:1), those from the Great Tribulation (7:10), and those victorious over the beast (15:3) are recognized. These groups are responding to God's redemptive work, to the elevated status He has conferred on them, and to His faithfulness in having brought them through fiery tribulation.[11]

Especially conclusive, chapters 18 and 19 contain the announcement of Babylon's overthrow and the people's overwhelming response to that news. A voice gathers and prompts congregational response:

> "Praise our God,
>   all you his servants,
>   you who fear him,
>   both small and great!" (19:5).

Then, "like the roar of rushing waters and like loud peals of thunder," the multitude shouts its response:

> "Hallelujah!
>   For our Lord God Almighty reigns.
>   Let us rejoice and be glad
>   and give him glory!" (19:6–7).[12]

The passage takes on the feeling and verve of Old Testament Davidic praise! The word *hallelujah* occurs four times in the space of six verses in chapter 19 and nowhere else in the New Testament or the Book of Revelation. Moreover, the act of prompting response constitutes a precedent for worship leaders to elicit congregational response here and now. (Be encouraged and take confidence.) If heaven's worshipers need prompters, how much more do earthly worshipers! Notice also, however, the brevity and the dignity of the prompting.

Response is also repeatedly underlined and punctuated in Revelation by corporate *amens*.[13] The Greek word for "amen" occurs more than 125 times in the New Testament, 99 from the mouth of Jesus. Worshipers used it commonly in Jewish synagogues and the early Christian church. Robert Coleman says "amen" means to affirm "that which is certain or reliable, that which can be trusted without question. . . . By saying amen, one not only expressed agreement with the statement of another, but also made it binding on himself."[14] He adds:

> Jesus often introduced His own words with the word *amen* or "truly, I say to you" (e.g., Matt. 6:2, 5, 16; 8:10; 10:23; 19:28; 24:34; 25:40), sometimes even doubling the amen (e.g., John 1:51; 3:3, 5, 11; 5:19). Such self-affirmation of the truthfulness of His message was a majestic expression of His authority. Amen may be found in other New Testament writings at the close of prayers and doxologies, strengthening their force (Rom. 1:25; 9:5; 11:36; 16:27; Gal. 1:5; Eph. 3:21; Phil. 4:20; Heb. 13:21). In its highest form, the word is used of Christ Himself (Rev. 3:14) which echoes Isaiah's reference to the God of the Amen, or truth (Isa. 65:16). Of course, when one thinks of the inspired Word, he realizes that all the promises of God in Christ ". . . are yes; wherefore also by Him is our Amen" (2 Cor. 1:20).[15]

The corporate *Amen* is a resource that Scripture uses imaginatively and we can learn to use effectively.

THE SCENE: REVELATION 4 AND 5

At once I was in the Spirit, and there before me was a throne in heaven with someone sitting on it. And the one who sat there had the appearance of jasper and carnelian. A rainbow, resembling an emerald, encircled the throne. Surrounding the throne were twenty-four other thrones, and seated on them were twenty-four elders. They were dressed in white and had crowns of gold on their heads. From the throne came flashes of lightning, rumblings and peals of thunder. Before the throne, seven lamps were blazing. These are the seven spirits of God. Also before the throne there was what looked like a sea of glass, clear as crystal.

In the center, around the throne, were four living creatures. . . . Day and night they never stop saying:

> "Holy, holy, holy
> is the Lord God Almighty,
> who was, and is, and is to come."
>   Whenever the living creatures give glory, honor and thanks to him who
> sits on the throne and who lives for ever and ever, the twenty-four elders
> fall down before him who sits on the throne, and worship him him who
> lives for ever and ever. They lay their crowns before the throne and say:
>
> "You are worthy, our Lord and God
>   to receive glory and honor and power,
> for you created all things,
>   and by your will they were created
>   and have their being."
>   (Rev. 4:2–11)

When we let Revelation 4 and 5 speak boldly, we find a model from which we can borrow and adapt at least several elements for corporate worship here and now. The scene in this passage contrasts sharply with our typical evangelical worship. Given our cultural context and Western mind-set, it may even seem shocking. The worship event is spectacular with pageantry, ceremony, light shows, sound effects, a visible division of responsibilities by participants, movement in a focal area, highly charged drama, candles, even incense. We have the makings of a media event with a reverential tone!

The focal area appears to be circular, akin to theater-in-the-round. At the center stands the throne where God is seated. A rainbow of emerald light encircles it. Immediately around the throne seven blazing lamps shine and four creatures "minister" to God incessantly day and night (7:15). Flashes of lightning, rumblings, and peals of thunder issue from the throne. In another, perhaps larger, concentric circle twenty-four elders on twenty-four thrones sit in white raiment and wear crowns of gold. The entire throne area seems separated from the "congregation" by a long approach that stretches out like a sea of glass, clear as crystal. With a little imagination we can picture the dazzling visual effects possible as shafts of flashing lightning play on the reflective glassy sea and the host of heaven dressed in reflective white.

Using Light and White

Visualizing this setting, let us consider the ways that four elements depicted here have been adapted in various contemporary worship services: the seven lamps, the sea of glass, the white dress, and the idea of continuous praise.[16]

In Lutheran services acolytes (young assistants) traditionally make procession down the aisle and into the pulpit area, where they light *candles* (symbolic of the Holy Spirit's presence) to commence the service. In addition, many Lutheran churches have an "eternal light" candle that burns, like those in Revelation, continuously day and night. Even the most unlikely aspect of the scene, the *sea of glass*, finds a contemporary counterpart in the architecture of the Brazil for Christ Church in Sao Paulo, which seats fifteen thousand people. It contains a "wall-to-wall band of four-foot mirrors" located beneath the pulpit. Worshipers facing the pulpit "see themselves" in this awesome wall mirror, which is like a reflective glassy sea

In some black churches in America, the elders' wives, dressed in *white* (symbol of purity or victory), gather in the front pews near the altar and sing and pray together as a prelude to evening Communion services. As worshipers enter the service, the praise is already in progress. These women, like the four living creatures, perform a ministry that conveys to the people an aura of *continuous praise;* and like the twenty-four elders, they function as a small, ministering choir.

The text of Revelation elsewhere clarifies the symbolic meaning of white linen:[17]

> "For the wedding of the Lamb has come,
>   and his bride has made herself ready.
> Fine linen, bright and clean,
>   was given her to wear."

(Fine linen stands for the righteous acts of the saints.)

> Then the angel said to me, "Write: 'Blessed are those who are invited to the wedding supper of the Lamb!'" (19:7–9).

White linen can be directly connected to the "wedding supper," which some view as having a symbolic connection to the Lord's Supper—another reason why "white" is appropriate at Communion services.

Concentric Circles

The circle imagery in Revelation (implied in 4:4; 5:11) can express important truths.[18] A circular seating arrangement visually communicates the idea of community and fellowship.[19] We can incorporate the circle into worship in various ways.

When you are gathered in a circle, point out that although God is now unseen, in heaven His throne will be at the center and God will Himself fill the space (21:22). Then quote 1 Peter 1:8, sing "The Lord's Prayer," and follow that with impromptu worship responses such as sentence prayers and memorized hymns and choruses. During "The Lord's Prayer" sturdily lift your linked hands on the words "for thine is the kingdom, and the power, and the glory" as a nonverbal expression of

God's power. (Many have found this to be a meaningful expression of worship.) Another extension of this geometric design may occur at the close of a service when the people form a large circle, link hands, pray, and sing "Blest Be the Tie That Binds."

For Communion services in the evening (in either small or large churches) the Lord's Table can be placed at the center with the people seated in-the-round. With the circle shape, form and meaning intersect: the Lord is at the center and we are fellowshiping around Him. In my home church we have used this pattern several times with great success. We invite the people to come to the table "when they are ready" (not in some prescribed order, row by row) and ingest the elements there or take them back to their seats. The freedom in this procedure results in an unrushed Communion service that allows time for reflection. Children like it too for the (subdued) movement and action. Special music, congregational singing, and moments of silence are all appropriate during this period.

The first time we did this, there was a lull after twenty minutes. No one came to the table. We therefore assumed everyone had partaken and proceeded to end the service only to find some had not. (It was hard to judge when everyone was done.) We solved that problem the second time by announcing when people were no longer coming to the table, "We will spend another few minutes reflecting on the Lord; if you have not yet partaken and desire to, please do so now."

Employing Nature Sounds in Worship

The idea of rumblings from the throne suggests another way to adapt the Revelation scene to contemporary worship. In the Old Testament God imaged Himself to humans in the elements of wind and fire, and the prophets and the poetical books extolled God's greatness through the metaphors of nature. In Revelation God issues rumblings, lightning, and peals of thunder as part of His response in the dialogue of worship. These emotive sights and sounds tend to transcend cultures.[20]

How exciting that for the first time in history through the use of synthesizers we can now at least attempt to depict this particular aspect of God's communication! After persistently experimenting with a synthesizer I have been pleased with producing a wide range of sounds from the most delicate, silky wind to the most driving, wailing hurricane imaginable, as well as sounds of surf, rain, hail, and awesome rumblings and claps of thunder. All these effects can be made to sound organic and not at all mechanical.

At Regent College in 1978 some co-workers and I incorporated some wind and storm sounds as an accompaniment to readings from the Psalms in an extended evening worship-Communion service. It was received enthusiastically, and many people told us their concept of God had been expanded. This end result is the key. *I do not advocate using music electronics just to be different or spectacular.* These resources are useful to the extent they help us to comprehend the grandeur of our Lord and *lead to actual worship.*

FACTORS ENCOURAGING A TRANSCENDENT EXPERIENCE

Other elements in Revelation worship that we can adapt are its scale and dimension, the quality of the sounds heard, and the bodily movements of the participants.

Breathtaking Scale

In Revelation, ten thousands upon ten thousands of angels are praising God in loud voices, joined by the voices of every creature in heaven and earth. This grand, choric effect is no less exciting in our corporate worship now. Most of us know the feeling of being in a packed worship space. The loud, resonant worship is overwhelming. We participate in something larger than ourselves.

Reverberant Acoustics

If we take a close, literal look at Revelation 5:13 (and I trust I am not exaggerating here), it seems that John is indicating he was able to discriminate the individual voices that constituted the whole: "I *heard every creature* in heaven and on earth and under the earth and on the sea, and all that is in them, singing." This contrasts sharply with the deadened acoustics in many modern churches.

> *Paul Wohlgemuth tells of an experience directing the Biola Chorale (on tour) in a Sunday evening service. A half-hour before the concert the choristers prayed that the Lord would make the concert spiritually meaningful and inspirational. But they struggled to communicate effectively as they sang. They felt as if they were singing alone and had trouble hearing each other. They simply could not generate the choral sound needed to envelop the choir and give each singer the extra emotion, energy, and excitement that was needed.*
>
> *"What stifled the life, inspiration, and thrill of singing?" the choristers asked after the service. One singer voiced her frustration and disappointment: "It seems the Lord didn't speak tonight." Paul responded to her, "If the Lord didn't speak, He didn't speak to the architect."*[21]

A nonreverberant worship space can discourage, even cripple, congregational response. Carpeted floors, cushioned seats, curtained backdrops, low ceilings, and acoustical tile can stifle the natural resonance and amplification of the human voice. Feeling alone and missing the supporting sound around them, people sing more self-consciously, tentatively, and inhibitedly. People miss the joy of blending, mixing, and merging their own voices with the corporate voice.

Church leaders generally don't understand that music demands a longer reverberation time than speech. Because Evangelicals often consider what precedes the sermon to be merely "preliminary," they underestimate the effect of acoustic factors on congregational response. We need to ask the question, "Do we want *both* a preaching and a people-response space?" We read in Revelation that the angels "cried aloud." Moreover, long reverberation times relate to the many resonant sounds we find in Revelation, such as the voice of God that resounds like "many waters" (1:15; see also 14:2).

Robert E. Coleman says:

> . . . all the songs about the throne involve corporate worship. There are no solos. Yet such is the unity of spirit, that the myriads of participants sound as if they have one voice. . . . the joyous shouting is likened to "the sound of many waters" as though a thousand Niagaras were cataracting over steep cliffs, or a hundred oceans were crashing on the shore. To use another figure, it is compared to "the sound of mighty peals of thunder" (19:6), splitting the heavens in rolling sonic booms.[22]

Corporate worship responses that sound like thunder have been reported on earth. In August 1980, 2.7 million Korean believers assembled on an airport runway for three days of worship and evangelism. A lot of people—comparable to filling the Los Angeles Coliseum more than twenty-seven times! It is said that when the people responded "amen" to the preachers, it rumbled like thunder!

The expression of our core values can be emboldened in environments of this magnitude, and people can be stirred to the depths of their being. At the time of those meetings in Korea, W. H. Brooks, pastor of my youth, was approached by a Korean in a hotel lobby with the words, "Do you know Christ as your Savior?" Relating this experience later, Brooks exclaimed, "Just imagine, this in *Korea!*" He went on to tell of a moving incident that occurred during the meetings.

"I was standing on a side platform looking down on the multitudes. I saw Korean students sitting on pieces of cardboard in the drizzling rain. One young man was praying, his hands outstretched to heaven. I left my seat, knelt beside him, and placed my hand on his shoulder. I asked God to give me the spirit and vision I sensed this young man had."

Arriving home, the pastor laid bare this experience to his wife. She responded, "Can you make it a *permanent* part of your life?"

Prostration

When I hear of stories of openness and commitment like this, I am stirred and affected. I pray, "God, help me to be this kind of a person." I further believe that the transcendency inherent in immense worship settings of this sort can powerfully influence us. Worship occurring on such an unprecedented scale can uniquely affect our response.

The use of the body in Revelation worship makes the response even richer and more complete. Precisely at this point many Evangelicals tend to stumble. We are haunted by the feeling that if our worship were more authentic and spiritual, it would be directed to God without the mediation of the senses and the body. But consider: If this were the case, should we not expect to find this condition existing in Revelation, where pure, spirit-to-spirit worship would have the best chance of taking place? But what do we find? In Revelation, worshipers fall prostrate on their faces. Clearly, in both heavenly and earthly worship the body has a role.

Worship in Revelation still involves the body, not just the soul. God elected to redeem not only our soul-spirit, but also our bodies (1 Cor. 15).[23] Our Lord, who was "infleshed" on earth, remains "infleshed" in heaven (albeit glorified flesh).[24] Moreover, physical expressions of worship can teach. Falling on our faces in worship publicly teaches us humility. To fall down is a visible, embodied definition of worship. The gesture appears inevitable in Revelation!

SIMULTANEOUS TEXTURES OF PRAISE

Worship in Revelation 4 and 5 becomes multidimensional in the sense that more than one action takes place at one time. Note carefully that the four living creatures around God's throne continuously praise Him with undulations of "Holy, holy is the Lord God Almighty, who was, and is, and is to come" (4:8). At the same time, at various points the twenty-four elders, angels, and creatures add their praise (by singing or speaking) to that of the four creatures. In addition, periodic rumblings come from the throne. In regard to sound, then, John experiences at least *three* textures simultaneously.

This idea of combining diverse yet complementary textures is a distinct feature of twentieth-century music.[25] (I have in mind here something akin to montage or collage in art—the combining of textures more radically diverse than, say, the simultaneous use of an organ, sung chorale, and aria in Baroque music.) How exciting to think that what composers are only now beginning to experiment with, God thought of first!

But the concept is not really foreign to us. Every day we experience multiple textures. In a shopping mall we simultaneously hear conversations, fountains, background music, cash registers, the shuffling of crowds. While driving we hear the noises of the radio, motor, horns, sirens, windshield wipers.

What about worship services? We have interpreted "let everything be done decently and in order" to mean "one thing at a time." Consequently our worship services are strongly (and sometimes excessively) linear.

The organized textures and actions we see in Revelation are not chaotic. They are intelligible and disciplined, but they have an element of simultaneity, of several things happening at once. They differ from the speaking in tongues of 1 Corinthians 14:27, where the church was advised to limit such speaking to one person at a time. By contrast, an entire congregation can pray aloud simultaneously. The effect is not at all chaotic. In mainland China, Singapore, and Korea, worshipers perceive this kind of prayer not as a charismatic phenomenon, but as a general practice in many church groups. The people verbalize their prayer in this way—yet not so loudly as to distract one another—and after several minutes a single person usually closes with a summation prayer.

> *A number of years ago, a missionary from South America joined the faculty of an evangelical college in the Midwest. He was popular with the students and faculty and was often asked to lead in prayer. On the mission field he had experienced some fellowship with believers who prayed out loud at the same time in their services. One day when leading the college assembly in prayer, he suggested, "As a change today, why don't we all pray out loud at the same time?" No one did. "I was not asked to lead in public prayer again for seven years," he told me!*

What a pity! A popular, appreciated person found himself blacklisted for seven years because he committed one "transgression" against the prevailing culture.[26] When a person miscalculates or rubs against the grain of the local culture, church leaders need to show love and sensitivity. Open the lines of communication and restore these people!

The professor's suggestion was not tolerated. Yet in heaven, worship appears to be an orderly, complex, and at times *multilayered unity*—even as the Godhead is a simultaneous, working unity. Perhaps some of us will be astonished at the worship practices in heaven.

The Pentecost Sunday service, which occurs seven weeks after

Easter, provides an appropriate time for multiple textures. The natural drama inherent in the Pentecost account lends itself to this approach. I once tried some multiple textures with a choir and a reader's theater that was favorably received in a blue-collar church.[27] I have also been successful in combining two singers in an antiphonal relationship (they sang the prayer of Francis of Assisi, "Eternal Life") while two readers, in echo fashion, simultaneously read through 1 Corinthians 13.

In these examples the basic technique floods the senses of people with more information than they can process. This tends to elicit from them a strong desire to select, sort, and integrate the details into a meaningful whole. In the Francis of Assisi number, for example, each pair of performers was echoing material back and forth simultaneously. All these happenings made for intensity. During the last fifth or so of the piece, part of 1 Corinthians was reread by one reader, unadorned and without the accompanying multiple textures—and the people really listened! The busyness of the multiple textures helped the simple rereading at the end to stand out boldly.

SUMMARY

Revelation worship is not just for the future. It confirms the validity of several principles for today's worship, including the priesthood of believers, the worship of Jesus, the use of instruments, costly worship, and the necessity of response. Several elements of Revelation worship can be adapted for contemporary worship, including the use of candles, white dress, continuous praise, circular seating, and nature sounds. Revelation worship favors the design of reverberant spaces and the use of physical movement. An interesting Revelation idea involves the creation of simultaneous textures of praise.

QUESTIONS FOR THOUGHT AND DISCUSSION

1. Why do you think the study of worship in Revelation has been widely neglected?
2. What underlying principles of worship in Revelation would you consider to be binding today?
3. Do you think the thesis that Revelation worship is practical for today is valid? Explain.
4. What do you find striking or shocking about Revelation worship?
5. Do you have a preaching space, a worship space, or both at your church? How can you use them in implementing ideas of Revelation worship?

6. What patterns from heaven's worship could be adapted to your local church worship?
7. Organize a class debate using the resolution "Revelation worship is practical for the church today." Divide the class and have each half face the other—one side in favor of the question, the other side against. Allow each side three minutes for advancing arguments and then three minutes for counterarguments. Any person on a side can advance any number of arguments. Decide on a winner, then have some free discussion.

CHAPTER EIGHTEEN

The Ultimate Drama

Drama—not Hollywood style, but liturgical drama—is a basic element in Revelation worship.[1] That shouldn't surprise us, for we've already seen that all worship involves drama in some form. The essence of drama consists of individual or corporate action, visible or mental. In Revelation 4 and 5 we read of two actions of great cost and great dramatic potential. First, the elders cast their crowns of authority before the throne. Second, the Savior takes the scroll and breaks the seven seals. We will take a closer look at that second dramatic action: Christ taking the scroll from the hand of God! When I think about this, I get excited. I can't wait to see it happen!

> Then I saw in the right hand of him who sat on the throne a scroll with writing on both sides and sealed with seven seals. And I saw a mighty angel proclaiming in a loud voice, "Who is worthy to break the seals and open the scroll?" But no one in heaven or on earth or under the earth could open the scroll or even look inside it. I wept and wept because no one was found who was worthy to open the scroll or look inside. Then one of the elders said to me, "Do not weep! See, the Lion of the tribe of Judah, the Root of David, has triumphed. He is able to open the scroll and its seven seals."
>
> Then I saw a Lamb, looking as if it had been slain, standing in the center of the throne, encircled by the four living creatures and the elders. . . . He came and took the scroll from the right hand of him who sat on the throne. And when he had taken it, the four living creatures and the twenty-four elders fell down before the Lamb. Each one had a harp and they were holding golden bowls full of incense, which are the prayers of the saints. And they sang a new song:
>
> > "You are worthy to take the scroll
> >   and to open its seals,
> > because you were slain,
> >   and with your blood you purchased men for God

> *from every tribe and language and people and nation."*
> *(Rev. 5:1–9)*

What a thrilling act! A mighty angel trumpets, "Who is worthy?" Then there's suspense. John weeps because no one worthy can be found. Next, climactically the Lamb, worthy at great cost, courageously advances toward the throne and takes the scroll from the One sitting there. Instantly everyone falls down in worship and awe. The action extends over time as each seal is broken. Notice also the element of surprise in the narrative. The *Lion* of Judah appears as a slain *Lamb!* This is both drama and deeply meaningful worship.

DRAMATIC INSIGHT DEMONSTRATED THROUGHOUT

This liturgically dramatic worship isn't limited to chapters 4 and 5 of Revelation. The book is full of it. Chapters 8 and 15 devote considerable space to descriptions of liturgical action. Throughout the book the worship scenes around the throne of God are rich with pomp and tumult and drama. Worshipers stand, prostrate themselves before the throne, burst forth into singing and shouting. Angels and beasts come and go bearing vessels. There is even dramatic silence.

After the seventh seal is opened in chapter 8, there are thirty minutes of silence. Imagine that! What an unerring instinct for the dramatic!

The *selection* of the 144,000 who sing the "new song" no one else can learn also points to drama (14:3).[2] That the 144,000 are martyrs makes the performance all the more evocative. In our services, too, choosing (insightfully) the right person to sing a song can add intensity to the occasion. For example, if a mother who has recently given birth to a child is selected to sing the second stanza of the hymn "Because He Lives" (text: "How sweet to hold a newborn baby . . ."), it brings a new dimension to the service.

Notice also that in the responses, the attention of worshipers focuses on God, not self:

> Great and marvelous are *your* deeds,
>   Lord God Almighty.
> Just and true are *your* ways,
>   King of the ages.
> Who will not fear *you*, O Lord,
>   and bring glory to *your* name?
> For *you* alone are holy.
> All nations will come
>   and worship before *you*,
> for *your* righteous acts have been revealed (15:3–4).

That's an important emphasis. Drama in worship should keep God at stage center. It shouldn't become a time to enlarge our own egos. People sometimes imagine that heaven will be boring with nothing to do. That's not what we find in Revelation. Worship there is filled with unresolved tensions and conflicts that affect the entire emotional climate in heaven. The martyred souls beneath the altar, impatient with prolonged waiting, cry out for justice ("How long, Sovereign Lord, holy and true, until you . . . avenge our blood"), and they are told "to wait a little longer" (6:10–11). Only later, in chapter 19, is this pent-up tension released in a tumultuous explosion of victory: "He [God] has avenged on her the blood of his servants. . . . Hallelujah!"[3]

Our worship here on earth should also reflect the elements of tension, crisis, and irresolution that we find in our own lives. The alert worship leader will find in the personal odysseys of the people opportunities for dramatic, meaningful worship.

THREE DRAMATIC PATTERNS

The design of Revelation worship shows dynamic, dramatic shapes and organized divisions of labor.

1. Dynamic Crescendo

Revelation 4 and 5 reveal a definite, planned progression of dynamics. A graduated crescendo culminates in a climactic response as the size of each group praising God increases exponentially. First there are four living creatures (4:8). Then twenty-four elders appear (4:10). Then they are joined by myriads of angels (5:11). And finally every creature "in heaven and on earth and under the earth and on the sea, and all that is in them" sings to Him who sits on the throne (5:13).[4]

What a practical idea! Doesn't it sound like something we could do? Consider this simple way to adapt the basic idea of crescendo to a typical church setting—perhaps as an ending to the Scripture reading.

Option 1		Option 2	
Leader:	Praise the Lord!	*Leader:*	Praise the Lord!
Choir:	Praise the Lord!	*Men:*	Praise the Lord!
Leader:	Praise the Lord!	*Leader:*	Praise the Lord!
Congrega-tion:	Praise the Lord!	*Women:*	Praise the Lord!
Leader:	Praise the Lord!	*Leader:*	Praise the Lord!
All:	Praise the Lord!	*All:*	Praise the Lord!
All:	PRAISE THE LORD!	*All:*	PRAISE THE LORD!

2. Balanced Participation

It is clear that God is not a respecter of persons in the design of Revelation worship. We see a balanced division of responsibility in participation. Every group category participates in a significant response that enhances the total dramatic effect of the worship experience: the four creatures (4:8), the twenty-four elders (4:10; 11:16–18), the angels standing around the throne (5:11), the souls under the altar (6:9), those victorious over the beast (15:12), the 144,000 (14:3), the great multitude (7:9; 19:1–3, 6–7), and every creature (5:13).

What about the identifiable groups in your congregation? With a little thought, you should be able to identify some (beyond simple male and female divisions) and find ways to involve them as groups in a meaningful congregational response.

3. The Concept of Stations

The concept of stations in the heavenly temple suggests dramatic possibilities. This concept has a history that relates back to the desert wanderings and the temple. The people of Israel marched in a prescribed formation in the Sinai desert. Furthermore, multiple choirs, stationed in various places in the Old Testament temple, performed antiphonal responses akin to the worship in St. Mark's Cathedral during the Renaissance in Italy.[5] This very likely occurred on festival days, given the organization of the Levitical musicians into twenty-four divisions. The concept of stations specifically appears in 2 Chronicles:

> He then stationed the Levites in the house of the LORD with cymbals, with harps, and with lyres according to the command of David (29:25 NASB).

In the Book of Revelation, the presence of stations appears in the overall pattern of references to angels with certain kinds of authority. Chapter 16 refers to the "angel in charge of the waters" (16:5), another angel has power over fire and comes out from the altar (14:18), and seven angels stand before the throne (8:2). The concept of stations is also evident in the placement of the four creatures, the twenty-four elders, and the 144,000 in concentric circles around the throne.

In our churches we could be more imaginative in stationing worship participants in various parts of the sanctuary. For example, a trumpet fanfare could be sounded from the balcony instead of the front. During the Scripture reading, portions could be read not only from the pulpit, but by selected members from their seats in the congregation. That way

Scripture would be perceived as emanating more from the people. Similarly the choir could be divided on occasion into two parts, one situated in the loft and the other somewhere else in the sanctuary. This might be especially effective if the music is of an antiphonal nature.

EMINENTLY PRACTICAL

I have used the ideas presented in this chapter in both church and college settings. In designing all-university chapel services for more than three thousand students at Biola, we have found Revelation worship ideas extremely valuable and workable for festive occasions (convocation, Christmas, and Easter).[6] They have brought to these events an aura of drama unmatched for the occasion.

For example, we adapted the idea of concentric circles by placing a small table with a solitary Jesus Candle in the center of the worship area. Representatives from the administration, faculty, staff, and students formed a small circle around the table. We had a twenty-four-person guitar choir (counterpart of the twenty-four harps in Revelation), two college choirs, the band, orchestra, piano, and synthesizer stationed in various places in the space. The students sat in various designated sectors in the round, according to their standing as undergraduates, graduates, and seminary students, and so forth. All these groups had their own responses at various points in the order of service.

At the same service we had a "Roll Call of Nations" (a way of introducing the international students attending Biola), hymn singing that integrated two choirs, a string orchestra, and responses of the people like the following, led alternately by a male and a female student:

Leader: Make a joyful noise to the Lord, all the lands!

North: Serve the Lord with gladness! Come into His presence with singing!

Leader: Know that the Lord is God!

North: It is He that made us, and we are His;
We are His people, and the sheep of His pasture.

* * *

Leader: Enter His gates with thanksgiving, and His courts with praise!

South: Give thanks to Him, bless His name!

Leader: For the Lord is good;

South: His steadfast love endures forever,
His faithfulness to all generations.

* * *

Leader: Praise the Lord! Praise God in His sanctuary
West: Praise Him in His mighty firmament!
Leader: Praise him for His mighty deeds;
West: Praise Him according to His exceeding greatness

* * *

Leader: Praise Him with trumpet sound;
East: Praise Him with lute and harp!
Leader: Praise Him with timbrel and dance;
East: Praise Him with strings and pipe!
Leader: Praise Him with sounding cymbals;
East: Praise Him with loud clashing cymbals!

* * *

Leader: Let everything that hath breath praise the Lord!
All: Praise the Lord!
Leader: Let everything that hath breath praise the Lord!
All: *Praise the Lord!*
All: PRAISE THE LORD!
All: **PRAISE THE LORD!**

When the people performed the "dynamic crescendo" in this liturgy (an idea borrowed from Revelation!), such a roar was heard, I can remember seeing heads snap back, jaws drop, and smiles of amazement break out. In these "teachable moments" students were genuinely awestruck. Together we experienced a new sense of transcendency. Some faculty members wept. They said that in eighteen years they had never seen anything like it.

On one occasion for Christmas we had *four processions* emanating from four locations on the campus (an administration building, a classroom building, and dorms). Singing carols as they went, the students, faculty, and staff of each procession followed separate routes to the assembly entrance, where we had an outdoor ceremony and then went in and worshiped.

At that time I recall leading a thousand-person procession headed by trumpeters, choir members, and a flag bearer. We were doing pretty well until the flag got caught in the trees! It was scary for a moment! We could feel the press of a thousand people behind us. When we arrived at our destination, the four processions swelled and then converged outside the gym area, each continuing to sing a different carol at the same time. For about thirty seconds the effect seemed wonderfully chaotic as each group kept singing (a little spontaneous California competition!).

A word of caution. If you undertake something like this in a local church setting, expect a certain amount of opposition. People have difficulty envisioning it as being practical. Until they actually see it in person they may not share your enthusiasm. That was the experience of close friends of mine who mounted something like this for their church missionary convention. No one believed it would work—not even the music director—but they kept plugging away. They told me, however, that the final result stretched and amazed everyone.

The same thing happened to me at Biola University. Just minutes before our first service of this nature, I recall the discouraged words of a faculty member: "We had better forget this next year . . . it's too complex . . . too many variables. . . ." He was voicing his fear that the service might collapse. Indeed, it was risky, and we were all holding our breath. But we had stepped out in faith and God mightily honored that. It was one of our finest moments!

TWIN PILLARS OF WORSHIP

It is easy to get caught up in the more dramatic moments of worship, the pageantry of it, and to lose sight of what is most important. Revelation brings us back to that. The spring of worship in Revelation rests on two controlling thoughts: (1) we worship God for He alone is holy; and (2) we worship God and the Lamb, for they alone are worthy of our worship.

For God, holiness forms the controlling concept. He cannot violate His own character. He was, is, and will always be holy (4:8). For us, God's worthiness is the controlling concept. We need a deserving Object for worship, or we lose our sense of direction and our worship lacks integrity. God's holiness determines His action. His worthiness makes possible the integrity of our response. *These twin pillars make worship work.*

1. Worthiness of God

In the Bible the marvelous expression "You are worthy" is unique to Revelation and relates to the character and acts of God and the Lamb. The phrase occurs three times and provides the lead thought of three response poems. The first "worthy" poem is addressed to the Father, the second and third to the Son. The first poem reads:

> You are worthy, our Lord and God . . .
> you created all things (4:11).

The second reads:

> You are worthy to take the scroll . . .
> because you were slain
>   and with your blood you purchased men for God. . . .
> You have made them to be a kingdom and priests (5:9–10).

The third reads:

> Worthy is the Lamb, who was slain,
> to receive power (5:12).

Note the emphasis: the Father is the worthy Creator, the Son the worthy Redeemer.[7] After these three poems a doxology of praise addresses the Father and Son together:

> To Him who sits on the throne and to the Lamb
> be praise and honor and glory and power,
>   for ever and ever! (5:13).

Aside from the undulations of "Holy, holy, holy" by the four living creatures, these four proclamations alone form the group responses of chapters 4 and 5.

As to the language of the corporate prayers and songs, at least three principles consistently apply.

First, prayers and songs are addressed to God (or the Lamb) and are performed directly to the Object of worship. Such a powerful idea deserves special emphasis.

The primary reason many of the newer worship choruses are so effective is that they address God directly in song. Songs like "Thou art worthy," "Thou, O Lord, art a Shield about me," "We Exalt Thee," "Lord, You are more precious than silver" accomplish this. The emphasis exactly parallels the Old Testament principle of singing and praying "to the Lord." By contrast, many of our beloved gospel songs are really testimony songs addressed to people in the worship space: "In my heart there rings a melody," "He Touched Me," even "Amazing Grace." Only secondarily do they deal with the worthiness of God. Thus they *may* lose much of their worship appeal in not directly pointing to the Object of our worship. Yet there are many staid, old hymns that—like the worship choruses—address God directly.

Second, language that relates to acts of God in history is relatively concise and objective.

Third, when worshipers contemplate the mighty Object of their worship and reflect on what He is and what is due to Him, the language begins to soar. We read of the threefold "glory and honor and power" (4:11), the fourfold "praise and honor and glory and power" (5:13), and the sevenfold "power and wealth and wisdom and strength and honor and glory and praise" (5:12). This kind of language has an extolling function that is cumulative, rhythmic, and climactic. David's prayer in 1 Chronicles embodies the same quality:

> Praise be to you, O LORD,
>   God of our father Israel,
>   from everlasting to everlasting.
> Yours, O LORD, is the greatness and the power
>   and the glory and the majesty and the splendor,
>   for everything in heaven and earth is yours.
> Yours, O LORD, is the kingdom;
>   you are exalted as head over all.
> Wealth and honor come from you;
>   you are the ruler of all things.
> In your hands are strength and power
>   to exalt and give strength to all.
> Now, our God, we give you thanks,
>   and praise your glorious name (29:10–13).

These texts clearly encourage the emotional side of worship. However, I want to sound a note of caution: we do not necessarily have to feel emotional joy (while we are worshiping) for our worship to be genuine.

2. The Holiness of God

At the church of my boyhood, the old 10 Avenue Alliance Church in Vancouver, British Columbia, there was emblazoned behind the choir loft in huge, Gothic, burgundy letters an inscription that read:

Holy, Holy, Holy is the Lord God of Hosts

That inscription seemed to me very important and mysterious stuff. The same kind of lettering was on the cover of our hymnbook too. I remember trying very hard Sunday after Sunday to figure out what it meant, but I just could not break the code. The shape of the ornate lettering was too hard to decipher.

I remember whispering one Sunday to one of the boys who sat beside me, "What does it mean?" I watched in excited amazement as he printed on paper the lettering in characters I could understand. I now had the letter sequence. Still I could not fathom the meaning of the words Holy *or* Hosts, *so I'd stare at them during the sermon.*

Now, many years later, I can still benefit by staring at those words. It still seems to me to be very important and mysterious stuff.

Holiness cannot fail to have tremendous significance in Revelation worship. It must be *the* key word. We read that day and night before the throne the four living creatures do not cease to say:

> Holy, holy, holy
> is the Lord God Almighty,
> who was, and is, and is to come (4:8).

In the deliberate design of Revelation worship, holiness acquires weight and importance not only through ceaseless repetition but through the status of the four living creatures—they are stationed nearest the throne. The threefold repetition "Holy, holy, holy" further underscores its importance. No other word in Scripture is repeated in this manner. It evokes association with the powerful theophany in Isaiah:

> Holy, holy, holy, is the Lord Almighty;
> the whole earth is full of his glory (Isa. 6:3).

The ceaseless repetition also serves to clarify a phrase uttered by Jesus:

> And when you are praying, do not use *meaningless repetition, as the Gentiles do* ["Do not keep on babbling like pagans": NIV], for they suppose that they will be heard for their many words (Matt. 6:7 NASB).

Because of this verse, I have been sparing in the past in the ways I have used repetition in worship. The ceaseless repetition of Revelation 4:8 seems to be unique to all of Scripture. It comes closest to functioning like a Hindu mantra—repetition of quite a different sort than that of Psalm 136, for example.[8] Some might be inclined to construe it as mere "babbling" or fear its excessive use as a mind-control technique. Clearly, neither is the case. A better perspective might be that "holiness" is God's central attribute and therefore the ceaseless repetition of the word is appropriate. This use of repetition in Revelation has helped free me in my thinking. Yet I urge caution. Constant repetition seems to me to be the single most powerful technique employed in the Book of Revelation.

KEEP ME OPEN, LORD

The Revelation model of worship must be regarded as a mature, considered expression of Christian worship. Yet it is vastly different from my experience of worship growing up in a fundamentalist-evangelical church environment. Perhaps that's your experience too. We tend to have a provincial attitude toward worship. (Someone has suggested that the last seven words of the church may be "We never did it that way before!") Yet I suspect that Revelation worship strikes a deep and longing chord within us. It also shows us the shape of what worship can be (as God sees it) when teaching and evangelism are no longer part of the "service." Worshipers in heaven are genuinely stricken and astonished by a comprehensive Awesomeness.

I sense the message is at once powerfully inspiring and *dangerous* — if means are confused with ends. The elements that comprise Revelation worship, as enthralling as they may be, are *no substitute for God Himself*.

If, however, we can keep the Object of our worship primary—"*I am the Alpha and the Omega*"—the vision is an exciting and liberating one for the church today. Revelation worship encourages us to think of God in big terms, even to "the far reaches of imagination."[9]

QUESTIONS FOR THOUGHT AND DISCUSSION

1. How important, structurally, is the dramatic event of taking the scroll in the Book of Revelation? What implications do you draw from this?
2. Worship in Revelation "is filled with unresolved tensions and conflict that affect the entire emotional climate in heaven." Explain the implications of this statement.
3. Explain the significance of the following statements: "For God, holiness is the controlling concept. . . . For us, God's worthiness is the controlling concept."
4. Holiness must be *the* key word in Revelation worship. Why?
5. "The elements that comprise Revelation worship, as enthralling as they may be, are *no substitute for God Himself.*" Discuss the danger implied in this statement.

RECOMMENDED READING

Blevins, James L. *Revelation As Drama.* Nashville: Broadman Press, 1984. (Contains a drama script for church performance.)
Coleman, Robert E. *Songs of Heaven.* Old Tappan, N.J.: Fleming H. Revell, 1980.

CHAPTER NINETEEN

Symbolism: Old But New

*Symbols are created when something interior and spiritual finds
expression in something by nature exterior and material. In form, symbols
may be "mental" or "metal," an idea in the mind or objective matter.*[1]

Our study of Revelation worship serves as a kind of review of all the
previous chapters of this book. For example, the preceding chapter
related to Old Testament drama, while this one relates to Old Testament
symbolism. In the following chapters we see a worship that is marvelously
inclusive and wonderfully mysterious. We see God the Creator-Artist at
work and gain insight into His concept of creativity. Revelation worship
will (if we let it) challenge, stretch, and free us.

Ever since the Reformation, Evangelicals have largely shunned the
use of symbols in worship, but worship in the Book of Revelation
employs them lavishly. What are we to make of that?

In this chapter I will make a strong case for the legitimacy of
symbols in Christian worship. I will maintain that while they are not
mandatory, we are free to use them. My goal is to present issues strongly
and encourage thoughtful consideration so that "iron may sharpen iron."
Readers who do not accept the whole argument may find parts of it valid.
I have also provided additional perspectives in the footnotes.

HAS THE TIME FOR SYMBOLS PASSED?

In his book *True Worship,* John MacArthur presents what I take to
be the traditional evangelical argument on the status of symbols in
Christian worship. Consider the following quotations from his book:

> [Jesus speaking to the Samaritan woman in John 4] was not denying
> all the symbols. . . . He was telling her the time was coming when *all
> the symbols would pass away,* and that there would not be a need for a
> physical temple, sacrifices, and priests. . . . Now there was nothing

wrong with the symbols, they were just that. . . . they were *just prodders of the mind*—symbols to cause His people to worship. But in the new covenant, the symbols became reality, and went *from the external to the internal* (italics added).[2]

The New Covenant *ended the ceremonial symbols* and the symbol of the temple. . . . Worship was *no longer prodded by an outward symbol*, it became an inward reality. The external reminder to worship, which occurred when the Israelites camped around the tabernacle, now occurs internally through the prompting of the Holy Spirit in the life of every believer (italics added).[3]

Is the view that all the symbols were "just prodders of the mind" (note the pejorative connotation) really supported by the Scriptures?[4] Or is there more to it than this?

Did the New Covenant *end* the symbols? Surely we must all agree that worship symbols are not ended in the Book of Revelation! Surely in heaven the altar, the lampstands, and the clouds of incense have an existence just as real as the twenty-four elders prostrating before the throne of God. And for us, the symbols are not ended in the sense that they also exist in our minds.

But what about the use of symbols in our earthly worship forms now? Did Jesus say in John 4 that symbols were ended? No. He declared that worship was not to be tied to a certain place (v. 21), but He was silent about symbols. Did Jesus teach that worship was to become *inward* rather than *outward?* Apparently not, though He did teach that true worship is spiritual in nature (v. 24).

If for the moment we accept MacArthur's distinction between external Old Testament worship and internal New Testament worship, Revelation presents us with a tantalizing problem. Clearly it doesn't fit the pattern. Why does Revelation revert to external worship? Does the presence of symbols in Revelation make worship there less spiritual? This seems wrong. Isn't the very appearance of "the Lamb" itself a symbolical presentation of the God-human paradox? The internal-external distinction just doesn't fit.

Finally, MacArthur argues there is not a *need* for symbols under the New Covenant. In response we could ask, "Why then should there be a *need* for symbols in Revelation worship at all with God present in reality? Isn't the Holy Spirit available to prompt believers in heaven too?" Yet external symbols abound! There is not an *efficacious* need for symbols in worship on earth or heaven. The need is not of that sort. Symbols do not save or possess merit. They are not essential, mandatory, or central in this sense.[5] Rather, it seems, God *chooses* to use physical symbols as vehicles of communication in heavenly worship in the same way that thunder and lightning are used to communicate God's transcendence and identity in Old Testament worship.

Moreover, there is a greater need for symbolic communication in large-group worship. More "vision," more drama (mental or visible), will keep people's attention. Accordingly, God designs in heaven a worship environment that affords opportunity for large-scale participation. He designs something to see, to feel, an environment involving liturgical action and drama—a worship that speaks to the whole person. Further, God requires a comprehensive mode of confession involving both word and gesture in which "every knee" bows and "every tongue" confesses that "Jesus Christ is Lord" (Phil. 2:10–11). From personal experience we know that communication involving the whole person is more powerful:

> Normally, the meaning of a thing thought is less powerful than the meaning of a thing heard, which in turn is less powerful than the meaning of a thing seen as well as heard. In turn the meaning of a thing heard and seen is less potent than meaning kinetically conveyed or grasped, i.e., through bodily motion. Meaning apprehended through touch and taste is still more vital than meaning kinetically or audibly experienced. (In this respect we apparently do not outgrow the instinct of infants to put objects into their mouths to evaluate reality.) And lastly, meaning involving several senses is obviously more vital than meaning involving only one.[6]

Symbols are part of the human condition. God created man a body-spirit, and in heaven man retains a glorified body and spirit. God apparently loves matter, and symbols speak to that condition. Man is everywhere a symbol-making, symbol-using being, just as the Creator is everywhere a symbol-making, symbol-using God.[7] The supreme manifestation of symbol in the Gospels is God expressed in human form in the Incarnation ("Anyone who has seen me has seen the Father"—John 14:9), and in Revelation by the Lamb ("looking as if it had been slain, standing in the center of the throne, encircled by the four living creatures and the elders"—5:6).

As mentioned previously, Revelation worship serves as a kind of review of all the previous chapters of this book. For example, the preceding chapter related to Old Testament drama, while this one relates to Old Testament symbolism. In the following chapters, we see worship that is marvelously inclusive and wonderfully mysterious. We see God the Creator-Artist at work and gain insight into His concept of creativity. Revelation worship *will* (if we let it) challenge, stretch, and free us in our desire to experience the presence of God!

JOHN'S STYLE

The Book of Revelation is thoroughly Hebraic and decidedly integrative. From the standpoint of the angels, aspects of the timeless worship occurring in heaven have been integrated into Old Testament worship forms. But from our human perspective it is as if numerous eddies, streams, and tributaries from the Old and New Testaments are feeding into Revelation worship. Either way, of the 404 verses in the Book of Revelation, approximately 265 contain allusions to the Old Testament. These 265 allusions involve some 550 Old Testament passages in all.[8] In what fashion does Revelation treat these allusions? Scholars say of John's style:

. . . he scarcely ever quotes a whole sentence. Everything he writes must be freshly phrased or at least combined. No author cites so little and alludes so much.[9]

He makes no sustained attempt at allegory or metaphor.[10]

[He] uses his allusions . . . for their evocative and emotive power. This is not photographic art. His aim is to set the echoes of memory and association ringing.[11]

. . . one symbol may have a variety of meanings.[12]

[He combines] in a single symbol ideas from many sources.[13]

John's symbolism is always undergoing kaleidoscopic change.[14]

Auditory and visual materials are most apparent.[15]

Revelation involves a resurgence of Old Testament imagery. Moreover, the language of Revelation is of an artistic rather than a scientific nature.

SYMBOLISM IN SCIENCE AND ART

Scientists use symbolism differently from the way artists do. The scientist *uses* symbolism and metaphor in thinking and conceptualizing, but the poet *explores* metaphor. In the act of invoking the scientific method and in writing up the results of research, the scientist (including the scholar in systematic theology) normally seeks a specialized, technical vocabulary where one word has one meaning. Dorothy Sayers explains:

It was the Royal Society who announced in 1687 that they "exacted from their members a close, naked, *natural* way of speaking . . . bringing all things as near the mathematical plainness as they can." Words . . . [were] not to be metaphorical or allusive or charged with incalculable associations—but to approximate as closely as possible to mathematical symbols: "one word, one meaning."[16]

The scientist, Sayers says, "writes down the letters Hg [mercury], and hopes that this time he has finally escaped the influence of the poet. The symbol Hg is (or is intended to be) *pure* symbol." The symbol is not intended to visually describe and interpret the substance, nor charge the reader's emotions—"it merely stands for the substance."[17]

The poet, by contrast, creates by metaphor. The poet "perceives a likeness between a number of things that at first sight appear to have nonmeasureable relation."[18] For illustration Sayers takes Shakespeare's famous line about the honeybee:

> The singing masons building roofs of gold.

Sayers comments:

> Now, the scientist who wants one word, one meaning, may very properly object to almost every word in this line. He will point out the word "singing" would be better confined to the noise produced by the vibration of the vocal cord; that bees have no vocal chords; . . . that bees are not, in the strict sense of the word, masons in a stone cutter's yard; . . . "roofs" (he will say) is an inaccurate description of a conglomeration of hexagonal cells; while the word "gold" is preposterous, seeing that neither the atomic structure nor even the colour of the product in question is correctly indicated by such a misleading word.[19]

The distinction between the scientific and artistic use of symbols applies to our study of Scripture as well. For example, in Paul's writings we find both kinds of usage. Some passages are poetic in character (1 Cor. 13), while others are more analytical, with technical words like *justification, sanctification,* and *propitiation.* The latter specialized words (or symbols) tend to carry more focused, invariable meanings. Words like *thunder* and *trumpet,* when used in poetic contexts, are more fluid and evoke a wide variety of sound and color associations that readily adapt to the hue of the particular context.

CONTINUITY WITH UNFOLDING NEWNESS

When we set the symbolism of the Old Testament alongside the symbolism of Revelation, we see continuity with unfolding newness. Revelation worship continues the Old Testament tradition, but it also adds new elements. Both the continuity and the newness exist at God's command and by His design because tabernacle-temple worship was meant to foreshadow heaven's patterns:

> They [the priests] serve at a sanctuary that is a *copy and shadow* of what is in heaven. This is why Moses was warned when he was about

to build the tabernacle: "See to it that you make everything according to the pattern shown you on the mountain" (Heb. 8:5).

The pattern revealed on Mount Sinai was a reflection of heaven's worship. The list below, moreover, shows that aspects of Revelation symbolism relate not only to tabernacle-temple worship, but more broadly to all the models we have studied.

Old/New Testament	Symbol	Revelation
	Pre-Sinai	
Genesis 2:9–10	Edenic river of life	22:1–2
Genesis 8:20	Altar (Noah)	8:3
Genesis 9:13	Rainbow (Noah)	4:3
Genesis 22:7	Sacrificial lamb (Abraham)	5:6
	Sinai	
Exodus 19:16	Smoke	15:8
Exodus 19:16, 19	Trumpet	8:2
Exodus 19:18–19	Thunder, lightning	4:5
	Tabernacle	
Exodus 16:33	Manna	2:17
Exodus 25:10	Ark	11:19
Exodus 25:31	Menorah	4:5
Exodus 27:2	Four horns of altar	9:13
Exodus 28	High priest vestments	1:13
Exodus 30:18; 1 Kings 7:23	Laver/sea	4:6
Exodus 30:35	Smoke, incense	8:4; 15:8
Exodus 37:9	Cherubim	4:6
	Temple	
1 Chronicles 9:23	Gates	21:12, 15,
1 Chronicles 24:1, 9	Twenty-four divisions/elders	4:4
1 Chronicles 25:1	Harps	5:8
	Synagogue	
Luke 4:17, 20	Scroll opened	5:7
	Pauline	
?	Concentric circles	4:4, 6; 5:6
Romans 7:25; Colossians 1:3	"Thanks be to God"	11:17
1 Corinthians 11:20	Meal fellowship	19:9
1 Corinthians 14:16	Doxological amens	5:14
1 Corinthians 14:26	Congregational participation	5:12

Continuity with newness appears to be a fundamental principle in God's creative approach to worship.

SCENE: CHRIST WALKING AMONG THE LAMPSTANDS

Let's look at the above symbols in greater detail. The scene in Revelation 1 is painted in priestly, liturgical hues. Though some of us may not be liturgically inclined, in fairness we must not sweep over this fact. We see Christ Jesus in high priestly vestments walking among the lampstands (symbolic of the church universal). John of Patmos says:

> I turned around to see the voice that was speaking to me. And when I turned I saw seven golden lampstands, and among the lampstands was someone "like a son of man," *dressed in a robe reaching down to his feet and with a golden sash around his chest* (1:12).

We see the long-flowing robe and sash and the lampstands, and we can imagine the lamplight. In dazzling glory Christ walks in this liturgical environment, just as ages ago, priests in the temple walked in the holy place and trimmed their lamps. The Book of Hebrews says Christ "serves in the sanctuary, the true tabernacle" (8:2). We see the same picture in Revelation 4 and 5 where Jesus advances to the throne and takes the scroll, an action involving liturgical movement.

In the Old Testament the high priest wore a full-length robe or cape with a sash (Exod. 28:4; 29:5). "Pomp and ceremony," comments Wenham, "served one end: the appearance of the glory of God. . . . elaborate vestments helped simple humans appreciate the majestic holiness of God."[20] The Aaronic garments were "for glory and for beauty" (Exod. 28:2 NASB); the more prestigious the office, the more splendid the vestment. In Revelation the symbolism of clothes emphasizes "the worth of Christ's ministry for his people,"[21] which is as "superior" to the priest's ministry "as the covenant of which he [Christ] is mediator is superior to the old one" (Heb. 8:6). Today choir robes perform a similar role in drawing attention to function rather than personality.

SYMBOLISM IN THE HEAVENLY TEMPLE

The Most Significant Symbols

The symbolism of the heavenly temple serves a number of functions. For one, it arouses our historical consciousness. For example, the *temple* revives memories of the tabernacle in the desert (Lev. 26:11–13). It was the place where God's presence dwelt, where He spread His tent. All sixteen references to the word *temple* in Revelation "designate the inner shrine rather than the larger precincts."[22]

The *ark*, normally hidden, is not a central manifestation in Revelation, yet it symbolizes intimate and abiding fellowship. It rekindles memories of the ark of the covenant in the Exodus.

The *twenty-four elders* have been taken as symbolic of the twelve apostles and twelve tribes of Israel or the twenty-four divisions of priests and musical Levites. I take them to stand collectively for all leadership of both the Old and New Testaments: elders as well as priests and musicians.[23] Seated on twenty-four thrones and wearing crowns and holding harps, they surround the throne. Their harps prompt and enhance congregational worship. When cued by the four living creatures, the elders intermittently rise, prostrate themselves in submissive worship, and then lay their crowns of authority before the throne. Only God remains seated.

A cloud of *smoke* appeared at strategic moments in Israel's history and was associated with God's presence on Mount Sinai, at the dedication of Solomon's temple, and at Isaiah's theophany.[24] In Revelation smoke is associated with God's glory and power:

> And the temple was filled with smoke from the glory of God and from his power, and no one could enter the temple until the seven plagues of the seven angels were completed (15:8).

The greatest and most pervasive symbol of power and authority in Revelation, however, is the *throne*. The word *throne* occurs forty-four times altogether, and it is found in all but five chapters (9, 10, 15, 17, and 18). Related words that emphasize the reign of God—words like *authority, power, rule, kingdom,* and *king*—occur seventy-seven times.[25] The vision of the throne, central to Revelation, is also central to the books of Ezekiel, Isaiah, and Daniel.

The Multiple Dimensions of Revelation Symbols

Revelation symbols often serve multiple functions and carry multiple meanings.[26] Functionally the *four living creatures* guard the throne with their watchful eyes (4:5), initiate and conclude portions of heaven's praise with their voices (4:9; 5:14), and trigger the first and last of the series of sevens.[27] Similarly, the *throne* area of chapter 4 functions variously as a heavenly court where the King reigns in untrammeled majesty, a heavenly synagogue where the scroll is opened, a heavenly temple where incense (symbolic of prayers) is offered on the altar, and as a "great white throne" where the Judge drums out the Accuser.[28] Or take the symbol of the *Holy City* (21:22). This master symbol of the last chapters of Revelation is not strictly a "city" as we would imagine it. It combines elements of the city of Jerusalem (21:11–21), the temple (21:22–27), and of an Edenic paradise (22:1–2).

Thunder and lightning symbols also serve multiple functions. They naturally evoke fear and awe. Yet when placed in the context of the rainbow and the twenty-four worshiping elders, the flashes of lightning and peals of thunder from the throne in Revelation 4 express unparalleled transcendence—not retribution.

In real life I have found the experience of thunder can be different in various parts of the country. In Vancouver, British Columbia, where I was reared, angry-looking clouds usually preceded thunder and lightning. The whole sky would be in motion, followed by jagged arrows of lightning and cracks of thunder. You could never be sure where lightning would strike. (I'd shudder inside as I watched it.) A live bolt could "arc" some nearby object—myself! Someone growing up in Vancouver could easily identify lightning with judgment.

In the prairies I once experienced an entirely different kind of thunder. We were traveling by car, the sun was setting, and splashes of brilliant orange and red were being reflected against the clouds. Suddenly the sky lit up with sheets of lightning that flared repeatedly and regularly for about half an hour while sonic booms of thunder echoed. Quite a show! I've never seen anything like it. It evoked in me feelings of awe, even a certain amount of fear, but not judgment—judgment was quite absent. "Sheet lightning" had a different effect on me than "arrow lightning."

These personal descriptions reflect two ways that the Book of Revelation employs thunder and lightning—for transcendence and retribution. The transcendent rumblings from the throne are matched and complemented by the sound texture of innumerable multitudes whose combined response also rumbles like thunder (14:2; 19:1). That is, God's thunder and the people's rumbling response could be envisioned as a gigantic antiphonal exchange in the dialogue of worship. On the other hand, the seven thunders (10:4) undoubtedly symbolize a series of terrifying judgments.

Thunder and lightning, therefore, can express either retribution or nonretribution, depending on the context. Some scholars do not seem to appreciate this variety: four passages in Revelation appear to use thunder retributively, while three do not.[29] Perhaps the lightning of chapter 4 could even be likened to the fireworks shows on Independence Day celebrations in the United States or like fireworks going off in sync with music. At the Hollywood Bowl, the Los Angeles Philharmonic orchestra annually presents just such a concert—which is understandably a favorite family event! Since sounds of thunder can be reproduced with synthesizers in today's worship, their use, particularly as windows to transcendence, has increasingly interested me. I note that for C. S. Lewis, too, "tasting" reality imaginatively (as he put it) became more and more important for him as he grew older.

A traditional counterpart to thunder in local congregations is the pipe organ. When the organist "pulls out all the stops," we can feel the very pews vibrating! At church we were unable to use the organ in our services for several weeks. Pastor Allen Hadidian remarked to me in passing the other day, "I miss the transcendence that the organ gives to our worship." Thunder and organ sounds are "ways of knowing." Don't underestimate this. Scripture doesn't. God doesn't.

Trumpet sounds, also, have rich connections to Old Testament life that continue through the Epistles to the Book of Revelation. They were blown to assemble the people, call them to repentance, or summon them to war. Trumpet blasts were blown to commence all the major feasts and the daily sacrifice, and to mark a new day, the Sabbath, new moons, and the new year. Trumpets, you will recall, sounded on Mount Sinai when Moses met with God, and they will announce Christ's second return. They proclaimed the accession of kings. In Revelation the seventh trumpet signals the heavenly "coronation anthem":

> The seventh angel sounded his trumpet, and there were loud voices in heaven, which said:
>
> "The kingdom of the world has become the kingdom of our Lord and of his Christ,
>   and he will reign for ever and ever" (11:15).

How exciting! Again, we have a differentiation of symbolic meaning illustrated, the first six trumpets announcing judgment while the seventh announces the kingdom.

The *bowls* also have multiple functions. Bowls of incense symbolize the prayers of the saints (5:8). The seven bowls provide a means for initiating seven plagues (16:1). God is alert to multiple uses in His use of symbols. We can learn from Him!

SUMMARY

Man is a symbol-making, symbol-using being, just as the Creator is a symbol-making, symbol-using God. In this chapter I have questioned the belief that the time and need for symbols has passed. I have sought to establish a strong connection between Old Testament and Revelation worship. Revelation worship blends continuity of the past with unfolding newness. Lightning, thunder, trumpets, and bowls fluidly express either judgment or transcendence. Smoke, lamplight, and altars are used. Symbols such as the "throne" and the "city" serve multiple functions.

Revelation symbols not only arouse our historical consciousness (i.e., our recollection of other Scripture passages), but also set our personal storehouse of memories ringing. Have you ever wondered why the 265 allusions to Scripture in Revelation are consistently short and paraphrased—so unlike the longer citations in (say) Hebrews? I believe a primary intent of John is not only to provoke the analysis of Scripture with Scripture for prophetic understanding, but to spark our imaginations, to open us up to new vistas of experience. Evoking in us a transcendent experience of God Himself is a tremendously important goal of the book. Revelation worship, old but new, encourages us to grow in experience and be stretched in understanding through symbolism.

A saying attributed to the Top Worship Consultant (who unfortunately is seldom consulted): "I like a little thunder with My worship."

QUESTIONS FOR THOUGHT AND DISCUSSION

1. Did the need for ceremonial symbols in worship end with the coming of the new covenant? Discuss.
2. "When we set the symbolism of the Old Testament alongside the symbolism of Revelation, we see continuity with unfolding newness." Discuss.
3. How is the symbolism that scientists employ different from that of artists?
4. In your view, is there a need for symbols in today's worship? Explain your answer.
5. "Meaning involving several senses is obviously more vital than meaning involving only one." Discuss, citing examples.
6. What symbols could you use to invoke transcendence in your church worship?

CHAPTER TWENTY

Worship With Mystery

As I was reading the Children's International Bible version of Revelation to my seven-year-old Jesse for the first time, he seemed to be very much into the basic story line. After a half-dozen chapters he jumped up and threw his hands in the air, shouting, "The world is coming to an end! The world is coming to an end!" Wanting to get a better idea of how he was coping emotionally, I asked: "What do you think of this book, Jesse?" He became absolutely still for a moment, then said, "It's strange, but good."

MYSTERY AND SYMBOLS

Revelation symbols tend to induce in us a sense of openness, wonderment, and mystery. Visually, for example, when did you last see a lamb with seven horns and seven eyes? Or take the four living creatures:

> The first . . . was like a lion, the second was like an ox, the third had a face like a man, the fourth was like a flying eagle. Each of the four living creatures had six wings and was covered with eyes all around (4:7–8).

The strangeness of these creatures—their wholly otherness—rivets our attention to the text. We recoil in wonder. Thunder, lightning, smoke, and incense also inject awe into worship. Their meanings, which tend to be more diffuse, cannot always be *wholly* perceived through rational, analytical means.[1] For example, what is the meaning of the thirty minutes of silence in Revelation 8:1? Or think of the mystery of the Trinity (1:4; 22:17). How can three be one? It does not yield to logical closure. Lack of closure can be unsettling to Western minds demanding absolute certainty and precise explanation—even on secondary issues not lending themselves to clear resolution.[2] Interestingly, in this respect the writer John does not always communicate visions that cohere visually.

Some are visually unresolvable.[3] Yet this too forms part of the communication style of Holy Writ.

Moreover, in Revelation (as in the rest of the Bible) some symbols *are* explained while others *are not*. For example, there are explanations for the seven stars and lampstands, the woman, the waters, and the fine linen (1:20; 7:15, 18; 19:8). Elsewhere, a clear explanation is given of the symbolic meaning of the Lord's Supper, but nowhere is a similar explanation given for the symbolism of the tabernacle furniture. Regarding the parables of Jesus, the disciples often ask, "What does this mean?" Sometimes an explanation is offered, sometimes not. When Jesus speaks metaphorically, His audience often mistakenly takes His statements too literally. C. S. Lewis says that trying to pin down Jesus' teaching into neat propositions is "like trying to bottle a sunbeam."[4] In one case in Revelation, a symbolic explanation presents not one, but two meanings— each itself symbolic:

> The seven heads are seven hills on which the woman sits. They are also seven kings (17:9–10).[5]

Cast in highly artistic form, some books in Scripture (such as Job, Song of Songs, and Revelation) place great interpretative responsibility on the reader.[6] Although the main points of these books may be uncontested (for example, God's complete victory over Satan in Revelation), students of Scripture have entertained widely differing perceptions of details. There is no consensus.

An article in *Time* reported that one hundred scholars could not even agree on the meaning of "Little Red Riding Hood":

> Nearly everyone agrees that the story . . . is an evocative tale of sex and violence, but exactly what it evokes is a matter of dispute among folklorists, anthropologists, Freudians, feminists and literary critics.[7]

Old Testament scholar Kevin J. Vanhoozer wonders whether theologians would have fared better! Believing that the purpose of the story of Red Riding Hood is, at the very least, to *warn* someone, he remarks:

> Many of the Old Testament narratives have a similar purpose. . . . [Scripture puts it the following way.] "These things happened to them as examples and were written down as warnings for us" (1 Corinthians 10:11). That is, the New Testament record was written down not only to convey information, but to *affect* its readers in certain ways.[8]

Certainly in our evangelical services people need clear and incisive teaching, but in our overweening disposition for propositional statements and analysis, the affective, aesthetic dimension (which is fundamental to worship involving the whole person) is often completely lost. We need greater appreciation for the public reading of narrative and poetic passages of Scripture—allowing biblical images to speak forth with power and beauty. Poetic images help instill a love for Scripture and delight in worship. Just as great preaching inspires, so great reading inspires.

When actor-director John Cochran reads Scripture at my home church, it's sheer music! Wonderful! And his reading reveals truth. I wish pastors would read more Scripture in the course of their sermons. In its own way, inspired reading can be as insightful and spiritually revealing as analysis, especially the reading of narrative. Vanhoozer remarks analogously:

> I, for one, have not come across a good paraphrase of Brahms' "Fourth Symphony." . . . someone has said that the whole Protestant doctrine of the human race is contained in Rembrandt's paintings . . . but a systematic theologian would be hard pressed to put this theology in propositional form.[9]

Don't misunderstand. We want analysis too! This book, for instance, offers plenty of it. But Evangelicals tend to esteem propositional statements and undervalue poetic passages. How tragic! Dallas Willard, calling for a commitment to the arts, put it poignantly in a chapel service at a Christian college:

> I don't want you to think of art as a little frill or whipped cream on the cake of life. It's more like steak and potatoes.[10]

Much of the "steak" in Scripture, including prophecy, comes cast in poetic form. C. S. Lewis disparages people who are on the lookout for information alone: "As the unmusical listener wants only the Tune, so the unliterary reader wants only the Event."[11] He says, "The most valuable thing the Psalms do for me is to express the same delight in God which made David dance."[12] We need to understand that some metaphors are "our only method of reaching a given idea at all."[13]

AMBIGUITY AND SYMBOLISM

A friend of mine read some of his poetry to an audience at Yale University. Upon finishing, he was caught off guard by some students who asked him, "Would you answer some questions concerning your symbolism?" He told me he didn't answer them. "I didn't feel comfortable talking about my poems."

This story fairly represents many artists. Some willingly explain the meaning of their work, but many hesitate. They would rather have their audiences discover the implications themselves. Artists are reluctant to put titles on paintings and often include cryptic or suggestive ones if any.

Similarly, composers are reticent about providing programmatic notes with symphonies. Filmmakers resist giving "interpretations" of their films. Believing that words alone cannot tell all they wish to say, they want the setting of the film, the characters, the way they are drawn—in short, their craft in the work itself—to convey that information within the art form.

Yet, where the people lack skills for understanding the "language" of a particular artistic medium, some explanation *is* needed. You have to strike a balance between giving too much, therefore preempting personal discovery, and too little, so that the people totally miss the point. In matters like these, the leadership of each church must discern the level of the people's capacity to make connections.

> *When we conducted an Advent candlelighting ceremony at my church for the first time, we received a positive response from children and adults alike. We also installed four banners, keyed to the four Advent themes. Each banner contained a single word and a symbol: promise (rainbow), hope (anchor), peace (tree), and waiting (star). Each week we highlighted a different banner and lit a different candle. To our surprise we found that few of the people grasped what we felt was obvious; they were not connecting the key word on the banner with the Advent ceremony theme for the day. So we had to articulate that relationship during the announcements. We might have handled this more creatively by addressing the children directly at the very outset: "Listen and watch for the next four Sundays. Can you discover in what way the Advent ceremony relates to the banners?"*
>
> *Since the Advent candlelighting ceremony was not part of our past church worship tradition, it proved important to build a bridge for the people into this alternative form of communication. We distributed copies of the Advent ceremony so that as parents, couples, and singles watched on Sundays, they could learn to do it themselves and be comfortable performing the ceremony at home with their family or invited friends after dinner during the week. In this way we sought to encourage the entire church to model worship and fellowship in their homes.*

Ambiguity in relation to the use of symbols remains an issue in many churches. Since symbols acquire meaning from their environment, ambiguity can be measurably reduced by placing symbols in a carefully prescribed *context*. Recall how in the Old Testament temple the worshiper offered his lamb (nonverbal communication) while the Levites sang to the Lord (verbal communication). This principle is basic to the strategy of Revelation and something to consider when using symbols in a local church context. In other words, the whole can inform the part.

For another example, consider that the thunder of Revelation 4 needs to be seen in context with the "Holy, holy, holy" of the four living creatures, the bowing of the elders, the rainbow of light, and the verbal responses of the congregation along with other thunder passages in Scripture.

In the same way, when taken together in Communion services, the readings, the dedicatory prayers, the hymns, the bread, and the cup all form a comprehensive and interactive form of communication. We can make the mistake theoretically of expecting too much of symbols, of requiring that symbols tell the whole story. In our services, symbols may communicate mystery and unboundedness, and the sermon (or words of accompanying explanation) a sense of definition—a happy contrast.

We need to be clear, however, that the whole direction of Western science and analysis aims at reducing mystery through explanation. A sense of mystery needs to be retained! The Trinity is mystery. The Incarnation is mystery. The blazing lamps around the throne (symbolizing the Spirit) present mystery. God describes Himself as "I AM WHO I AM" (Exod. 3:14). This kind of language is "odd," to say the least, and deliberately arouses a sense of mystery. It defies analysis. It's like saying "A rose is a rose is a rose is a rose"—some undefinable extra is added in each repetition. The meaning must be *caught;* it does not belong anywhere in a scientist's vocabulary. But it does in ours. A faith such as ours, founded on the supernatural, fundamentally demands mystery.

FOUR DEANS, FOUR SYMBOLS

I recall thinking of Revelation worship one day as I was involved in planning an all-university worship service at Biola designed to express what we were as an institution. I was scheduled to meet with the four deans on the matter. I wanted to introduce some symbolism into the event but had difficulty thinking what precisely would be comfortable to the people and appropriate for the occasion. Some ideas gradually came to mind. I was quite nervous in presenting them to the deans because I did not know how the group would react. My premonitions proved correct. They expressed some natural hesitancy, especially when they realized they were to be the performers in front of a large audience! After talking back and forth, we agreed on something with which each felt comfortable. I could tell, though, that I had touched a sensitive nerve.

This is what we decided. In our floor plan for the event, everyone was seated in the round in four quadrants (north, south, east, west) with a small table at the center. The top administrators (president, provost, the four deans, and student leaders) were seated nearest to the table, then the musicians (choirs, band, string orchestra, and twenty-four guitar players), the faculty and staff, and finally the graduate and undergraduate students. The third part of the actual worship program went like this:

Presentation of Songs and Symbols to the Lord

Rosemead School of Psychology
The Healing Oil Outpoured
Talbot School of Theology
The Open Bible
Song: "O Worship the King" (Talbot)
School of Intercultural Studies
The Towel of Servanthood
School of Arts and Sciences
The Jesus Candle
Song: "Seek Ye First the Kingdom of God"

A student assisted each dean, who explained the symbol, offered a prayer, and performed a symbolic gesture at the table in the center.

—The dean of the Rosemead School of Psychology explained it trained Christian counselors to minister emotional and spiritual healing to hurting people. He committed his students to the Lord and then poured oil into a flask.

—Holding the Bible for all to see, the dean of the Talbot School of Theology pledged to keep a high view of Scripture and asked the student beside him to lead the Talbot students in singing "O Worship the King."

—The dean of the School of Intercultural Studies spoke of maintaining a servant's heart, not lording it over others on mission fields.

—The dean of the School of Arts and Sciences prayed that the graduates and undergraduate students would be "light" in their places of employment, communities, and churches, then he lit the Jesus Candle. The person with him, accompanied by a guitar choir of twenty-four players, then led the students in "Seek Ye First."

After a meditative piece by the symphonic band, the above-mentioned leaders formed a "circle of prayer" (another symbol) around the table as Dr. Clyde Cook, president of Biola, led the entire university in prayer. More was involved in the symbolic presentations than I have space to describe, but the result proved an effective (and elegant) way to reinforce some core values of the university in the context of worship.

Revelation ideas can be implemented in local church worship in much the way we did this at Biola. Even small churches can obtain some of the Revelation feeling by having Communion in the round with the table in the center. People then come to the table and partake.

THEOLOGY OF SPACE: MOVEMENT AND GESTURE
AS SYMBOL

The symbolism of movement and gesture can also be used to illustrate important principles of worship in local church situations. In a small fundamentalist church I had a men's chorus make procession down the aisle, face the pulpit with their backs to the congregation, and sing in unison "The Lord's Prayer" (Malotte) to begin a Sunday morning service. The piece and the movement powerfully set a tone for the whole service. Visually the men communicated the idea that they were singing to the Lord, not to the people. Many in the congregation grasped the symbolism. They understood that the words and the visual gesture reinforced each other.

This turned out to be so successful that I tried to replicate it at another fundamentalist church where I served as a worship consultant. Rehearsing this piece with the men, I encountered strong opposition from one person in the group. We all discussed the issue he raised, and I sensed that though a number of the men stood with me, we were divided. I tried to clarify my intent: "By facing toward the front, the altar area, we are symbolically facing God, not the people. We are communicating that we are singing to Him, and focusing the congregation on God, not us."

My explanation only complicated matters for this man. He objected to my using the word *altar*. He said something to the effect, "We don't believe in altars at this church." I wanted to read Revelation 5:7 and other Scripture passages to him, but I could see the plot thickening and decided to back off from the idea. It was more important at that time to preserve my relationship with my brother and pursue the matter with him later individually. In talking about this incident with the pastor later, I learned that the church had worked through the issue of symbols sometime ago when a disagreement arose over the use of the cross. They decided to allow a cross symbol on the outside of the church, but put up no permanent, physical cross inside, out of respect for the second commandment. I cite this experience to reassure you that I am aware of different views and feelings on this matter. The intent of this chapter, however, is to let Scripture challenge us, above and beyond the comfort of whatever tradition we may have inherited.

We as Evangelicals can become more sensitive to what we are communicating visually, gesturally. When we stand at the front facing the people and waving mikes in our hands, we may be unintentionally conveying the impression we are performing, even entertaining, Hollywood style. For this reason some churches—Lutheran and Episcopal, for example—place the choir and organ in the balcony out of view of the people or facing each other in the choir loft at right angles to the congregation. I am not necessarily suggesting that Evangelicals ought to get out their hammers and tear down choir lofts centered behind their pulpits or that pulpits must be set to the side. I am suggesting we should be more aware of the visual-gestural messages we are generating, even unconsciously. Heaven's worship has a theology of space that is well thought out, sensible, and appropriate: all the people face the One seated on the throne. If God considered this form significant, should we not consider spacial placement significant too?

WHY AREN'T SYMBOLS IN THE GOSPELS AND EPISTLES?

You may be asking, "If symbols are so important, why are they not used in the worship practice reported in the Gospels and Epistles?" Why, for example, don't candles appear in those New Testament books? Good questions! To be honest, we may have to be satisfied with a less-than-conclusive answer. I'm reminded of the suave response one of my English professors gave to a question I asked in my undergraduate days. With a wry smile my professor replied: "I'm not very good at that kind of question, Barry. Would you care to ask another?" Please consider the following points.

First, the absence of symbols in the early New Testament church may mean their use is *not required or mandatory*. However, since no specific prohibition against symbols is found either, and since symbols are extensively used in the Old Testament and in the Book of Revelation, their use may be *permissible*. That is the position I take in this book. The use of symbols is no more mandatory than having a choir, but it does deserve a second look by Evangelicals.

Second, while we don't have texts in the Gospels and the Epistles that confirm the use of symbols in the New Testament church, this should not be sufficient grounds for prohibiting their use in local churches. If we followed this principle of New Testament precedents consistently, a lot more than liturgical symbols would have to go. There would be no place for choirs, musical instruments, solos, banners, the Lord's Table decorated with an open Bible, a prayer altar, Sunday school, baby dedications, invitations for salvation, church denominations, or even buildings constructed specifically for churches. Even such scripturally based practices like responses of "hallelujah" or prostrations would not be allowed.

Yet regarding prostration, for example, we have evidence that it remained a form of personal worship (at the very least) in the culture, although it is not specifically mentioned among corporate worship practices. In the Gospels there are two accounts of people prostrating themselves before Jesus (Matt. 9:18; Luke 17:15), and Acts tells of Cornelius falling at Peter's feet in reverence. While Peter corrected him for doing this ("Stand up," he said, "I am only a man myself"), he did not seem to think prostration itself illegitimate.

Given this evidence for prostration in the New Testament culture and in the Old Testament narrative, would it be wise to conclude that early Christians did not practice prostration because specific instances cannot be found in local church or synagogue practice in Scripture? Hardly! Perhaps we could construct a principle like this: *We should examine worship practices in the light of the entire pattern of Scripture as well as extrabiblical documents that shed light on Scripture and culture.*

Some have argued that the Gospel of John—a book rich in symbols—teaches that worship ought be *spiritual* rather than *symbolic* (except for the Lord's Table and baptism). They argue that the very *presence* of so many symbols in John—Christ is the Word, the Light, the Bread of Life, the Good Shepherd, etc.—coupled with the *absence* of any explicit use of such symbols in worship is significant.

However, John is not concerned with Christian worship practices or forms anywhere in his Gospel. His focus is entirely different. He uses imagery—like the *flock* (10:1–16) and the *vine* (15:1–11)—to emphasize the individual's personal relationship and union with Christ Himself.[14] The shepherd calls each sheep by name (10:3–5); each branch is individually nurtured from the parent stem (15:4–5). Ralph P. Martin elaborates:

> John's view of the church governs his concept of worship: the church is made up of individual followers who are joined one-by-one to the Lord, and the worship they offer springs directly out of an experience of enriched individualism.[15]

The term *church* does not occur anywhere in John's Gospel either. He is not concerned with corporate expression. Therefore, to select the Gospel of John as the authority on the issue of symbols in corporate worship is a mistake. Nevertheless, in 1 Corinthians Paul focuses directly on the nitty-gritty issues related to worship practice; so does John in the Book of Revelation.

We can also make an argument based on the notion of progressive revelation. The Gospels and Epistles were probably written and in circulation well before the Book of Revelation. Since John's vision of heavenly worship had not yet been given, the full extent and import of Hebrews 8:5 could not have been revealed. Therefore, we can't know the many ways in which the Book of Revelation (written around A.D. 90) might have influenced worship in the early church had it been available.

The point I want to emphasize is that the Book of Revelation is pivotal. Revelation worship can swing the balance: it gives impetus for a more liturgical kind of worship when viewed as a model for worship here and now. God designed Revelation worship. *He* uses symbols in worship. And so may *we* when we worship Him.

TEMPLE AND SYNAGOGUE ARE COMPLEMENTARY

Interestingly, God chose throughout Bible history to keep the vision of the temple (with its symbolism) before the hearts of His people. The temple was only temporarily out of view.

The temple concept begins with the movable tabernacle in the desert wanderings, continues with the Solomonic temple, the second temple rebuilt under Nehemiah and Ezra, and finally Herod's remodeling of it around the time of Christ. Between A.D. 70 and 90 the temple concept temporarily falls from view. Around A.D. 90 God reveals to John a vision of the heavenly temple, a Christianized version of the Old Testament temple—which *reestablishes* in the minds of God's people the temple symbols.

Jewish Christians attended both the temple and the synagogue until the former was destroyed in A.D. 70. The temple and synagogue enjoyed a complementary relationship to one another: the temple emphasized symbolism, and the synagogue, the Scriptures. Jewish Christian church worship practices were indebted primarily to the synagogue, which in turn owed a debt to the temple. Jesus made symbolism part of Christian worship in instituting the Lord's Table and baptism.

WHY WAS REVELATION WORSHIP REVEALED?

The basic question remains: "Why did God choose to describe the worship in heaven in such copious detail?"

The Book of Revelation gives us, among other things, a revelation of heavenly worship practices. Why did God give us that? Is it intended to be a model for us today, or is it exclusively for the future?

I contend that it already influences us. Its images, so vivid and captivating, have lodged themselves in our memories through hymns saturated with them. But beyond this, Revelation balances its use of all the arts and appeals to the whole person. Its liturgical ideas have demonstrated, practical value. I would even go further and say that as God has revealed His creativity in the forms of Revelation worship, so we are encouraged as creators (with a small "c") not only to borrow and adapt from Revelation, but to exercise our imagination for His glory in our worship of Him here and now.

QUESTIONS FOR THOUGHT AND DISCUSSION

1. "In our services, symbols may communicate mystery and unboundedness, and the sermon (or words of accompanying explanation) a sense of definition." Discuss.
2. "A faith such as ours, being founded on the supernatural, fundamentally demands mystery." Discuss.
3. If symbols are so important, why are they not used in the worship practices reported in the Gospels and Epistles?
4. If we take the principle of New Testament precedents to an extreme, it will stifle innovation and cultural adaptation. Comment.
5. Why did God choose to describe in such detail the worship in heaven?

RECOMMENDED READING

Hoon, Paul Waitman. *The Integrity of Worship*. Nashville: Abingdon Press, 1971.
Webber, Robert E. *Evangelicals on the Canterbury Trail: Why Evangelicals Are Attracted to the Liturgical Church*. Waco, Tex.: Word Books, 1985.

CHAPTER TWENTY-ONE

Product of God, Creator-Artist

He who was seated on the throne said, "I am making everything new. . . . It is done" (Rev. 21:5–6).

Have you ever wondered how Evangelicals *suddenly* transported to heaven might react to Revelation worship? The transition could be difficult. Some of us might have salty responses! Tighten your seat belts!

Imagine the criticism God would receive from Evangelicals like us who arrive in heaven and find the roar of the congregational response too loud, the thunder and lightning too unsettling, the four living creatures too weird, the thirty minutes of silence too long, the prostration too embarrassing, the undulations of "Holy, holy, holy" around the throne too repetitious, the tabernacle furniture too Catholic, too symbolic! Or what about Evangelicals who find the idea of vestments too showy, the material outlay too expensive, the ceremony too elaborate, the incense too strange, or phrases like "We give thee thanks" too liturgical, stilted, and confining?

I can further imagine these same Evangelicals poised to do some carping . . . until they remember the alternative and change their minds!

INCLUSIVE WORSHIP

When we are in fact transported to heaven, I suspect even the most critical among us will be swept off our feet in awe and wonder. The words "we never did it this way before" will take on new meaning! To bring all the cultures of the world together in unity will be quite a feat. Only God could do it. And He will! We know from observing God's work in the created order that He loves variety and thinks comprehensively. Let's look at the ways God exercises His creative choice in projecting to us an inclusive, universal worship.

First, an inclusive symbol introduces inclusive worship. Revelation worship appears to be initiated by the four living creatures,[1] who function as an inclusive symbol.[2]

> The first living creature was like a lion, the second . . . like an ox, the third had a face like a man, the fourth was like a flying eagle (4:7).

The creatures symbolize "whatever is noblest, strongest, wisest, and swiftest."[3] In other words:

lion = noblest
ox = strongest
man = wisest
eagle = swiftest

The creatures probably "stand in some way for the whole of creation,"[4] since the number four in Revelation seems to symbolize the world. John sees the four angels "standing at the four corners of the earth, holding back the four winds" (7:1).

Second, worship in heaven is immense in scale and unimaginable in variety. People from *every* "nation, tribe, people and language" form part of the total response:

> After this I looked and there before me was a great multitude that no one could count, from every nation, tribe, people and language, standing before the throne and in front of the lamb (7:9).

As the Psalmist had predicted universal worship (Ps. 86:9), now the multitudes in heaven declare its advent: "All nations will come and worship before you" (15:4).

But the canvas of praise is still broader. Not only the angelic and redeemed orders, but *all of creation* sing to God. Every creature "in heaven and on earth and under the earth and on the sea" participates. The phrase "all that is in them" emphasizes inclusiveness:

> Then I heard every creature in heaven and on earth and under the earth and on the sea, and *all that is in them,* singing (Rev. 5:13).

Clearly Revelation worship stands within the tradition of (and broadens) our understanding of Psalm 150: "Let *everything* that has breath praise the LORD" (v. 6).[5] The four living creatures are the mechanism for igniting this praise. Since they are in appearance part angelic, part human, part creaturely, every created being can identify with some aspect of these symbolic beings.

Recall also that the worship setting is apparently a configuration of concentric circles. Have you ever tried to lead thousands of people seated about you in the round? I have. It is less than satisfactory because the leader's back is always toward someone, so he or she tends to move around in the space (facing this way and that) to alleviate the problem. There really is no solution—besides having four leaders, animated as one, prompting the assembly. If we visualize it, this is exactly what we have in Revelation 4! Note also the word *whenever:*

> *Whenever* the living creatures give glory, honor and thanks to him who sits on the throne . . . the twenty-four elders fall down before him who sits on the throne, and worship him (4:9–10).

Whenever can be translated "when" (NASB) or "as often as." In either case a certain coordination of the four creatures and the twenty-four elders occurs; an apparent cause-and-effect relationship or simultaneity exists between them.[6] The four living creatures trigger the universal worship response and the twenty-four elders (and the rest of creation by implication) then follow.

Third, the modes of response are comprehensive in scope, involving both verbal and nonverbal communication, prostration, and singing. Genuine inward worship is complemented by outward manifestation. All nations, all animals, all nature (earthquake, lightning, thunder), all arts (the visual, the aural, ceremony, drama, movement, pageantry), all senses (including olfactory), all manner of symbols (furniture, articles, animals, architecture), and all orders of beings (angelic, human, creaturely) contribute to worship. The direction of the Revelation model is toward inclusiveness.

Fourth, God chooses to give music and song a magnificent place in Revelation worship. Music is one of the most inclusive and integrative art forms. We can expound on the relationship of music to language (poetry and prose forms), to drama (opera), to time (both clock and psychological time, altered states of consciousness, memory, proportion/mathematics), to dance (movement), to space (sound movement, localization), sound color (timbre, resonance), to people (social dimension), and to abstract and graphic notation. Music is a multidimensional art form. The chart by Hodges, shown below, offers a descriptive model of music's interdisciplinary nature.

Fifth, the unity that God has achieved between the peoples in heaven illustrates another aspect of His creativity. Not just concerned with the form of worship (symbols and the like), God desires a unity of deep, real, abiding qualities. The words that introduce the *united,* congregational song of Moses and the Lamb express these values:

> They held harps given them by God and sang the song of Moses the servant of God *and* the song of the Lamb (15:2–3).

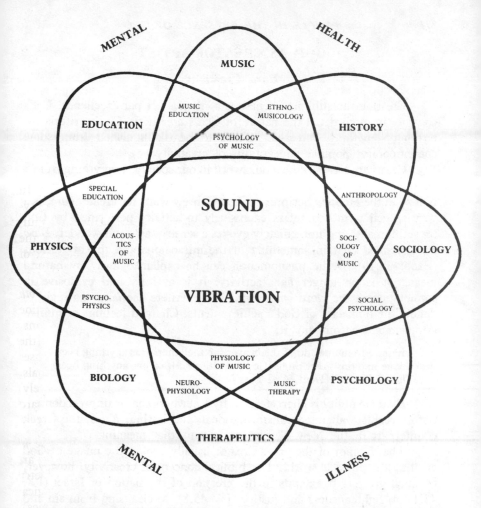

Descriptive model ("molecule") of the interdisciplinary world of music psychology. Adapted from Donald A. Hodges, ed., *Handbook of Music Psychology* (Lawrence, Kans.: National Association of Music Therapy, 1980).

One song rings out in *complete* harmony. There is no longer any controversy between the law and the gospel, nor any hostility between Israel and the church. The ultimate reality of Ephesians is fulfilled as Israel and the church are made truly one in Christ:

> His purpose was to *create* in himself one new man out of the two, thus making peace, and in this one body to reconcile both of them to God through the cross by which he put to death their hostility (Eph. 2:15–16).

GOD AS CREATOR-ARTIST

Bara Creativity

Creating the sublime oneness is a creative act par excellence! Let's consider in more detail the nature of God's creativity. God's criteria for terming something "creative" needs to be distinguished from some contemporary, popular conceptions of creativity.

Creativity has become a buzzword in our society. Everything from a child's scribble to Einstein's theory of relativity is considered creative. Not so in the Hebrew Scriptures! The Hebrew word for create, *bara*, is a very special term.[7] It refers exclusively to activity performed by God (never humans) and immediately evokes a sense of awe and wonder. *Bara* activity must contain something of the miraculous and the mysterious (Exod. 34:10). If the phenomenon can be explained away by natural means, it is no longer *bara* activity. It is as lofty and explosive in connotation as the word *omnipotent*. Bible writers use *bara* sparingly to denote the pinnacles of God's achievements. Charged feelings of human astonishment accompany it:

> Inquire from one end of the heavens to the other. Has anything been done like this great thing [God's creative act], or has anything been heard like it? (Deut. 4:32 NASB).

Bara creativity is characterized by a newness that is unprecedented, unforeseeable, valuable, transformational, and lasting. *Ktizo*, the Greek counterpart in the New Testament, retains that meaning.

The thought of the great Creator usually evokes the image of God creating the physical world. The biblical concept of creativity, however, is much greater. It extends to the creation of the nation of Israel (Isa. 43:1), to righteousness and justice (Isa. 45:8), to cleansing from sin and psychological healing (Ps. 51:10), to regeneration (2 Cor. 5:17; Eph. 4:24), and it leads inexorably to praise and joy (worship). That is, God's creativity includes not only physical, sociological, ethical, and spiritual kinds of construction, but the construction of praise and joy:

> For behold, I *create* new heavens and a new earth. . . . be glad and rejoice forever in what I *create;* For behold, I *create* Jerusalem for rejoicing (Isa. 65:17–18 NASB).

"Jerusalem for rejoicing." Revelation worship has to do with rejoicing! Worship is the arena where the full rein of God's creativity finds joyful expression.

Newness centrally characterizes *bara* activity. In biblical literature the word *new* (*chadash*), like the word *bara*, is used sparingly in reference to significant events. In eight instances *new* occurs in immediate conjunction with the word *bara*.

But what is the nature of *bara* newness in Scripture? What kind of newness is involved? How can it be described? What are its features, its criteria?

1. *Bara* newness is unprecedented (Isa. 43:15–21)—the first of its kind, that which did not exist before, that which is irreducible to something known, the unheard of.
2. *Bara* newness is humanly unforeseeable (Num. 16:30). It has the quality of surprise, of hidden things brought to light—the quality of the unexpected and unpredictable.
3. *Bara* newness is valuable (Gen. 2:9; Isa. 41:17–20). It cannot be novelty for novelty's sake. It must solve a problem, serve a function, be workable, yet beautiful, fitting, elegant.
4. *Bara* newness is transformational in that it can become part of tradition and undergo transformation, re-creation (Gal. 6:15; Eph. 2:15).
5. *Bara* newness is lasting. It does not lose its luster after repeated examination and contemplation. This is a newness that never perishes.

With a little reflection the reader will discern these same criteria operative in the design of worship in Revelation 4 and 5. From beginning to end Revelation worship gives us a lesson in *bara* creativity!

Moreover, in the Old and New Testaments *bara* creativity is power theology. It urges upon the observer a rethinking of everything, a transformation of one's worldview:

> "That they may see and recognize,
> And consider and gain insight as well,
> *That the hand of the Lord has done this,*
> And the Holy One of Israel has created it."
> (Isa. 41:20 NASB)

Bara creativity forces the observer to expand his awareness to acknowledge God.

"Behold I Make All Things New"

The full weight of these criteria lie behind the momentous statement "Behold I make all things new"—the first time God specifically "speaks" in the Book of Revelation (21:5 KJV). How enlightening!

Creativity is central to God's character. The eternal Creator is and forever will be creating. Swiftly come His words "It is done" (one word in the Greek). *"Done!"* God has the power to bring the vision to life, to realize it. "Inspiration and perfection, wish and fulfillment, will and accomplishment"—these coincide spontaneously and simultaneously.[8]

Sometimes believers intimate that the practice of continuous praise in heaven will be boring. Don't believe it! That is an impossibility given the *creativity* of our God! Knowing what we do about God, what are the probabilities that He will stop creating? Zero! God is the inexhaustible, eternal Creator. Like any true artist, He is always interested in the "next step." Heaven will never be boring.

The statement "Behold I make all things new" sets off a new rhythm in the Book of Revelation. We see God, the sublime Artist, the unrivaled Architect, again at work. The Holy City comes down out of heaven from God, a perfect cube (perfect replica of the shape of the Holy of Holies) in Revelation 21. The concept of the Holy of Holies is now expanded and becomes, as it were, an enormous, symmetrical city, 1,400 miles long in every direction (21:16). Decorated with every kind of precious stone, it gleams with twelve pearly gates and twelve foundation stones. The streets are paved of "pure gold, like transparent glass." A river, clear as crystal, flows from the throne of God and from the Lamb. On each side of the river stands the tree of life "for the healing of the nations."

Notice that the symbolism continues! The Edenic and temple symbolism is retained and transformed! God apparently does not discard His ideas and creations. He is ever re-creating, ever renewing, ever transforming. He is the consummate Artist and Developer.

Symbols in the Book of Revelation have not passed away! The Judeo-Christian God is a symbol-making, symbol-loving God. Symbols in Revelation provide a vehicle for joy, for glory, for creativity of expression, for multilevel and elegant communication, for commemoration. The Maker of all things beautiful is ever, and forever will be, the lover of light, color, sound, drama, and ceremony.

INTIMACY IN WORSHIP

We saw in Revelation 4 that a sea of glass "separated" the worshipers from the throne area. Similarly in times past (Genesis), the archangel guarded the entrance to Eden after the Fall, and later the veil barred entrance to the Holy of Holies (Exodus). Now in the final climactic progression of Revelation, the convergence toward possession continues. The movement is steadily toward intimacy. The focus is now on personal relationship: people forever in the presence of God!

> And I heard a loud voice from the throne saying, "Now the dwelling of God is with men, and he will live with them. They will be his

people, and God himself will be with them and be their God. He will wipe every tear from their eyes. There will be no more death or mourning or crying or pain, for the old order of things has passed away" (21:3–4).

Father Gregory Elmer comments:

> . . . in heaven we shall know face to face. Yet we shall not have a clear and distinct comprehensive vision of God, as if God were an object as objects are in the external world. God is SUPREMELY MYSTERY, and the revelation of Jesus is not the exhaustion of that mystery into clear and perspicuous doctrines, but intimacy with that Mystery, a Mystery no longer a rebuff to us, but close. . . . The overwhelming polyvalent and ontologically superessential and utterly ineffable God will be close, and our mind will be sublated in our heart, and our mind and heart together will be released in our spirit, and our spirit will be carried away into a Waylessness and a Wandering in the Infinite Abyss of Godhead . . . beyond all symbols.[9]

This relationship of knowing God "face to face" is available to all who thirst for it. With steady hand John pens these last, sublime words:

> . . . his servants will serve him. They will see his face, and his name will be on their foreheads. There will be no more night. They will not need the light of a lamp or the light of the sun, for the Lord God will give them light. And they will reign for ever and ever (22:3–5).

> The Spirit and the bride say, "Come!" And let him who hears say, "Come!" Whoever is thirsty, let him come; and whoever wishes, let him take the free gift of the water of life (22:17).

> Amen. Come, Lord Jesus (22:20).

QUESTIONS FOR THOUGHT AND DISCUSSION

1. Revelation worship holds the key to all the models. Discuss.
2. "Music is one of the most inclusive and integrative art forms." Discuss.
3. Will worship in heaven be boring? Explain your answer.
4. When, in your opinion, is something truly creative?
5. Should the word *creativity* be used of the work of humans? Explain.
6. Can you articulate the biblical concept of God's creativity and show how He manifests it in the worship found in Revelation?

Appendix 1
Rationale for Implementing Worship

The following philosophy was developed by a worship committee for its congregation. It aims to provide practical guidance through potential problems rather than speak comprehensively on the elements of worship. Thus music is more prominent than prayer and Scripture reading in this statement.

We, as members of _____, desire to continually grow in our understanding of God's person and character. He is infinitely worthy of our worship.

I. *Definition of Worship*. Worship is the act of declaring to God His worth, affirming who He is and what He has done, and responding to Him in praise, adoration, thanksgiving, and awe.

II. *Responsibilities of the Worship Committee*. The committee shall be responsible to encourage worship in the Sunday services, in small groups, and within the family. The Sunday morning responsibility includes the provision of music, prayer, Scripture reading, the design of the service, and the coordination of the ushers.

III. *Priesthood of Believers*. We affirm that worship is the responsibility of the people. For this reason we give high priority to encouraging a tradition of vibrant congregational singing. We regard the congregation as our first and foremost choir. Soloists, choirs, welcome, and announcements should not be allowed to crowd out the time allotted to congregational praise. We also desire to have worshipers (i.e., our people) lead in Scripture reading and prayer.

IV. *Order of Service*. We seek to achieve an integrated service that flows. Although the essentials of our morning service include prayer, Scripture reading, singing, an offering, and the sermon, we seek variety in the service from week to week. In the ordering of the service, the arrangement can consist of a number of short items or consist of long, continuous sections (e.g., ten minutes of uninterrupted singing). Both can be effective, and we plan to use both means. Additionally, at times we may incorporate a "morning praise" pre-service for the purpose of teaching new and old hymns and choruses, preparing our people for worship, and for instructing our people concerning worship.

Prayer, Scripture reading, and congregational praise should not be considered "preliminaries" before the sermon. We seek a service that is truly a worship service.

V. *Performance*. Worship entails a performance dimension whereby the people are the performers, the leaders are the prompters, and God is the audience. Our focus is to minister first to the Lord and then to one another. In this way we can guard against the kind of performance that is ego based and entertainment oriented. In general, the selection of worship leaders/contributors should be based on skill, giftedness, and the demonstration of a credible Christian lifestyle.

VI. *Formation of the Choir*. We desire to hold off forming a choir that would perform regularly until we have sufficient resources, and until there is a strong call from the congregation and singers themselves for it. It has been our custom, however, to mount a choir during the Christmas and Easter seasons.

VII. *Balance*

A. *Balance of Receiving and Responding*. Many evangelical services are really teaching services (not worship services). The people come to "get" something from the main event, the sermon, rather than to offer something (praise) to God. Actually both are critical and need not be antithetical or ranked in some priority, but can be complementary. We desire both to receive and to respond.

B. *Balance of Simple/Complex*. Often our worship will be simple, heartfelt, and unadorned. But at other times it may be rich and elaborate in ceremony, pageantry, drama, and symbolism, as befits the occasion.

C. *Balance of Hymns and Choruses* (Eph. 5:19). The young people should be encouraged to learn the great old hymns (which often contain great lines of theology) and become acquainted with their rich historic past. The adults should be willing to learn fresh, new choruses. Contemporary choruses are a particularly effective means of communicating to the nonchurched, new Christians, and children who attend our services. Each must respect the other and be willing to stretch and grow.

D. *Balance of Worship/Fellowship/Evangelistic Hymns*. In the Sunday morning services we will *mainly* seek hymns that put the emphasis upward on our relationship with God (i.e., singing "to" the Lord, Eph. 5:19; Col. 3:16; Rev. 5:9–10, 12–13). Generally the lyrics should address God and speak of who God is and what He has done (is doing, will do), rather than talk of our own experience. At the same time, relational fellowship hymns (i.e., "addressing" and "admonishing" one another, Eph. 5:19; Col. 3:16), evangelistic hymns (1 Cor. 14:24), and nineteenth-century hymns with sentimental value need not be excluded.

E. *Balance of Oral Vs. Written Tradition.* In the oral tradition one learns from a teacher (without the use of any printed medium) and repeats the material until everything in the end result is memorized. Material is getting into one's long-term memory traces—it is being internalized. The material then becomes available for singing at home, at work, or while driving on the freeway, thus making possible the scriptural injunction to sing and make melody in your heart (Eph. 5:19). Contrariwise, in the written tradition the learner reads the new or old material, and memorization is not a critical component.

In our congregational singing on a given Sunday morning, we intend to sing some things by memory and to read some things. We feel we should always be working toward the long-term goal of having the people memorize (as much as possible) all choruses and hymns. Accordingly, we may repeat a hymn or chorus of outstanding value on consecutive Sundays to aid the process of memorization. There is the added benefit also that when our people know pieces by memory they are freer to focus on God rather than the printed page.

F. *Balance of Intimacy and Transcendency.* Our God is both personal and majestic. Therefore we desire to project both a sense of intimacy and a sense of God's power and greatness for our worship.

G. *Balance of Sound Sources.* We encourage the use of a wide variety of sound sources, even though the human, corporate voice (congregational choir) is the essential element. In the Old Testament the sound sources included string, woodwind, and brass instruments and did not exclude percussion instruments.

H. *Balance of Verbal Proclamation and Symbolical Communication.* The verbal elements of prayer, Scripture reading, and singing should be balanced with the symbolic communication such as the Lord's Supper (observed monthly).

VIII. *Adaptation to the Southern California Culture.* When we can do so without biblical compromise, we will willingly adapt/adjust to our culture's patterns in order to communicate in a relevant way the timeless truths of Scripture.

IX. *Dynamic Document.* This document is clearly dynamic in nature and will require further adjustment as our church grows.

Submitted by the Worship Committee
(Permission is granted to reproduce this statement of philosophy.)

Appendix 2
Worship Participation Form

Author-pastor Ray Ortlund developed this form to hand out to worship participants. You may want to use something similar in your church. It can serve as a reminder to participants of what their role is and when. It also sets down some basic guidelines.

To: Worship Participants
From: Raymond C. Ortlund

PART IN SERVICE: _____

DATE AND TIME: _____

Leading in worship is an awesome and marvelous responsibility. Thanks for your participation.
I want to ask these things of you:

1. Dress conservatively in a suit.
2. Be at the planning time or be filled in on the service by one who was there so you can get in on any last-minute changes. (Planning time: _____)
3. Notice the context of your prayer. Come out of a hymn or anthem and lead into another act.
4. The Prayer of Praise is two minutes of glorifying God. It is not a time of asking for us, but of centering on God Himself.
5. The Pastoral Prayer (four minutes) should begin with brief adoration, then confession, petition, and end with thanks. Speak for the people to God, not for God to the people. Voice the congregation's cry to God.
6. Think through your prayer carefully. No "off-the-cuff" praying. You need not read it, but be well prepared.
7. "Think back row and balcony!" This will help you project so they can join you in prayer.

8. Plan to stay on the platform as a demonstration of how to worship and listen.
9. Don't talk, write, hum, or look around to size up the congregation. Worship! Give full attention to what is going on at the moment.

Thanks for listening! God bless you and give you joy in serving Him.

Appendix 3
A Worship Service Based on the Public Reading of 1 Thessalonians

Arranged by Wayne Peterson, May 1986. Drawn from the *New International Version*, the *New English Bible*, *The New Testament in Modern English* by J. B. Phillips, and the King James Version.

GENERAL INSTRUCTIONS

The Live Reading. Organize an entire service around the reading of 1 Thessalonians. Punctuate the reading of the whole book with hymns, prayers, and the offering. If you have flexible seating, divide the congregation into antiphonal reading groups (A and B, or East and West), so that the two halves face each other separated by a center aisle. Reading sections labeled "Leader" may be read by the pastor, "Elder" by a respected male leader, "Mrs. X" by an older woman (preferably a person recently widowed). Or make up your own reader designations. Place a microphone (M) at the back of church for the elder and widow. Feel free to substitute your own selection of hymns and choruses.

Preparing the Congregation. The entire printed text should be handed out during the prelude. At the beginning, explain the nature of the service to set people at ease, and practice reading a passage or two antiphonally. Announce that the apostle Paul is "going to visit us today" and that a time of sharing will conclude the service. Then after announcements and welcome (and perhaps a hymn), begin the reading.

An Appearance By Paul. During the prayer time, have an individual dressed like Paul in a flowing robe and sandals steal in and seat himself at a desk positioned on the platform. After the prayer, have a tape begin with ten or fifteen seconds of quill-scratching sounds as Paul takes a quill and writes. Then have a taped voice read 1 Thessalonians 2:17– 3:13. During the offertory prayer, Paul can secretly leave the platform.

Sharing Time. After the reading, take a roving mike and invite the congregation to share what they gained from the reading.

1 THESSALONIANS

Leader: From Paul, Silvanus, and Timothy

Group A: to the congregation of Thessalonians

Group B: who belong to God the Father and the Lord Jesus Christ.

Leader: Grace be unto you from God our Father and the Lord Jesus Christ.

I. Paul's Thanksgiving for the Thessalonians

Group A: We always thank God for you all, and mention you in our prayers continually. We call to mind, before our God and Father, how your faith has shown itself in action, your love in labor, and your hope of our Lord Jesus Christ in fortitude.

Group B: We know, brothers, that God not only loves you but has selected you for a special purpose. For we remember how our gospel came to you not as mere words, but as a message with power behind it—the convincing power of the Holy Spirit.

Leader: That is the kind of men we were at Thessalonica. And you, in your turn, followed the example set by us and by the Lord.

Group A: The welcome you gave the message meant grave suffering for you, yet you rejoiced in the Holy Spirit; thus you have become a model for all believers in Macedonia and in Achaia.

Group B: From Thessalonica the word of the Lord rang out, and not in Macedonia and Achaia alone, but everywhere your faith in God has reached men's ears.

Group A: No words of ours are needed, for they themselves spread the news of our visit to you and its effect: how you turned from idols, to be servants of the living and true God, and to wait expectantly for the appearance from heaven of His Son Jesus, whom He raised from the dead, Jesus our deliverer from the terrors of judgment to come.

Leader: You know for yourselves, brothers, that our visit to you was not fruitless. We had, as you know, suffered and been treated with insults at Philippi, and we came on to you only because God gave us courage. Whatever the strain, we came to tell you the gospel of God.

Group B: Our message to you is true, our motives are pure, our conduct is absolutely above board. We speak under the solemn sense of being entrusted by God with the gospel.

Group A: We do not curry favor with men; we seek only the favor of God, who is continually testing our hearts. Our words have never been flattering words, as you have cause to know; nor, as God is our witness, have they ever been a cloak for greed. We have never sought honor from men, from you or anyone else, although as Christ's own envoys we might have made our weight felt; but we were as gentle with you as a nurse caring fondly for her children.

Group B: With such yearning love we chose to impart to you, not only the gospel of God, but our very selves, so dear had you become to us. Remember, brothers, how we toiled and drudged. We worked for a living night and day, rather than be a burden to anyone, while we proclaimed before you the good news of God.

Group A: We call you to witness, yes and God Himself, how devout and just and blameless was our behavior towards you who are believers. As you well know, we dealt with you one by one, as a father deals with his children, appealing to you by encouragement, as well as by solemn injunctions, to live lives worthy of the Lord who calls you into His kingdom and glory.

Group B: And so we are continually thankful to God that when you heard the word of God from us you accepted it, not as a mere human message, but as it really is, God's word, a power in the lives of you who believe.

Group A: For you, my brothers, have followed the example of the churches of God which have come into being through Christ Jesus in Judea. For when you suffered at the hands of your fellow countrymen you were sharing the experience of the Judean Christian churches, who suffered persecution by the Jews.

Group B: It was the Jews who killed their own prophets, the Jews who killed the Lord Jesus, and the Jews who drove us out. They do not please God, and are in opposition to all mankind. They refused to let us speak to Gentiles to tell them the message by which they could be saved.

Group A: All these years they have been adding to the full record of their sins and finally the wrath of God has fallen upon them.

Hymn: "How Firm a Foundation"
Prayer Thanking God for His Faithfulness

II. Paul's Longing to See Them

[Drama segment: Paul is seated at the writing desk; spin tape with the quill sound and the voice reading what follows.]

My friends, when for a short spell you were lost to us—lost to sight, not to our hearts—we were exceedingly anxious to see you again.

So we did propose to come to Thessalonica—I Paul, more than once—but Satan thwarted us. For after all, what hope or joy or crown of pride is there for us, what indeed but you, when we stand before our Lord Jesus at His coming. It is you who are indeed our glory and our joy.

So, when we could bear it no longer, we decided to remain alone at Athens, and sent Timothy, our brother, and God's fellow worker in the service of the gospel of Christ, to encourage you to stand firm for the faith and, under all these hardships, not to be shaken. For you know that this is our appointed lot. When we were with you we warned you that we were bound to suffer hardship; and so it has turned out as you know. And thus it was, that when I could bear it no longer, I sent to find out about your faith, fearing that the tempter might have tempted you and my labor might be lost.

But now Timothy has just arrived from Thessalonica, bringing good news of your faith and love. He tells us that you always think kindly of us and are as anxious to see us as we are to see you. And so, in all our difficulties and hardships your faith reassures us about you. It is the breath of life to us that you stand firm in the Lord. What thanks can we return God for you? What thanks for all the joy you have brought us, making us rejoice before our God while we pray most earnestly night and day to be allowed to see you again and mend your faith where it falls short?

Now may our God and Father Himself and our Lord Jesus Christ clear the way for us to come to you. May the Lord make your love increase and overflow for each other and for everyone else, just as ours does for you. May He strengthen your hearts so that you will be blameless and holy in the presence of our God and Father when our Lord Jesus comes with all His holy ones.

Hymn: "Joyful, Joyful We Adore Thee"
*   or "We are One in the Bond of Love"*
Offering
[Paul leaves during offertory prayer]

III. Living to Please God

Leader: Finally, brothers, we instructed you how to live in order to please God, as in fact you are living. Now we ask and urge you in the Lord Jesus to do this more and more.

Elder: You know what instructions we gave you by the authority of the Lord Jesus. It is God's will that you should be holy; that you should avoid sexual immorality; that each of you should learn to control his own body in a way that is holy and honorable, not in passionate lust like the heathen who do not know God. No man must do his brother wrong in this matter, or take advantage of him, because as we told you before with emphasis, the Lord punishes all such offenses. For God calls us to holiness, not to impurity. Therefore, he who rejects this instruction does not reject man, but God who gives to you His Holy Spirit.

All: Now about brotherly love we do not need to write to you, for you yourselves have been taught by God to love each other. And in fact you do love all the brothers throughout Macedonia. Yet we urge you brothers to do so more and more. Make it your ambition to lead a quiet life, to look after your own business, and to work with your hands as we told you, so that your daily life will win the respect of outsiders and so that you will not be dependent on anyone.

Leader: We wish you not to remain in ignorance, brothers, about those who sleep in death, you should not grieve like the rest of men, who have no hope.

All: We believe that Jesus died and rose again. So it will be for those who died as Christians; God will bring them to life with Jesus.

Mrs. X: For this we tell you as the Lord's word: we who are left alive until the Lord comes, shall forestall those who have died; because at a word of command, at the sound of the archangel's voice, and with the trumpet call of God, the Lord Himself will descend from heaven, and the dead in Christ will rise first.

After them, we who are still alive and are left will be caught up with them in the clouds to meet the Lord in the air. Thus we shall always be with the Lord. Console one another, then, with these words.

Leader: Now, brothers, about times and dates we do not need to write to you, for you know very well that the Day of the Lord will come like a thief in the night. While people are talking of peace and security, suddenly calamity is upon them. It will come as sudden as the pangs that come upon a woman with child. There will be no escape.

Group A: But you, brothers, are not in darkness that this day should surprise you like a thief. You are all sons of the light and sons of the day. We do not belong to the night or the darkness. We must not sleep like the rest, but remain awake and vigilant. Sleepers sleep at night and drunks are drunk at night, but since we belong to the day we must keep sober, armed with faith and love as armor, and the hope of salvation as a helmet.

Group B: For God did not destine us for the terrors of judgment, but to receive deliverance through our Lord Jesus Christ. He died for us so that, whether we are awake or asleep, we might live together with Him. Therefore encourage each other and build each other up, just as in fact you are doing.

Hymn: "Come We That Love the Lord"

IV. Paul's Charge

Leader: Now we ask you, brothers, to respect those who work hard among you, who are over you in the Lord and who admonish you. Hold them in the highest regard in love because of their work.

Group A: You must live in peace among yourselves. And we would urge you, brothers, to admonish the idle, encourage the faint-hearted, support the weak, and to be very patient with all.

Group B: See to it that no one pays back wrong for wrong. Aim always to do the best you can for each other and for all men.

Group A: Rejoice always.

Group B: Pray continually.

Group A: Give thanks in all circumstances.

Group B: This is what God in Christ wills for you.

Group A: Do not put out the Spirit's fire.

Group B: Do not treat prophecy with contempt.

Group A: Test everything, hold on to the good.

Group B: Avoid every kind of evil.

Leader: May God himself, the God of peace, sanctify you through and through.

Group A: May your whole spirit, soul, and body be kept blameless at the coming of the Lord Jesus Christ.

Group B: He who calls you is to be trusted, He will do it.

Group A: Brothers, pray for us also.

Group B: Greet all our brothers with a holy kiss.

Group A: I charge you before the Lord to have this letter read to all the brothers.

All: The grace of the Lord Jesus Christ be with you!

(Permission is granted to reproduce this order of worship.)

Appendix 4
The Easter Story: Reader's Theater for Six Readers

The reading requires two narrators and four readers. The narrators should stand at the opposite sides of the stage area, facing each other but slightly turned toward the congregation. The four readers together serve as a crowd. Suggestion: use a pen highlighter on your headings to cue your speaking parts.

Reader 1:	(Man) Christ; member of the Sanhedrin
Reader 2:	(Woman) Mary, the mother of James
Reader 3:	(Man) Pilate; angel at the tomb
Reader 4:	(Woman) Mary Magdalene
Narrator 1:	(Man)
Narrator 2:	(Woman)

THE EASTER STORY

Narrator 1: At the conclusion of three years of ministry, Jesus of Nazareth, the Christ, turned His eyes and thoughts toward Jerusalem. Accompanied by His disciples, He traveled to Bethany. He entered Jerusalem on the Monday before the Passover.

Narrator 2: The crowds gathering in the city for Passover went wild. When they heard that this Jesus of Nazareth was entering the city, they shouted acclamation for the miracle worker.

Readers 1, 2, 3, 4 (simultaneously as a crowd repeat cries of acclamation at least once)

Reader 1: Peace in heaven, glory in the highest.
Reader 2: Hosanna to the Son of David.
Reader 3: Hosanna to the King of Israel, David's seed.
Reader 4: Hosanna to the Messiah.

Narrator 1: Four days later, the cheers and hosannas had turned to jeers and curses.

299

Narrator 2: They were crying to Pilate to release Barabbas. They were crying to crucify Jesus of Nazareth, the Christ.

Reader 3:
(Pilate) Who shall I release to you? Jesus who is called Christ, or Barabbas?

Readers 1, 2, 4: Barabbas! Give us Barabbas! Barabbas! Give us Barabbas!

Reader 3: Then what shall I do with Jesus who is called Christ?

Readers 1, 2, 4: Crucify Him! Crucify Him! Crucify Him!

Reader 3: Why? What evil has He done?

Readers 1, 2, 4:
(louder) CRUCIFY HIM! CRUCIFY HIM! CRUCIFY HIM!

Narrator 2: And so, filled with foreboding, Pilate handed Jesus of Nazareth over to them to be crucified.

Narrator 1: The soldiers wove a crown of thorns, put it on His head, and arrayed Him in a purple robe.

Narrator 2: They mocked Him, crying, "Hail, King of the Jews." They repeatedly struck Him.

Narrator 1: They led Him out, bearing His own cross to the place called the Skull, which is called in Hebrew "Golgotha."

Narrator 2: And there, between two thieves, they nailed His hands and feet to the cross. They raised it skyward, dropped it into a socket in the rocky hillside, and crucified the Son of God.

(PAUSE)

Narrator 1: Pilate had written a title and it had been placed on the cross. In Latin, Greek, and Hebrew it read "King of the Jews."

Narrator 2: As Jesus hung on the cross, dying by degrees in agony, there was darkness from the sixth to the ninth hours.

Narrator 1: As the end approached, and after Jesus had cried out as God turned from Him, He had fulfilled all prophecy concerning His coming. He spoke His last.

Narrator 1:
(Jesus in agony) It is finished. Father, into your hands I commit my Spirit.

Narrator 2: And he breathed His last.

(PAUSE)

Narrator 1:
(dramatically) At that instant, the curtain of the temple was torn in two from top to bottom. The earth shook, boulders were split, tombs were opened and many of the bodies of the righteous were raised.

Narrator 2: The soldiers saw the earth quake. They were awestruck. Finally, the centurion spoke.

Reader 3: Surely, this innocent man was the Son of God.

Narrator 1:   The crowd that had followed to see the spectacle, when they saw these things take place, turned for home beating their breasts.
(PAUSE)

Narrator 1:   To prevent the bodies from hanging in Jerusalem on Passover Sabbath, the Jews asked that the soldiers break the legs of the three men who had been crucified so that they would die quickly.

Narrator 2:   So the soldiers came and broke the legs of the two thieves. But coming to Jesus, they saw He was dead already.

Narrator 1:   One of the soldiers pierced Jesus' side with a spear. Blood and water instantly ran from the wound.

Narrator 2:   When evening had come, Joseph of Arimathea, who was a respected member of the Sanhedrin and a secret disciple of Jesus, went to Pilate. He asked permission to take away the body of Jesus.

Narrator 1:   Pilate was surprised that Jesus could already be dead. He summoned the centurion. When Pilate learned that Jesus was indeed dead, he granted the body to Joseph.

Narrator 2:   Joseph bought a linen shroud. He and Nicodemus, who had first come to Jesus by night, took down the body of Jesus.

Narrator 1:   They wrapped the body in the shroud and laid it in Joseph's own new rock-hewn tomb. Joseph unlocked the great stone and allowed it to roll to the door of the tomb. He and Nicodemus departed.

Narrator 2:   Mary Magdalene and Mary the Mother of James were there, sitting opposite the sepulcher. They saw the tomb and how His body was laid. Returning home, they began to prepare spices and ointments to anoint the body. On the Sabbath, they rested according to the commandment.
(PAUSE)

Narrator 1:   The next day, the chief priests and the Pharisees gathered before Pilate.

Reader 1:
(member of the Sanhedrin)   Sir, while He was still alive, the impostor said, "After three days, I will rise again." Please order the tomb made secure until the third day to prevent his disciples from stealing the body and telling the people "He has risen from the dead." The last deception would be worse than the first.

Narrator 1:   Pilate considered, then replied.

Reader 3:   You have a detachment of soldiers. Make it as secure as you know how.

Narrator 1:   So a seal was placed on the stone and a guard was posted. The stage was now set for the central event of all human history.

(*PAUSE*)

Narrator 2:   Sometime before dawn there was a great earthquake, for
(*brightly, with ex-*   an angel of the Lord descended from heaven, rolled open
citement)   the great stone door, and sat down upon it.

Narrator 1:   His face was as brilliant as lightning and his clothing as white as snow. Seeing him, the terrified guards trembled and fainted dead away.

Narrator 2:   When the Sabbath had passed, Mary Magdalene, Mary the Mother of James, and Salome bought spices to anoint the body. Very early, before dawn, on the first day of the week they left for the tomb. They spoke among themselves.

Reader 2: (*Mary,*   But who will roll the stone away from the door for
mother of James)   us? It is very large.

Narrator 2:   As they stepped into the tomb, they did not find the body. They were puzzled. Two men appeared before them in dazzling garments. The women were frightened. As they knelt and bowed, one of the angels spoke to them.

Reader 3:   Do not be afraid. I know you seek Jesus who was crucified. He is not here. He is risen. Go quickly and tell His disciples that He has risen from the dead.

Narrator 2:   They returned from the tomb and told this to the eleven and all the rest.

Narrator 1:   But the disciples did not believe them. Peter and John ran to the tomb. John outran Peter and reached the tomb first. John stooped to look in. Peter caught up and ran into the tomb. They saw the linen shroud, and the napkin which had been on His head not lying with the rest of the shroud, but rolled up in a place by itself. Then John stepped into the tomb, and he saw and he believed. Peter and John then slowly returned home.

Narrator 2:   Mary Magdalene was overwrought with grief, and confused. She stood weeping outside the tomb. Stopping to look in, she saw two angels in white, sitting where the body of Jesus had lain. One at the head, one at the foot. They spoke to her.

Reader 3:   Woman, why do you weep?

Reader 4:   Because they have taken away my Lord, and I don't know where they've taken Him.

Narrator 2:   Mary then turned and saw Jesus standing near her.

Reader 1:   Woman, why are you weeping, and who do you seek?

Narrator 2:   Thinking He was the gardener, Mary turned away in her grief.

Reader 4:   Sir, if you have carried Him away, tell me where you have laid Him and I will take Him away.

Narrator 2:   Then Jesus spoke her name, gently.

Reader 1:   Mary

Reader 4:   Teacher!
(with surprise and delight)

Narrator 2:   Mary threw herself at His feet.

Reader 1:   Mary, do not hold Me, for I have not yet ascended to the Father. But go to My disciples and tell them, "I am risen." Tell them I am ascending to my Father and your Father, My God and your God.

Narrator 2:   Mary went to the disciples. She told them.

All: HE IS RISEN! HE IS RISEN! HE IS RISEN!

Notes

CHAPTER 1. OLD TESTAMENT PRINCIPLES

1. Graham Kendrick, *Learning to Worship as a Way of Life* (Minneapolis: Bethany House, 1984), 173.

2. Bruce Leafblad, *Music, Worship, and the Ministry of the Church* (Portland, Oreg.: Western Conservative Baptist Seminary, 1978), 44.

3. Gordon J. Wenham, *The Book of Leviticus* (Grand Rapids: Eerdmans, 1979), 17.

4. Ibid., 21. "The Mosaic blueprint features only one set of institutions; they centered on worship. Later in history prophets (other than Moses) appear. Later too the monarchy is established . . . but at first there was only worship. The institutions of the idea community are summed up in sacrifice, the central tabernacle, and the priesthood" (Lawrence O. Richards, *A Theology of Children's Ministry* [Grand Rapids: Zondervan, 1983], 22).

5. See Colin Brown, ed., *The New International Dictionary of New Testament Theology*, vol. 3 (Grand Rapids: Zondervan, 1978), 544ff.

6. R. A. Finlayson, "Holiness, Holy Saints, in *New Bible Dictionary*, ed. J. D. Douglas (Grand Rapids: Eerdmans, 1962), 530.

7. See a classic work on the subject: Rudolf Otto, *The Idea of the Holy*, trans. John W. Harvey (reprint, New York: Oxford University Press, 1971).

8. R. C. Sproul, *The Holiness of God* (Wheaton, Ill.: Tyndale House, 1985), 38.

9. I do not want to appear judgmental in reference to this church, because I have not personally attended there, and I do not have knowledge of their philosophy of worship and ministry.

10. Wenham, *The Book of Leviticus*, 32. Calling this distinction "arbitrary and artificial," he advocates a "slightly different approach."

11. See W. Bingham Hunter, *The God Who Hears* (Downers Grove, Ill.: InterVarsity Press, 1986), 20, 28–29.

12. Mary Douglas, *Purity and Danger* (London: Routledge and Kegan Paul, 1966), 44, 51–54, 57.

13. Michael Newton, *The Concept of Purity at Qumran and in the Letters of Paul* (London: Cambridge University, 1985), 6.

14. Menahem Haran, "The Priestly Image of the Tabernacle," *Hebrew Union College Annual* (Cincinnati: Hebrew Union College, 1965), 36:216.

15. Ibid.

16. Wenham, *The Book of Leviticus*, viii.

17. Ibid., 58.

18. Ibid., 78.

19. Harmonically I tend to play straight triads, secondary dominants, wide octaves, and open fifths (Greek sounding) when attempting to communicate transcendency; and richer sonorities (sevenths, ninths, thirteenths, raised elevenths) and modal harmonies (à la Vaughan Williams) when communicating intimacy. There are exceptions.

20. Wenham, *The Book of Leviticus*, 35.

CHAPTER 2. NEW TESTAMENT PRINCIPLES

1. B. F. Westcott has this to say of worship "in spirit and truth": "The words describe the characteristics of worship in one complex phrase, and not in two coordinate phrases. Worship involves an expression of feeling [worship in spirit] and a conception of the object [worship in truth] towards whom the feeling is entertained. . . . Judaism (speaking generally) was a worship of the letter and not of the spirit (to take examples from the time): Samaritanism was a worship of falsehood and not of truth. By the Incarnation men are enabled to have immediate communion with God, and thus a worship in spirit has become possible: at the same time the Son is a complete manifestation of God for men, and thus a worship in truth has been placed within their reach. These two characteristics answer to the higher sense of the second and third commandments, the former of which tends to a spiritual service, and the latter to a devout regard for the 'name' of God, that is for every revelation of His Person or attributes or action. 'The first strikes at hypocrisy, the last at idolatry'" (reprint, *The Gospel According to St. John*, [Grand Rapids: Eerdmans, 1971], 1:73).

2. Ibid.

3. Leon Morris, *The Gospel According to John* (Grand Rapids: Eerdmans, 1971), 270. However, some like George Eldon Ladd take "worship in spirit" to mean worship "empowered by the Spirit of God": ". . . 'spirit' [4:23] refers to the Holy Spirit and not to inner 'spiritual' worship as opposed to outward forms. . . . Because the Holy Spirit is to come into the world, men may worship God anywhere if they are motivated by the Holy Spirit. . . .
"The contrast here is not so much between the world above and the world below as between worship in the former time and worship in the new era inaugurated by Jesus. The contrast is between worship in Spirit and truth as compared with worship in Jerusalem or Gerizim. . . . The 'Spirit raises men above the earthly level, the level of the flesh, and enables them to worship God properly'" (*A Theology of the New Testament* [Grand Rapids: Eerdmans, 1974], 225).

4. Alvah Hovey, *Commentary on the Gospel of John* (Valley Forge: Judson Press, 1885), 119. Alternatively, Ladd's interpretation avoids the dualism of inner and outer: "Worship in truth to the Greek ear would mean worship in reality as over against the unreality of empty forms. This, however, is not the Johannine meaning. . . . Worship in truth . . . means worship mediated through the person of Jesus, and inspired by the Holy Spirit" (*Theology of the New Testament*, 292). See also Leon Morris (*The Gospel According to John*, 293–96) on "worship in truth."

5. Some commentators emphasize that Jesus is contrasting a worship in the spirit to a worship in material things—i.e., a worship characterized by liturgy, vestments, sacrifices, strictness of detail, and personnel (such as the presence of a

properly consecrated priest). This must be indirectly inferred from the text, however. A Southern Baptist commentary has different emphasis: "To worship *in spirit* does not mean that all holy places and material aids should be abandoned but that the creative, life-giving power of God should infuse whatever human forms are utilized by the cultus" (*The Broadman Bible Commentary* [Nashville: Broadman Press, 1970], 9:254).

So also an American Baptist commentary: "This rational worship will not indeed reject outward rites, but it will use them only as helps and expressions of spiritual service" (Hovey, *Commentary on the Gospel of John*, 118).

E. W. Hengstenberg strikes a good balance: ". . . the present declaration of Christ is directed against the externals of worship, only in so far as they lay claim to an independent significance. If we extend it further, we should not promote, but destroy the worship of God in spirit and truth; for man, as a corporeal creature as well as a spiritual being, needs the external to lead him to the spiritual, and the spiritual life must be stunted if this support be withdrawn. Yet from the declaration of our text we derive the rule, that all accumulation of externals of worship, which so easily overmaster instead of stimulating the spirit, are to be avoided" (*Commentary on the Gospel of John* [1865; reprint, Minneapolis: Klock & Klock Christian Publishers, 1980], 239).

6. Arthur W. Pink, *Exposition of the Gospel of John*, 3 vols. (1923; reprint, Grand Rapids: Zondervan, 1968), 206–9.

7. Donald P. Hustad maintains that historically many of the deeply ingrained anti-Romanist, anti-liturgical, and anti-aesthetic attitudes that have shaped our evangelical heritage in large part, stemmed from the Separatist movement (*Jubilate! Church Music in the Evangelical Tradition* [Carol Stream, Ill.: Hope, 1981], 118.

8. I contend that the apostle John's dualism simply does not have anything to do with the antithesis Pink erects. George Eldon Ladd asserts, citing John 8:23: "The dualism of John is primarily vertical: a contrast between two worlds—the world above and the world below. 'You are from below, I am from above; you are of this world, I am not of this world' " (*A Theology of the New Testament*, 223).

9. "Recent scholarship has recognized that such terms as body, soul, and spirit are not different, separable faculties of man but different ways of viewing the whole man. . . . [In contrast, for Plato] the body was not *ipso facto* evil, but it was a burden and hindrance to the soul. . . . In Hellenistic times, the body, belonging to the world of matter, was thought to be *ipso facto* evil by the gnostics. . . . most of the philosophers of Greece followed Plato in his view of soul and body, and that it was so impressed upon the civilized world that 'no man can discuss the relation of soul and body today without encountering some resurgence of the Platonic view' " (Ladd, *A Theology of the New Testament*, 457–58).

Ladd further summarizes Pauline teaching on the body: ". . . the body can become an obstacle, but it is not a hindrance of itself." My view is that Pink was influenced (no doubt unconsciously) by vestiges of a Neoplatonic, nonbiblical dualism—if not on the intellectual level, then certainly on the emotional level. Anti-Roman Catholic feeling also unquestionably shaped his thought.

10. Calvin M. Johansson, *Music and Ministry: A Biblical Counterpoint* (Peabody, Mass.: Hendrickson Publishers, 1984), 16.

11. Hustad, *Jubilate!* vii–xi.

12. Ladd says that in the Pauline Epistles "*Psyche* [soul] . . . refers to man as a thinking, working, and feeling person. *Pneuma* [spirit] is man's inner self viewed in terms of man's relationship to God and to other men. . . .

"There is one difference between Paul and the Old Testament. The central term for man in the Old Testament, in the intertestamental literature, and in the rabbis was *nephesh* or *psyche*. In Paul it is *pneuma*. 'Spirit' has made a dramatic advance, *psyche* a dramatic retreat. . . . *pneuma* took the leading role" (*A Theology of the New Testament*, 460–61).

13. William Temple, *The Hope of a New World* (London: Macmillan, 1940), p. 30.

14. William Temple, *The Church and Its Teaching Today* (London: Macmillan, n.d.), p. 15.

15. Ralph P. Martin, *The Worship of God: Some Theological, Pastoral, and Practical Reflections* (Grand Rapids: Eerdmans, 1982), 210.

16. Matthew 28:19; 2 Corinthians 13:14.

17. Paul Waitman Hoon, *Integrity in Worship* (Nashville: Abingdon Press, 1971), 114–15.

18. G. Van der Leeuw further relates the arts as a whole within the framework of the Trinity. He sees (1) dance and drama in the rhythm, movement, and countermovement of God the Father's creation; (2) word, picture in the Son; and (3) music in the intangible, unseen work of the Holy Spirit (*Sacred and Profane Beauty: The Holy in Art*, trans. D. E. Green [London: n.p., 1963], 328–40). Also, an interesting study that relates the doctrine of the Trinity to the creative process is Dorothy L. Sayers's *Mind of the Maker* (1941; reprint, Westport, Conn.: Greenwood Press, 1970).

19. Kenneth Tollefson, "Nehemiah, Model for Change Agents: A Social Science Approach to Scripture," *Christian Scholar's Review* 15, no. 2 (1986): 123.

20. Ralph P. Martin believes that controversy over the meaning of the Communion service is a thing of the past: "The last two generations have seen a remarkable coming together of Christians, a sharing of insights, and a cross-fertilizing of traditions that has sought to go back to a more firmly rooted biblical understanding. . . . A remarkable meeting ground has resulted as Roman Catholic interpreters have drawn away from the notion of a physical change (implied in transubstantiation), and Protestants have explored what the elements become when the Word is spoken over them . . . in some sense they have power to convey and actualize. . . . The common ground is seen in such terms as 'transsignification' or 'trans-finalization' . . . the bread is no longer as it came from the baker's oven but receives a new 'signification' . . . [the new emphasis is on] reliving the past through its creed and liturgy . . . calling Yahweh's past deeds out of the 'pastness' into a living 'present' . . ."(*The Worship of God*, 145–47).

21. Communication from Dr. Curtis Mitchell, Talbot School of Theology, February 1987.

22. See discussion on confessing Jesus as Lord in Ralph P. Martin, *The Worship of God*, 177–78.

23. Kenneth C. Haugk lists thirteen barriers to "equipping the saints." See "Lay Ministry: The Unfinished Reformation," *Christian Ministry* (November 1985): 5.

24. William Nicholls says: "[worship is] the supreme and only indispensable activity of the Christian church. It alone will endure . . . into heaven, when

all other activities of the Church have passed away" (*Jacob's Ladder: The Meaning of Worship* [Richmond: John Knox Press, 1958], 9). See also Ralph P. Martin: ". . . worship is more than just a facet of church life. It underlines and informs our understanding of all we believe and cherish concerning God and his design for the church and the world. . . . We submit that no statement of the church's raison d'etre comes near to the heart of the biblical witness or the meaning of church history unless the worship of God is given top priority. The church exists for this above all else (*The Worship of God*, 209).

25. Bruce Leafblad, *Music, Worship, and the Ministry of the Church* (Portland, Oreg.: Western Conservative Baptist Seminary, 1978), 21.

26. Ibid., 21–39.

27. Jack W. Hayford, *Church on the Way* (Grand Rapids: Zondervan, Chosen Books, 1983), 52.

28. Ibid., 48–49.

29. Ibid., 78–80.

30. Ibid, 51.

31. See the readable, inspirational book by his wife, Anne Ortlund, *Up With Worship* (Glendale, Calif.: Regal Books, 1975).

32. Personal communication, 22 February 1987.

33. Ronald Allen and Gordon Borror say: "These three aspects can be visualized in several ways: (1) upreach, (2) inreach, and (3) outreach; or (1) God, (2) ourselves, and (3) others; or (1) to worship, (2) to edify, and (3) to evangelize; or (1) love God, (2) love one another, (3) love the world for their salvation" (*Worship: Rediscovering the Missing Jewel* [Portland, Oreg.: Multnomah Press, 1982], 55).

34. Ibid., 57.

35. Hustad, *Jubilate!* 64.

36. Daniel Reeves and Ronald Jenson, *Always Advancing: Modern Strategies for Church Growth* (San Bernardino, Calif.: Here's Life, 1984), 120–21.

37. Ibid., 64–65.

CHAPTER 3. LEARNING FROM THE PATRIARCHS

1. Alvin Toffler, *The Third Wave* (New York: Morrow, 1980), 198.

2. "The Changing American Family," *Chicago Tribune*, 26 November 1979, sec. 1.

3. Lawrence O. Richards, *A Theology of Children's Ministry* (Grand Rapids: Zondervan, 1983), 186.

4. Ibid., 187.

5. Robert D. Hess, "Experts and Amateurs: Some Unintended Conse-quences of Parent Education," in Mario D. Fantini and René Cardenas, *Parenting in a Multicultural Society* (New York: Longman, 1980), 150–56.

6. Ibid., 156.

7. Richards, *A Theology of Children's Ministry*, 191.

8. Ibid., 196.

9. Ibid., 193.

10. We could also reexamine the titles we give worship leaders. For example, we use the titles "director of music" or "minister of music." These titles tend to place the emphasis on performance rather than ministry. Alternative titles

that point better to the goal of the position are "director of worship," "minister of worship," or even consider the insightful title that Roman Catholics often use: *pastoral musician.*

11. Charles M. Sell, *Family Ministry: The Enrichment of Family Life Through the Church* (Grand Rapids: Zondervan, 1981), 218.

12. Ibid., 219.

13. See Joel Nederhood, "Should We Have Daily Family Devotions: Yes," and Enos Sjogren, "Should We Have Daily Family Devotions: Not Necessarily," and also Harold H. Hess, "Should We Have Family Devotions: No," in *Eternity* (March 1971): 14ff.

14. Sell, *Family Ministry,* 221.

15. Richards, *A Theology of Children's Ministry,* 75.

16. See parallel passage in Deuteronomy 11:18–19. Also see 1 Thessalonians 2 and Titus 2.

17. Richards, *A Theology of Children's Ministry,* 24.

18. Paragraph drawn from Richards, *A Theology of Children's Ministry,* 126, 158, 250, 387. Read Richards on Piaget (59–62, 141–42). Piaget's research indicates "there is a distinct sequence to cognitive growth, and that at early stages many concepts simply cannot be grasped by young children." Richards asks, "How many of the concepts we try to teach through the Bible stories are beyond the ability of children to comprehend? How many of the applications demand ways of thinking that are simply beyond the young?"

19. Ibid., 402.

20. Ibid., 402–3.

21. Ibid., 159. See also Richards's discussion of Kohlberg's stages of moral reasoning (149–63).

22. Adapted from Richards, *A Theology of Children's Ministry,* 159.

23. Ibid., 239.

24. Ibid., 261.

25. Read Luke 1:46–55 together.

26. *Family Life Today* 2, no. 12 (November 1976): 21.

27. Ibid., 19.

28. For some great ideas on family reunions and building family memories, see Edith Schaeffer, *What is a Family?* (Old Tappan: Revell, 1975), 19–33, 198–205.

29. *Family Life Today* 2, no. 12 (November 1976): 18.

30. Ibid. I included "bananas" because our kids sometimes give bizarre answers!

31. Ibid., 21.

32. *Family Life Today* 2, no. 7 (June 1976): 20.

33. This story is adapted from Patricia and Donald Griggs, *Teaching and Celebrating Advent,* rev. ed. (Nashville: Abingdon Press, 1980), 8–9. This booklet has good ideas for family Advent ceremonies as well as Advent puzzles, cutouts, and other activities.

34. *Christianity Today* (4 April 1986).

35. Sell, *Family Ministry,* 269.

36. This suggestion may not be appropriate for older children if you have agreed to respect their right to privacy.

CHAPTER 4. BALANCE OR CHAOS?

1. Oscar Cullmann, *Early Christian Worship*, trans. A. Stewart Todd and James B. Torrance (Naperville, Ill.: Alec R. Allenson, 1956), 26.

2. *Good Things Come in Small Groups: The Dynamics of Good Group Life* (Downers Grove, Ill.: InterVarsity Press, 1985), 22–26.

3. Ferdinand Hahn, *The Worship of the Early Church*, ed. John Renmann, trans. David E. Green (Philadelphia: Fortress Press, 1973), 68.

4. See Jacob Neusner, "The City as Useless Symbol in Late Antique Judaism," in *Major Trends in Formative Judaism: Society and Symbol in Political Crisis* (Chico, Calif.: Scholars Press, 1983), 29–40.

5. A basic assumption in this and the next three chapters is that Ralph P. Martin's thesis (Synagogue + Lord's Table = NT Worship) is too simplistic (*Worship in the Early Church* [Grand Rapids: Eerdmans, 1975], 26–27). Instead we should think in terms of great freedom and variety (pluralism?) in the structure of worship in the New Testament as a result of the Council in Jerusalem (Acts 15). My views are similar to Hahn's on this issue although I prefer to focus on only the extremes of the continuum and demonstrate a difference between the synagogue and Corinthian worship (Hahn, *The Worship of the Early Church*).

6. On the ideas of Mary Douglas, see the discussion by Frank C. Senn, *Christian Worship and Its Cultural Setting* (Philadelphia: Fortress Press, 1983), 68–75. Douglas takes the view that churches need to make a choice between a worship which is ritualistic or effervescent. In Paul's model, however, there is no apparent either-or dichotomy, but rather an integration.

7. The term "body-life" stresses participation in a group where people experience a sense of interplay and interdependence as they do in a family setting.

8. Ralph P. Martin adds that "[the body metaphor] has the further merit of being a universal, transcultural association. All human beings recognize the language of the body, and both the ideas of physicality and personhood ('body' meaning 'self'-identity , as in the expression 'everybody' = everyone) are to the fore in Pauline anthropology" (*The Spirit and the Congregation: Studies in 1 Corinthians 12–15* [Grand Rapids: Eerdmans, 1984], 21).

9. See Phillip Sigal, "Early Christian and Rabbinic Liturgical Affinities: Exploring Liturgical Acculturation," *New Testament Studies* 30:63–90.

10. 1 Corinthians 12:3; 16:22.

11. 1 Corinthians 14:16; 1 Chronicles 16:36

12. Cullmann, *Early Christian Worship*, 32.

13. W. C. van Unnik, "Dominus Vobiscum: The Background of a Liturgical Formula," in *New Testament Essays in Memory of T. W. Mason*, ed. A. J. Higgins (Manchester, England: University of Manchester Press, 1959), 294.

14. Graham Kendrick, *Learning to Worship as a Way of Life* (Minneapolis: Bethany House, 1984), 173.

15. Aspects of Corinthian worship appear to have continued historically. A quotation from Tertullian (ca. A.D. 160–220), a leader in the charismatic Montanist movement, expresses the body-life model in worship practice: ". . . anyone who can, either from the Holy Scripture or from his own heart, is called into the middle to sing to God" (*Apologiticus*, ch. 39, para. 18). Quotation is from the article "Music of the Early Christian Church," in *The New Grove Dictionary of Music and Musicians*, ed. Stanley Sadie (Washington, D.C.: Macmillan, 1980), 4:364.

16. This chapter takes the view that Paul positively endorses the idea of maximum participation in 1 Corinthians 14:26. Ralph P. Martin takes a quite different view. He maintains that Paul is describing and not implicitly prescribing. Martin says that when Paul repeats the verb "each one *has*" five times in 14:26, he is very likely intending "to hold up the Corinthian individualism to reproof" (Martin, *The Spirit and the Congregation*, 78).

Lois Barrett sees size as the distinguishing feature of contemporary house churches: "I have sometimes explained the difference between the house church and a sanctuary church as a difference in place. . . . But now, I'm moving toward seeing the "house" as a symbol for the issue of size, which is the real issue.

"Size makes a difference in what happens. I know through my own experience and through reading the studies of social scientists that smaller groups allow people to participate more in what is going on. The smaller the church, the closer the interaction" (*Building the House Church* [Scottdale, Pa.: Herald Press, 1986], 19). See her chapter on house worship (45–56).

17. Alexander B. MacDonald, *Christian Worship in the Primitive Church* (Edinburgh: T. and T. Clark, 1935), 17. By contrast, the footnotes to Acts 15:4–22 and 15:12 in *The NIV Study Bible* (Kenneth Barker, ed., [Grand Rapids: Zondervan, 1985]), point out that in Jerusalem the people in the general assembly did not decide the issue at hand, but listened to the decision reported by the elders. For a discussion of three forms of church government (episcopacy, presbyterianism, and congregationalism) see *The Evangelical Dictionary of Theology*, ed. Walter A. Elwell (Grand Rapids: Baker, 1984), 238–41.

18. There seems to be a problem here. The group dynamics of maximum participation seem to require *small* groups, yet the Scriptures say there were *"many"* Christians in Corinth, and Paul "stayed there for a year and a half teaching them the word of God" (Acts 18:10–11). At least two solutions seem possible: (1) more than one house church may have existed in Corinth (see Acts 2:46 for support for this pattern in Jerusalem); (2) more than one room (or building) may have been used for worship and teaching in Gaius's household. Some large households were virtually small communities with multiple structures including an adjoining hotel. A household could include "not only immediate relatives, but slaves, freedmen, hired workers, and sometimes tenants and partners in trade or craft" (Wayne A. Meeks, *The Urban Environment of Pauline Christianity* [New Haven: Yale University Press, 1983], 57, 75–76). See also subsequent notes.

19. R. Daniel Reeves and Ron Jenson, *Always Advancing: Modern Strategies for Church Growth* (San Bernardino, Calif.: Here's Life, 1984), 28.

20. Small groups are ideal for grooming leaders in small, mid-sized, and large churches. Large churches particularly benefit by the formation of small cell groups. The leaders of small groups need to be held accountable to the elders or pastor.

21. Eddie Gibbs, ed., *Ten Growing Churches* (N.p.: Marc Europe, British Church Growth Association, 1984), 169: "We find it does not work to have pastoral leaders also leading their own group, though they often take the lead when they visit a group."

22. Ibid. Further: "The house groups are a great help in keeping unity within the body. Problems can go unnoticed for weeks in a large congregation, but in a small closely knit group, it is hard to hide one's feelings" (169).

23. Martin Luther envisioned the possibility of three kinds of services: (1) Latin service, (2) German service, and (3) small-group house service he termed "a truly Evangelical Church Order" for earnest Christians who "profess the Gospel with hand and mouth." He visualized the third group's meeting "in some house in order to pray, read, baptize, receive the Sacrament and do other Christian works." For them, "the many and elaborate chants would be unnecessary. There could be a short, appropriate Order for Baptism and the Sacrament and everything centered on the Word and Prayer and Love." Yet, he said, there was presently no call for such a thing. But if there were, he would support it (quoted in Bard Thompson, *Liturgies of the Western Church* [New York: World, 1961], 125–26).

24. *Good Things Come in Small Groups*, 24.

25. Ibid., 29.

26. Ministry-time team members are carefully selected by the pastor and elders and are trained for this ministry.

27. If standing is awkward, the persons coming forward may sit on the first row of seats set aside for that purpose. The invitation to come forward can also be given at the conclusion of the service, as at the Anaheim Vineyard Church.

28. Personal conversation, August 1986.

29. Often the Sunday evening service is a good place to implement new ideas. This was Pastor John Sutherland's intention at St. Andrew Lutheran Church in Whittier, California, also. He presented to the church council the idea of having a healing service in the evening as outlined in their book of *Occasional Services* (1982); but the council suggested "why not have it on Sunday morning instead." That is how the church "stumbled" into a healing service. Fearful that it might be perceived as "kooky," Sutherland prepared the way with an article in the church bulletin defining healing in a broad way (i.e., body, mind, and spirit).

He relates, "That first Sunday I preached a cautious sermon on how God heals in different ways, using the Greek word *soteria* (salvation-health) as the central thought. Then my assistant and I invited people to come forward to the altar railing for prayer. To my complete surprise, 95 percent of the 275 people present came forward! Our healing service is now one of our most popular services; a team of eight ministers. People invite their friends and neighbors. Total strangers have come forward. The service now occurs regularly on the fifth Sunday of the month (four or five times a year), and we print a clarifying statement in the church bulletin on that day."

30. Unchurched visitors and those who are not comfortable offering prayer in a small group may find this approach confrontational. Consider devoting a Sunday evening to training your people how, so these others will feel comfortable. Talk through the concept and act out a small-group ministry time, eliciting feedback and suggestions from your people.

31. Perhaps one disadvantage of this approach over the long term is that the momentum (rhythm) of the service is broken. Nevertheless, some churches are happy with this method.

32. Arthur E. Paris, *Black Pentecostalism: Southern Religion in an Urban World* (Amherst: University of Massachusetts Press, 1982), 74. See also a report on the Church of the Cherubim and Seraphim in Britain by J. G. Davies, *Liturgical Dance: An Historical, Theological and Practical Handbook* (London: SCM, 1984), 200–201.

33. Ibid., 73–74.

34. Paul sarcastically labels these people "kings" (1 Corinthians 4:8).

35. I find Graham Kendrick's entire discussion highly pertinent, valuable, and born of much practical experience (*Learning to Worship as a Way of Life*). See the chapter on "Leading Worship II," and page 170 in particular.

36. MacDonald, *Christian Worship in the Primitive Church*, 26.

CHAPTER 5. EXTRAORDINARY VARIETY!

1. Oscar Cullmann, *Early Christian Worship*, trans. A. Stewart Todd and James B. Torrance (Naperville, Ill.: Alec R. Allenson, 1956), 26.

2. See Acts 4:24ff.; Mark 14:26 (from the Hallel, Psalms 115–18); James 5:13.

3. Ralph P. Martin, *The Worship of God: Some Theological, Pastoral, and Practical Reflections* (Grand Rapids: Eerdmans, 1982), 52. For Jewish setting see Revelation 4:8, 11; 15:3–4; for incarnational canticles see Luke 1:46–55; 2:29–32; and for Christological hymns see John 1:1-18; Philippians 2:6-11; Colossians 1:1-15; 1 Timothy 3:16).

4. Ibid., 53.

5. Some psalms directly address the self in the context of worship: "Why are you in despair, O my soul? . . . Hope in God. . . . O my God, my soul is in despair. . . . Therefore I remember Thee" (Psalm 42:5–6 NASB).

6. Alexander B. MacDonald, *Christian Worship in the Primitive Church* (Edinburgh: T. and T. Clark, 1935), 18.

7. From a conversation with Prof. Robert Harrison, historian at Biola University, 8 September 1986.

8. R. Daniel Reeves and Ron Jenson compare major forms of ecclesiastical government—episcopal, presbyterian, and congregational—to monarchical, republican, and democratic governmental structures (*Always Advancing: Modern Strategies for Church Growth* [San Bernardino: Here's Life, 1984], 128).

9. Wayne A. Meeks, *The First Urban Christians: The Social World of the Apostle Paul* (New Haven: Yale University Press, 1983), 29.

10. Ibid. See also John E. Stambaugh and David L. Balch, *The New Testament in Its Social Environment* (Philadelphia: Westminster Press), 1986.

11. Gerd Thiessen writes: "Paul speaks not of a 'house-congregation' (as in Philemon 2) but of the 'whole congregation.' From this it could be concluded that the congregation also met at other places, but in smaller groups. . . . In any event, the whole congregation met at Gaius', and that presupposes that he had sufficient space at his disposal, since the congregation at Corinth was large . . . (Acts 18:10). Thus we may infer high social status for Gaius. In addition, there is the matter of other people found frequenting the house. From here Tertius writes the letter to the Romans. That makes it appear as if other tasks were customarily performed in this house. There also seem to have been contacts with the 'city-treasurer' Erastus, whose greetings are conveyed at the very end of Romans as if he had just stopped by (*The Social Setting of Pauline Christianity: Essays on Corinth*, ed. and trans. John H. Schutz [Philadelphia: Fortress Press, 1982], 89). Josef A. Jungmann, Roman Catholic historian and liturgist, tells a fascinating story about the continued existence of house churches. He says that research has revealed that the appellation *saint* was sometimes added to the name of church at a much later date on the false assumption that it enshrined a martyr.

Saint Clement's Church was one. Its name came about as a natural consequence of the fact that it was Clement's house. That is, there was nothing particularly saintly about Clement other than being the person who donated the property for church use (*The Early Liturgy to the Time of Gregory the Great,* trans. Francis A. Brunner [Notre Dame, Ind.: University of Notre Dame Press, 1959], 13). ˒

12. Romans 16:23; 1 Corinthians 16:19. Prof. Robert Harrison (Biola University) believes the household was not the only arena for worship, but in Paul's urban setting it probably was his primary tool for evangelism.

13. Meeks, *The Urban Environment of Pauline Christianity,* 52.

14. Thiessen writes: "Corinthian citizens were not only on the rise socially; the city had also experienced a rapid economic upturn, as excavations confirm" (*The Social Setting of Pauline Christianity,* 100). See also C. F. D. Moule, *The Birth of the New Testament,* 3rd ed. (New York: Harper & Row, 1982), 201ff.

15. Thiessen, *The Social Setting of Pauline Christianity,* 107.

16. Ibid., 163–64. The common solution today is a potluck.

17. Ibid., 165–66.

18. Donald McGavran, *Understanding Church Growth* (Grand Rapids: Eerdmans, 1970), 198. Critics of the church growth movement have charged that the principle of social homogeneity is unbiblical. Some disagreement might be dispelled if church growth people clarified the principle and its implications in more detail. I merely observe (with others) that the Corinthian church seems to have been socially diverse, and Paul worked to achieve oneness under these conditions.

CHAPTER 6. BACK TO THE FOUNTAINHEAD

1. What is interesting is that at the very time when English people appear to be departing from the Anglican church in large numbers to become involved in free-worship formats, college students in the Chicago area are leaving the free worship of evangelical churches to become liturgical Episcopalians (as reported in Robert E. Webber, *Evangelicals on the Canterbury Trail* [Waco, Tex.: Word Books, 1985]). This demonstrates once again that forms need to be infused with spiritual vitality. For information on house churches in nineteenth-century England, see Deborah M. Valenze, *Prophetic Sons and Daughters: Female Preaching and Popular Religion in Industrial England* (Princeton: Princeton University Press, 1985), 25ff.

Norm Wakefield describes his multihouse congregation (Shared Life Fellowship) that meets in homes in Phoenix, Arizona: "We meet together twice a week, Sundays and Thursdays. On Sunday the first half hour or forty minutes is spent together. During this time children and adults sing together and are free to share. Often during this time we have a feature where children talk one-on-one with adults or share in small groups. We have each person tell his favorite Bible story or describe a favorite teacher or tell about one time each felt loved.

"Also, we periodically have all-age Bible studies on Thursday nights. These are designed to involve first graders through adults. We include puzzles, games, and other activities. Everything is done in small, mixed groups of adults and children. . . . To keep anyone from taking over the leader role, we'll have instructions like, 'Let the person closest to age 12 . . .' and 'The person whose birthday is closest to November will now . . .' We try to get everyone involved in all these studies on the same level, whatever their age" (quoted in Lawrence O. Richards, *A Theology of Children's Ministry* [Grand Rapids: Zondervan, 1983], 201).

2. Joyce V. Thurman, *New Wineskins: A Study of the House Church Movement* (Bern: Verlag Peter Lang, 1982), 86.

3. Ibid., 9.

4. Carl Lawrence, *The Church in China* (Minneapolis: Bethany House, 1985), 88–90.

5. Address by J. I. Packer at Talbot School of Theology, 10 November 1983.

6. See David O. Moberg, *The Church as a Social Institution: The Sociology of American Religion* (Englewood Cliffs, N.J.: Prentice-Hall, 1962).

7. All quotations not specifically noted are from an address by Packer given at Talbot School of Theology, 10 November 1983.

8. Russell P. Spittler claims: "So far as any published 'systematic theology' is concerned [in the Pentecostal Tradition] . . . there simply is no such Pentecostal theology. Even the *interest* to produce such a work has barely surfaced" ("Scripture and the Theological Enterprise: View from a Big Canoe" in Robert K. Johnston, ed., *The Use of the Bible in Theology/Evangelical Options* [Atlanta: John Knox Press, 1985], 57–58).

9. J. I. Packer listed these weaknesses ("disfigurements") in the charismatic movement in his address at Talbot School of Theology (10 November 1983; tape TC-5221): (1) elitism, (2) sectarianism, (3) emotionalism, (4) anti-intellectualism, (5) illuminism ["readiness to trust unchecked words from God . . . from folks who have gained a reputation as prophets"], (6) charismania ["measuring growth and maturity . . . by the number and impressiveness of people's gifts"], (7) super supernaturalism ["affirming the supernatural in a way that exaggerates its discontinuity with the natural . . . leads to an underestimate of God's ordinary slow, patient, providences . . . and ordinary means of grace"]. He also said: "Not all charismatics fail in all these ways."

10. These factors are culture dependent; for example, in Canada people tend to dress more formally.

11. Quoted in Thurman, *New Wineskins*, 8.

12. A somewhat similar phenomenon today is the emergence of church growth consultants.

13. Thiessen lists seventeen persons connected in a leadership-facilitating capacity with Paul.

14. Packer, Talbot address, 10 November 1983.

15. Read Tim Stafford's provocative article, "Intimacy: Our Latest Sexual Fantasy" (*Christianity Today*, 16 January 1987), and ask yourself, "How does the subject of this article relate to the strong need for worship expressed by many today?"

16. For a similar pattern see Judson Cornwall, *Let Us Worship* (South Plainfield, N.J.: Bridge, 1983), 153–58.

17. Packer, Talbot address, 10 November 1983.

18. Throughout both chapters on Pauline worship, I am thinking of lay or part-time worship leaders.

19. Did you hear the story of the guy with the guitar who was leading worship on Sunday morning? He stopped to do a little sharing: ". . . and late last night in the midst of this great distress, and emotional and spiritual turmoil, the

Lord gave me a song. And I'd like to sing it for you now. By the way, I have already copyrighted it, and if you use it, I'll sue the socks off you!"
20. Donald P. Hustad is a former organist for the Billy Graham crusades and a former director of the Sacred Music department at Moody Bible Institute. He recently retired as professor of church music and V. V. Cooke Professor of Organ at Southern Baptist Theological Seminary, Louisville, Kentucky.
21. Donald P. Hustad, *Jubilate! Church Music in the Evangelical Tradition* (Carol Stream, Ill.: Hope, 1981), 50–51.

CHAPTER 7. PATTERNS FOR PROTESTANTS

1. In this book, synagogue worship follows after the Pauline model for two reasons. First, the representative form of leadership through elders seems more suited to managing larger groups than the congregational form of Corinthians (the models of this book are sequenced according to size). Second, the synagogue continued to influence Christian worship through the remainder of the first century and on into the fifth century.
2. Christopher Rowland, *Christian Origins: From Messianic Movement to Christian Religion* (Minneapolis: Augsburg, 1985), 71–80, 299–301. For further information ask about the Caspari Center for Biblical and Jewish Studies in Jerusalem (Jews for Jesus, P.O. Box 1454, Studio City, CA 91604). A summer course on "Early Judeo-Christianity" was offered by Ole Chr. M. Kvarme, 1985.
3. The oldest Graeco-Jewish documents mentioning synagogues date back to the dedication of a synagogue to Ptolemy III (247–221 B.C.) and his queen Bernice, according to Emil Schurer (*The History of the Jewish People in the Age of Jesus Christ*, ed. Gesa Vermes, Fergus Millar, and Matthew Black, rev. ed. [Edinburgh: T. and T. Clark, 1979] 2:425). See also Moshe Dothan's article "Research on Ancient Synagogues in the Land of Israel" in *Recent Archaeology in the Land of Israel*, ed. Hershel Shanks (Washington, D.C.: Biblical Archaeology Society, 1984) relating to synagogues from the second temple period.
4. Abraham E. Millgram, *Jewish Worship* (Philadelphia: Jewish Publication Society of America, 1971), 83.
5. Jacob Neusner, *A History of the Mishnaic Law of Appointed Times.* (Leiden: E. J. Brill, 1982), 3:168–69.
6. The attendant's task was to bring out the scroll and afterward to replace it, as well as begin and end the Sabbath by blowing a trumpet.
7. Even today this act is central to the unfolding drama of synagogue liturgy.
8. A synagogue ruler (singular) is cited in Luke 13:14.
9. Ralph P. Martin writes: "As far as we can piece together the format of the synagogue service, three elements stand out: the praise of God, and the reading and exposition of Scripture. . . . the primary emphasis does seem to fall on *praise* . . . Scripture, read and applied, was given a central place side by side with praise, although in public worship the reading of Scripture was accorded precedence over the rabbis' homily" (*The Spirit and the Congregation* [Grand Rapids: Eerdmans, 1984], 60).
Further: "But the homily [Rabbi's sermon] still held a lower rank than the actual reading of Scripture, and it was given only if a person competent to give the exposition was present. This explains the scene in the synagogue at Pisidian

Antioch (Act 13:15), where Paul is invited to give a 'word of exhortation' to the assembled congregation" (Martin, *The Worship of God* [Grand Rapids: Eerdmans, 1982], 103).

10. It is also fair to say that the New Testament church was born with a sermon, that is, Peter's address beginning in Acts 2:14: "Preaching entered late in the life of the ancient Israel, but it was there from the start of the new Israel, the Church. . . . the Church came to birth *with preaching* and *preaching came to birth with the church* (D. W. Cleverley Ford, *The Ministry of the Word* [Grand Rapids: Eerdmans, 1979], 53). See Ralph P. Martin for biblical models on the sermon and for historical perspective on its development, in his chapter "The Role of the Sermon" in *The Worship of God* (101–123).

11. Joseph Gutman, "Synagogue Origins: Theories and Fact," in Joseph Gutman, ed., *Ancient Synagogues: The State of Research* (Chico, Calif.: Scholars Press, 1981), 51–52.

12. Lee I. Levine, ed., *Ancient Synagogues Revealed* (Jerusalem: Academic Press, 1981), 3ff.

13. Schurer, *History of the Jewish People*, 424. See also the extensive essay on the synagogue by Wolfgang Schrage in Gerhard Kittel and Gerhard Friedrich, *Theological Dictionary of the New Testament*, trans. G. W. Bromiley (Grand Rapids: Eerdmans, 1971), 7:782–852.

14. Ibid., 425.

15. Schurer gives mTam 4:3; 5:1 as support. Further: "Josephus regards its origin [the custom of reciting the Shema] as so remote that he sees it as having been laid down by Moses himself [Ant. iv 8, 3 (212)]" (*History of the Jewish People*, 455).

16. Schurer cites mBer 1:1–4.

17. Hoffman says that "synagogal liturgical decisions are akin to catechetical statements" and that liturgical recitation is equivalent to "theological polemic" (Lawrence A. Hoffman, "Censoring In and Censoring Out: A Function of Liturgical Language," in Gutman, *Ancient Synagogues*, 22).

18. The remainder of the Shema may be found in Deuteronomy 11:13–21 and Numbers 15:37–41.

19. Also Mark 8:29; Acts 2:36; Romans 1:3–4; 10:9; 1 Corinthians 12:3.

20. John H. Leith, *Creeds of the Church: A Reader in Christian Doctrine From the Bible to the Present* (Richmond: John Knox Press, 1973), 5.

21. Since the Council of Chalcedon (A.D. 451), the Constantinopolitan Creed, popularly known as the Nicene Creed, has been attributed to the Council of Constantinople (A.D. 381).

22. Two versions of the prayer exist, the Palestinian version and the Babylonian version, of which the former is considered the oldest and probably comes closest to what might have been said during the time of Christ. See Schurer, *History of the Jewish People*, 459–60.

23. See Lawrence A. Hoffman's interesting view of tannaitic liturgy. He says some aspects of the liturgy are cognitive—i.e., they speak of the God of history and what He has done. Other aspects of the liturgy are less cognitive. They are "marked by fluidity of sound and rhythm." Words are not used so much for their information carrying quality as for their function of pointing and fixing the worshiper's concentration on the "master image" (God). Like a spinning wheel, the words are interchangeable, endless, and form the shape of the eternal. The wheel is spun, so to speak, and the "spokes disappear, leaving the master

image." "Specific semantic meaning," Hoffman says, "is subservient to the general symbolic image" ("Censoring In and Censoring Out," 26–30).

24. Schurer, *History of the Jewish People*, 2:460–61.

25. Ferdinand Hahn, *The Worship of the Early Church*, trans. David E. Green (Philadelphia: Fortress Press, 1973), 33.

26. See Hahn, *The Worship of the Early Church*. Also see Schurer, *History of the Jewish People*, 462–63, and F. F. Bruce, *The Gospel of John: Introduction, Exposition and Notes* (Grand Rapids: Eerdmans, 1983), 215.

27. Gerhard Delling, *Worship in the New Testament,* trans. Percy Scott (Philadelphia: Westminster Press, 1962), 93.

28. Alexander B. MacDonald, *Christian Worship in the Primitive Church* (Edinburgh: T. and T. Clark, 1935), 73.

29. Schurer, *History of the Jewish People*, 451.

30. It is reasonable to envisage Jewish boys' schools as existing at the time of Christ, for they were flourishing in every town and province by about A.D. 63 (Schurer, *History of the Jewish People*, 419).

31. To obtain a copy of de Lange's paper "A Woman in Israel," write the Associate General Secretary, Campion Hall, Oxford OX1 1QS, United Kingdom, and ask for collected papers of the Ecumenical Society of the Blessed Virgin Mary, 1975 conference at Birmingham, England. De Lange, who is a rabbi, is lecturer in Rabbinics at Cambridge University.

32. Nicholas de Lange cites Tosefta Megilla iv (iii), II, Babylonina Talmud, Megilla 23a. Scripture indicates women could offer prayer in the temple or synagogue (1 Sam. 2:1–10; Luke 1:46–55).

33. Christopher Rowland says: "Despite various attempts to show that various types of lectionary patterns antedate the fall of Jerusalem [A.D. 70] . . . there is no evidence to suggest that the three-year cycle was in existence during the second temple period [i.e., before A.D. 70]" (*Christian Origins*, 45).

34. A lectionary of planned Scripture readings based on the Christian calendar year is available in the appendix to Robert E. Webber's *Worship: Old and New* (Grand Rapids: Zondervan, 1982), 213–22.

35. The reason why 1 Corinthians does not make mention of the public reading of Scripture is that Paul is addressing the problem areas of their worship; therefore some of the basics that were unproblematic presumably go unmentioned.

36. For help in implementing a reader's theater in your church, see Todd V. Lewis, *RT: A Reader's Theatre Ministry* (Kansas City, Mo.: Lillenas, 1988).

37. Acts 4:5, 8, 23. See also the notes for Acts 15:4–22 and 15:12 in the *NIV Study Bible* (Kenneth Barker, ed. [Grand Rapids: Zondervan, 1985], 1674).

38. Schurer, *History of the Jewish People*, 429, 431. In the larger cities a council of elders represented the Jews of the whole city, probably through officers chosen by each congregation.

39. Ibid., 431. Schurer says in the same paragraph that as far as is known since the post-exilic period, "the mass of the people . . . nowhere exercised jurisdiction."

40. Schurer writes: "tMeg 4:21: 'The elders sit with their face to the people and their back to the sanctuary. The ark stands with its front to the people and its back to the sanctuary. . . . When the priests confer the blessing, they stand with their face to the people and their back to the sanctuary. The synagogue minister

(here as prayer-leader) stands with his face to the sanctuary, and likewise all the people are turned to the sanctuary' " (*History of the Jewish People*, 449, fn. 107).

41. Wayne A. Meeks, *The Urban Environment of Pauline Christianity* (New Haven: Yale University Press, 1983), 35.

42. Ibid., 131, 133.

43. See also C. Peter Wagner's discussion on "modalities" and "sodalities"(*Leading Your Church to Growth* [Ventura, Calif · Regal Books, 1984], 142–65).

44. Meeks, *The Urban Environment of Pauline Christianity*, 133–34. The references for the three lists are 1 Corinthians 12:8–10, 28–30; Romans 12:6–8; Ephesians 4:11.

45. Ibid., 70.

46. Handout, "Rabbinic Teachings Regarding Women," from Allen Ross's course (Rabbinical Interpretation of Old Testament, course no. 138), semantics department, at Dallas Theological Seminary.

47. De Lange, "A Woman in Israel." Rehearsing this ceremony would be an excellent educational experience for children in Christian homes.

48. Ibid.

49. A. C. Bouquet, *Everyday Life in New Testament Times* (New York: Charles Scribner's Sons, 1953), 210. Many churches in India, however, still segregate the sexes.

50. "Jewish Music" in *The New Grove Dictionary of Music and Musicians*, ed. Stanley Sadie (Washington, D.C.: Macmillan, 1980), 9:632. The article cites the Babylonian Talmud, treatise Berakst ch. 3 para. 24a as support.

51. For an excellent "case study" of women's roles in the church, see J. I. Packer's essay "In Quest of Canonical Interpretation" in Robert K. Johnston, ed., *The Use of the Bible in Theology/Evangelical Options* (Atlanta: John Knox Press, 1985), 46–54.

52. Donald P. Hustad, *Jubilate! Church Music in the Evangelical Tradition* (Carol Stream, Ill.: Hope, 1981), 58.

CHAPTER 8. THE LEGACY

1. I have chosen the Puritans as a representative group from the Protestant Reformation because their ideas concerning worship contrast strongly with the Roman Catholic church.

2. According to Gerhard Delling, "[in Judaism] congregation confession of sin prayers occupied considerable place—but the New Testament shows no trace of it" (*Worship in the New Testament*, trans. Percy Scott [Philadelphia: Westminster Press, 1962], 93).

3. Nicholas de Lange reports that baptism was "practiced regularly by certain pietist sects, and was required as part of the admission of converts to Judaism" ("A Woman in Israel," collected papers of the Ecumenical Society of the Blessed Virgin Mary, 1975 conference at Birmingham, England). Phillip Sigal makes the same point in "Early Christian and Rabbinic Liturgical Affinities: Exploring Liturgical Acculturation," *New Testament Studies*, 30:66–67. He relates the "halakhic" approach in baptizing proselytes to the chapters on baptism (20–22) in Hippolytus, *The Apostolic Tradition* (ca. A.D. 220).

4. Alexander B. MacDonald, *Christian Worship in the Primitive Church* (Edinburgh: T. and T. Clark, 1935), 68.

5. This alternative view is held by Prof. Robert Harrison, historian at Biola University.

6. Robert E. Webber, *Worship: Old and New* (Grand Rapids: Zondervan, 1982), 49. Justin Martyr's document is accorded real importance by churches that espouse a liturgical form of service.

7. Justin Martyr, *First Apology*, ch. 67, in Cyril Richardson, ed., *Early Christian Fathers* (Philadelphia: Westminster Press, 1953), 287–88.

8. William D. Maxwell, *A History of Christian Worship: An Outline of Its Development and Forms* (Grand Rapids: Baker, 1982), 11.

9. For an enlightening discussion of the authority of tradition versus the authority of Scripture, see Robert E. Webber, "An Evangelical and Catholic Methodology," in Robert K. Johnston, ed., *The Use of the Bible in Theology/Evangelical Options* (Atlanta: John Knox Press, 1985), 137–58.

10. Revelation 5:8; 8:2, 6, 13; 9:14; 14:2; 15:2.

11. W. D. E. Oesterley, *The Jewish Background of the Christian Liturgy* (Oxford: Oxford University Press, 1925), 96.

12. Eric Werner, "The Conflict Between Hellenism and Judaism in the Music of the Early Christian Church," *Hebrew Union College Annual* 20 (Cincinnati: Hebrew Union College, 1947). See also Donald P. Hustad, *Jubilate! Church Music in the Evangelical Tradition* (Carol Stream, Ill.: Hope, 1981), 41–44.

13. Other aspects of Greek culture were influential in Palestine according to John E. Stambaugh and David L Balch: "Theaters and amphitheaters were built, by Herod in Caesarea, for example, and even in Jerusalem, where various kinds of games were celebrated: gymnastic and musical games, chariot racing, and animal baiting (Josephus, Antiquities 15:267–291)" (*The New Testament in Its Social Environment* [Philadelphia: Westminster Press, 1986], 414–15).

14. Werner, "Conflict Between Hellenism and Judaism," 414–15.

15. "Anti Hellenism led to the opposition of the Pharisees (rabbis) to the use of instruments in worship" ("Jewish Music" in *The New Grove Dictionary of Music and Musicians*, ed. Stanley Sadie [Washington, D.C.: Macmillan, 1980], 9:632).

16. Ibid., 9:623.

17. Ralph P. Martin, *The Worship of God: Some Theological, Pastoral, and Practical Reflections* (Grand Rapids: Eerdmans, 1982), 6–7.

18. Ibid., 8.

19. Gordon S. Wenham writes: "It is true that in the NT it is hard to find covenant terminology and structures, but that does not mean the principles enshrined in the OT covenant have disappeared" (*The Book of Leviticus* [Grand Rapids: Eerdmans, 1979], 33).

CHAPTER 9. DRAMA

1. Leviticus 16:21; Deuteronomy 21:6–9.

2. Erik Routley, *Words, Music and the Church* (Nashville: Abingdon Press, 1968), 129, 136. Part 4, "The Dimension of Drama," is insightful.

3. See the classic statement on this in Constantin Stanislavski, *An Actor Prepares*, trans. Elizabeth Reynold Hapgood (New York: Theatre Art Books, 1936), 31–50.

4. Robert E. Webber, *Worship Is a Verb* (Waco, Tex.: Word Books, 1985), 55–56.

5. John N. Vaughan, *The World's Twenty Largest Churches* (Grand Rapids: Baker, 1984), 153.

6. See an interesting discussion of when *not* to lay hands on the sick by an Assemblies of God church planter overseas: David E. Goodwin, *Church Planting Methods* (DeSoto, Tex.: Lifeshare Communications, 1984), 69–72.

7. Webber, *Worship Is a Verb*, 83. See also Ben Patterson, "Worship as Performance," *Leadership* 2, no. 3 (1981): 49–52.

8. For a work by a Roman Catholic writer on "narrative theology," which combines theory and practice and which brings philosophical insights into the storytelling process, see William J. Bausch, *Storytelling: Imagination and Faith* (Mystic, Conn.: Twenty-third Publications, 1984). For drama plays, clown, mime, and banner resources, write the Contemporary Drama Service (Box 7710-S4, Colorado Springs, CO 80933: Meriwether Publishing LTD) and ask for a catalog. If you wish to introduce drama in your church, school, or college, consider inviting the Thai Folk Drama Troupe, a Christian troupe directed by Allan and Joan Eubank, Payap University, L.P.O. Sansai 101, Chiang Mai 50000, Thailand.

9. Routley, *Words, Music and the Church*, 150–52.

10. This idea is based on a quotation from Kierkegaard. The concept is useful to make a point, but needs some amplification. God's role is actually more complex. He is not only the audience but also the initiator as well as interactor in worship. Lutherans in their philosophy of worship, for example, view God primarily as the initiator and the people as the responders.

11. Ben Patterson, address at Talbot Chapel, Biola University, 14 February 1985. I cannot confirm from my own study that the "major efforts in instruction" occurred during the week, but Patterson may be correct. Alternatively, in regard to the distinctive Patterson makes between teaching and response, many would envision the role of sermon in the dynamic of worship as follows: we come to God and He comes to us as the Word is proclaimed in the sermon.

12. One of my students saw a pastor file his nails during a Sunday morning solo and tell jokes to the person next to him during the hymn singing. "He didn't even have a hymnal on the platform. Needless to say," the student responded, "I had difficulty listening to his sermon. I became angry." Similar stories could be told of the behavior of musicians. This kind of nonsense is inexcusable.

13. Ronald Allen and Gordon Borror, *Worship: Rediscovering the Missing Jewel* (Portland, Oreg.: Multnomah Press, 1982), 144.

CHAPTER 10. SYMBOLISM

1. This story may be found in *Exploring Hebrews* by John Phillips (Chicago: Moody Press, 1977), 141–42.

2. Graham Kendrick, *Learning to Worship as a Way of Life* (Minneapolis: Bethany House, 1984), 142–50.

3. Ibid., 143.

4. Gene Edward Veith, Jr., *The Gift of Art: The Place of the Arts in Scripture* (Downers Grove, Ill.: InterVarsity Press, 1983), 54.

5. David A. Miller, "Neuropsychology and the Emotional Component of Religion," *Pastoral Psychology* 33 (1985): 267. My thanks to Prof. Tony Wong (Rosemead School of Psychology at Biola University) for this reference.

6. Jerre Levy, "Right Brain, Left Brain: Fact and Fiction," *Psychology Today* (May 1985): 43–44.

7. Miller, "Neuropsychology and the Emotional Component of Religion," 269.

8. Levy, "Right Brain, Left Brain," 44.

9. This is the position of Prof. Sherwood Lingenfelter (School of Intercultural Studies, Biola University). Note, he does not claim that other cultures are programmed differently or are genetically different, but that their value-reward system may favor one hemisphere over another.

10. Miller, "Neuropsychology and the Emotional Component of Religion," 270.

11. I am well aware that candles and other forms of symbolic communication have been abused in the past.

CHAPTER 11. FINE ARTS

1. William A. Dyrness argues as follows in "Aesthetics in the Old Testament: Beauty In Context," *Journal of the Evangelical Theological Society* 28 (1985): 428: ". . . the prohibition in the second commandment has primarily to do with false worship and not with the attempt to reflect God in images. The line is drawn between God and idols but not between God and images. . . . God refuses us the right to make an image of himself because he has made such attempts unnecessary. He himself has given adequate reflection of his character in his created order, especially in men and women. These 'images' are to call forth praise for the maker (Psalms 8; 19)." For a more stringent view of the second commandment, see J. I. Packer, *Knowing God* (Downers Grove, Ill.: InterVarsity Press, 1973), 38–44.

2. Francis A. Schaeffer, *Art and the Bible* (Downers Grove, Ill.: InterVarsity Press, 1974), 12.

3. Note the abstraction. In reality pomegranates are not blue.

4. Menahem Haran, "The Priestly Image in the Tabernacle," *Hebrew Union College Annual* (Cincinnati: Hebrew Union College, 1965), 36:206–7.

5. Gene Edward Veith, Jr., *The Gift of Art: The Place of the Arts in Scripture* (Downers Grove, Ill.: InterVarsity Press, 1983), 47. My thinking has been heavily influenced by Veith in my writing this chapter.

6. Ibid., 46–48.

7. Ibid., 47.

8. Ibid., 67.

9. Ibid., 64–65.

10. Ibid., 65.

11. Ibid., 21.

12. Personal communication, Talbot School of Theology, 1986.

13. For more detail see Barry Liesch and Tom Finley, "The Biblical Concept of Creativity: Scope, Definition, Criteria," *Journal of Psychology and Theology* 12 (1984): 188–97.

CHAPTER 12. DAVIDIC PRAISE

1. Jack R. Taylor, *The Hallelujah Factor* (Nashville: Broadman Press, 1983), intro. and 108.

2. Ibid., preface, 16.

3. G. Johannes Botterweck and Helmer Ringgren, eds., *Theological Dictionary of the Old Testament* (Grand Rapids: Eerdmans, 1980), 4:249.

4. Ralph P. Martin, *Worship in the Early Church* (Grand Rapids: Eerdmans, 1975), 11. Also, the word *bless* means "to kneel."

5. Botterweck and Ringgren, eds., *Theological Dictionary of the Old Testament*, 4:249.

6. A second Old Testament word for worship, *abodah*, is translated "service." The corresponding Greek word in the New Testament is *latreia*. See Colin Brown, gen. ed., *The New International Dictionary of New Testament Theology* (Grand Rapids: Zondervan, 1978), 3:550–55.

7. Ronald Barclay Allen, *Praise! A Matter of Life and Breath* (Nashville: Nelson, 1980), 60.

8. Ibid., 64–65.

9. Ibid., 200.

10. Ibid., 170.

11. Taylor, *The Hallelujah Factor*, 25.

12. William Hendriksen, "Exposition of Pastoral Epistles," *New Testament Commentary* (Grand Rapids: Baker, 1957), 103–4.

The Scripture references are as follows:

Bowing the head (Genesis 24:48; Exodus 12:27; 2 Chronicles 29:30; Luke 24:5);

Standing (Genesis 18:22; 1 Samuel 1:26; Matthew 6:5; Mark 11:25; Luke 18:11, 13);

Lifting the eyes (Psalms 25:15; 121:1; 123:1–2; 141:8; 145:15; John 11:41; 17:1; see Daniel 9:3; Acts 7:55);

Kneeling (2 Chronicles 6:13; Psalm 95:6; Isaiah 45:23; Daniel 6:10; Matthew 17:14; Mark 1:40; Luke 22:41; Acts 7:60; 9:40; 21:5; Ephesians 3:14);

Hands spread out or lifted (Exodus 9:29; 17:11-12; 1 Kings 8:22; Nehemiah 8:6; Psalms 63:4; 134:2; 141:2; Isaiah 1:15; Lamentations 2:19; 3:41; Habakkuk 3:10; Luke 24:50; 1 Timothy 2:8; James 4:8);

Prostrating (Genesis 17:3; 24:26; Numbers 14:5, 13; 16:4, 22, 45; 22:13, 34; Deuteronomy 9:18, 25; Joshua 5:14; Judges 13:20; Nehemiah 8:6; Ezekiel 1:28; 3:23; 9:8; 11:13; 43:3; 44:4; Daniel 8:17; Matthew 26:39; Mark 7:25; 14:35; Luke 5:12; 17:16; Revelation 1:17; 11:16).

Two other prayer postures not included in the chart occur one time each: *head between the knees* (1 Kings 18:42), and *striking the chest* (Luke 18:13). The above postures may be done in combinations.

13. "The Celebration Song" can be found in *Maranatha! Music Praise and Worship Collection* (Costa Mesa, California, 1987). See *Maranatha! Music Praise Chorus Book* (distributed by Word, Inc., 1983) for "King of Kings."

14. Interestingly, although we don't shout it, we sing it! Jack R. Taylor's list of songs using the Hallelujah includes: "All Creatures of Our God and King," "Praise My Soul the King of Heaven," "Come Christians Join to Sing," "Revive Us Again," "Satisfied," "Low in the Grave He Lay," and "Christ the Lord Is Risen Today."

15. Taylor, *The Hallelujah Factor*, 45.

16. Some readers may feel I have not focused sufficiently on the abuses connected with the raising of hands in some charismatic circles. First, I don't think this is at root a charismatic issue per se. Second, I do not consider myself a charismatic. If there are abuses, I think it is the responsibility of charismatics themselves to speak to this (see Chuck Smith, *Charisma Vs. Charismania* [Eugene, Oreg.: Harvest House, 1983]). I am trying to obey the teaching of Jesus: "Why do you look at the speck of sawdust in your brother's eye and pay no attention to the plank in your own eye? . . . You hypocrite, first take the plank out of your own eye, and then you will see clearly to remove the speck from your brother's eye" (Matt. 7:3–5).

17. Taylor, *The Hallelujah Factor*, 84–85.

18. Ibid., 86.

19. Ibid., 85.

20. Chuck Smith, *Charisma Vs. Charismania* (Eugene, Oreg.: Harvest House, 1983), 132.

21. Taylor, *The Hallelujah Factor*, 83.

22. Ibid., 86.

23. Kenneth Barker, ed., *The NIV Study Bible* (Grand Rapids: Zondervan, 1985), 99 note on 9:29.

24. Abraham E. Milligram, *Jewish Worship* (Philadelphia: Jewish Publication Society of America, 1971), 49–50.

25. Taylor gives some practical advice on how to deal with individuals who protest the implementation of praise (*The Hallelujah Factor*, 103–110).

CHAPTER 13. THE ORGANIZATION OF DAVIDIC PRAISE

1. H. W. Beecher, *Lectures on Preaching*, 2nd series (1873; reprint, New York: n.p., 1973), 115.

2. R. H. Mitchell, *Ministry and Music* (Philadelphia: Westminster Press, 1978), 11.

3. Robin A. Leaver and James H. Litton, eds., *Duty and Delight: Routley Remembered* (Carol Stream, Ill.: Hope, 1985), 89–91.

4. Mitchell states: ". . . within the free-church theological education little or no attention is given to developing a theology of church music. The pastor's three or four years of preparation for ministry may have included virtually no important training or experience in the field of music" (*Ministry and Music*, 13). Hustad concurs: "Most of our seminaries and Bible Colleges do not require courses in worship for the minister in preparation (except for studies in homiletics and preaching)" (*Jubilate! Church Music in the Evangelical Tradition* [Carol Stream, Ill.: Hope, 1981], 167).

5. Norman W. Regier, "Self-Evaluation of Pastor's Church Music Education and the Resultant Philosophy of Music in the Worship Service" (Ph.D. diss., University of Missouri–Kansas City, 1985), 26.

6. J. W. Schwarz, "The State of Church Music Education for Ministerial Students in Protestant Seminaries in the United States," *Dissertations Abstracts International* 36, 1600A (University Microfilms no. 75-19043), 65.

7. Ibid., 92.

8. Leaver and Litton, *Duty and Delight*, 98.

9. J. F. White, "Liturgical Scholars: A New Outspokenness," *Christian Century*, 98:107.

10. I asked Dr. William Lock, director of graduate studies in church music at Biola University, "How do you think this division came about?" He thought that some kind of shift may have taken place with the Reformation. In the Catholic church the priests were also the choir, and many priests (like Martin Luther) were accomplished singers. As the importance of the sermon was established in the Protestant church and pastors were not part of the choir, their involvement with music decreased. Yet Luther and Calvin themselves were very much involved with musicians in the creation of hymnals. Lock further added that in the late nineteenth and early twentieth centuries evangelists like Billy Sunday worked hand-in-glove with their song leaders.

The split seems to have become pronounced during the thirties and forties when music programs began to be established in universities at the same time evangelical seminaries were burgeoning. Both pastors and musicians became "professionals." Before this, musicians would do whatever the pastors wanted, but now the musicians had ideas, expertise, and standards of their own that they received from secular institutions. The split has been exacerbated in recent years.

11. The rare example set by Ronald Allen (Old Testament scholar) and Gordon Borror (church musician) in co-authoring *Worship: Rediscovering the Missing Jewel* (Portland, Oreg.: Multnomah Press, 1982) needs to be applauded. They are full-time faculty members at Western Conservative Baptist Seminary in Portland. This kind of integrative effort is a model to all and deserves high praise. The institution where I teach music, Biola University, is also doing something positive. Church music students enrolled in the master's program take four-to-six core courses that are also required by the theology students. Thus the prospective church musicians have an opportunity to rub shoulders with students who are preparing for the ministry. We have the advantage of a complete music department and school of theology within a block of each other.

12. Leaver and Litton, eds., *Duty and Delight*, 97.

13. Ibid., 93.

14. Ibid., 91-2.

15. Robert E. Webber, "An Evangelical and Catholic Methodology," in Robert K. Johnston, ed., *The Use of the Bible in Theology/Evangelical Options* (Atlanta: John Knox Press, 1985), 139-40.

16. The studies by Schwarz (1975) and Regier (1985) that I have cited show that during this ten-year period most evangelical seminaries have made no adjustment or accommodation in their curriculum to give further emphasis to worship.

17. See Nehemiah 12:47; 13:4-5. Also see Alfred Sendrey, *Music in the Social and Religious Life of Antiquity* (Madison, N.J.: Fairleigh Dickinson University Press, 1974), 261-64; and John E. Stambaugh and David L. Balch, *The New Testament in Its Social Environment* (Philadelphia: Westminster Press, 1986), 98-99.

18. Menahem Haran suggests that the priests and Levites lived in the Levitical cities "without distinction. They had a little pasture land outside the city for keeping livestock. This land was not for generating wealth, but for general sustenance, and was to be theirs perpetually" (*Temples and Temple Service in Ancient Israel* (Oxford: Oxford University Press, 1978), 112–13.

19. See James D. Newsome, Jr., ed., *A Synoptic Harmony of Samuel, Kings, and Chronicles: With Related Passages From Psalms, Isaiah, Jeremiah, and Ezra* (Grand Rapids: Baker, 1986). The volume contains an excellent table of contents and index.

20. Nehemiah 7:73; 11:1–3, 18, 20.

21. The modular organization can be pieced together by considering the following passages and is corroborated from ancient extrabiblical sources:

Hamlets: 2 Chronicles 31:15, 19; Ezra 2:70;

Forty-eight Levitical cities: Numbers 35:1–8;

Lots: 1 Chronicles 25:8 (young and old alike, teacher as well as student, cast lots for their duties);

Week-long performances: 1 Chronicles 9:25 (their brothers in their villages had to come from time to time and share their duties for seven-day periods); 2 Chronicles 23:4 (the priests and Levites who come in on the Sabbath); 2 Chronicles 23:8 (arriving and departing on the Sabbath);

Concept of division still operational in New Testament: Luke 1:5, 8;

Twenty-four groups performing together for the festivals: Nehemiah 12:24 (division corresponding to division).

22. See Dale E. Ramsey, *Sing Praises: Management of Church Hymns* (St. Louis: Christian Board of Publications, 1981).

23. "Ten percent of the average service attendance is a valid approximation of the people ideally involved in the music ministry. Therefore, it is reasonable that eight or nine people in a church of eighty-seven could have some basic music gifts. In a church of three hundred, a reasonable goal is thirty in the choir" (Robert D. Berglund, *A Philosophy of Church Music* [Chicago: Moody Press, 1985], 106).

24. H. L. Ellison in *The New Bible Commentary*, ed. Donald Guthrie, rev. ed. (Downers Grove, Ill.: InterVarsity Press, 1970), 381.

25. Also 2 Kings 3:15 and Psalm 48:2, 3.

26. 1 Chronicles 25:5; 2 Chronicles 29:30; 2 Chronicles 35:15.

27. R. Laird. Harris, ed., *Theological Wordbook of the Old Testament* (Chicago: Moody Press, 1980), 1:275.

28. C. F. Keil and F. J. Delitzsch, *Biblical Commentary on the Old Testament* (Grand Rapids: Eerdmans, 1950), 7:270.

29. E. L. Curtis and A. A. Madsen, *A Critical and Exegetical Commentary on the Books of Chronicles*. The International Critical Commentary (New York: Charles Scribner's Sons, 1965), 276.

30. Menahem Haran says, "In the biblical period, that is, at its pre-exilic stage, prayer belonged to the periphery of cult and was not a part of cultic activity. Its place was outside the priestly circle, which held sole responsibility for all cultic matters within the temple precincts. To my mind, then, defining the priestly service in the first temple period as 'a soundless worship' . . . was certainly right" ("Priesthood, Temple, Divine Service: Some Observations on Institutions and Practices of Worship," *Hebrew Annual Review* [1983]: 131).

31. For Mattaniah, compare Nehemiah 13:13 with 11:17, 22.

32. Keil and Delitzsch take this phrase to mean the musicians exhibited "intelligent playing" in the service (*Biblical Commentary on the Old Testament*, 7:465).

33. "Temple (Herod)," in *Encyclopaedia Judaica* (New York: Macmillan, 1971), 15:971. There is also a tradition that as the S. S. Arizona sank during the attack on Pearl Harbor, the naval band aboard continued to play.

CHAPTER 14. MUSICAL STYLE

1. There are about twelve references, including 1 Chronicles 15:16, 19, 28; 16:5, 42.

2. Stanley Sadie, ed., *The New Grove Dictionary of Music and Musicians* (New York: Macmillan, 1980), 9:618.

3. Ibid., 9:622.

4. Alternatively, "prophesy with" in 1 Chronicles 25:1 may mean to "prophesy with the aid of" as in the sense of singing accompanied with the aid of instruments (1 Chron. 25:6).

5. J. H. Eaton, "Music's Place in Worship: A Contribution from the Psalms," in *Prophets, Worship and Theodicy* (Leiden: E. J. Brill, 1984), 92–93. See Psalms 47:5 (exaltation); 98:6 (combination); 150:3.

6. Ibid., 93.

7. Exodus 15:20; 2 Samuel 6:5; Psalms 149:3; 150:4.

8. 1 Chronicles 15:28; 25:6; 2 Chronicles 5:12; 29:25; Nehemiah 12:27.

9. 1 Chronicles 6:39; 16:5. I do not mean to imply that Asaph was awarded the position *because* he was a percussionist.

10. 1 Chronicles 26:6; Nehemiah 11:22–23.

11. I Chronicles 16:37, 41; 25:2; 2 Chronicles 29:30; Ezra 2:41; Nehemiah 11:17; 12:46.

12. Sadie, *New Grove Dictionary*, 9:622.

13. At the Annual Carpenter's Home Church Audio/Music Seminar for church music directors, held 29–30 July 1986 in Lakeland, Florida, "many attendees expressed an interest in moving away from the exclusive use of large pipe organs" and showed enthusiasm for using MIDI and synthesizers in church contexts. There was discussion on how to integrate synthesizers into worship music. About "80 percent of the participants were already using synthesizers in their churches" according to *Roland Users Group* 4, no. 2 (1986).

Also, on the market at present is the Kat Midi Controller, an electronic mallet keyboard with rubber bars and having the look of a vibraphone or marimba. Notes can be sustained by holding down the mallet. The Kat "can help mallet players get involved in more contemporary forms of music and open a lot of doors for mallet players that have previously been closed" (*Professional Percussionist* [March 1987]). I am grateful to Dr. Ed Childs for this information.

Don Muro reports: "Electronic church organ companies such as Allen and Ridgers are now offering MIDI interfaces as options on their more recent models. AOB, another large electronic church organ company, recently installed an organ with one of its keyboards MIDIed to Casio synthesizer; the synthesizer's volume level can be controlled by the organ's swell pedal. The JLCooper Oran MIDI retrofit kit, which works with most pipe and electronic organs, has a 61-note input, a transpose function, sub- and super-octave doubling, a built-in program change sender, and a note-splitter" ("Organists Plug in: Praise the Lord and Pass the MIDI Cables," *Keyboard Magazine* [December 1987]: 21).

I am currently using synthesizers (Roland JX 10, D50, and MKS 20) over acoustic pianos for the greater part of the service in leading worship in local churches. Moreover, mere economics will very likely influence young churches to move strongly in this direction. Current synthesizers and samples offer flexible, sophisticated sounds at a fraction of the cost of acoustic instruments—and they are portable! Who wouldn't prefer to cart a ten-pound digital grand piano module around if the sound production was nearly comparable to a piano?

Readers wanting information on how to form a rhythm section at church can learn from two Hollywood studio musicians experienced in church needs. See the book and demonstration cassette *The Celebrated Tom Keene/Fred Petry Rhythm Section Book* (Alexandria, Va.: Alexandria House, 1978).

14. Donald P. Hustad, *Jubilate! Church Music in the Evangelical Tradition* (Carol Stream, Ill.: Hope, 1981), 275.

15. See Eric Werner's articles "Music" and "Musical Instruments" in *The Interpreters Dictionary of the Bible* (New York: Abingdon Press, 1962), 3:457–76.

16. The Jews were fond of drone harmony. Eaton says, ". . . from the lute and double oboe drone harmony was well known, notes being sustained under or over the melody" ("Music's Place in Worship," 96).

17. Hebrew music at the time of the second temple may have been influenced by Greek music. We know from Greek music theory that Greek scales were not even organized according to octaves (for example, the sense of closure [finality] we perceive in the C major scale of c^1 to c^2), a basic premise of Western music.

18. An antiphonal alignment of the Levitical divisions seems to be indicated: "And the heads of the Levites were Heshabiah, Sherebiah, and Jeshua . . . with their brothers opposite them, to praise and give thanks, as prescribed by David the man of God, division corresponding to division" (Nehemiah 12:24 NASB). Also Ezra 3:10–11; Nehemiah 11:17; 12:9b. For verses on stations see 2 Chronicles 5:12; 29:25–26; 30:15–16; 35:4, 10, 15. Stationing and antiphonal responses remain useful ideas today.

19. See T. W. Hunt, *Music in Missions: Discipling Through Music* (Nashville: Broadman Press, 1987).

20. See Paul Waitman Hoon, *The Integrity of Worship* (Nashville: Abingdon Press, 1971), 95ff., for an interesting discussion on tradition.

21. Mosaic (Ps. 90), Davidic (Ps. 51), post-exilic (Ps. 147:2), new song (Pss. 33:3; 96:1; 98:1; 144:9; 149:1).

22. Menconi Ministries, P.O. Box 306, Cardiff, CA 92007.

23. Harold M. Best, "Church Relatedness, and Higher Education" (Reston, Va.: Proceedings of the National Association of Schools of Music, 1979), 215.

24. Frank E. Gaebelein, *The Christian, the Arts, and Truth: Regaining the Vision of Greatness* (Portland, Oreg.: Multnomah Press, 1985), 94.

CHAPTER 15. MOVEMENT IN WORSHIP

1. Martin Blogg, *Dance and the Christian Faith—Dance: A Form of Knowing* (London: Hodder and Stoughton, 1985), 68. Blogg and J. G. Davies have written especially well on dance and worship.

2. Missionary letter, 23 March 1986. Some Canadian-American readers may have been enlightened by seeing the "African Children's Choir" sing and worship with compelling movement.

3. Blogg, *Dance and the Christian Faith*, 68.

4. Ibid., 67–68.

5. Ibid., 11. Adapted.

6. J. G. Davies, *New Forms of Worship Today* (London: SCM, 1978).

7. J. G. Davies, *Liturgical Dance: An Historical, Theological and Practical Handbook* (London: SCM, 1984), 86.

8. Ibid., 86.

9. Ibid., 87–88.

10. For an excellent exposition of *basar* ("flesh"), see Hans Walter Wolff, *Anthropology of the Old Testament* (Philadelphia: Fortress Press, 1974), 26ff.

11. Davies, *Liturgical Dance*, 88.

12. Matthew 24:22; Romans 13:1; 1 Corinthians 1:29.

13. See the excellent, extended discussion by George Eldon Ladd, *A Theology of the New Testament* (Grand Rapids: Eerdmans, 1974), 466ff.

14. These three points adapted from J. G. Davies, *Liturgical Dance*.

15. George Eldon Ladd comments: "Galatians 5:19ff. makes clear that when 'flesh' is used in a moral sense it does not necessarily have any physical meaning, since most of the sins ascribed to the lower nature (*sarx*) could well be practiced by a disembodied spirit" (*A Theology of the New Testament*, 472–73).

16. James Hastings, *Dictionary of the Apostolic Church*, 2 vols. (N.p.: n.d., 1915–18).

17. Michael Marshall, *Renewal in Worship*, rev. ed. (New York: Morehouse, 1985).

18. Davies, *Liturgical Dance*, 23.

19. Ibid., 28.

20. Ibid., 33.

21. Ibid., 24.

22. Ibid., 127.

23. Ibid., 138.

24. Blogg, *Dance and the Christian Faith*, 154.

25. Ibid., 133.

26. Ibid., 56.

27. Ibid., 148.

28. Ibid., 171.

29. Ibid., 100.

30. Ibid., 147.

31. Ibid., 93.

32. Ibid., xviii.

33. Ibid., 28.

34. Ibid., 84.

35. Ibid., 91.

36. Ibid., 109.

37. Ibid., 142.

38. Ibid., 78.

39. Ibid., 79.

40. Ibid., 79.

41. Byron Spradlin at Talbot School of Theology chapel, Biola University, April 1987.

42. Davies, *Liturgical Dance*, 77. See also John Ephland's "Praising God with Dance," *Christianity Today* (7 February 1986): 75, which describes the dance teams of several Chicago-area churches.

43. Blogg, *Dance and the Christian Faith*, 50.

44. Ibid., 22. See Matthew 15:10–20.

45. Ibid., 49–50. See 1 Corinthians 8, 10.

46. Ibid., 63.

47. Ibid., 132.

48. Some ideas may be found in *Dancing Christmas Carols: A Sourcebook for Adding Movement and 'Gesture to Christmas Carols*, ed. Doug Adams (San Jose, Calif.: Resource Publications, 1978). It has choreography suggestions by members of the Sacred Dance Guild of the United States and Canada. The guild is not an evangelical organization.

49. This song can be found in *Maranatha! Music Praise Chorus Book* (Costa Mesa, Calif.: Maranatha! Music, 1983), distributed by Word, Inc.

50. The tune can be found in *Maranatha! Praise and Worship Collection* (Costa Mesa, Calif.: Maranatha! Music, 1987).

CHAPTER 16. CELEBRATING FESTIVALS

1. Lyle E. Schaller, *The Middle-Sized Church: Problems and Prescriptions* (Nashville: Abingdon Press, 1985), 30.

2. Historically the coming of the Spirit coincided precisely with the Old Testament Feast of Weeks (also called the Feast of Harvest or the Feast of First Fruits), fifty days after the Sabbath of Passover week (our Easter). That places Pentecost Sunday in late May or early June. See Acts 2:1; Exodus 23:16; Deuteronomy 16:10; and Leviticus 23:15–16.

3. For an interesting and supportive introduction to the liturgical year seen through the eyes of an Evangelical, read Robert E. Webber, *Worship Is a Verb* (Waco, Tex.: Word Books, 1985), 153–72. See also by Webber, *Worship Old and New* (Grand Rapids: Zondervan, 1982), 161–73.

4. See Eddie Gibbs, ed., *Ten Growing Churches* (Marc Europe: British Church Growth Association, 1984), 22, 38, 112–13, 115.

5. Charles M. Sell, *Family Ministry: The Enrichment of Family Life Through the Church* (Grand Rapids: Zondervan, 1981), 218.

6. The command to celebrate occurs frequently in Scripture. Here are some references from Exodus alone: 5:1; 12:14; 23:14; 31:16; 34:22.

7. Adapted from Hayyim Schauss, *The Jewish Festivals: History and Observance*, trans. Samuel Jaffe (New York: Schocken Books, 1962), 170–84.

8. Translation by Phillip Goodman in *The Sukkot and Simhat Torah Anthology* (Philadelphia: Jewish Publication Society of America, 1973), 5.

9. Ibid., 9.

10. *Sukkah*, 3:9; 4:5. See Jacob Neusner, *A History of the Mishnaic Law of Appointed Times*, part 3: "Sheqalim, Yoma, Sukkah," translation and explanation (Leiden: E. J. Brill, 1982).

11. The Hebrew name for the feast is Sukkoth (meaning "huts"). There are at least three excellent sources of information: (1) Neusner, *History of the*

Mishnaic Law of Appointed Times, 3:127–75; (2) Goodman, *The Sukkot and Simhat Torah Anthology;* and (3) Martha Zimmerman, *Celebrate the Feasts of the Old Testament in Your Own Home or Church* (Minneapolis: Bethany House, 1981).
12. Culled from *Sukkah* 5:1–4.
13. *Sukkah* 5:1.
14. John White, *Excellence in Leadership: Reaching Goals With Prayer, Courage and Determination* (Downers Grove, Ill.: InterVarsity Press, 1986), 48.
15. Schaller, *The Middle-Sized Church*, 30.

CHAPTER 17. OUR HEAVEN ON EARTH

1. John F. Walvoord says of Revelation: "Few books . . . provide a more complete theology" (*The Revelation of Jesus Christ* [Chicago: Moody Press, 1966], 30–31).
2. An exception may be the Jerusalem council (Acts 15).
3. J. W. Bowman, *The Drama of the Book of Revelation* (Philadelphia: Westminster Press, 1955).
4. Gerhard Delling takes an opposing view. He maintains that our earthly worship "in its innermost essence is a copy of the heavenly," but that this similarity does not extend to the "details of external reproduction." Heavenly worship is parallel to earthy worship (*Worship in the New Testament*, trans. Percy Scott [Philadelphia: Westminster, 1962], 48). Similarly, Jacques Ellul asserts that Revelation is for the future: "we must not try to manufacture it with our techniques and metaphysics here and now" (*The Humiliation of the Word*, trans. Joyce Main Hanks [Grand Rapids: Eerdmans, 1985], 255); see also 237–42.
See also the provocative paper by David E. Aune, "The Influence of Roman Imperial Court Ceremonial on the Apocalypse of John," *Papers of the Chicago Society of Biblical Research*, 28 (1983): 5–26). Aune concludes that "John's depiction of the ceremonial in the heavenly throne room has been significantly influenced in its conceptualization by popular images of Roman imperial court ceremonial" (22). He says, "I must reject the widely-held notion that the heavenly liturgy of the Apocalypse is a projection of the liturgy of the earthly church" (7). Rather, "John's thought world is sufficiently syncretistic that its complexities cannot be understood apart from a consideration of the traditions of the Graeco-Roman world" (23).
On the other hand, Father Gregory Elmer, OSB, says that the Catholic and Orthodox traditions see the ongoing heavenly liturgy "not only as the model for earthly liturgy, but as the archetypal or paradigmatic liturgy itself (Hebrews 12:22–24). . . . the closing words of the Prefaces in the Catholic Sacramentary run something like 'Angels and Archangels, and all the saints of heaven ceaselessly praise Your Name. May our voices blend with theirs as they sing their unending hymn of praise, "Holy, Holy, Holy"'" (personal communication from Saint Andrew's Priory, Valyermo, California, 23 March 1987).
5. My sincere thanks to Dr. Daniel Bauman (San Diego) and Dr. Lowell Saunders (Biola University) for help in clarifying the thesis.
6. Revelation 5:13; 7:10; 19:1–3, 6–8.
7. Father Gregory firmly objects to the judgments in this paragraph. He maintains it is "biblically inadmissable" to use a book like Revelation "written in apocalyptic genre" as a "basis for judgments about history. Apocalyptic is

generally suffused with a despair of history." He further asserts that the Middle Ages were not free from historical conditioning: "There were undoubtedly liturgical distortions in the Middle Ages, but there was a fundamental liturgical adaption [by the Catholic Church] to the times. Besides, the Middle Ages were a vastly different world from ours" (personal communication, 23 March 1987).

To his comments I respond that there was undoubtedly some adaptation to the times, but add that the Catholic church was also a *profound shaper* of the times, and needs to take responsibility for its liturgical decisions, just as Protestants must take responsibility for distortions in their own worship today.

Jews during this period, for example, continued to practice a congregationally oriented liturgy regardless of changes in the culture. Jewish schools existed by and large not to impart a "classical education," but primarily to teach Hebrew and the Torah so people could assume a leadership role in a congregational form of worship. See Emil Schurer, *The History of the Jewish People in the Age of Jesus Christ*, ed. Geza Vermes, Fergus Millar, and Matthew Black, rev. ed. (Edinburgh: T. and T. Clark, 1979), 2:419.

From my reading of Scripture and extrabiblical literature, not only Revelation worship but also Pauline and synagogue worship appears to be strongly congregational. This concurrence encourages a strong endorsement of the Reformation principle of the priesthood of believers. To this, Father Gregory responds: "Their participation [people in the Middle Ages] was through silence and contemplation on art and its symbols. And I would subscribe to the call of the Second Vatican Council [1962] that the congregation have a more active verbal and explicit participation" (23 March 1987).

8. Delling, *Worship in the New Testament*, 119. Acts 7:59 and Philippians 2:9–11 encourage us in the direction of praying to Jesus, but Revelation provides explicit, confirming examples in a liturgical context.

9. In the NASB, the word *latreuo*, used here as "service," is elsewhere translated "worship" or "worshiper" (Phil. 3:3; Heb. 9:9; 10:2). Also, the Hebrew word *abodah* and its Greek equivalent *latreia* are translated "service" and are frequently used in relation to worship, as in the sense of "service" of worship. See Colin Brown, gen. ed., *New Testament Theology* (Grand Rapids: Zondervan, 1978), 3:550–55. Also see Clinton Morrison, *An Analytical Concordance to the Revised Standard Version of the New Testament* (Philadelphia: Westminster Press, 1979), 651.

10. Revelation confirms what we have learned elsewhere (2 Sam. 24:24; Matt. 26:7–10; Mark 12:41–44), namely, God values costly worship.

11. Robert H. Mounce comments on Revelation 5:9: "Every new act of mercy calls forth a new song of gratitude and praise" (*The Book of Revelation* [Grand Rapids: Eerdmans, 1977], 147).

12. See also 19:1–3 (multitude), 4 (four living creatures and twenty-four elders). The word *hallelujah* occurs only in Revelation (19:1, 3, 4, 6) and nowhere else in the New Testament.

13. Revelation 1:6–7; 3:14; 5:14; 7:12; 19:4; 22:20–21.

14. Robert E. Coleman, *Songs of Heaven* (Old Tappan, N.J.: Revell, 1980), 89.

15. Ibid., 90.

16. For alternative views of the symbolism in Revelation, a handy reference is Kenneth Barker, ed., *The NIV Study Bible* (Grand Rapids: Zondervan, 1985).

17. We can safely assume that the color of the linen is white; see Revelation 3:4–5, 18; 4:4; 6:11; 7:13–14; 19:14. White has also been interpreted as meaning "victory," e.g., the white horse of Revelation 6:2.

18. Menahem Haran thinks of the graduated holiness in the tabernacle in terms of "concentric circles" ("The Priestly Image in the Tabernacle," *Hebrew Union College Annual* [Cincinnati: Hebrew Union College, 1965], 206–7). See also the outstanding discussion of circle shapes by David E. Aune, "The influence of Roman Imperial Court Ceremony on the Apocalypse of John," *Papers of the Chicago Society of Biblical Research* 28 (1983): 4–6.

19. In North American churches the circle may communicate a certain leveling of all the people—"democracy"—before God. See Patricia C. Brady, *Has Anything Really Changed? A Study: The Diocese of Victoria Since Vatican II* (Winfield, B.C.: Wood Lake Books, 1986). Brady deals extensively with the symbol of the circle in the Vatican II reforms: "For a long period, the pyramid has been a dominant symbol in our culture, suggesting as it does power at the top supported by a broad base. Now, once again, the circle has become a dominant cultural and religious symbol, which best expresses the shift from hierarchical to collegial structures, a shift which has occurred in the Church as a result of the teachings of Vatican II. . . . I will show how the circle symbolizes integration, wholeness and unity" (15).

20. This is more appropriately a question for cultural anthropologists to pursue.

21. Paul Wohlgemuth, "Acoustical Tile Has Robbed Us," *Gospel Herald* 70, no. 19 (10 May 1977): 377. By contrast, many cathedrals in Europe, including those exhibiting romanesque and gothic architecture, provide enough echo to create a numinous impression. The builders of these structures used stone, the golden section, and other number relationships to create resonance that makes it a pleasure to sing in these spaces.

22. Coleman, *Songs of Heaven*, 141.

23. George Eldon Ladd writes: ". . . redeemed, glorified existence will be somatic existence, not a 'spiritual,' i.e., nonmaterial mode of being. Glorification will include the redemption of the body (Romans 8:23). . . . Paul describes it as a 'spiritual body' (1 Corinthians 15:44). . . . [it] involves a real body, however different it may be from our mortal physical bodies. . . . The survival of personality that is often presented as the essence of the Christian hope is a Greek teaching and is not the equivalent of the biblical hope of a fulfilled redemption" (*A Theology of the New Testament* [Grand Rapids: Eerdmans, 1974], 465).

24. Hebrews 2:14; John 1:14.

25. Musicians schooled in music history will recognize a historical precedent in the masses of Guillaume de Machaut and the pieces composed with multiple texts in the fourteenth and fifteenth centuries in Europe.

26. I heard of another college professor who prepared his students for this type of prayer by saying, "Today we are going to practice God's omniscience."

27. Interestingly, rehearsing this material in a congregation that includes educated business executives, I met with opposition and had to scrap the idea.

CHAPTER 18. THE ULTIMATE DRAMA

1. James L. Blevins, amillennialist professor of New Testament interpretation at the Southern Baptist Theological Seminary in Louisville, has incorporated

into his commentary a drama script of the Book of Revelation (which his students presented at the seminary) for churches wishing to mount a performance. See his *Revelation As Drama* (Nashville: Broadman Press, 1984).

2. See Austin Farrer, *The Revelation of St. John the Divine* (Oxford: Clarendon Press, 1964), 160.

3. See G. B. Caird on the word *soteria*, which he translates as "victory" (*A Commentary on the Revelation of St. John the Divine* [London: Adam & Charles Black, 1966], 100).

4. J. Messyngberde Ford, *Revelation* (New York: Doubleday, 1975), 95.

5. Personal conversation with Dr. Richard O. Rigsby, Talbot School of Theology, Biola University, May 1984.

6. I am grateful to Dr. Clyde Cook, president of Biola University, for his support, enthusiasm, and participation on these occasions.

7. Paul Waitman Hoon is critical of those who make the "worthship" of God—the acknowledgment of His supreme value—the "systematizing theme for theological reflection" on worship. He believes theologies built upon the proposition that the word *worship* stems from the word *worthship* distort thinking by taking this concept "as the primary rather than as a derivative point of departure." It distorts by implying that the "initiative in worship lies with man." Worship he says, is "more than an exercise in discriminating and identifyng value." Moreover, ascribing worth is not distinctively Christian, for it can be applied equally to "the dance of the sun worshiper or the prayer wheel of the Oriental, to the rites of a mystery cult or the thought of a philosopher." He maintains, "The category of value in biblical thought is secondary to the categories of being, decision, and action" (*The Integrity of Worship* [Nashville: Abingdon Press, 1971], 91–94).

I cannot see how Hoon's line of thinking, however, relates to the *biblical* use of "worth" in Revelation. The term as used in Revelation 4 and 5 relates precisely to "categories of being, decision, and action." Worthiness refers both to the character and acts of God and the Lamb. So for me, his discussion, unless I have misunderstood him, largely misses the mark.

8. Father Gregory Elmer's critique of this chapter provides a Catholic perspective on repetition: "I know this saying of Jesus is a classic text for those traditions which sparingly use repetition. . . . but look again! What Jesus is clearly saying is that the pagans use repetition in order to WIN a hearing from God or the gods (see the practice of the priests of Baal in their contest with Elijah around Mt. Carmel). He is saying nothing about using repetition in a prayer of RESPONSE to God's love, which is what ALL Christian prayer is (otherwise prayer is just a subtle form of "works" used to gain or earn God's love). Repetition is entirely appropriate in a prayer of response, especially as that prayer moves toward the kind of ecstasy very much endorsed by the Scripture, the jubilation evidenced by David as he danced before the Ark . . . etc.

"Moreover, repetition is a form of mantra. It jams the business or ego-centered mind, and allows the heart to open up. This is the sense of the Rosary. A prayer for body, mind and spirit: the wood beads occupy and remind the body of what we're doing, namely, praying, and help us keep centered. The repeated prayer works like a mantra and puts the busy mind to rest. The visualization of scenes from the life, death, and resurrection of Christ open the heart to that union with God Paul mentions in Romans 8, in which the Spirit prays for us with groanings beyond all words.

"Besides, anyone who is in love knows that sincere repetition of affirmation only serves to increase the mutual enjoyment of the lover and the beloved.

"The whole point being that repetition used to finagle and wheedle, or snare God's attention is against the second commandment which forbids us to use religious language to try to manipulate or catch God, forbids us because God has already given Himself freely and personally to us. But repetition in praise is simply the jubilation of ecstatic love. My real suspicion is that the Anglo-American cultural suspicion of ecstasy is what's really at stake. Everyone in England in the seventeenth century was so keen on 'rational' worship!" (Personal communication, 23 March 1987).

See also note 23, chapter 7, on tannaitic liturgy and "master image."

9. Harold M. Best's phrase in his provocative article "There is More to Redemption than Meets the Ear: An Inquiry into Christian Responsibility in Music," *Christianity Today* 18, no. 21 (26 July 1974): 12–18.

CHAPTER 19. SYMBOLISM: OLD BUT NEW

1. The definition was adapted from material in Paul Waitman Hoon, *The Integrity of Worship* (Nashville: Abingdon Press, 1971), 219.

2. John MacArthur, Jr., *True Worship* (Panorama City, Calif.: Word of Grace Communications, 1983), 76.

3. Ibid., 56. This chapter was sent to John MacArthur, Jr., before publication to allow him the courtesy of responding. He wrote to me: "I was not saying that symbols were no longer a part of worship. I was speaking of the symbols of the tabernacle and the features of the Old Covenant. These symbols found their fruition in the finished work of Christ. Obviously there is still room for symbols in worship; i.e., baptism and communion" (14 April 1987).

MacArthur's letter contained no further response to the "internal-external" duality, the words "end" or "need," his tone of language (e.g., "prodders"), or the other questions raised. From his communication it seems clear I have not misstated his position. For him, the symbols in the tabernacle (altar, incense, etc.) "are no longer part of worship." He appears to limit the symbols to two: baptism and Communion. I cannot be sure he has understood the position I take in this chapter and the next. His cordial response, however, was appreciated.

4. Here is a Catholic perspective. Father Gregory Elmer, OSB, objects to both the disqualification of the temple symbol and to the phrase that symbols are "prodders of the mind": "The use of even an external and physical symbol, such as the temple, is not condemned, for we read in Acts that after the Pentecost, the disciples met in the temple for the daily liturgy of the hours! [Acts 2:46]. . . . The notion that symbols are shabby concepts or only aids to the mind . . . is just neo-platonism. We need symbols . . . because reality is altogether richer than logic and it is irreducible to reason. . . . It is the whole person, body, mind, and spirit, who worships, not just the mind. . . . [therefore] we need physical symbols such as church buildings, art, liturgical vestments, incense, etc., and we need words spoken and sung, and we need silence for the spirit" (personal communication from St. Andrew's Priory, Valyermo, California, 23 March 1987).

5. Even to Abraham the sign of circumcision was not efficacious (Rom. 4).

6. Hoon, *The Integrity of Worship*, 313. However, I contend that we must guard against inferring that this kind of worship is more worthy, better, or more genuine than an unadorned, Puritan style of worship.

7. For a Roman Catholic view on symbols see Karl Rahner, "The Theology of the Symbol" in *Theological Investigations*, trans. Kevin Smyth (Baltimore: Helicon, 1966), 6:221–54. He says: ". . . the concept of symbol . . . is an essential key-concept in all theological treatises . . . God's salvific action on man, from its foundation to its completion, always takes place in such a way that God is the reality of salvation, because it is given to man and grasped by him in the symbol, which does not represent an absent and merely promised reality but exhibits this reality as something present (245).

See also archaeological material from Eretz Yisrael, studied and interpreted by E. Testa, *Il Simbolismo dei Giudeo-Cristiani* (Jerusalem: Franciscan Printing Press, 1961–1981) for a plethora of early Judeo-Christian symbols (e.g., the cross as Trinitarian, as mast of a ship, as a serpent, as a ladder, as the tree of life, as a royal sign, etc.). Considerable pluralism is implied in the imagery. Also consult Timothy Polk, "In the Image: Aesthetics and Ethics Through the Glass of Scripture," *Horizons in Biblical Theology: An International Dialogue* 8 no. 1 (June 1986).

8. B. F. Westcott and F. J. A. Hort, *The New Testament In the Original Greek* (New York: Harper, 1882), 184–88. See a chart which lists the distribution and number of Revelation allusions in each Old Testament book in Merrill C. Tenney, *Interpreting Revelation* (Grand Rapids: Eerdmans, 1957), 104. See Roger Nicole, "New Testament Use of the Old Testament," in *Revelation and the Bible*, ed. Carl F. H. Henry (Grand Rapids: Baker, 1958), 135–52. Also see William J. Dumbrell, *The End of the Beginning: Revelation 21–22 and the Old Testament* (Grand Rapids: Baker, 1985). Lastly, *The Jerusalem Bible* (1966) prints in italics words in Revelation that are alluded to elsewhere in Scripture.

9. Austin Farrer, *The Revelation of St. John the Divine* (Oxford: Clarendon Press, 1964), 30.

10. G. B. Caird, *A Commentary on the Revelation of St. John the Divine* (London: Adam & Charles Black, 1966), 64.

11. Ibid., 25.

12. Ibid., 61.

13. Ibid., 108.

14. Ibid., 61.

15. E. H. Peterson, "Apocalypse: The Medium Is the Message," *Theology Today* 26 (1969): 137.

16. Dorothy L. Sayers, *Letters to a Post-Christian World: A Selection of Essays* (Grand Rapids: Eerdmans, 1969), 89.

17. Ibid., 85.

18. Ibid., 92.

19. Ibid.

20. Gordon J. Wenham, *The Book of Leviticus* (Grand Rapids: Eerdmans, 1979), 151.

21. Ibid., 140

22. Kenneth Barker, ed., *The NIV Study Bible* (Grand Rapids: Zondervan, 1985), 1935.

23. J. Messyngberde Ford has numerous references on Revelation 4:4 (*Revelation* [New York: Doubleday, 1975]).

24. Exodus 40:35; 1 Kings 8:10-14; 2 Chronicles 7:2–3; Isaiah 6:4; Ezekiel 10:3–4. See Ford, *Revelation*, 258, for many Old Testament references.

25. Robert E. Coleman, *Songs of Heaven* (Old Tappan, N.J.: Revell, 1980), 15.

26. Interpretation is also often difficult. Twenty-one interpretations have been suggested for just the four living creatures! See R. C. H. Lenski, *The Interpretation of St. John's Revelation* (Columbus: Wartburg Press, 1943), 179.

27. At the creature's command ("Come!"), the horsemen ride out the judgment of the seals (6:1–5); later a creature gives the seven bowls to seven angels (15:7).

28. Caird, *Commentary on the Revelation*, 61.

29. Revelation 6:12; 11:13, 19; and 16:18 use thunder and lightning in the retributive sense, while 4:5; 14:2; and 19:6 (especially) do not. Tenney (*Interpreting Revelation,* 171) and others regard lightning and thunder exclusively as symbols of God's retribution and judgment. Robert H. Mounce, however, takes them as "symbolic of the awesome power and majesty of God" (*The Book of Revelation* [Grand Rapids: Eerdmans, 1977], 136). See also Psalm 77:18, which accents transcendency, not judgment.

CHAPTER 20. WORSHIP WITH MYSTERY

1. Revelation 17:9. On symbolism see also the interesting perspective of Frank C. Senn, *Christian Worship and Its Cultural Setting* (Philadelphia: Fortress Press, 1983), 6, 8, 50, 68, 73–77, 103, 111.

2. J. I. Packer says: "Evangelicals have not always noted the complexity of the hermeneutical task; indeed, sometimes they have let themselves speak as if everything immediately becomes plain and obvious for believers in biblical inerrancy, to such an extent that uncertainties about interpretation never arise for them. . . . It is the way of Evangelicals to expect absolute certainty from Scripture on everything and to admire firm stances on secondary and disputed matters as signs of moral courage. But in some areas such expectations are not warranted by the evidence, and such stances reveal only a mind insufficently trained to distinguish certainties from uncertain possibilities" ("In Quest of Canonical Interpretation," in Robert K. Johnston, ed., *The Use of the Bible in Theology/Evangelical Options* [Atlanta: John Knox Press, 1985], 48, 52).

3. Leon Morris lists the following irreconcilables—1:17; 6:8; 8:7 with 9:4; 8:12; 14:4; 17:1 with 3; 20:3, 13 (*The Revelation of St. John* [Grand Rapids: Eerdmans, 1983], 55).

4. C. S. Lewis, *Reflections on the Psalms* (London: Geoffrey Bles, 1958), 113.

5. See Morris, *The Revelation of St. John,* 209–210. The *NIV Study Bible* cites 17:10 as an example of the "fluidity of apocalyptic symbolism."

6. See the sixfold communication model, which has direct relevance to the Revelation communication style, in Robert Scholes, *Semiotics and Interpretation* (New Haven: Yale University Press, 1982), 20–21, 31.

7. *Time* (19 March 1984): 41.

8. Kevin J. Vanhoozer, "The Semantics of Biblical Literature: Truth and Scripture's Diverse Literary Forms," in *Hermeneutics, Authority and Canon*, ed. D. A. Carson and John D. Woodbridge (Grand Rapids: Zondervan, 1986), 73–

74. An outstanding article that respects both the propositional and literary integrity of Scripture. See also Robert Alter, *The Art of Biblical Poetry* (New York: Basic Books, 1981).

9. Ibid., 73.

10. Address at Biola University, 31 March 1987. Dr. Willard, an Evangelical, is chairman of the philosophy department at the University of Southern California, Los Angeles.

11. C. S. Lewis, *An Experiment in Criticism* (London: Cambridge University Press, 1961), 30.

12. Lewis, *Reflections on the Psalms*, 45.

13. C. S. Lewis, "Bluspels and Flansferes: A Semantic Nightmare," in *Selected Literary Essays* (New York: Cambridge University Press, 1969), 258.

14. Ralph P. Martin, *The Worship of God: Some Theological, Pastoral, and Practical Reflections* (Grand Rapids: Eerdmans, 1982), 206–7.

15. Ibid., 207. See also his entire discussion, 200–208.

CHAPTER 21. PRODUCT OF GOD, CREATOR-ARTIST

1. This description in Revelation bears similarities to Isaiah 6:2; Ezekiel 1:4–21; and Psalm 99:1.

2. G. B. Caird, *A Commentary on the Revelation of St. John the Divine* (London: Adam & Charles Black, 1966), 64.

3. Henry Barclay Swete, *The Apocalypse of St. John*, 3d ed. (London: Macmillan, 1911), 71.

4. Leon Morris, *The Revelation of St. John* (Grand Rapids: Eerdmans, 1983), 90.

5. John F. Walvoord, *The Revelation of Jesus Christ* (Chicago: Moody Press, 1966), 26. Walvoord notes the striking variety of animals used in Revelation symbolism; he points out references to Christ as the lamb, to horses, locusts, scorpions, a calf, leopard, bear, eagle, vultures, fish, and unnatural beasts.

6. John Peter Lange, *Commentary on the Scriptures: Revelation,* trans. and ed. Philip Schaff (1871; reprint, Grand Rapids: Zondervan, n.d.), 148–49, 158.

7. This section on *bara* creativity draws heavily on Barry Liesch and Tom Finley, "The Biblical Concept of Creativity: Scope, Definition, Criteria," *Journal of Psychology and Theology* 12 (1984): 188–97.

8. Leonard Stein, ed., *Style and Idea: Selected Writings of Arnold Schoenberg* (New York: St. Martin's Press, 1975), 214.

9. Personal communication from St. Andrew's Priory, Valyermo, California, 23 March 1987.

Scripture Index

339

Index of Songs, Hymns, and Hymn Tunes

Index of Subjects and Persons